CRUNCH

A MILLION SNOWY STEPS ALONG THE PACIFIC CREST TRAIL

DANIEL WINSOR

March 2021

Published in the United States by Daniel Winsor.

www.hikerbeta.com

Trade paperback ISBN: 9798704622451

Cover design by Rose Miller

Maps by Aubrianna Winsor

Editing by Susan Edwards

Internal formatting by Daniel Winsor

Cover photograph by Daniel Winsor

Printed in the United States of America

10   9   8   7   6   5   4   3   2   1

To my wife, Melanie.

*Thank you for your ultimate love and support through the PCT, and for reading all those **very** rough drafts... and telling me they were good.*

To Zoey, my first-born daughter and the second love of my life.

Thank you for entertaining yourself slapping the toilet in the other room through all those editing sessions. I hope reading this one day puts a smile on your face.

Author's Note

To write this book, I mostly relied on personal notes I recorded in my tent each evening, but also utilized online research and consultation with the people who appear in the book. Some of the events, places, and conversations in this memoir have been recreated from memory, which isn't perfect. Ask Mel how many times she's had to close the utility knife after I've used it to open Amazon boxes, or close cabinet doors behind me, or about the socks left at the foot of the bed, or about—you get the point. It's a miracle I'm still allowed inside the house.

I have changed the names and identifying characteristics of many of the individuals in this book, as well as some places, but the events are as close to factual as I could possibly get them.

Pacific
Crest Trail ----------

Reno, Nevada

Lake Tahoe

Sacramento

Sonora Pass

Highway 120

Tuolumne Meadows

Agnew Meadows

Mammoth Lakes

San Francisco

Bishop

Kearsarge Pass

Forester Pass

△ Mt Whitney

Lone Pine

Horseshoe Meadows

California

Kennedy Meadows

the
Pacific
Ocean

Los Angeles

San Diego

Campo

Mexico

N
W — E
S

I'm not telling you it's going to be easy; I'm telling you it'll be worth it.

—Art Williams

1

GOLDEN GIRL

"Thank *GOD*. I couldn't take *one more second* in that frozen hell!"

Two men I instantly recognized as thru-hikers strolled into our campsite. There wasn't much of an initial greeting, but a campfire was an open invitation to welcome themselves into our evening.

Apparently.

"Oh *stahhp*," the second hiker gave his flustered partner an eye-roll, one that could only be bred from weeks of hiking together. "It was *five* miles. And look! You made it! It wasn't that bad, was it?"

Under bushy eyebrows, the first hiker's eyes tightened into a dramatic glare. "Slim. I could've *dhhied*. Anymore of that, and I swear—I'll be off the PCT the next day."

Slim sighed and shook his head, as if resigning to a stubborn spouse, then joined my wife, my parents, and me around the fire. I didn't know much about the PCT, just that it stood for the Pacific Crest Trail and was a footpath spanning thousands of miles, all the way from Mexico to Canada.

"Hi there. Slim." Slim extended a grimy fist to bump. "And this is Golden Girl. You folks hiking the John Muir Trail?"

"Just a section," my father sat up a bit straighter and with an edge of pride in his tone added, "but we're hiking about eighty miles of it."

"Oh, that's a nice short trip," Slim replied, to our collective sense of slight. Frankly, he was lucky my exhausted mother didn't come flying across the campfire in the general direction of his jugular.

My father forced a patient smile. "I'm assuming you boys came from Muir Pass today? We're headed there in the morning. How was it?"

"It was," Slim shot a nervous glance over his shoulder at Golden Girl, who'd gone to set up his tent, "a little snowy."

A dramatic, "HUMPH," puffed out of Golden Girl.

Slim rolled his eyes again. "It was *five* miles of snow, man."

"It. Was. *HELL*, Slim."

Golden Girl had a name that matched him about as perfectly as one could. It truly was as if Betty White herself had put on a bear costume, a pair of colorful, short shorts, and a backpack. His mannerisms belied the dirt-mottled, muscled legs and unfettered beard of a weathered outdoorsman.

"So Slim and Golden Girl, those are—I mean, those aren't your *real* names, right?" I asked, worried I'd offend these strange characters if their possibly alcoholic parents had indeed scribbled "Slim" and "Golden Girl" on their hospital papers.

"They're trail names. Most people on the PCT have one. It's kind of a game. We suggest nicknames for each other to use while we hike to Canada."

Golden Girl's snippy voice called over from inside his partially erected tent. "I obviously did *NOT* pick mine."

The side of Slim's mouth lifted into a guilty smile. "I mean, come on."

The five of us around the fire shared a suppressed chuckle.

"So five miles of snow," I said, "that's kind of a long stretch, huh?"

I was worried about my mother, who wasn't as much into backpacking as she was into doing whatever it took to spend time with her vagrant son. She was joining us for a week in the backcountry, but all the bugs and lack of heated bathrooms were challenging her love for me—and any stretches of snow weren't exactly going to help.

"Maybe for some of us." Slim glanced back in the direction of the preoc-cupied, shorts-straining ass protruding from Golden Girl's tent. "But it's what? June 20-something? The first hikers out here went over Forester Pass on *May 15th*. There were twelve- or thirteen-mile stretches of snow then, even with the last winter being so dry."

My mind was instantly blown. "People are out here in the middle of *May*?"

That was all it took. A seed was officially planted.

For several years, I'd been living in the world-class playground of the Eastern Sierra with my wife, Melanie. We'd fallen in love with the climbing, the backpacking, the peak bagging—all of it was full of mind-blowing beauty and challenge. Typically (in our mediocre world, at least) the Sierra weren't considered open for business until late June, when at long last, the winter ice would recede enough to allow the dirt trails to reappear. The Sierra held unparalleled beauty during the summer months, but I couldn't imagine them still buried in snow. The High Sierra, a portion of the range lined with thirteen- and fourteen-thousand-foot peaks, was notorious for unreal amounts of snowfall. Mammoth Mountain often recorded more than *fifty feet* through decent winters.

I stared into the campfire, the wheels in my head spinning with curiosity.

A couple groups of hikers strolled by camp, exchanging greetings and reminding me although we were in the middle of the backcountry, we were also on a trail traversed by thousands of visitors each summer. It was referred to as the John Muir Superhighway by the half-joking, half-embittered locals.

CRUNCH

So in the middle of May, I pondered, *You could not only see these canyons and peaks in their most rare, snowbound state, but you'd also have the most popular hiking corridor in America—**to yourself**?*

I wanted to be that May 15th guy. I wanted to be the legendary one they spoke about in hushed tones of admiration around campfires. I wanted to be that madman out there in the middle of the vast wilderness, pitting himself against the heartless Sierra with only his pack, gear, ice axe, and boot-spike…things—the ones with the metal pokies.

Uhh, buddy? An internal voice of reason spoke up, *You know almost nothing about snow, other than how to shovel it or snowboard down it.*

It was true. In fact, I'd spent four years in New York getting rather whiny every time a fresh blanket of that white evil settled on the driveway.

Stick with what you know, maybe save the Sierra heroics for someone else.

When we awoke the next morning, Slim and Golden Girl had already packed up and left, and our family of four slipped and slid over those five miles of sunbaked slush Golden Girl had been grumbling about. Not one of us was successful staying on our feet, our average pace was solidly below *one mile per hour*, and everyone summited Muir Pass with new tweaks and bruises. If you were to ask my mother, she'd tell you it was terrible. But in my head, unannounced to anyone but that dumbfounded voice of reason, a fire had been lit.

I was going to find a way into the snowbound Sierra.

* * *

It took over a year to bring it up.

Not because I was scared of Mel's reaction, but because of the magnitude of the commitment. On principle, I tended to stubbornly stick to my word—so I needed to watch what came out of my mouth.

"Next spring, I want to attempt the entire High Sierra PCT section before the snow melts."

Melanie and I were sitting under a favorite boulder in the sunny Buttermilks, outside of Bishop, California.

"If the winter is another mild one, I'd shoot for starting in the beginning of March. Kennedy Meadows to Sonora is 300 miles," my faced scrunched in apology, "which would take five or six weeks."

In our mobile life, I was asking a lot to be gone for so long. We lived in a twenty-seven-foot trailer equipped with 150 gallon fresh water capacity and four solar panels to allow us to boondock wherever parking was free and rocks were nearby to climb. But our home had to be moved every two weeks to keep peace with the local authorities. Packing it up was a chore, driving it was a chore, but *parking* that monster—was the *worst* of the chores. Being left alone with two stubborn huskies *and* our trailer was definitely asking for too much.

"Okay," Melanie replied, with the nonchalance of a woman who'd just been informed I'd considered buying a new shirt, and not that I abandon her for weeks on end to go risk my life in the mountains. "But why just the Sierra section? You'd be hiking a lot of the PCT already, including the hardest stretch. Why not start at the border?"

"I mean, that would be a *long* time. I think people take five or six months to hike the whole thing."

She shrugged. "Having you gone wouldn't exactly be easy, but when else are you going to be able to try something like this? One day, we'll be done with this life, and be in jobs or having kids. This could be a good time to do it."

Truthfully, the idea of walking for two or three thousand miles (for I had no actual clue how long the full PCT was) seemed like a rather unpalatable idea. Impressive, sure, but not one I'd ever considered. I did enjoy the annual backpacking trip, but the longest I'd hiked was just over a hundred miles. Aside from that, I typically resisted any extra walking in my life. I'd long professed hiking wasn't worth the effort unless there was an epic wall to climb at the end of it. So was walking for six months something I genuinely wanted to do?

One morning, before another day of climbing, I hopped on my computer out of curiosity, just to see how rare the feat of hiking the PCT actually was. I couldn't imagine more than a handful of insane athletes completed that mission each year.

"*Seven hundred and fifty people*?!" I was stunned. "*Wow...* That many people walked the entire trail in just one summer?"

I shook my head and sat back in my chair. Apparently, I'd placed thru-hiking on too lofty a pedestal.

"If 750 people could do it, it *can't* be that hard."

I closed my laptop and stared at the door of our small home.

"Can it?"

The part of me leaning toward trying the full trail had been tempted by the opportunity to attempt a rare, elite challenge. That number was a bit of a letdown. Not enough to shut down all desire, but certainly high enough to underestimate what I was getting myself into.

"I think I will start at the border," I called over to Mel from the back of the trailer. "Maybe a thru-hike won't be that bad."

I figured in reality, I had little to lose. There could be no harm in having her drop me off at the southern monument. To be honest, even completing 700 desert miles just to reach the gates of the High Sierra at Kennedy Meadows seemed—*unlikely*. Nothing about backpacking that far sounded appealing, but there could be no harm in getting out of the truck and walking until I could pout northward no further. Mel could come pick me up to dry my tears and fast-forward my hike whenever I felt like seeing the snow as originally planned.

"Okay."

And in the clouds above the Sierra, close to their divine perch atop Dick Peak, the mighty trail gods chuckled for the first time.

2

LESSONS

With a trembling hand, I checked my watch for the sixteenth time since I'd slipped into my sleeping bag.

"Only two a.m.?" I groaned through chattering teeth. "This night is never going to end."

Moonlight shimmered off my frozen breath crystallized on the tent walls. Even tucked into a pricey down sleeping bag, and wrapped in layers of thermals and scratchy wool, my limbs were freezing. I hadn't felt my toes in hours. My brain cycled through bouts of panic, one minute reassuring me I'd be all right, and the next demanding I get up to flee the awful night I'd set up for myself. But it was below zero and very windy; night-hiking through the snow with insufficiently warm gear *seemed* like a bad idea, unless my only goal was to be on the news.

It was February, just one month before I was supposed to set off on the Pacific Crest Trail. The winter so far had been big. Not just enough to give me my snow to walk on, but *record-setting*. My hopes for a mild snowpack had been dashed by Christmas. From the comfort of our trailer in Bishop, we'd had a front-row seat to the steady stream of blizzards pummeling the Sierra, month after month after month.

I had hiked into the Eastern Sierra along closed winter roads to spend one night around 9,000 feet to test my meticulously prepared Sierra backpacking setup. Six miles into my planned ten, I triggered a small avalanche. Shaken, I decided to cut my hike short and camp next to a small stream I came across.

Winds picked up; the severe cold not only prevented my stove from working, but also rendered my fingers incapable of striking a lighter. I gave up on cooking to gather some water, which wasted no time freezing solid in my bottles. With all of my layers on, a bout of shivering started up I couldn't suppress. It was frightening. Even in gloves, my fingers were inoperable, and it took an excessive amount of time and effort to erect my tent through pulsing gusts.

I eventually made it into my sleeping bag inside the poorly pitched tent but spent the rest of the evening fearing every upcoming gust. If the tent collapsed on top of me, I'd be forced back out into the elements to fix it. And without enough warmth to stop shivering *inside* my sleeping bag—that felt like a worst-case scenario.

I'd never experienced a night that long. The sun finally arrived after fourteen miserable, dark hours. Mel was waiting at the same highway gate where she'd dropped me off. I returned to her rather shell-shocked. I was exhausted, starving, thirsty, and sunburned in the oddest of places from the sun's reflection off the snow. I looked and felt like hell, and it had been a grand total of twenty-four hours since she'd last seen me.

"I shouldn't try the High Sierra in the snow," I told her with the downtrodden gaze of a man who'd felt the full repercussions of his own poor planning.

"Let's get you warm before you make any big decisions."

3
SNOW

Running my fingers across the cold monument marking the southern terminus of the Pacific Crest Trail was beyond surreal. For months, I'd obsessed over the day I'd be standing next to that cluster of grey pillars. It was shorter than I'd expected.

I exchanged greetings with Aika, a petite Asian woman a few years my senior who was also starting her trek. Two guys in their early twenties were pounding Monster energy drinks, preparing wisely for the miles ahead.

I said goodbye to Melanie, held her in a hug for an extra few seconds, and walked to the first bit of actual trail. I stopped to look back uphill toward that exalted monument standing in front of the rusty U.S./Mexico border wall, took a deep breath, then turned to face the vast expanse of chaparral and desert between me and the Sierra.

That heavy first step north forever imprinted itself in my memory, and through the first mile, I repeated the same mantra in my head over and over.

You're just going for a walk.

My thoughts were already in the snowy mountains. There was a lot of uncertainty ahead of me, and to say I was confident would be a massive overstatement. I still didn't know if I was even capable of hiking the initial 700 miles through Southern California, and I *really* didn't know if I'd prepared enough to attempt the Sierra.

It wasn't long before I walked up on the energy drink duo sitting alongside the trail with their shoes off, tending to blisters. An abnormally excessive amount of sweat was beaded on their foreheads. I found that humorous, and I'll be honest—a bit reassuring.

The wide trail was lonely. Despite being on one of the most famous trails on the planet, I spent the majority of the day alone. Overcast skies and cold gusts kept me moving. Traditionally speaking, March 26 was an early start date, but it was much later than I'd originally planned.

The winter had delivered a dense snowpack to the Sierra range. The start of 400-plus miles of buried trail were just a few weeks in the future, far from long enough for the snow to go anywhere. Most hikers with a lick of sense had already made plans to skip around the snow, but I was dead set on drawing a straight line through it.

Just the thought made my hands shake, like a boxer headed into a title fight. Never mind I still had to walk the distance from Texas to the Pacific Ocean before I actually had to step into the ring.

My plans had shifted over the winter with every new layer of white on those jagged peaks. I'd originally wanted to start on the first of March, but once 2017 started breaking records, I'd chickened out, opting to aim for a typical mid-April starting permit.

"I'll get *plenty* of snow travel if I'm in the Sierra in July," I'd assured Mel, doing my best to ignore the pit of shame from deserting my aspirations to see the Sierra in May.

But it turns out the universe wasn't going to allow me to derail so easily.

The popularity of the PCT had been exploding. It wasn't clear why, but the best-selling book and subsequent movie *Wild* was typically the scapegoat on the online forums, where embittered sixty-year-olds reminisced in all caps about the good old days, when there were only three hikers in the entire world, they navigated by map and compass, and would go years without seeing another soul on the trail. In a world full of social media addicts, I figured it had more to do with the ability to broadcast the beauty of something like the PCT directly to the pockets of the desk-bound masses. But either way, what had once been a rare objective attempted by fewer than a hundred people each year had swollen to *thousands,* creating heated competition over permits.

Permits were limited to fifty people starting the trail each day, which to the unaware, butterfly-chasing, rock-scaling dummies in Bishop, seemed like *plenty* to go around. I was completely oblivious that people would be waiting with a pot of coffee and trembling fingers for the very *second* the website allowed them to submit an application.

In January, just one day after permits had gone live, we drove out of the mountains to where we had internet access at our favorite donut-shop-adjacent coffee joint. I opened my laptop with the smug grin of a guy who was on top of things, but that grin soon collapsed.

"What's wrong?" Mel asked.

The white paper bag holding my morning donuts sat undisturbed next to me for *minutes*—an eerie scene undoubtedly frightening her.

"*All* the dates; every single permit for *any* start date in the month of April, is taken." I shook my head in disbelief. "I'm too late."

I could've thrown my damn coffee across the room (but not the donuts. Throwing donuts? Absurd.). I went ahead and put in for the best available date, March 26, solidifying an adventure I'd semi-attempted to weasel my way out of.

The snow kept piling up at Mammoth Mountain Ski Resort. January broke a single-month record. Friends living in Mammoth started having to dig trenches, literal hallways of white ice with walls twenty feet high, just to reach their front doors.

And it didn't stop there.

The resort recorded 400" of snowfall. Then 500". Then 600".

I set off on countless trail runs and training hikes, putting as many snow miles under my feet as I could handle, figuring the more I prepared, the more reassured I would be—but the exact opposite seemed to be happening. The more I uncovered how little I knew, the more rattled I felt. I spent more than just the one overnight at North Lake with open eyes and chattering teeth. Staying dry, warm, and fed in the snow felt borderline impossible. A sinking fear crept into the background of my days, a fear amplified by every new snowstorm.

I was sure my Sierra plans were over my head. I'd wanted a challenge, *but* I'd wanted a normal challenge, not a historic challenge! But part of me *detested* the fear I felt, and wouldn't allow me to back away. I continued to adjust my gear and shove myself into painful lessons through cold, wind, blizzards, and freezing rain. I figured out layering. I practiced pitching my tent in the snow efficiently. I researched avalanche safety, both online and through long conversations with friends who were professional guides, backcountry skiers, and ski patrol members.

By mid-March, the amount of water the snowpack held was unprecedented. Some winters (in the years we've been capable of measuring, at least) had dropped more inches of snow, but inches of snow is a garbage way to measure a snowpack. Snow inches can be light and fluffy, or dense and icy. 2017 had been gifted with the latter.

I had plenty of reasons to back away, but as the days closed in on March 26, my fear shifted into resolve. Not because I'd convinced myself what I was planning was safe or even smart, but because the opportunity to do something great was approaching.

Hiking through the PCT in 2017 wasn't going to be just another year of manicured dirt alongside 750 others. It was going to be hard. Real Hard.

Maybe impossible.

4

700

After a full night of pretending, I opened my eyes and sighed, letting out a visible column of breath into the moonlit tent.

I was lying at the front gates of the Sierra, and I'd been awake for what seemed like hours. Hell, maybe I'd never actually fallen asleep. I adjusted my position in my sleeping bag for the twentieth time. Well, it wasn't *mine*. I'd swapped out my trusty thirty-degree bag for Melanie's twenty-degree. It was a last minute switch to not only have a warmer setup, but also shave an extra three ounces off my back—a shrewd move with genius written all over it. The only slight issue was I *barely* fit inside the tube of slippery green nylon, so unless I laid in perfect mummy-pose, I pushed into parts of the bag too hard, which compressed the down and created cold spots.

I probably just need to get used to it, I thought. *Maybe try to lie still instead of spending the entire night twirling like a damn eggbeater?*

The southern 700 miles had been a roller coaster. There were stunningly beautiful stretches in the chaparral and snowy ridgelines, spaced out by waterless, monotonous sections through the low deserts. I was proud of every step I'd taken—but I'd tortured my feet to their limit.

CRUNCH

I'd spent eight days off the Pacific Crest Trail and home in Bishop trying to recover. In the mornings, I quite literally couldn't stand on my feet. Instead of healing, the sharp pain in my heels was getting *worse* by the day. I didn't have health insurance, but I *did* have an internet connection and plenty of free time. Relying on my polished self-diagnosis skills, I'd narrowed it down to either a slew of strained muscles, advanced breast cancer, or—perhaps most likely—a bad case of plantar fasciitis.

Plantar fasciitis is the plague of the thru-hiking world. It's the inflammation of the tendon running along the underside of the foot's arch. While resting, that tendon contracts and hardens, pulling on the boney underside of the heel, making it excruciating to walk or stand on hard surfaces.

It's a good thing there aren't many hard surfaces on the PCT.

I'd spent those days in Bishop *trying* to rest, but the stress around the upcoming trek through the Sierra kept me moving. I packed and repacked my backpack. I spread out my resupplies over and over, covering every surface in our cramped trailer (to Mel's delight, I'm sure), trying to balance filling holes in my calories with shaving any excess weight from my intimidating load.

In Southern California, my pack had rarely touched twenty-five pounds, and I'd arrived at Kennedy Meadows hobbling like a ninety-year-old who'd been run over by a train—well, in the interest of accuracy, let's make that a *ninety-three-year-old* who'd been run over by *two* trains. Now, food alongside my heavier clothing layers, bear canister, ice axe, crampons, and alpine snowshoes had my pack pushing *fifty* pounds. Since twenty-five pounds on dry trail had damn near crippled me, I tried not to think about what fifty pounds on snow was going to do. Unlike through the first 700 miles, there would be no restaurants, no towns, no resorts, no showers, no beds, no electricity, no help, and no easy escape for hundreds of miles. I needed to be packed light enough to move through the mountains fast, but being under-prepared would mean bailing, being rescued—or much worse. Sorting through my gear explosions in the trailer, every item going into my pack was vital. Ten minutes later, every item was a complete luxury I was guaranteed to regret.

Hanging in my head was a vision of clinging to the edge of a cliff, dangling over seething whitewater, my fingers being pried apart one by one from the weight of my pack until the last finger opened, sending me plunging into the imaginary abyss with a final cry of, "Damn you, toothbruuuuush!"

Mel occasionally interrupted my obsessing with vegetables. She was on a personal mission to ensure I occasionally sat down to ramp up my nutrition before heading into the backcountry. Her rather dubious theory was a solid diet of Pop-Tarts and gummies shaped like penguins hadn't been sufficient to heal my over-taxed feet.

Day and night, I'd scoured my brain, trying to find what I'd forgotten. There had to be something. Sleep was obviously needed to recover, but the stress surrounding the weeks to come wouldn't allow it. My furrowed brow was a permanent fixture for the time I was home. If I wasn't hobbling back and forth between the "necessary" pile and the "luxury" pile, I was sitting brow-furrowed, often in front of vegetables, lost in thought.

Several hikers had already moved into the Sierra, but far more were pooling at the Kennedy Meadows hiker hangout, a restaurant/retreat called Grumpy Bear's. As expected, fear had begun to fester. Hikers skipping the Sierra were stalling there, making sure any fresh arrivals knew precisely how dangerous and impassible the snow was, regardless of whether any of them had personal experience in the Sierra or with snow travel in general.

Driving into Kennedy Meadows the previous evening, we'd quietly passed Grumpy Bear's to get straight to the campground. I didn't need to hear how screwed I was.

I already knew that.

A hundred yards short of our campsite, I'd hopped out of the truck exactly where Mel had picked me up eight days earlier. A short length of PCT I hadn't yet hiked cut through the campground, and I wasn't going to leave any stretches of the trail untouched, if I could help it.

I'd learned my personal standard of successful completion of the PCT was a style referred to as "connected steps" thru-hiking, often derogatorily referred to as "purist" thru-hiking by those who took offense to the idea.

Connecting steps is what it sounds like: literally hiking from point A to point B, with no exceptions—Mexico to Canada, stepping along as much of the PCT as legally possible. Officially closed sections were negotiated by mapping out a way to hike around them using side trails and/or roads. The goal was to arrive at the Canadian border with the ability to say, "I walked from Mexico to Canada," with no asterisks, no ifs, no ands, and no buts to tack on. I was a naive newcomer to the world of thru-hiking, so to me the rules for successfully hiking a long trail had seemed rather simple and straightforward. It was a trail. So if one desired to *complete* the trail—one had to *hike the whole trail*.

Simple, right?

This was apparently incorrect.

I'm being serious.

You see, 2,650 miles is *really* freaking far. That might seem obvious, but few people who start the PCT really have a solid grasp on what 2,650 miles even means, myself included. It's seven million steps. If you started counting on January 1, and did nothing else aside from count numbers and sleep eight hours each night, in a never-ending cycle of wake-count-sleep, wake-count-sleep, you'd reach seven million on May 2, likely in a hoarse whisper, chained to your bed in a mental hospital.

Every hiker is a purist on day one. The PCT is a romantic idea for its suitors tying their shiny laces at the southern monument, but that romanticism lasts from day one through about day one-and-a-half. Within a hundred miles, most people are over the concept of hiking the whole trail, and spend the rest of the PCT searching for shortcuts. The realization of just how far 2,650 miles is produces a creative spectrum of loose definitions of what a successful thru-hike should entail.

One day, while I was sitting at the Paradise Valley Café, just over a week into the trail, a crew I didn't recognize proudly announced their PCT-hiker identity to the waitress, whose face slacked into the unimpressed gaze of one who'd been beaten over the head with that same proclamation 9,000 times before. Those proud PCTers promptly hitched a ride to Idyllwild to pass a fire closure—one that wasn't happening for another fourteen jaw-dropping (and coincidentally *uphill)* trail miles. In the time it took me to eat my weight in cheeseburgers, I watched three subsequent groups do the same.

It dawned on me right there: *Those 750 names on the PCTA website, those weren't people who walked from Mexico to Canada. Those were 750 people who'd **taken credit** for hiking from Mexico to Canada.*

I found that realization encouraging, actually. As the definitions of a complete thru-hike softened around me, my personal resolve became further cemented to not only experience every open mile of trail, but to literally walk from border to border, whatever it took—through the hard parts, the snowy parts, the boring parts, the asphalt parts—all of it.

My convictions didn't make me many friends, however. With most hikers complicit in not hiking all of the miles, the guy hiking all the miles is kind of a problem. I embraced the "purist" label at first, but it was used derogatorily more often than not. I didn't find it hurtful; it just didn't make any sense. Nobody referred to a marathon runner as a purist for running all 26.2 miles. Some rare thru-hikers didn't use electronics, never slept indoors, refused to hitchhike, or even *hiked barefoot.* That all felt a hell of a lot more like "purist" hiking than what I was doing. I hitchhiked (but only to get in and out of towns), used the hell out of electronics, had zero problem sleeping in hotels, and I was certainly going to utilize every bit of technical gear (and you know, *shoes)* to get me to Canada.

At the end of the day, as long as I was the one facing my increasingly scruffy self in the mirror, I didn't care what others thought of me or how I was hiking my hike. Connecting steps was part game, part insane, part irritating, and four parts masochistic—but I'd wanted a challenge that took more grit and conviction than what 750 people had.

Of course, my whole arbitrary game would potentially be derailed by the Sierra within the week, but until I was forced off my connected path, I was going to walk every step, even if it was a hundred boring yards through a campground. Ninety-nine-point-nine percent of hikers wouldn't think twice about skipping it, but in my stubborn world, those hundred yards would forever haunt me.

At the end of the campground hike, there'd been a campsite with a tent and two people sitting outside it. I reflexively nodded in their direction, then returned my eyes to the trail.

"Beta!" one of the hikers called out.

I shot my eyes back over to the couple. It took a few seconds to realize who it was.

"Oh my God, Road Dog! Vagabond Runner! I didn't recognize you!"

I'd met the middle-aged duo briefly almost a month earlier. Road Dog's beard was now hiding most of his face, like most of us men on the trail, but both he and his wife had lost an alarming amount of weight. Of course, 700 miles of backpacking had ensured we'd *all* shed any extra pounds—but it was more than that.

Their spirits certainly didn't match their shriveled physiques. Road Dog proudly told me they'd taken *one* rest day since they'd hit the trail. I'd taken close to ten, and had still arrived in Kennedy Meadows three steps away from the pirate surgery (you know, the one where you get the peg legs). They'd pushed for weeks straight to connect with us, and were geared up to *continue* their incredible streak of no rest days right on into the Sierra the next morning.

I really shouldn't be awake, I thought to myself, staring at the dark cuben fiber tent wall inches from my face.

A cold spot on my hip forced a half-eggbeater to face the other wall for the seventh or eighth time. My mind simply wasn't going to let me sleep. After eight full rest days, lying in Kennedy Meadows, *hours* from taking my first steps into the Sierra backcountry—I was exhausted.

A rustle in the tent next to mine was reassuring. I checked my watch.

Two a.m.

Maybe I'm not the only one struggling to sleep.

One of my best friends, Miguel, had taken a month off work to tackle the Sierra with me. We'd been friends for over a decade since going through the Navy's nuclear training program together. Miguel was farm-boy strong, and tough as nails. He also had an affection for sufferfest trail-running events with the forehead-slapping, why-didn't-I-think-of-that business model of charging people money to swim through electrified mud pits. Miguel was also familiar with much of the terrain we were going to hike through—in summer, at least.

If there was any shred of comfort, it came from having him there. Like most ex-military who'd seen the horrors of a boot camp shower (that's thirty seconds of ninety-seven peripheral wangs while being verbally abused), or a submarine (that's six months trapped underwater with 130 peripheral wangs while being verbally abused), a hike in the snow simply paled in comparison.

Mel had crashed in the backseat of our truck in a pile of old sleeping bags we'd used many times, our trusty "dirtbag motel." I pondered for a second whether she was also struggling to sleep, but I knew better. I'd spent five years being jealous of Melanie's miraculous ability to sleep, pretty much no matter where. Wolves could've dragged her out of the truck and eaten her hours ago, and she'd still be asleep.

At 4:58 a.m., still before both of our alarms, Miguel and I reconvened at the campsite's picnic table. I sent a desperate prayer up to the trail gods to let whatever small naps achieved between all the eggbeatering be enough to get me through the day. Melanie soon joined us and whipped up some oatmeal while Miguel and I executed one last gear check.

"Gooood morning!" a cheery Road Dog called into camp. "You two psyched for this? We could barely sleep!"

I smiled at the sight of two bright faces. "Yeah, me neither."

I couldn't believe Road Dog and Vagabond Runner were there, smiling and ready to go after blowing through Southern California in *under a month*. They were at least a decade my senior, and the five weeks I took to reach Kennedy Meadows had about killed me.

Miguel hefted his behemoth pack off the picnic table, grunting under the load. "I can't wait until we eat the weight out of these things."

Road Dog shrugged. "We did pretty good with our weight. Not too much heavier than they were in SoCal, actually."

That lifted an eyebrow. "Really? Damn, man. I feel like I've got two packs on."

Miguel looked at me. "You think we're over-packed?"

"I honestly don't know. We'll see, won't we?"

I gave Melanie a long hug. With the whole crew there, it wasn't as long as I wanted.

"Please be safe," she said. The tension behind her green eyes was a gut-wrenching reminder of just how much I had to lose. "I love you."

"We will." A small lump formed in the back of my throat, a common side effect of telling baseless lies to your loved ones. "I love you too."

All of us said our goodbyes, thanked Melanie and headed toward the trailhead. We walked in anxious silence, four-wide across the asphalt campground road.

We had everything. We were ready. The snowy Sierra awaited.

5

BETA

All of the social media apps on my phone had long been deleted. Online PCT forums were a breeding ground of anonymous dark prophets, who enjoyed forecasting the devastation awaiting the idiots attempting the Sierra. Their pessimism wasn't completely misplaced. Accidents in the mountains had already happened. A week before, one strong hiker almost froze to death. He exited Kearsarge Pass and quit his entire PCT hike right then and there.

Another infamous badass had stormed into the Sierra after averaging forty-plus-mile days through Southern California, but then went missing. He reappeared in the Eastern Sierra desert after bailing over an obscure pass with tales of ten-degree nights and falling into hidden caverns under the snow. He left to hike the Appalachian Trail instead.

The online doomsayers *loved* highlighting those juicy stories. Success was far less interesting than failure. It was terrifying to watch hikers I admired bailing from the Sierra. So I just—stopped watching. Might not have been the right answer, but I couldn't handle the added stress of the online fear machine. In reality, I had no idea how my mindset and skills compared to my fellow Sierra suitors, but if I knew one thing, it was this: I was going to see for myself.

Our team of four slipped into the still forest at dawn, safety and security officially in the rear view. Over a month of snow was in front of us with countless, unknown obstacles, and no easy escape. I ran my gear through my mind over and over, still searching for what I'd forgotten. I was coming up empty though. It was simply time to walk.

Miguel led the way. He'd been training hard at home for this adventure, and it showed. His nervous excitement and fresh legs set him on a feverish pace ahead of the three PCT hikers. Road Dog, Vagabond Runner, and I theoretically had a month-long warm-up hike, which should've meant we'd all be mileage-destroying powerhouses—but that wasn't the case. It was hard to tell whether the first 700 miles were an overall benefit or drawback. The arches of my feet certainly weren't happy I was back to walking.

Within a few miles, the South Fork of the Kern River came into view, which thankfully had a well-built bridge spanning it. We had miles to put behind us, but couldn't help but stop to stare at the muddy, swollen torrent overflowing its banks.

I'd stressed to Miguel how difficult some of the creek crossings were potentially going to be. Sifting through journals online, I had read about accidents, deep wades, and full-on *swims*.

As we neared the far side of the bridge, Miguel turned back to me with a childish grin and leaned in so I could actually hear him over the chaos flowing beneath us. "I don't know, man. That really wasn't so bad."

I laughed. That was exactly why I'd wanted Miguel by my side.

My nagging left foot started emanating familiar pains, slowing my pace. I was hoping my rest days were going to be enough for the foot to heal, but five weeks of foot abuse clearly needed more than one sleepless week to reverse. My teammates pulled ahead until I was hiking alone, with only my thoughts to keep me company. The pleading look on Melanie's face was haunting me. I loved that girl more than I could explain, and more than I worried about losing my own life during this trek, I worried about losing my life with her.

BETA

Our families hadn't exactly been excited about our 2013 decision to leave our secure jobs and sell everything out of our luxury townhouse to move into a rather, how to put this nicely—*methy* 1981 RV. But since the moment the military had dropped us in San Diego, Mel and I had averaged seeing each other a whopping three days *per month*.

After just the first night we spent in our empty townhouse, I dropped Mel and her green canvas seabag off at the pier to check in with the USS Vinson, which shipped out to sea later that day for three weeks. When she got home, she was allowed off the ship for a whopping 36 hours before reporting back to the ship for another two week underway, and that basic schedule persisted with no real end in sight. The Navy was a cruel master when it came to family life, and although I enjoyed my cushy civilian job, and all the fleeting thrills of pricey dinners and buying high thread-count sheets for rarely visited bedrooms, I spent the vast majority of my time in our house alone. I really just wanted Melanie back. I wanted to be outside with her next to me, climbing rocks in the alpine sun. I wanted less stuff and more memories. Mel's time with the Navy ended, and after a combined fourteen years of our lives being controlled by military orders, we had a chance to take a leap.

Long before we were ever in a relationship, I'd taken Mel to show her my small, dusty climbing gym where I'd been setting routes. She'd recently gone snowboarding for the first time, and broken her wrist on *the second run of the day*—needless to say, she was still open to new hobbies. With powerful grace and control born from years of ballet, her wrist still confined in a splint, she climbed the entire wall with essentially one usable arm. From there, we were partners. Not in the boyfriend/girlfriend sense, that didn't happen for over a year (for **this** level of manly magnetism is, eh, easy to ignore it turns out).

When we'd first met in the Navy, Melanie was always down for a chat in the engine room, a trip to the climbing gym, or to meet up to get something to eat. She became a great friend during my home remodel, where she'd find me covered in drywall dust, eating meals of Reese's peanut butter cups and expired frosting. She would stop by Subway on the way and sit me down in front of a sandwich, insisting I stop working long enough to ingest some real food. She slid into best-friend territory when she'd drive half-an-hour almost every day, even after our fourteen-hour workdays, to join me under that horrific white dust to help me get my home put back together.

I eventually weaseled in a kiss on a flight heading home from a rare climbing trip to Las Vegas, and we'd been inseparable ever since. Our time pulled apart in San Diego was heart-wrenching, but we'd taken the drastic step to fix it. So then, after three straight years of being at each other's side 24/7, the idea of willfully taking myself back out of that situation to go risk my life along the PCT was conflicting, to say the least.

Still within ten miles of Kennedy Meadows, I was hobbling along the trail again, as if I hadn't taken a single day off. With my teammates out of sight, I stopped at an inviting stump under a large, leafless tree. I propped my pack's weight on top of a fallen branch, groaning through the absurd bliss of the tension lifting off my shoulders. Sweat rolled down my forehead. My feet burned inside my insulated boots.

Everyone else seemed to be doing well, certainly better than how I felt. I fought to suppress surges of panic.

*Should I consider quitting while I'm still able to retreat back to Kennedy Meadows? While I'm still, I don't know—**alive??***

An uncaring gust of wind tugged at my pack straps.

"You're not doing this because it's easy, but because it is hard," I muttered to myself, paraphrasing John F. Kennedy's famous words for the hundredth time.

I couldn't remember when I'd first heard that quote, but the concept—that hard things are worth doing, simply because hard things are worth doing—had resonated deeply with me. There certainly was something uncomfortable about being too comfortable, too domesticated, too civilized, too—soft.

You don't need to be the strongest person out here; you just have to keep going.

I caught up to my team in front of the last bridged creek leaving Kennedy Meadows, the second crossing of the South Fork of the Kern River. We stopped for lunch along the bank, assembling tortillas filled with various backpacking, non-perishable goos. The sheer volume of the swollen river was a humbling sight. We were headed to the source of all of that water, with hundreds, maybe *thousands*, of creeks to cross, and only a select few had bridges.

After lunch, the trail pitched uphill into Cow Creek Canyon. Miguel plugged in his headphones, again taking off in a strong gait ahead of us. I'd known Miguel for a long time, and classic rock was his go-to. Sure enough, even under his oppressive load, off-key caroling to AC/DC drifted back through the air.

Between heavy breaths, Road Dog said, "*Man*, that guy's amped."

Miguel's high spirits invoked a certain jealousy. *I* wanted to feel that good. I wanted to skip along the trail and sing into the pines, even with this fat, demon child clinging to my back. But his energy was a good thing. We were going to need all the collective drive we could get, and he was filled to the brim. He stayed in front of the pack, often out of sight, but belted out the occasional, vaguely recognizable ballad from Queen or Whitesnake so we knew he was still alive.

"Hey, Beta," Road Dog shouted ahead to me, using my trail name, "We have a name for Miguel yet?"

"Not yet. I figured you'd be on it though."

Road Dog had actually suggested Beta as my trail name when we first met, on my second day on the trail. We'd stopped to say hello, but once he and his wife had found out I was from Bishop, *and* planning on tackling the Sierra, our brief pleasantries shifted into an hour-long strategy session.

Road Dog wanted to know everything I was planning from gear, to snow travel, to tackling passes and rivers. I didn't know *everything,* but I'd certainly done my homework and trained enough to have a rough plan. Road Dog was an intense listener, completely absorbed in my words. It finally took his wife to break up the conversation.

"We should probably let him go. I'm sure he has miles to hike."

It took a second for him to even register what she'd said. "Oh, right," but his piercing blue eyes brightened. "Hey, do you have a trail name yet?"

"Not yet, but it's only my second day out here."

Vagabond Runner smiled and rolled her eyes. "He loves this."

"How about Golden? Because, ya know, you're *Golden* when you get to the Sierra."

I laughed. While it would be a badass trail name, it had a bit too much bravado to it, a humiliating choice if I ended up failing in a not-so-golden manner.

"Or Free Solo! Because you and your wife are *free,* mobile, off the grid—and *solo*, because you're hiking alone. It has to do with climbing, too."

It took a second to register all the meaning he'd just pulled into that one name. The guy had skills.

"Or Beta!" He left Free Solo in the dust before I'd even had a chance to think. "Because you gave us the *beta* on getting through the Sierra."

That one resonated. In climbing, "beta" refers to detailed information on how to unlock a tricky sequence. What holds to use, what fingers to put where, what body position to focus on—that was all beta. It had to do with climbing, it nodded toward me being the go-to guy for information (never mind I knew about as much as everyone else who'd never crossed the Sierra in the snow), and it wasn't as ego-stroking as Golden.

Admittedly, it was extremely early for a trail name, but Beta stuck.

At the outlet of the Cow Creek drainage, we caught back up with Miguel standing in front of a gushing creek. His headphones were out, and he turned to us with a shocked laugh.

"This thing is seasonal, isn't it?"

The stream was raging outside of its banks. Cow Creek was indeed usually reported dry at some point throughout the summer.

"Not this season, I'm guessing."

It was too swift to cross at the trail, so we headed upstream a bit to jump across a constriction. While it wasn't a hard crossing, it certainly wasn't *nothing*.

BETA

Within minutes of our camp near Olancha Pass, snow started to appear on the trail. My boot compacted a small patch of ice for the first time with a satisfying *crunch*. We'd talked about this, planned around it, trained for it, and second-guessed it for many, many miles. Now, here we were—Sierra ice officially underfoot—standing on one end of a vast, remote expanse of snow, soaring mountain passes, and raging rivers.

We crossed our first small snowbridges, kicked our first steps into the soft slopes, and executed a couple shaky boot-skis. It had all been hypothetical for so long.

Now, it was real.

6
AMPED

Spider-webbed ice covering my tent walls was illuminated by the dawn light, and I sighed in relief. Even though I was exhausted, sleep had been fitful in temps teetering on the edge of too low for my gear. As a cherry on top, winds had beaten the tent around for most of the night, but had finally calmed at 2:16 a.m.

How did I know it was 2:16? Because I was awake. I was awake before, during, and after that damn wind had finally settled down. I couldn't get away from cold spots inside Mel's sleeping bag. Eggbeatering through the night, I'd found plenty of time to contemplate the outcome of no sleep coupled with giving Jabba the Hutt a piggyback ride through hundreds of miles of snow.

I shivered through packing everything up, anticipating the backwards fact I'd be warmer once I was outside the tent in all my layers. A typical tactic was to preheat my hiking clothes by sleeping with them inside my bag, but with barely enough room for just me in there, my clothes had been relegated to spending the night out on the tent floor. That frozen-dew-encrusted pile of fifteen-degree fabric sat in cruel wait, while I tried to remind myself I'd voluntarily arrived in my current reality.

"One, two… *uhnn*… three!"

I slid out of my sleeping bag and stuck each of my warm, bare thighs into my ice pants, followed by a warm foot into each ice sock. I *technically* had a clean ice shirt to change into—but after a prolonged staring contest, my sleeping thermal was promoted to the prestigious rank of hiking thermal.

I flipped over and stretched into the down dog yoga pose, pushing into the walls of my tent, grimacing through tight, painful pulling in the tendons running along the bottom of my feet. If I had any hope of making it to Canada, I needed all the help I could scrape together. Melanie was a bit of a yogi and had made me promise I'd take the time to stretch twice a day. With her being a beautiful girl, and me being a boy in the tutelage of a beautiful girl, I'd agreed without a second thought. If those green eyes had suggested I begin each morning with a few hearty flicks to the testes, I would've been onboard. But with those eyes hundreds of miles away from the guy pushing into an ice-encrusted tent wall, mashing ice flakes into his hair and his previously dry sleeping thermal, my commitment to those twenty seconds was already wavering. My whole body trembled through ten Mississippis.

The last two Mississippis might've been closer to Misspis.

A hot cup of coffee appeared under the flap of my tent. "Morning, buddy. Drink up!"

I vowed right then my firstborn would be named Miguel, or eh, Coffee… It would take some thought. I suppose Melanie would want to weigh in on the decision as well.

Women.

I emerged from my tent, groaning into the serene morning. My partners all looked a hell of a lot better than I felt.

I shook most of the ice off my tent and crammed it into my backpack with stinging hands. By seven a.m., we were moving steeply uphill into the life-affirming warmth of the sun. Not one of us had feeling in our hands and feet.

By 7:05, packs were down and layers were being shed in desperation. The fifteen-degree morning was no match for slogging our packs up a snowy mountainside.

We passed frozen mud puddles and gushing, icicle-lined creeks. It was a wonderland, one of the most beautiful sections of hiking I'd ever witnessed. Small, hidden streams had carved out a network of hollows below the uniform, flat surface of the snow. The roof of the hollows varied from several feet thick, to paper thin. Postholing—the maddening art of a foot unpredictably punching through the surface into one of those voids, or just into soft snow in general—was bad news for the ankles of overloaded hikers.

Out of curiosity, unsure how thick a snowbridge had to be to trust, I stepped up onto an arch only an inch thick and spanning several feet. With the stream only six inches below, I braced for a safe collapse—but it easily held my 230 pounds.

"Wow," I said, "stronger than I thought."

The terrain steepened further and the trail disappeared entirely under a broad snowfield. After several hundred yards hiking in a general upward direction, we had no real idea where we were in relation to the PCT. We all stopped to catch our breath, and for the first time of many, pulled out our GPS to get our bearings.

Somewhere under the ice, a faint rumble was coming from a buried creek.

Are there underground rapids big enough to swallow a hiker? I pictured breaking through the surface like a trapdoor had released under me, then being swept under the snowpack, gasping for air in the dark against rushing ice water. *I wonder what you would die from first? The cold? Or would you drown?*

"Looks like the trail angles across that slope there," Road Dog cheerfully announced, snapping me out of my paranoid daydream.

We moved into heavier snow under the cover of trees, where the flat surface morphed into steep, uneven drifts around the trunks of weathered pines. Moving up and over every mound of ice was slippery, tenuous, and difficult work.

Almost simultaneously, we all dropped our packs. It was crampon time.

I would like to say we all strapped our shiny array of aggressive spikes to the soles of our boots like a crew of veteran mountaineers. That we threw our packs on in slow motion and marched across the snowfield with commanding confidence, like the stars of a heroic, inspiring movie with an unnecessary amount of sweeping drone footage and crashing cymbals, maybe even a random explosion or two.

That didn't happen.

This had been a moment I wasn't exactly looking forward to. Our collective experience with snow traction was pretty much nothing. I'd spent a decent number of miles in snowshoes, but when it came to crampons, all of our combined experience resided within me—being the ten minutes I'd tried them on the week before.

During my rest days in Bishop, I'd dropped Melanie off for a winter hike at the Onion Valley trailhead, but before leaving the parking lot, I strapped on my shiny new Black Diamond Contacts (incorrectly a few times, but eventually nailed it). I stepped up a nearby hillside mimicking some mountaineer guys on YouTube, then slipped and slid back down, greatly looking forward to sitting again. My feet were in an incredible amount of pain, and I had next to zero desire to put my full weight on anything but my ass.

And that was it.

For a half-hour, we sat in the snow strapping and re-strapping our crampons onto our boots. Everyone seemed to be leaning on me, but I felt almost fraudulent giving advice. I'd spent a lot of time in the Sierra, logging hundreds of summer miles and standing on top of dozens of peaks—but we weren't in the Sierra I knew.

While I was trying to help Miguel strap on his crampons, Road Dog asked, "Like this, you think?"

I glanced over and gave him a confident, "Sure, looks good."

... .

They were on backwards.

[Cut to drone footage and cymbals crashing]

It took until all packs were on for me to realize Road Dog and Vagabond Runner's front crampon points were at their heels. I sheepishly apologized and their packs went back down. It wasn't the most reassuring moment for a crew heading into hundreds of miles of mountaineering. We were a group of skydivers ripping the tags off our parachutes.

"We're doing great, team," I said. "These things do go on our feet, right?"

The beautiful weather and firm snow were perfect learning conditions to share what little knowledge I had with my fellow novices. Blind leading the blind at its finest. Lucky for us, crampon skills are more borne from experience than from YouTube theory, and we had a generous number of experience-building miles through mild snow before we reached the steep mountain passes.

The terrain switched between snow and dirt dozens of times. Many short, north-facing downhills were snow patches bookended by dirt. Rather than don crampons for just thirty yards of snow, we dabbled further in the art of boot skiing. Instead of stepping through the snow, the idea was to *slide* down, like a socked child gliding over a polished floor. The learning curve was far from linear though. In a repeating cycle, I'd become overly confident in my budding skills, then find myself flying sideways down the slope, emitting the unique squeal of a grown man shoveling slush up his shirt. I'd stagger back up against the awkward weight of my pack, clear my nipples of melting snow, and trudge back uphill toward my scattered trekking poles and self-esteem.

A hillside covered in freshly jettisoned belongings was known as "yard saling." Sometimes, when one of our beloved teammates was in a groaning pile at the base of a gear-strewn slope, we'd call over empathetic things like, "Hey buddy, how much for those gloves?" or "What can I get for a nickel?" or "How much for the snowy klutz there?"

When our egos couldn't handle any more boot skiing, we tried glissading on our butts. It was certainly safer, but the snow was often too soft, and it was debatably less humiliating to be force-scooting through the slush like a popsicle-wielding child running laps on a playground slide.

Uphill trudges were slow. Downhills went fast. A snowbridge several inches thicker than the one I'd tested that morning appeared arcing over the trail. I confidently hopped up onto it, only for the entire thing to immediately collapse, as if I'd hopped up onto a bridge of Styrofoam.

The unexpected drop was only a couple feet, but my knees delivered a sharp, painful message: Any further falls than this, and walking out of the mountains may not be an option. Even though the afternoon temps were still below freezing, the snowbridges had curiously become weaker throughout the day.

Creeks waiting for us in the hundreds of miles ahead kept us experimenting with snowbridges. Some of those creeks were notorious torrents with a sordid track record, but I was banking on a major benefit to hiking this early in the season: It was all but guaranteed snowbridges would be spanning some of them. The general *stability* of snowbridges was a big unknown, however. Falling back onto a muddy trail was one thing, but breaking through the middle of a snowbridge over whitewater was, well—*another* thing, to put it mildly. After enough sampling, I found an afternoon bridge had to be five or six inches thick to hold my weight, compared to the one-inch thickness that had held me that morning!

We arrived at our planned camp, the usually bone-dry Gomez Meadow, which was surrounded by streams and sheets of flowing snowmelt. Eight miles for the day was on the short side, but this spot positioned us as low as possible for the night. We were just below 9,000 feet, but we'd soon be pushing into the High Sierra and camping at an unavoidable 11,000 feet—maybe higher.

We found a great campsite at the far side of the meadow, with plenty of logs and flat tent sites. Miguel set out the solar panel to charge our electronics in the remaining sunlight.

"So you're the guy in charge of the electricity, I see." Road Dog's eyes had a familiar gleam. "What do you do for living, Miguel?"

"I'm an operator at a power plant."

"And you and Beta met in the Navy, right? Also doing stuff with electricity?"

"Yeah, operating nuclear plants on submarines."

His intense eyes lit up. "Amped! It's the perfect trail name for you. You're the electricity guy; both here, being in charge of the solar panel, with the Navy, *and* at your job. Add in the singing and charging down the trail and you're just—*AMPED!*"

Miguel chuckled. "Do I get a trail name? I'm not hiking the PCT. Really, I'm only hiking a small fraction of it."

"Nonsense. You're on a more difficult hike than the ninety percent of people skipping around this section. I'd say you deserve a trail name more than most."

To our surprise, a solo hiker approached camp. We hadn't seen another PCT hiker since we'd left Kennedy Meadows. Road Dog went over to invite him to camp with us. There was strength in numbers, especially in the backcountry.

When the hiker got closer, I recognized him. "Oh wow, it's Fireball."

I'd met the quiet Korean on our very first day on the Pacific Crest Trail. We'd camped together, along with a dozen others who hiked those twenty miles from the monument. He was a nice guy, but he spoke almost zero English. I actually wasn't sure he knew his trail name was Fireball. I'd just started calling him that after he'd pulled out a full fifth of uber-sweet, cinnamon-flavored Fireball whiskey from his pack the day we'd met. He thought it was just normal whiskey, and that first sip—hadn't gone over well.

I hadn't seen Fireball since, and I was impressed to see him all the way out there and tackling the Sierra. Alone, at that! But he promptly broke the conversation off with Road Dog and continued along the trail.

Road Dog made his way back to camp scratching his head. "He said his name is Fireball. He was very insistent about hiking four more miles. Didn't want to camp here."

As we settled into our tents for the night, I pulled out my inReach—a satellite device I carried primarily for its ability to call in an SOS if needed. It was also capable of retrieving weather reports and exchanging text messages. The device was fairly reliable, but the delays between messages coming in and going out were highly variable. The satellite signal didn't like tree cover, cliffs, canyons, clouds—many of the things I was constantly around. So messages transmission would range from 10 minutes to an entire day.

I sent out a weather report request, which came back with surprising speed this time.

Uh oh. Looks like the Sierra isn't done dishing out the challenge this year.

Snow was coming. A hefty *seventy percent* chance forecasted for the day after tomorrow.

Snow in May wasn't out of the ordinary. Snowstorms often popped up into June. In fact, the Sierra was infamous for the occasional blizzard in *July.*

Is it a good idea to proceed into a storm? Just a couple inches of powder and we'll be in avalanche territory. It could take days for the new snow to consolidate.

I sent a message to Melanie, telling her about the storm. I wanted to know her thoughts, maybe get some advice from my usual backcountry partner. But a half-hour later, I hadn't heard from her. The message might've still been trying to send, or maybe her reply was still trying to reach me. There was no way of knowing for sure.

I rolled over and pulled out a note Melanie had scribbled onto a scrap of paper and snuck into a meal she'd dehydrated for me. I read it for the fourth time that day, then a fifth and a sixth.

This rice was made with super energetic magical powers. Your feet will feel better from the anti-inflammatory properties, and the veggies will give you good nutrients and antioxidants to bring you home healthy to me. Love you!"

I smiled. I missed her.

We'd spent weeks apart at a time while I'd hiked through Southern California, and I'd contemplated quitting the PCT altogether *several* times because of it, when I'd been at my lowest. Mel had been my adventure partner for over four solid years. I wanted her to be right there, to tell her about the snow and discuss our options. I wanted to hear her logic, her suggestions, what *she* believed I was capable of trekking through—or not trekking through.

I tucked the note carefully back into my bag of essential items and slid into my tight down tube for the night. My thoughts attempted to wander back to the threat of snow, but they were no match for my exhaustion after two nights of poor sleep and the hard hiking in between.

7
FIREBALL

By 6:30 a.m., we were on the trail. My left foot struggled to warm up, sending wincing flashes of pain from my heel with every step. The first couple of miles were nice and flat headed toward the ominously named Death Canyon Creek. The information I'd gathered barely mentioned it, only noting it typically dried into stagnant pools later in the season.

The four of us were stopped in our tracks at the bank of a six-foot-wide channel of rushing water.

"Were we supposed to have a big crossing this morning?" Amped asked.

I shrugged. "I... guess so."

The options were limited, and a bit crap. The two safest choices were a six-foot leap at the trail, or a bushwhack through a downstream thicket of reeds growing out of the creek. To my eyes, the first option was impossible. A long jump with fifty pounds on my back was bound to go poorly for the kid whose high school track and field coach forgot he was on the team. At some point I'd just stopped going to practice and no one noticed.

I was that good.

Without a second thought, Amped rocked back and sprinted toward the creek like a bull headed to maul a particularly fluorescent matador. He hucked all 240 pounds of his collective mass across the channel, barely sticking the landing on the other side—but he made it.

Road Dog and Vagabond Runner *also* took off and leapt successfully across the creek! The nurturing, maternal part of my brain stopped in for an encouraging pep talk.

Just jump, you wuss!

Six feet wasn't a record-setting long jump, but I'd spent the morning struggling just to walk. The reed bushwhacking option looked uncomfortable, but it was likely less humiliating than a full-effort leap into the middle of the creek.

I entered the thicket, awkwardly wedging my boots into reed crotches to stay above the water. Stiff branches threaded through my pack and clothes, trying their damnedest to stop my progress. On repeat, I stepped forward until I couldn't move, then reversed enough to unthread whatever branch had needled its way through my pack strap, waist strap, water bottle holder, wallet etc. After enough f-words to cement my spot in hell, I reached the middle of the thicket, the point where all the reeds were growing away from me.

From the shore, a dammed mass of branches looked like a solid bridge to finish the crossing, but the branches barely took any weight before it collapsed, gifting me with a soggy foot for the day. I was staring across a four-foot gap to a boulder on the opposite bank. After all that struggling, I had to jump anyway. A wise voice told me to go back through the reeds and jump across where my team had—but my prideful dipshittedness is *not* to be trifled with.

My crossing was taking an awful lot longer than everyone else's, and I could feel my teammates watching me, likely with some degree of thinning patience in the cold. I prayed they couldn't see the beads of struggle sweat on my forehead.

"Oh yeah, this way isn't so bad!" I called over.

I eyed the opposite bank intensely, as though if I were to stare at it hard enough, it would give up and come closer. Amped walked over to the bank.

"You good, bud?" he shouted over the creek.

"I'm all right!"

I wasn't all right, and Amped knew it. He dropped his pack and shuffled down the loose dirt to stand on the bank as close as he could get. I summoned all the force I could and kicked off my rear foot—which did nothing more than fire down through the reeds and into the whitewater.

You're going in, my mind informed me in a calm, matter-of-fact tone, like a secretary informing a boss about a missed call.

But to my surprise, my downward trajectory into the creek changed. Amped extended over to grab the haul loop on my pack, dug into that farm-boy strength, and hauled me over to the bank like I was a damn baby sheep.

But to be clear, I am *NOT* a damn baby sheep, but a 170-pound grown man with a fifty-pound pack on.

A familiar tent was pitched nearby, our buddy Fireball, who was, um— nowhere *near* four miles farther down the trail.

"Good morning!" we all called over with friendly smiles.

Fireball raised his eyes from a steaming tin to return an awkward head nod, but turned away, seemingly to avoid any further interaction. I shook it off and dug deep, commanding myself to give him the benefit of the doubt. It was just confusing to me that he wouldn't jump at the security of being part of a crew.

A couple miles later, Fireball caught us trudging up a long set of switchbacks. He surprised us with a stop to talk.

"Ehrressupry, M...T... R?" Fireball carefully asked, scanning the four of us for any signs of comprehension.

"You have a resupply at Muir Trail Ranch? MTR?" I asked.

His eyes lit up. "Yes!"

"Oh." My face scrunched. "Crap."

MTR is a popular resupply in the middle of the High Sierra—typically. But this year, Muir Trail Ranch was still closed. *Way* closed. It wouldn't be open to host hikers for *months*. Arriving at the deserted ranch hungry and expecting a resupply could be disastrous.

I'm not going to be able to explain this to him—unless I know more Korean than I think.

I brushed the thought aside before my stupid brain started entertaining the idea that I knew a single shred of Korean.

"MTR?" I asked.

Fireball smiled and nodded his head.

"Is closed."

He smiled and nodded more.

I demonstrated every negative gesture I could think of; an "x" with my arms, I shook my head, made a stank face—he just kept nodding.

"You can't go there. There are no people at MTR."

After a thoughtful pause, Fireball smiled again. "MTR! Yes!"

He took out his phone and opened the navigation app, which was peppered with Korean symbols. Fireball confidently pointed at the general spot where MTR was located, almost a hundred miles from where we stood.

"MTR," he repeated, tapping on the screen.

I scanned his pack for an SOS, GPS, or navigation device aside from his cell phone. I didn't see one, but that wasn't exactly surprising. There was quite a blasé approach to navigation equipment among thru-hikers, even those entering the Sierra. In the interest of maintaining packs as light as possible, many were relying solely on phone apps, often with no form of backup navigation or way to contact help. Even bringing paper maps was hotly debated, despite the fact that they weighed essentially nothing.

But really, what could happen to an electronic, water-sensitive, cold-intolerant potato chip on a hike through a never-ending expanse of snow and water?

Most of us were using the same phone app as our primary navigation tool. Even without cell service, it used the phone's GPS chip to roughly locate your position relative to the buried PCT. While the app worked unarguably well, there was no way I'd be betting my mortality on a smartphone. Sure, it was tempting to lighten my pack by ditching my inReach, and who *wouldn't* want to shave a cool half-ounce by leaving paper maps at home? But all those were complacent errors with consequences not to be fully appreciated until you found yourself with a dead phone in the middle of the snow, hundreds of miles from civilization, no idea which way to hike, and zero trails to follow.

If Fireball strolled into a shuttered MTR, he'd be at least a day away from an exit, and that's only *IF* he knew which direction to hike. Escaping with his life would be a roll of the dice.

I dragged my finger around his phone and repeatedly stressed his need to exit at Kearsarge Pass for a resupply instead of heading deeper into the backcountry.

He smiled a lot and nodded more.

Fireball tucked his phone into its pocket and walked away. I tried to forget about it. After all, I barely knew the guy, and he seemed rather resistant to befriending us. As a fellow hiker, I wanted to help him stay safe, but I couldn't reasonably ensure the safety of a man who didn't speak English and refused to hike or camp with us. Short of hogtying and loading him onto my pack, there was nothing I could do.

And if you hear about his death in two weeks? Would you have done anything different right now?

Overcast skies and cold, bullying gusts escorted in the storm. It took over a mile of huffing and puffing up steep switchbacks until we warmed enough to remove puffy jackets, beanies, and gloves. Around 10,700 feet, we stopped for lunch at a breathtaking perch, high above the expansive Owens Valley to the east, the same desert valley where my little town of Bishop sat about a hundred miles north.

Traction was hard to figure out the rest of the day. Every time we'd get sick of sliding around in boots and taking humiliating tumbles, crampons would go on just in time for us to find dirt around the next bend. Moods were dropping. The afternoon miles were lengthening.

Fireball's footprints were ahead of us as we closed in on Diaz Creek, our goal for the night. His imprinted steps veered left unexpectedly, heading downhill along a snowy hillside. GPS confirmed that Fireball had headed in a ninety-degree vector from the trail. I broke off from his prints, sticking to a level path around the mountainside, accompanied by sharp twinges of guilt.

Shouldn't we go looking for him? What if he gets lost?

"That's not your problem. He came out here alone. Leave him alone," I lectured myself under my breath.

Amped was chomping at the bit behind me, wanting to move faster, ready to get the day over with. He pushed into the lead, but only long enough to step onto an unassuming patch of snow that collapsed under him, swallowing his entire lower half. With a pained grunt, he landed in the innocuous trickle responsible for carving the large void. After a minute to let the shock subside, and a high step to single-leg squat back out of the pit, he graciously handed the lead back to me.

The afternoon was warm as we made our final descent into the Diaz Creek drainage. Crampons were no longer biting in the slush and we stumbled through exhausting progress, taking turns picking ourselves back up off the snow. All day, Vagabond Runner had trailed behind us, but the distance grew until she was nowhere in sight. We set our packs down to rest and regroup. Fifteen long minutes later, right as we were about to backtrack to find her, she finally appeared.

She looked exhausted, and her typically big, infectious smile had been beaten down to a struggling grin.

"How're you doing, Vagabond?" I asked.

"Phew, I'm eh—*crashing*. Pretty hard. I just feel hungry, even after our lunch *and* my snack bar."

"Your snack *bar*? Singular? Is that all you're eating between meals?"

Amped and I had packed about a thousand calories in snacks alone for every day, and we were easily mowing through it and wanting more. A single bar was good for 300 calories *at best*.

"Yeah." She sensed the thinly veiled concern in my eyes. "But that's what we've had through the whole trail, and it's been fine. The hiking is a bit tougher now, obviously... I'm probably burning more calories than before." She closed her eyes and sighed. "But I'll be fine. Let's keep moving. I can't wait to get into camp!"

She smiled, forever in high spirits.

Arriving at Diaz Creek, we found a dry campsite slotted between rolling mounds of melting snow. Road Dog went to work to get a campfire going. An old trail rake was leaning against a tree. While I was still trying to postulate how and why a rake was all the way out there, Amped was gleefully grooming his tent spot.

Like they say, you can take the boy out of the farm...

We gathered around the campfire, each of us with our prepared dinners.

"Man, I've been looking forward to this all day!" Road Dog said.

"All day? Are you both hiking hungry?" I asked, miserable at just the thought.

"We've got our meals covered," Vagabond Runner said, "but just having the one snack is rougher than we'd thought."

"Do you think you have enough to get to Kearsarge Pass?" I asked, doing my best not to appear alarmed—for fear of them knowing my *exact* feelings.

"We've got enough food," Road Dog answered in a stern tone that sounded like he was trying to convince all four of us, including himself.

Vagabond Runner gave him a side glance, but returned her eyes to the fire, making no signals of agreement.

I'd been overly hungry on the trail more than once. Hiking into Big Bear, California, I'd under-packed my food and spent thirty punitive miles followed by a below-freezing night with an empty stomach. That desperation of hiker hunger coupled with no access to food, no way to fix it, was deeply etched in my memory.

"This is how we packed all the way through Southern California," Road Dog reiterated. "It worked." He stared into the fire, thinking back along the trail. "Although there's also no town food now. We were stopping somewhere for a big meal every few days. Maybe that's the difference."

Several very hard days were between us and the next chance to bolster our food supply. Across camp, sitting in front of Road Dog and Vagabond's tent were their bear canisters. Curiously, they were the smaller BearVault model. My BearVault was the largest that manufacturer offered, and I'd stuffed it to its absolute capacity.

My eyes widened. One of the small, blue canisters—*was empty.*

Again trying to not appear too alarmed, I locked eyes with Amped and nodded to direct him to look over at their tent. He instantly saw it too.

"Is that canister *empty?*" Amped reflexively asked in misery, as if he was its owner.

Road Dog glanced over. "Yeah. But we've got a big food bag in the tent. We'll be fine, I promise."

Vagabond Runner remained silent. Amped dropped it, not wanting to make anyone upset. I didn't doubt our partners would be able to survive and even smile through their discomfort, but I also didn't want to watch them suffer. The depths of my concerns stayed off my tongue, but roamed freely through my mind. I was finding it tough to force myself to be okay with others' decisions. They were on their own journey. I couldn't expect to keep everyone happy, warm, and fed. I could barely do that for myself.

As darkness was setting in, Fireball walked by camp on a side trail off the PCT. I was relieved to see him alive—but he'd clearly lost the trail again. We called out to him, and he returned a quick wave and a glazed-over smile, but avoided any further eye contact and scurried along, holding a manic pace in the wrong direction.

The hints were adding up, and it was obvious he wasn't going to join us. I could sympathize with him though. I'm sure translating conversations was exhausting after these long days. If I were hiking alone in South Korea, I'd probably want some solitude as well, just to focus on the hike itself. But as I was watching his colorful pack wander out of sight in the opposite direction of the trail, it took everything I had not to go grab him by the pack-strap and sit him down next to the fire.

Clouds had gathered overhead. I sat in the vestibule of my tent and sent out another satellite request for a forecast in our area. It came back with a ninety percent chance of freezing rain and snow the next day, and a seventy percent chance of snow for the two days after. Highs were barely above freezing.

"Uh oh," I muttered.

Movement several hundred yards away, across Diaz Creek, caught my eye. It was Fireball, bushwhacking through heavy brush in the low dusk light, thankfully moving back toward the trail.

What are the odds he knows what's coming?

8

THE STORM

MAY 15, 2017
DIAZ CREEK

"Ohhhh thank God."

I silenced my unnecessary alarm and clicked my headlamp on. The night was brutal. Sleep had been punctuated with shivering wake-ups every forty-five minutes. Each time, I'd hesitantly opened my eyes praying that time had flown past, but every check was met with disappointment. Every single one. The night was 900 hours long, at least. There was something quite stressful about having no escape from being too cold. I spent the perpetual darkness in twirling desperation, searching for a position that didn't involve cold spots. It was official: My choice to exchange my quilt (in which I'd slept comfortably down to ten degrees) for Mel's bag was a *colossal* mistake. If it were at all possible, I would've *gladly* transported from the long, sleepless night back to that stroke of genius moment to deliver a precisely aimed boot to my own groin. The weight savings of several measly ounces was *not* worth it.

Above the stubborn time on my phone screen, the date stood out: May 15. I smiled, reminiscing back to my conversation with Golden Girl and Slim. Now here I was, in the Sierra in the middle of May, just like I'd wanted. My smile lowered a bit. I wasn't exactly the hero of campfire legend I'd romanticized. That guy probably wouldn't have packed his wife's fun-size sleeping bag.

I moved through my miserable morning routine of ice pants and obligated stretching, then groaned my way into the standing position outside my tent. I felt like a 103-year-old the day after running a marathon. Seemingly every muscle I owned was sore, but I was happy to have all my layers on, and not still be shivering in Mel's tiny down refrigerator.

Amped was a bit more comfortable through the night. From his journal:

In the morning when it's twelve degrees outside the comfort of your sleeping bag, it's tough to will yourself out into the day. I do it. I hear the zippers of my fellow hikers and it wills me out. Getting an early start in this environment is important and I would later learn the extent of it.

My red fingers stung as feeling returned to them. I broke into a precious breakfast I'd been saving for a morning where I needed a pick-me-up: a Bobo's Bar. Bobo's Bars were a rare treat, since they were on the pricier end. Mel had snuck one into my resupply as a surprise, and in this world where money was meaningless but heavily processed and packaged foods were gold, I was beyond excited for an upgraded breakfast. But as I peeled the plastic back, all of my Bobo's excitement evaporated.

Mold. All over the bar. I broke off a piece and there was even fuzzy, white webbing throughout the inside of the bar. A bit of exaggerated panic surged through me. I flipped the packaging around to find the tiny, printed expiration date, which was still a year off.

"That's great," I bitterly muttered.

Calories were carefully planned out and scheduled. In spite of the bear canister stuffed with fifteen pounds of food sitting in front of my growling stomach, there was no longer breakfast for that morning. I stared at my ruined meal, considering the consequences of chowing down the moldy bar anyway. But if there was one way my life could get even less comfortable, it would be giving myself the gift of exposing my bare ass every ten minutes to squirt out my terrible decisions in a snowstorm.

I sulked my way just outside of camp and kicked a shallow recess in the ground, then dropped the Bobo's Bar into it. I kicked a bit of dirt onto the bar in gentle reverence, like I was burying a beloved family pet. It was obviously necessary, objectively inedible, and now covered in dirt—but I still wanted to eat it.

I sat back down in camp to lace up my boots. Amped showed up with a big mug of coffee again and handed it to me. He'd spotted me having my Bobo's funeral, and broke off a chunk of his breakfast waffle.

"Here bud, eat something. Today's going to be tough."

* * *

August 20, 2005. Twelve years earlier.

I yawned under a row of fluorescent lights over a textbook of tightly spaced words explaining reactor theory. It was a Saturday and perfectly quiet, the only acceptable volume in our military setting. No music, no talking, just the overhead buzz of those lights. Ten other freshly shaven sailors were spread throughout the classroom, trying to cram in the ridiculous amount of knowledge the Navy expected from their budding nuclear operators.

We were all about ten months out of boot camp, in the midst of the most academically rigorous program the military had to offer their enlisted sailors. School had been my entire life for those ten months, and not in the typical college sense, where freshmen could sleep through lectures, skip assignments at their leisure, and still manage to pass their classes. The Navy's nuclear program demanded perfection and allowed effectively zero time for anything but study. Where college students found time to drink, hang out with their friends, collect STDs, and maybe even go to the occasional movie, I'd only known my seat under those buzzing lights, my seat at the chow hall, or my stiff, military-issue mattress.

I hadn't made friends. My girlfriend I'd entered the military with had long since dumped me for another guy back home, and for good reason. I was 2,000 miles away, there were no cell phones allowed for sixteen hours of my day, and my focus was elsewhere. Drinking alcohol underage or smoking weed had the potential to land me in a world of humiliation along with a demotion in rank (and therefore pay), so I didn't. Six months in, I'd earned the privilege to head out to the civilian world to visit restaurants and maybe even try my hand at picking up another girlfriend with my tight haircut and immaculate uniform. I'd even bought a nice truck with the money I'd earned, but it sat unused in a big parking lot, collecting dust alongside many others.

A fellow sailor, a light-skinned Mexican guy with the last name Ramos lettered across the front of his uniform, approached me in the sparsely populated classroom. I'd studied around him for our entire time in South Carolina, but we'd exchanged few words.

"Winsor, you want to be roommates in Prototype?"

I was nervous to be involved in breaking the strictly enforced silence, but it was the weekend, and our superiors were likely out having a life instead of trying to find underlings to make examples out of.

"Sure," I replied, without a second thought.

Prototype was the next phase in our training, the last six months before we'd head out to the fleet to operate the plants onboard aircraft carriers and submarines. We needed roommates to fill our military-issued apartments, a tough proposition without friends. Externally, I'd kept to myself, indifferent to most people around me. Internally, I was angry. Lingering teenage frustration and confusion consumed any thoughts unrelated to nuclear power.

Joining the Navy had been a Hail Mary move. At seventeen, I was sleeping on the floor of my best friend's room. My relationship with my parents had soured over my rejection of the family religion, Mormonism. I'd grown up in the religion until almost sixteen years old, when I'd decided I wasn't onboard with the next big step for Mormon teenagers: the mission.

From age nineteen to twenty-one, Mormon boys were expected to venture out across the planet to convert others into the religion. I hadn't necessarily been unhappy going to church. I had many good friends there, and through the church-sponsored chapter of the Boy Scouts I'd made a lifelong, intimate connection with the outdoors. But unlike the claims of my fellow Mormons, I'd never felt the overwhelming feeling of truth about the gospel itself. Through tears in their eyes and wavering voices, they'd testify of a life-altering moment where the Holy Spirit had descended into their soul to assert, without a doubt, that God was real and Jesus loved them, and the Mormons were right, and the path to eternal happiness was a bargain at just ten percent of their income.

I watched those testimonies with a torturous guilt. I'd never experienced anything close to that, and it wasn't for lack of trying. I'd gotten onto my knees a dozen times, doing my best to close my fifteen-year-old eyes and faithfully ask God for a verification that the Mormon church was the one true gospel, but the big man upstairs must've been struggling to get a message through all those fleeting teenager thoughts of video games, skateboarding, and boobies. I was supposed to be taking committing steps toward a mission, where I'd theoretically be heading abroad to tell other people to believe in something I didn't. Shamefully hidden in the depths of my mind, I'd long decided a mission wasn't going to happen.

When I told my parents, it had been in an immature, teenage fashion, and it put an instant rift in our relationship. I remember my ex-Green Beret father looking me sternly in the eyes to deliver his unflinching directive: "In this house, we go to church. While you're living under this roof, you'll abide by the rules of this house."

So I'd left. Even though I'd only tried to back away from the Mormon mission, not so much from the church community itself, my world became increasingly uncomfortable as the gossip spread. I hadn't fully thought through the consequences, and in the already chaos-soaked years of adolescence, I lost the vast majority of my friends and alienated my family almost overnight. My relationship with my parents deteriorated into almost total silence. My Mormon friends at school formed a measured distance between us, as they'd been taught to keep themselves in the presence of "good" influences, just like I'd been taught. It felt like the whole world was talking about me behind my back, and I retreated back into myself like a turtle into its shell.

My best friend, Seth, was the only non-Mormon friend I had, and his parents took me in with no resistance I was aware of, although there must've been some real concern about supporting a miserable, hormone-addled eating machine. They generously offered what they could, which was their fridge and the bit of carpet next to Seth's bed.

I'd been raised with an instilled fear of leaving the Mormon faith. I was assured if I left, I'd be in for eternal misery—and my life would fall apart. That had always rubbed me the wrong way. It felt like I had invisible razor wire surrounding my life. But through my senior year, that threat seemed to be inching ever closer to reality.

I had a terrible job pushing carts in the Arizona heat for $5.15 per hour, a 1988 mufferless Jeep Cherokee that only ran on occasion, and a girlfriend who was clearly cheating on me. I stayed with her, not because I was overly fond of our relationship, but because I simply didn't have enough love in my life to be picky. I played increasingly rough with alcohol and engaged in more and more self-destructive behaviors.

I feared the Mormons were right. I'd landed myself in hell, and I hadn't even died yet.

I wouldn't say I was suicidal, but if there'd been an easy switch to turn it all off, I would have. Being alive wasn't particularly enjoyable. All of my heartache and stress and misery going away didn't exactly seem like a bad deal.

I hated where I was and who I was becoming. After arriving at the realization I had no prospects for my future, no family, a lousy girl-friend, and only one real friend, my interest was piqued by a chipper guy with a buzz cut wandering between classes in our high school. He was a foreign entity in my world, but he was put together, happy, and looked like someone people respected. He was administering a test called the ASVAB (Armed Services Vocational Aptitude Battery). It was a no-harm-no-foul exam that would not only give me some gauge of my career aptitude, but would also get me out of an hour of French III, where my very, very Mormon partner wouldn't stop telling me how fervently she was praying for my soul.

I had good grades and quite enjoyed how good I was at math and science, but had zero guidance toward college. I didn't know about scholarships, didn't have money, and didn't have parents or grandparents with money.

The ASVAB turned out to be a spatial reasoning and logic test, which seemed rather simple to me. I received a call from every branch of the military the next week, after scoring in the highest percentile on the test.

THE STORM

I'd never really thought the military sounded like a fun idea, but I picked the offer with the biggest sign-on bonus and initial rank, and six months later I was across the country in Great Lakes, Illinois, getting yelled at by a much less chipper guy with a buzz cut for folding my underwear wrong. We were forced up early and demeaned. I locked eyes with grown men taking dumps while I did the same, got poked and prodded with dozens of needles, had my wisdom teeth yanked two minutes after being informed it was happening whether I liked it or not, and endured many other instances of debasing humiliation and discomfort.

But, for my situation being *logically* terrible, I was satisfied. I wasn't happy, but I'd been given a purpose. I'd been helicoptered out of my situation in Arizona like a sheep rescued from a cliff ledge and dropped into a new environment, a fresh meadow where a black sheep could start over.

In Prototype, in our three-bedroom apartment crammed with four sailors, Miguel Ramos and I had clicked. I opened up to him about my internal misery, confusion, and anger. He was the first person to hear the total mess going on between my ears. Aching for some semblance of family in my life, I told him I'd been on the fence about going back to Mormonism, to finally throw in the towel on my stubborn resolve to be myself. All it was going to take was a phone call to announce my return to the fold, and my shame-ridden nightmare would be over!

Miguel wrapped me up in a big, burly hug without hesitation. "Screw that, man! *I'm* your family now. You can have my family too!"

I appreciated the sentiment but figured it was an empty gesture. But Miguel wasn't messing around. He took me into his life like a brother. No matter how separated we were, even while he was routinely 200 feet underwater in a steel tube for six months at a time, he would call me, send me messages, emails—whatever it took to check in with his adopted sibling.

* * *

"Thanks, man."

I savored the bit of cold waffle as if I'd never eat again. My hiker hunger was back in full force.

"Gotta keep you alive out here," he said. "That's why you brought me, right?"

I laughed. "That, and to sample the postholes for me."

I knocked the frozen mud off my snowshoes and crampons, then strapped them to my pack. Dark clouds were forming around the peaks to the north. Our goal for the day was big, fifteen miles to Rock Creek—and we were walking directly into a snowstorm. Temps were already low at Diaz Creek, and we were heading into higher, colder elevations. If we kept moving, we'd be okay.

Vagabond Runner and Road Dog emerged from their tent smiling, pumped to tackle the hard day ahead. Amped had his typical no-big-deal attitude. I seemed to be the only one who wasn't one hundred percent confident in how the day would end, but that's how I'd always been in the backcountry. Maybe it was my inner Boy Scout, forever paranoid I hadn't fulfilled his Be Prepared motto.

Just as our boots were back on the Pacific Crest Trail, innocent snow flurries drifted down from the darkening sky. Within a couple miles of camp, fresh crampon tracks in the dirt made it clear our Korean friend had again camped just beyond us. I again pushed the mild offense aside, chalking it up to our cultural and language barriers. There would be plenty of time to sob into my pillow later.

We caught up to Fireball standing at the base of a steep snowdrift blocking the trail. In obvious frustration, he was kicking at the drift with the outside edge of his boot, but the snow had frozen bullet-hard overnight. After a morning of following his crampon prints in the dirt, they were now curiously strapped to his pack, in a moment where they would be of perfect utility.

Fireball shot a nervous glance over his shoulder, then spun back to resume kicking with renewed vigor, as if a band of notorious thugs were closing in. I didn't understand this guy. Had one of us gone for a sleepwalk and shat in his pillowcase? He attempted to weight a shallow foot placement, which collapsed, causing him to wobble and slide the few inches back down to where he'd started. Without any progress up the drift, the full depth of his nightmares were realized when our smiling quartet caught up to him.

"Hello, Fireball." The friendly tone in my voice was getting harder to maintain. "How'd your hiking go yesterday?"

His eyes darted among the four of us, without answering.

"Are you okay?" I asked.

"No good. Night, *so* eh, cold. I, eh, no sleep."

His crampon tracks had started close to 10,500 feet, almost a thousand feet higher than where we'd camped, which meant the poor bastard had likely been sleeping in single digit temps. In his heavily broken English, he communicated he'd spent most of the night awake, boiling revolving batches of water for his Nalgene bottle to cuddle in his sleeping bag.

I strapped my crampons on and French-stepped up the drift, angling my toes downhill and weaving my feet with enough care to avoid slashing my own calves. I moved slowly with exaggerated movement, hoping Fireball could gather what little I knew about crampon technique to help keep him moving forward. He strapped on his crampons and followed us up the ice with success.

A mile later, we stopped for a break at the junction for Trail Pass, a common PCT exit point to reach Horseshoe Meadows, where there was a parking lot and a long mountain road leading down to Lone Pine in the Owens Valley. Fireball also paused for a rest, leaving him wide open to be assaulted by some friendly conversation.

"How far are you hiking today, Fireball?" I asked.

His translational wheels turned for a few seconds. "Fifehteen mile."

"How many miles did you hike yesterday?" Vagabond Runner asked.

He cocked his head with a confused look, as if he'd already answered that question. "Fifehteen mile."

I couldn't help but do some quick math, and he'd surely been a few miles short of fifteen, based on where we'd camped, but I brushed it aside. "Are you hiking fifteen miles today? Or fifteen miles *every* day?"

"*All* days. Fifehteen."

Oh boy.

"No matter what?" Amped asked, concern in his eyes.

Setting a strict daily mileage on dry trail was fine, but in the mountains, it was far from wise. River crossings and mountain passes had ideal windows of opportunity throughout the day—and downright dangerous ones. You had to think about elevation and snow levels. A rigid mileage goal had placed him sleeping uncomfortably for the night, but later, it could put him on avalanche-prone slopes in the unstable afternoons or push him to cross rivers during the heaviest flowrates.

Fireball nodded. "Fifehteen mile. All days to MTR."

My stomach knotted back up. My warning hadn't gotten through. Fireball promptly departed the junction, chipping away at his fifteen miles.

"You think he knows the significance of Trail Pass? Or where any other bail points are if he needs them?" Road Dog asked.

"I don't know," I answered. "I hope so."

Snow flurries had been off and on, but the intimidating, dark sky remained above. We were all still dry, warm, and after a quick consensus—ready for more, so we cut our break short and continued uphill along the PCT in crampons.

Traversing the hillside above the gorgeous, snowbound Horseshoe Meadows, we were essentially walking along the forty-degree side of a giant bowl of ice. The angled snow was a nightmare on the ankles. Facing downhill and cross-stepping one foot after the other would've been more comfortable, but five miles of it would take an eternity. So we stayed facing perpendicular to the slope and gritted our teeth through the building misery of our ankles jacked over, strained under the heft of our packs.

We weaved through dense pines, attempting to maintain our elevation through the traverse. The sun-warmed trees had created deep cones around them known as tree wells. Some wells were amazingly deep, up to twenty feet!

Fireball's footsteps were the only prints in the otherwise pristine snow. I was about to insist we take a short rest to let our ankles decompress, when a big mess in the snow appeared. Fireball's crampon prints led to the top of a fifteen-foot slide mark into a tree well. A set of *boot prints* resumed from the bottom of the slide.

Over the next snow berm, Fireball sat on a tiny sloped ledge in the snow, a blown-apart crampon in his lap. His gloves were off, and with wet, red fingers, he was threading what looked like one of his boot's laces through the crampon eyelets.

The overwhelming urge to forcibly pull him into our group resurfaced. Our team glanced between each other with the same pain. Fireball was obviously out of his element—like all of us were—but he was alone, and I wasn't confident his preparation was enough for the task at hand. I had great respect for anyone with the courage to dive into the unknown. I wanted to cheer him on, to be supportive of whatever journey he was on, but *goddammit*—I also didn't want to hear something catastrophic had happened, and then have to live with the guilt of not proactively trying to help.

"Fireball," Vagabond Runner called down, "Are you okay?"

Without looking at her, he nodded once in the affirmative.

She glanced at me, then turned back toward him. "Why don't you join us today?"

Again without looking at her, he shook his head.

"Do you need anything?" Vagabond Runner asked, unable to hide the pain in her voice.

One more negative head shake.

"You can't help someone who doesn't want help," I muttered to Vagabond.

We continued ahead of Fireball through the endless ankle-torqueing. The ball of my right foot was beginning to form a blister from the skin being repeatedly stretched sideways. The hillside was starting to wear on everybody, alongside another discomfort we hadn't seen coming.

Thirst.

We hadn't seen water since we left camp that morning, and our bottles had collectively dried up. Well—I suppose *technically* we'd seen tons and tons of water—but all in a more solid form than we preferred for drinking, and in a bizarre twist, no one was in the mood for slushies.

Melting snow in our stoves was always an option, but what I'd been referring to as "flurries" officially outgrew my optimism. It was dumping, and stopping for a relaxed melting session was now out of the question.

A reportedly reliable water source ended up being buried in snow still, so we pressed on toward a second source.

Also buried.

A sense of growing unease was building inside me.

"Water, water everywhere and not a drop to drink, huh?" Vagabond Runner gave me a struggling smile. Her lips were pale and starting to tremble.

Water was suddenly a real problem, a real damn weird problem, at that. In these conditions, our team wasn't going to be able to stop and melt snow without setting up some kind of shelter first. Winds picked up, driving the temperature down and pushing discomfort into our jackets and sleeves. Everyone was getting cold, but Vagabond Runner was clearly the most vulnerable. Watching the worry in Road Dog's eyes, I was grateful to not have Melanie there for the first time. That girl needed a parka to get through the Walmart produce section. I couldn't imagine having her in a twenty-degree snowstorm, many miles from anything warm.

Amped led the way through the disorienting storm, attempting to draw the most efficient line through the drifts. I kept my phone out to give him helpful prompts like "trend uphill" or "maintain elevation" or "find better friends."

On a south-facing hillside, we stumbled across a seep, essentially an exposed patch of soggy dirt. It was far from ideal to stop moving, but almost more than we needed warmth, we needed water. Our team made a quick decision to capitalize on the opportunity and started digging a sump where water could collect into a pool to submerge our water bottles.

The wind worked hard to strip our warmth while we stood still around our muddy seep. It took time for the muddy water to fill the sump, it took time for the sump to turn clear, it took time to fill our eight water bottles, and it took time to get packs organized and back on our backs.

It took too much time.

High winds and heavy snow continued building. Vagabond Runner fell silent. She'd added bread bags to her gloves as a vapor barrier, but the addition was either too little, too late, or both. Everyone, especially her loving husband, could see her escalating misery, but none of us could offer any remedy. We were all in the same battle, struggling against the same adversary.

As we neared the Cottonwood Pass junction in whiteout conditions, two silhouettes appeared through the haze, headed in the opposite direction.

Who would be out here in these garbage conditions headed south?

Amped pulled his hand out of a glove and delivered an ear-piercing whistle to get the mysterious duo's attention. It worked. The two silhouettes stopped, then started moving our way. The mask of the whiteout gradually lifted as we got closer. One figure was a stocky woman and the other was a tall, lanky man—in *shorts*.

"He's not wearing shorts, is he?" I asked. "There's no way…"

Amped replied, "I'm pretty sure it's shorts."

I doubled down. "There's no way. It has to be shorts over leggings *or something*."

But as the man appeared from the whiteout, sure enough. Homeboy was standing out in the twenty-degree blizzard in a light jacket, short shorts, and microspikes on his trail-runners.

Before I could say normal human stuff like "Hello" or "How's it going?" my brain blurted out, "Duuude. **Shorts**?!"

He chuckled, then replied in a thick Swiss accent, "I no need. Legs not get cold."

It took a slight headshake to refocus enough to undrop my jaw and ask where they were headed.

"Lone Pine," the woman replied. "We're moving too slow each day to make it to Kearsarge Pass. We're calling it."

They looked like they'd stepped right off the trail in Southern California; pack size, shorts, microspikes. I knew down to the damn *ounce* what could be left at home and what couldn't, and there was no way their warmth and/or food was built up for the Sierra.

But what did I know? Maybe the Swiss typically hiked naked, and what I was seeing was their version of heavy winter packing. Maybe I was an

American sissy who needed a fifty-pound pack, food, and "body heat" or whatever. They both seemed only mildly uncomfortable, even with snowflake-bedazzled leg hair.

These two maniacs are bailing out of this and we're not? Is continuing a mistake? Do I need to say something?

Our crew watched with unspoken jealousy as the couple disappeared back into the whiteout. It took a few minutes to get our bearings. Our phones weren't responding well with wet screens and frozen fingers.

I didn't want to be the first to quit. That felt like a job for the weakest link. But Amped seemed solid. Road Dog and Vagabond Runner were quiet, but it was unclear to what extent their combined, unflinching psych was capable of overriding discomfort.

We reached the Cottonwood Pass junction at the peak of the blizzard. Four steep, rugged, unknown miles from us was the Horseshoe Meadows parking lot, where Mel could theoretically meet us within a matter of hours. None of us wanted to take that detour—one that we'd have to eventually reverse to pick up where we left off—but it was our only chance to escape.

This was it. We either bailed to safety or we ducked our heads and pushed further and higher into the storm—and into a stretch of backcountry where bailing would be very difficult, if not impossible. Snow collected around our boots with incredible speed. All of us had the same nervous eyes, but no one wanted to say it. After all, *technically*, all of us were fine. Uncomfortable, sure, but objectively missing an acute reason to bail.

So, we put our backs to Cottonwood Pass—and resumed hiking.

With every trudging step further from safety, a lump in my throat grew. My thoughts circled, pumping out questions that quickly outran any answers.

Are we being safe? Is this too much or am I worrying too much? Is it time to toughen up or are we in danger? Was that guy really in shorts?

We took some partial cover in a grove of trees to shift into snowshoes and get on top of the building layer of powder. Exchanging crampons

60

for snowshoes went quickly for me and Amped since we'd primarily trained in snowshoes, but Road Dog and Vagabond Runner remained on the ground for quite a while. Then it dawned on me.

This is their first time putting on snowshoes.

Unlike the bluebird learning environment we'd been gifted to figure out crampons, we now stood in the polar *opposite* environment. Road Dog and Vagabond were visibly exhausted, freezing, and desperate to get moving again. With gloves off, fiddling with the myriad plastic straps using wet, red fingers, a loud thought pushed into the forefront of my mind.

Get out of here.

Through trembling fingers, our partners adjusted and readjusted each strap. To my great relief, they stood up ready to go! But a few steps later, their snowshoes had loosened, and they plopped back down in the snow to try again. I'd never heard anything but positive encouragement come out of these two, but they exchanged curt, frustrated words.

Amped proceeded ahead, walking in circles fifty yards away in an attempt to stay warm. From his journal:

Road Dog and Vagabond Runner struggle to get their snowshoes on as the temperature drops and it turns into a whiteout. It's getting dangerous. Especially for Vagabond Runner, who has zero body fat to burn. She shivers as the snow dumps four, six, eight inches.

I tried to help, but their binding system was different from mine. The wet cold had seeped in around my neck and sleeves, and a shiver started I couldn't suppress.

Please let them figure this out faster, I pleaded with the trail gods—who were probably too busy torturing us to hear.

Every minute felt like an hour. Eventually, Road Dog and Vagabond Runner stood with snowshoes ready to go.

"All right, let's do this!" Road Dog shouted next to a still-silent Vagabond Runner. Amped was chomping at the bit, clearly ready to keep hiking too.

So we kept hiking.

The snow continued to pile around us, nearing a full foot. Whipping winds tugged at our cinched jacket hoods. We were still almost *ten miles* from Rock Creek. A scant six had taken half the day already.

Amped slowed until his team was close enough to speak. "Everyone all right?"

Nobody answered, but all four of us were unable to hide our discomfort. Everyone was wet. Everyone was freezing. Temps had bottomed out, and the storm showed no signs of calming. We'd crossed the line. We *were* cold. Now we were *too* cold.

My snowshoes weren't visible, buried under the powder we'd been trudging through. Even if we somehow made it to Rock Creek safely, we'd be surrounded by avalanche-prone terrain. We'd potentially have to sit still for days until the sun could consolidate and stabilize the new snow. Nobody had the food margin for that.

My stubborn determination to not be the weak link faltered, and I forced out some of the most difficult words I've ever had to speak.

"We should talk about bailing while we still can."

Bailing was going to add eight miles of hiking and thousands of feet of elevation change getting off and returning through Cottonwood Pass, but Road Dog agreed first, and without hesitation.

"Look, if you had to even bring it up, there's really nothing to discuss. All of us either need to be in, or we all need to get out."

Vagabond Runner agreed, smiling for the first time in hours. Amped was also onboard.

I sent a message to Mel, requesting she make the drive from Bishop to pick us up at Horseshoe Meadows. The inReach struggled to push the message through the thick blanket of clouds above, and I tucked it back into my jacket with crossed fingers. We pivoted our aim toward safety, lifting everyone's spirits a bit—but the raging storm above kept a lid on any premature celebration. We weren't done yet.

I took the lead back to Cottonwood Pass, retracing our recent steps into a disorienting world of white. We reached the broad, flat top of the pass where a lonely Forest Service sign post welcomed our arrival. I squinted back into the pure white of the blizzard from where we came.

Does Fireball have any way of knowing where to escape? That safety and warmth is just a few miles away?

We aimed northeast off the pass, down a treeless stretch of steep snow. This was avalanche territory, but our options weren't exactly plentiful. I searched for the Swiss couple's footprints for reassurance, but they were nowhere to be seen, likely long since filled in by the storm.

I was *certain*—that guy couldn't have been wearing shorts.

We hesitated at the top of an aggressively pitched slope. Officially out of options, we turned to face the mountainside and kicked steps into the deep powder to begin the slow process of down-climbing. We went one hiker at a time. One slip could potentially take the entire team out, like a bowling ball slamming through an aligned set of pins. As Vagabond Runner made her way down, my thoughts again returned to Fireball.

Does he have the gear or food or knowledge to stay safe out here? Are we abandoning him? What if he doesn't make it? Would we be partially responsible? Would—I—be responsible?

Safely off the steep slope, we launched into a rapid pace, anxious to put the remaining downhill miles behind us. The Horseshoe Meadows parking lot was three miles away, where there would be a warm truck and a beautiful girl waiting to whisk us off to safety. I hadn't paused to check if my message had pushed through the storm, partly because I was dreading the answer. Hiking all the way down to the Owens Valley would tack on a massive length of road-walking to our day.

Visibility increased and winds calmed as we surrendered our hard-fought elevation. Spirits lifted and we began to smile and joke around with each other once again—but a message broke through the storm from Melanie, putting an end to our almost-happiness.

Horseshoe Meadows Road, the road Melanie had to drive up to come get us, was closed.

CRUNCH

We didn't have *two* more miles to walk, we had *fifteen* miles to walk. Lucky for my pissed off arches, thirteen miles of that was on tendon-punishing asphalt. I put my head down on the handle of my trekking poles.

"Noooooo," I groaned in exasperation.

Fifteen miles was a giant day in the snow by itself. We were still shy of ten for the day, but it had felt like thirty. I was ready to lie down and take the SOS button on my inReach for a test drive. The bill for touching that thing was what? $35k?

Worth it.

Maybe I'd push the damn button twice. Have the authorities send one chopper for us, and another filled with pizza. Lost inside my own pouting misery, I'd forgotten to externally share the news.

With hesitation, Amped asked, "Is something wrong?"

From Amped's journal:

The message comes in. The road to Horseshoe Meadows is closed. For real closed. Thirteen miles closed. I just laugh. Of course. This is why we get up early. We'll need every bit of daylight trying to get out of the mountains.

In sobered silence, we resumed marching across the huge snowfield in Horseshoe Meadows. The snowfall ground to a gracious halt right as we reached the campground. All of us opened our bear canisters in greedy anticipation, ready to do some damage. If there was a silver lining to a twenty-five mile day of snow and asphalt, it was that we could finally eat *as much as we wanted.*

Four Pop-Tarts, five tortillas, two tuna packets, a Snickers, and half of a jar of peanut butter disappeared before I felt even a twinge of satisfaction. I stopped there, seeing as how I was still thirteen miles from the nearest shot of insulin.

Out of nowhere, my stomach started cramping within the first mile along the deserted, snowy road. Amped was, well—Amped, and took off well ahead of the group. I fell behind, taking pictures and dealing with the consequences of not owning any shred of self-control.

The road walk was as monotonous and long as I'd assumed. My left foot protested almost immediately. The entire road was reportedly closed due to rock-fall. Turned out it was ONE rock, with plenty of room to drive around said rock. In a heroic act of retribution, I peed on it.

A limp set in on the way down to the Owens Valley. I cursed whoever made the decision to keep the road closed. Didn't they know there was a small group of insane people who would need a ride out of a snowstorm in mid-May?? With my discomfort clearly someone else's fault, I put my trekking poles away and grabbed a tiny bottle of wine out of my pack. I'd been saving it for a successful summit of Forester Pass—the highest point along the Pacific Crest Trail at 13,200 feet—a pass we were now running from.

Eventually, we dropped below the clouds, where the sweeping views of Owens Valley and the town of Lone Pine below opened up. It was a beautiful sight. Cell service returned and I was able to give Melanie a call, which helped distract from the desire to saw off my left leg and duct tape a trekking pole to the remaining stump.

After thirteen of the longest miles of my life, right as the sun dipped below the horizon, our Sierra-battered team reached the gate where Melanie was parked. She gave each of us a big hug, and revealed the spread of donuts and hot coffee she'd picked up for us.

Beautiful, smart, donuts, AND coffee?? It's just—go me, ya know?

We piled into the truck, glad to be safe, but I couldn't help but already think forward with white-hot dread to what was coming. Committing to that seventeen-mile, 7,200-foot drop to escape the backcountry meant if I wanted to maintain my connected steps, I was going to have to *reverse* that to get back to where I'd left off. My only hope was that Horseshoe Meadows Road would open in the next few days. With the only obstacle to opening being a rock with a bit of pee on it, the odds seemed strong Inyo County could handle it. Government road crews were known for their speed and efficiency, after all.

I shot a prayer up to the trail gods, confident *this* time, they'd surely appease me.

From Amped's journal:

The total for the day would be twenty-five miles and an estimated 7,500 calories. The physically hardest day of my existence, and a humbling experience. We approach and see Mel's smiling face. It reminds me of the sun on this icy day. I don't say anything but give her a big hug because we make it out alive. I feel so emotional that I have to just stay quiet during the drive to keep the tears back. Grateful for all I have in my life, this is the day everyone should experience.

We sat down at a small cafe in the sleepy town of Lone Pine and regaled Melanie with tales from our first week in the Sierra. We'd failed, but were alive to tell the story, and this failure would just be an intermission, not the final chapter.

But—that wasn't how everyone was feeling. Road Dog and Vagabond Runner were exhausted. We all were, but they were in dire need of a break. The next day would mark their first zero-mileage day in 500 tough miles. We agreed to watch the weather and figure out a good time to head back up Horseshoe Meadows Road together, but I got the feeling Road Dog and Vagabond Runner wouldn't be coming back with us.

Truthfully, sitting in that cozy restaurant with nary a snowflake in sight, I was on the same page. It was a struggle to remember why the hell I'd wanted to hike through the snow in the first place. In that moment, none of it mattered. We feasted on the calorie-dense bounty the shocked waitress set before us; elated, comfortable, and unable to think of anything beyond the next plate of food.

9
THE EYE

MAY 16-17, 2017
BISHOP, CALIFORNIA

From the comfort of a heated trailer, parked in the sweeping, desolate Volcanic Tablelands, we watched swirling clouds pummel the backcountry.

Amped and I incessantly checked the weather, in perpetual debate over the best timeframe to return to the mountains. The only thing capable of pulling my attention from the weather was food. An *absurd* amount of food. A *shameful* amount of food. If gluttony was indeed a sin, I'd be looking for the basement elevator when I arrived in hell.

Of course, *my* idea of food was fourteen trips to the donut shop each day—but Mel was right back at sitting me down with vegetables, as if she didn't even *care* about all the brow-furrowing. Deep down, even *I* knew I needed nutrition more than I needed another donut run.

But I wasn't about to say it out loud.

My mind was only half home. The rest circled around the approaching unknowns.

How much more snow is going to be back there? When is it going to be safe to cross? How much terrain will be avalanche territory now? Is it responsible to head back out? Should I call it good and skip up north with the rest of the PCT hikers?

There *were* silver linings to being forced out of the mountains, such as the moment of pure ecstasy when I removed Mel's dollhouse sleeping bag forever from my life and pulled in my trusty quilt for a reunion hug and a heartfelt apology. I also added a sleeping bag liner to further combat the low temps, not giving a single, solitary *shit* about how many ounces it weighed. It could've been made out of lead, concrete, and anthrax and I would've maintained the same giddy whistle while tossing it in my pack. Sleeping was an area I couldn't afford to save weight on. I needed warmth at night as much as I needed my damn Snickers bars.

You heard me.

The looming obstacle waiting for us when we returned was Forester. It was the most notorious of the High Sierra passes, where even summer hikers had to navigate the dreaded Forester Ice Chute: twenty feet of stable, frozen footprints across a gully...

Okay, so the PCT *isn't* a particularly dangerous hike.

But for us, the entire southern aspect of Forester Pass, thousands and thousands of vertical feet, was guaranteed to be one gigantic ice chute. Switchbacks blasted into the ascent to the pass would be filled in and smoothed over into one sweeping sheet of steep ice. As a fun bonus, a fresh, unstable layer of snow was now delicately coating the pass, lying in wait for the first unbridled hiker toot to unleash an entire mountainside of entombing snow upon them.

While I stress-ate donuts by the window, Melanie geared up for her alpine adventure of the season: bringing us a resupply over Kearsarge Pass. Most PCT hikers exited the Sierra at Kearsarge for some rest and a resupply. But if all went according to plan, Mel's help would allow me and Amped to skip the Kearsarge exit, giving us eighteen straight days to make progress in the backcountry.

Both Mel's and my alpine experience had always been in rock climbing, avoiding ice and snow at all costs to cling to that sweet, sweet dry granite, but our avoidance had its pitfalls. During the summer of 2016, Mel and a good friend hiked into the backcountry to tackle the eleven-pitch route Venusian Blind, as well as Mt. Sill (14,154 feet). On that trip, they spent many punishing miles avoiding snow travel, fighting through hellish scree adjacent to highways of smooth ice. The extra time and exertion in the scree resulted in their standing at the base of Mt. Sill exhausted and out of time, forcing them to turn around.

This year, while I was busy attempting to cripple myself by walking unreasonably far, Mel was on a mission to figure out crampons and snow travel. Bringing our resupply over Kearsarge was just one part of her plan to gain experience, boost her alpine fitness, and also help me and Amped.

Two days after we'd exited at Lone Pine, we woke to blue skies and a strong sun. If my ski patrol buddies weren't lying to me, the new snow layer needed a couple days of warm, full sun to soften and refreeze over-night into the consolidated snow beneath. A handful of sunny days were forecasted, so we settled on plans to hike back up Horseshoe Meadows Road the next day, theoretically to rejoin the PCT the day after that, hopefully giving enough time for the terrain to stabilize.

I sent Road Dog and Vagabond Runner a text to tell them our window had arrived. The delayed reply was sad, although not necessarily surprising.

They weren't coming.

It was for the best, but we'd gone through some trying times as a band of four, cutting our teeth together in the early season. It was going to be difficult to proceed without them. Road Dog and Vagabond Runner were going to flip further north and continue from there to the Canadian border, then come back for the Sierra section during the fall, when smart people hike it.

Talking to them on the phone, I could hear the pain in their voices. We had many discussions about what we wanted our PCT hike to look like, and we shared the goal to move in a continuous path north—but part of a lifetime of success in the outdoors is knowing when to back down.

News came of a seasoned, well-known mountain guide failing *twice* to get up and over Forester Pass with his group just before the storm. One expedition had resulted in a helicopter evacuation.

I was hoping for better news from the several hikers ahead of us. It wasn't happening though. The only hikers we heard from were two other parties who'd bailed out to Lone Pine, just as we had, but had decided to skip twenty PCT miles ahead and reenter the Sierra through Whitney Portal, rather than reversing the Horseshoe Meadows Road walk.

I'll be honest, that was a tempting skip. The road to Whitney Portal was open, for one, which meant no thirteen-mile, 7,000-foot climb on asphalt. It would also give us a viable excuse to skip those twenty miles of the High Sierra between Horseshoe Meadows and Mount Whitney, saving us two days of snow travel. The precedent had already been set by those parties ahead, and it was doubtful anyone would question my decision if I decided against returning to Horseshoe Meadows.

But I was never going to be able to convince myself skipping was an option. My stubborn objective wasn't *most* of the PCT. It was **the** PCT.

Every. Damn. Step.

With the hikers ahead steering away from Horseshoe Meadows, that positioned us to be the first post-storm team to cross the shunned stretch of trail between Cottonwood Pass and Whitney, a prospect I found rather unnerving. A wise tenet of avalanche safety was to never be the first across a fresh layer of snow.

That's rough advice for the guinea pigs.

10

THE ROADWALK

Amped and I were awake at three a.m., assembling our packs under a lone trailer lamp. Both of us silently combed through our gear, attempting to convince ourselves we were ready for eighteen days straight in the frozen backcountry.

Mel soon replaced our worries with coffee and bagels. She'd put something healthy and green on mine, inducing one last furrow.

The original plan had been for her to pilot the truck back to Horseshoe Meadows Road so we could sleep during the hour-long drive—a rather cute idea. While the truck rumbled along through the pitch-black desert, both Amped and I sat with eyes wide open, staring down our thoughts.

Thank God Amped is still here, I thought—over and over.

We arrived at the base of Horseshoe Meadows Road as the sky shifted into the dark red of an impending sunrise. It wasn't below freezing, but it was close, even down below 5,000 feet. I shouldered my pack, my whole soul groaning under the reloaded weight.

I kissed Melanie before turning back toward the same gate we'd been so relieved to exit from less than seventy-two hours earlier. A large sign read "Do Not Enter: Pedestrians," which had damn near given me a heart attack when I'd first seen it on our way out. If I couldn't reenter at Horseshoe Meadows, the options to maintain my thru-hike were grim. Thankfully, a quick call to Inyo County cleared it up. They didn't mind a couple hikers using the road to get back to the PCT, although it took a few minutes for me to convince the man we voluntarily *wanted* to go into the backcountry.

"There's still snow back there, son," he'd informed me.

…

He wasn't wrong.

The goal for the day was to reverse the road to regain the first 6,000 feet we'd lost bailing from the backcountry. Thirteen dry miles wouldn't normally be much to fear, but in snow boots, with reloaded bear canisters and all metal traction gear stowed on our packs, we were we in for a slog.

Construction trucks wound up the narrow, switch-backing road behind us. We did our best to step aside to minimize our presence. Part of me worried in spite of our informal permission to violate the gate sign, one of the trucks would pull over and demand we walk back down. But behind that worry was a fleeting hope some kind soul would have pity and give us a ride. I cared very much about hiking every step of the actual PCT, but with a similar magnitude, I cared very little about hiking bonus miles to and from the PCT.

But apparently, giving a ride to two vagrant men with ice axes wasn't going to happen. Three different trucks passed us. All three times, the drivers crept by with craning necks and looks of pure bewilderment, as if they'd passed two polar bears wearing pants.

The miles passed slowly, but they passed. Step after step after step of monotonous asphalt flowed below me. The last time I'd watched the same asphalt flow by, I'd been elated to escape our collective cold, wet, and miserable state. It felt odd to be reversing it. My left foot was angry again, but in defiance of logic, I almost welcomed the return of that familiar pain. It was the feeling of northward progress, a necessary evil in my world.

Other than one last ceremonious pee on the rock responsible for the closure, the road walk passed by uneventfully. I couldn't help but notice out of those three construction trucks, not one of them was attending to Pee Rock, the only kind-of obstacle on the entire road.

By 10:30 a.m., we reached the end of the asphalt at Horseshoe Meadows campground. Back above 10,000 feet, the ambient temperature was about the same as when Melanie had dropped us off, even with the strong sun overhead.

"It's so nice out," Amped said. "Should we keep going?"

"Seems like a shame to waste such a perfect day, but we've got to let the sun consolidate the new snow. I didn't bring my shovel to dig you out from under any avalanches."

He chuckled and set his pack down next to an unlocked pit toilet and a row of bear boxes for the night.

Ah, luxury.

Amped sliced up some salami and cheese to enjoy in the serene afternoon. Reclined against the bear boxes, we talked about the unknown miles ahead. Amped had his usual confidence in us. He trusted me more than I deserved, and I prayed my limited Sierra snow experience would be enough.

From Amped's journal:

The early afternoon was a blessing and a curse. It afforded us a nap, but gave us more time to think about the days to come.

Minus the occasional nose-curling waft from the pit toilet, it was a perfect camp. We turned in for the night while the sun was still in the sky, wanting to get some quality sleep before the temperature dropped.

11

ROCK CREEK

"It's not supposed to get any colder, right?" Amped asked behind exhausted, red eyes.

I pulled the laces of my boots tight with a grin. "That's what the weatherman said, and who can you trust if you can't trust the weatherman?"

Amped had coffee ready for both of us. I thanked him, to which he returned a groggy grunt. The twelve-degree night had indeed been brutal, and challenged the limits of our gear, but my trusty quilt coupled with the sleeping bag liner was a drastic improvement. I'd also made the effort to boil some water and pour it into my Nalgene for a cuddle buddy, so I'd slept well through the eleven hours we were in our tents.

Amped—did not.

Our aspirations for a pre-dawn departure were sidelined by the frigid morning. Both of us moved slowly packing up camp, drinking coffee, and taking one last dignified dump sitting on an actual toilet. Sure, it wasn't perfect. The seat held a flesh-stinging cold, and multi-layered stains whispered tales of a lifetime spent beneath the poor aim of hovering campers who'd apparently been eating nothing but TNT and carne asada burritos. Kicking off the day's aerobic activity in a confined space where lungs allowed only short, terrified sips of air, taking in *just* enough tainted oxygen to avoid losing consciousness wasn't *ideal*—but a toilet is a toilet. In the sea of ice ahead, whatever waited for us the next time nature called was *bound* to be less comfortable.

Right out of camp, the trail disappeared under snow, and we took a minute to strap on our crampons. We stepped through the wickedly cold, still meadow under the bluest of skies. The crisp, rhythmic sound of our shiny spikes biting into the ice was oddly pleasing.

Crunch, crunch, crunch, crunch

*Did I—**miss** that sound?*

That didn't seem right.

The four miles to regain the Pacific Crest Trail at Cottonwood Pass flew by on the hard snow. The alpine sun was out strong, already working to bake the ice into mush, but the night had been cold enough that it was going to take a while. Nearing the top of the pass, we reached the steep headwall of snow we'd down-climbed in the storm several days prior. The deep, loose powder the storm had been dumping on top of us had been softened in the sunny afternoons and forged during the nights into a slab of steep concrete.

With our axes at the ready, we faced our crampon's front points downhill and cross-stepped up the sixty-degree incline. I sent a quick prayer up to the abandoned voicemail machine of the trail gods that my limited practice would be enough to arrest a fall. An unarrested slide would send me squealing (in a manly register) down to pinball through the thick treeline we were gaining more and more elevation above.

After a thirty-four mile detour through snow and asphalt and 14,400 feet of elevation change, we stepped back onto the PCT. At 11,500 feet, our highest elevation yet, we passed by the solidly frozen Chicken Springs Lake. We crossed the outlet, or perhaps it was part of the lake itself (there was no real discernible difference between the two), then came face to face with a wall of snow. A curled cornice hung at its lip, like an ocean wave suspended above us, frozen in time. Our GPS confirmed the trail walked straight into it, so we started walking along the wall, away from the PCT's path. It only took a couple hundred yards to find a spot to gain the guarded ridge, where we joined a fresh set of mountain lion prints.

"How is anything awake?" I asked. "There can't be much to, um… eat."

Finishing that sentence felt unsettling.

Oh stop. You're just as likely to get eaten by a T-Rex.

No one had ever been killed on the PCT by a mountain lion—but there also weren't many PCT hikers silly enough to go strolling into mountain lion territory before the lion *food* had come out of hibernation.

We followed the lion prints for a long stretch. Remarkably, they were following the exact line of the trail, even with it being buried many feet under us. After a couple miles, we reached a large, cliff-lined bowl of snow with a buried lake fed by buried streams.

In the bright white, sun-reflecting arena of softened snow, our pace dropped precipitously. It was only ten a.m., still *definitely* below freezing, but apparently the snow cared little about ambient temperature. Our steps began sliding, which at first didn't faze us, but after slipping our way around the entire cirque, we reached a series of melted out slabs of granite and jumped at the chance to get off snow.

Our pace doubled over the sunbaked stone. At the end of the slabs, neither of us was ready to venture back into the slush, so we stopped to enjoy the hostile beauty around us over some lunch. Certainly, if we didn't feel like stepping back into the softening snow now, *more* time for it to *further* soften would help.

The mountain lion track had been the only sign of life aside from our own line of footprints behind us. From our perch atop the slabs, our last hour of hiking was visible around the large cirque, a distance that wouldn't take ten minutes once the snow was gone. Our path was an offensive line through an otherwise pristine, flowing piece of white artwork. We were a bib-adorned toddler who'd taken a red crayon and scratched it across the *Mona Lisa*.

While I chewed on a tortilla stuffed with peanut butter and Nutella, my mind wandered to Fireball. We hadn't seen or heard any sign of him.

A cliff towering a thousand feet directly above us was capped with a massive, physics-defying cornice hanging twenty feet out into space. With how quickly the snow had softened that morning, it was guaranteed the cornice wasn't going to be around for much longer. Those tons and tons of ice tumbling down the cliff like a runaway freight train would certainly be a sight to see—just not while eating lunch on the tracks. A bit of paranoia set in, and I hurried through my last few bites of lunch, struggling to generate enough saliva to contend with my pasty choices.

We entered Sequoia National Park, signifying our official entry into the High Sierra. At least, that's what our GPS indicated. The actual sign was underfoot somewhere, buried deep in the snowpack.

Stopping to check GPS every quarter-mile became the most time consuming and draining part of the day. The big landmarks around us—such as canyons and mountain peaks—were hidden by trees, and without generally heading up or downhill, there was a permanent sense of being lost.

After our seventy-sixth stop to check our path, Amped had gone silent, which wasn't like him. He rarely went long without chatting, joking, or singing to himself. I maintained the lead at the same pace we'd been hiking all day, but he fell behind. I stopped more frequently, each time patiently waiting for him to appear through the trees. At one stop, with my eyes down on my inReach, trying to decipher whether we were lost above the trail, or lost below the trail, Amped caught up.

Uncharacteristically curt, he asked, "Can we take a break?"

Something was off. *I* was the weakling in this relationship, not the Mexican bull in pants I'd brought along with me.

"Sure, bud."

Breaking meant more time for the sun to further soften the snow, but Amped knew that as well as I did. He unstrapped his right crampon, then took off his shoe and sock with a grimace. His big toe was red and swollen. Two days into the backcountry, and with sixteen days of heinous hiking ahead of us, it wasn't exactly good news.

"The crampons are digging into my toe. I don't think I'll be able to keep them on."

So in the middle of a fourteen-mile stretch of solid snow, Amped's crampons went on his back. I kept mine on but did my best to navigate the mildest possible path so he could follow without any traction. Fortunately for Amped, he had a great friend leading the way who would do whatever he could to avoid the steep parts. *Un*fortunately for Amped, the Sierra is basically one big steep part. He slipped and slid around, picking himself up off the snow more times than a guy with a swollen foot would prefer.

Running water had been tough to come by, so when we heard a stream running somewhere below us, we stopped. It took some searching, then a kick through the snow to reach the subterranean creek. Holding a bottle between my two cramponed boots while I filtered drinking water was a bizarre sight. Many online armchair hikers, no doubt giving advice from the challenging environment of their mother's basement, had assured me that in the Sierra, perhaps the dumbest three ounces one could carry was a water filter.

One particularly sage basement-dweller had offered his stable perspective, "It's F@$@^#% SNOWMELT!! WHAT COULD YOU POSSIBLY BE SCARED OF DRINKING IN FRESHLY MELTED F^$*#^$ SNOW, YOU F$*#^*$ *IDIOT*!!"

Certain this fella was just having a hard day—possibly because his mother was late with the damn Sunny-D and Oreos—I'd replied, "I'm trying to one hundred percent avoid Giardia out there, not ninety-nine percent avoid it. The three ounces is worth it to me."

Assuming a rational answer would quell the insults was naive, I'll admit.

Filtering water wasn't something I was willing to compromise. Any risk of contracting crippling diarrhea, while multiple days from any toilets to live on top of, was too much. My commitment to getting through the Sierra demanded I take every step to increase my odds of success. If I still failed, then fine, but if I failed because I couldn't carry three ounces to filter my water each day, then ended up having to be helicoptered to safety because I no longer owned control of my butthole, well that— would be rather upsetting.

Rock Creek sent a rumble through the trees long before we actually laid eyes on it. We hoped to camp on the far side of the creek, which meant executing our first major, bridgeless crossing. Still without crampons, Amped did his best to stay on his feet, but one steep slope after another kept taking his feet out from under him. We swapped places, so he could navigate whatever path he felt was safest. It went well until one slip sent him accelerating out of control down the snow. He dug in his trekking poles and boots to stop his slide toward the creek far below, an arching rooster tail of ice following him. A loud *snap* sent his snowshoes dragging erratically behind him.

Right before the creek, a tree well finally swallowed Amped. I took a breath I didn't realize I was holding.

"You all right?"

With a pained groan, Amped slid his pack off to inspect the damage. Cradling the pack in his lap, he held up the blown-apart remnants of what *used* to be straps that secured his snowshoes.

"You know how the worst days produce the best days of writing?" He looked up at me with exhausted eyes. "Today's going to be a **great** writing day."

From Amped's journal:

Out here, you don't have much. You carry only what you need to survive. You begin to love this stuff that takes care of you and you, in turn, want to take care of it. The broken strap elicits an irrational rage of emotion.

Amped rigged his pack to temporarily hold his snowshoes, and we continued tenuously down the slope. Not a half-mile later, Amped hopped into a boot-ski down a fifty-foot, fifty-degree patch of snow. Twenty feet into the slide, he *again* went down hard, leaving a trail of scattered trekking poles and clothing items on the slope behind him. This time, he let out a furious growl and shot back up to trudge uphill to collect his gear with a certain degree of visible rage.

It took every ounce of self-control I owned *not* to make a yard sale joke.

But I *really* wanted to know if he'd consider selling the trekking poles individually.

On that angle, the snow was soft enough to boot-ski with my crampons on. I slid until the metal points created too much drag, then easily stepped out the rest of the slope, still on my feet. There was a sour look on my partner's face.

"What?" I asked.

"That's really starting to piss me off," he bluntly replied.

I'm sure he was just joking.

…

Sure-*ish*.

We began following the bank of Rock Creek almost a mile upstream from the PCT crossing, taking inventory of every potential way across. There was a good amount of flow, but nothing too extreme. It certainly didn't match the seething torrent of doom my internal pessimist had envisioned.

Neither of us wanted to settle for an icy wade right before we stopped for the night. We found a reasonable crossing, where a thick snowbridge spanned the deepest channel, and connected to a large log stretching over the rest of the creek.

Amped went first, working his way across the bridge, prodding the snow ahead with his trekking pole to search for any thin sections he could potentially break through. One stab sent a large block of the overhanging bridge crumbling into the whitewater. Amped carefully lowered the last couple feet onto the log and tight-roped his way to the other bank.

I followed behind him in his compacted steps. Amped was a good deal heavier than I, so theoretically whatever held his weight would also hold mine. I lowered down from the snow, sinking my long, sharp crampon points into the soft wood. It was a satisfying attachment, like stepping onto a magnet with iron boots. I walked across in surprising security, and stepped onto the north side of our first big creek crossing. We both smiled for the first time in hours.

"Maybe we *can* do this," Amped said.

We wandered through frozen, soft marsh alongside the creek until we found a meadow with a patch of dry ground. There was sun to charge our electronics, a nice stream flowing right through camp, and even a spring bubbling straight out of the ground!

I set up my tent and wandered down to the creek to use the snowmelt to ice my aching feet. My left foot was doing much better in the rigid support of my boots, but it was still unhappy with all the walking. I basked in the late afternoon sun, enjoying the solitude with my numb foot submerged, its fussing wonderfully removed from my existence. The beauty surrounding me was otherworldly, almost too much to take in with the senses.

"You certainly don't get to experience this without earning it," I muttered.

With one numb leg, I hobbled back into camp, where Amped was already tucked in for the night, despite the sun still hovering well above the horizon. I draped my wet socks over a nearby branch to dry, jotted a few notes in my journal, and joined him.

Not in his tent, in my own. Amped was never one for a post-hike spooning.

He'll come around.

12
WUMPH

MAY 20, 2017
ROCK CREEK

I pulled back my tent flap to lace my boots for the day. There was no sign of Amped stirring. Seeing as how the earlier we got started, the better the snow would be, sleeping in would've otherwise been a problem—but Amped had taken a beating the previous day, and he needed as much quality rest as he could scrape together. I capitalized on the opportunity to enjoy a quiet, leisurely breakfast in the crisp morning.

The night had been below freezing, but still ten to fifteen degrees warmer than the last—downright *balmy*. I'd slept well, and from the muffled snores coming from across camp, so had Amped. This was good news because I wasn't entirely confident either of us would be sleeping that night, enroute to Forester Pass. We weren't going to be able to weasel our way out of camping above 11,000 feet.

Once I started packing up breakfast, Amped jolted awake. With the panic of one who'd slapped the snooze button one too many times, he started scrambling to get his things packed. The socks I'd draped over the tree branch to dry—weren't dry. They were ice, frozen solid into stinky, gravity defying U's.

We had camp collapsed and on our backs minutes later, once Amped had broken the world record for fastest camp pack-up, and I'd figured out how to safety pin blocks of ice to my backpack.

Out of curiosity, I wandered over to Rock Creek, specifically to check the water level. From everything I'd read online, it had been foolish to cross a creek in the afternoon. The basic theory made sense: freezing overnight temperatures slow the rate of water feeding creeks, resulting in morning crossings being lower and therefore safer than afternoon crossings. I was expecting Rock Creek to be choked down a bit, but—the creek was *higher*. The previous night, the snowy bank overhanging the creek had been about a foot above the water. Now, the water was mere inches from touching the overhang.

We departed camp, stepping over the dead ground spring we'd collected water from the evening before. The overnight cold had strangled it into a glass puddle. A bizarre, frozen marsh was just outside camp. It all looked like stable, icy grass, but random steps kept breaking through the "grass" into deep, brown water.

The ascent out of the marsh was south facing, and a stretch of dry switch-backs took us up to a saddle where the terrain flattened and the snow returned. Our water source for the morning was just more snowpack. That was all right though; the water in our bottles from Rock Creek was untouched. We both knew we needed to stay hydrated, but drinking ice water in twenty-five-degree weather wasn't exactly appealing.

In the endless snowdrifts, hiking in a straight line was an awful, draining approach involving many more ups and downs than we needed to subject ourselves to. We hashed out a navigation method where Amped led the way, focused on finding the path of least resistance through the maze of drifts and tree wells. I remained behind him with my phone out, giving prods in the right direction to keep us within the same general area of the buried PCT. We flew through a tough section of dense trees, then up and over a small pass in one continuous movement, a massive improvement over feeling lost and stopping every quarter mile.

After we crossed through an untouched white meadow, dirt trail appeared—so we stopped to put our snowshoes away. Two minutes later, naturally, the snow was back. We kept moving, our stubbornness winning against our pesky better judgment. But eventually, when we tired of bruising our hip bruises, we humbled enough to put traction back on.

And more dirt was waiting around the next corner.

At Crabtree Meadows, Whitney Creek was the next challenge. It was a crossing that reportedly required some care in the early season. A massive butt-glissade dropped us into the creek's drainage, where we headed upstream into the meadow to look for snowbridges. At the PCT crossing, a swift wade was almost guaranteed, so we didn't bother checking it out. A message was scratched into a bank of exposed dirt there, a message we would never see but would hear about later.

It read: "Help. Hiker Breeze 1 mile," with an arrow pointed east.

We merged with another set of mountain lion prints to cross the first upstream snowbridge we came across. We made our way back toward the PCT in a long arc through the meadow.

A bit later, we reached the trail junction with the world-renowned John Muir Trail. We'd both spent a lot of time on the JMT, and I'd envisioned a picturesque moment with the snowy trail sign—but it was still entombed somewhere below our feet.

Hitting the JMT junction meant we were officially on familiar, eh—*ground*, so to speak. Sun-faded footprints appeared from those hikers who'd skipped ahead to hike up Whitney Portal. Signs of other people were a comfort after two days alone with peckish lion prints.

The trees thinned as we neared the notorious Wallace Creek, and all of those comforting footprints vanished, erased by the sun. We again aimed to intersect the creek as far upstream as possible, hoping to find intact snowbridges like we'd found at Rock Creek. Our topographic maps made the terrain seem mellow enough.

An hour later, we stood on top of high ridge above the creek, panting like dogs. We'd fought up and over a series of short, steep ridgelines through softening snow, and a sweeping view of the creek verified what we'd feared. We'd climbed WAY above Wallace Creek, and—to add a bit of salt to the wound—there wasn't a snowbridge in sight, even from our elevated perch. I wandered to the edge of the ridge to peer down its north side. I was staring down the face of the cliff.

"Ohhh *crap*." I looked over at Amped. "We might've just put a lot of effort into stranding ourselves."

Reversing the string of ridgelines we'd struggled through seemed like a more daunting task than a damn swan-dive down the cliff. We traversed the ridge, checking to make sure we were still cliff-bound every dozen yards.

"This might work," Amped called over.

He was looking down an intimidating slope, wickedly steep, close to seventy degrees. I wasn't sure our snowshoes were capable of it. A taunting forest hung below the slope, waiting for an unlucky hiker to pinball through.

It was our only option, or—more accurately—the only one we could stomach. Swapping trekking poles for ice axes crossed my mind, but the pinballing would commence long before an axe could help. I stepped backwards off the ridge, placing the fate of my mortality in the row of metal spikes underfoot, a very similar feeling to rappelling off the edge of a rock face.

Our morning had been going relatively well, full of smiles and jokes, even fighting through the ridgelines—but a tense silence accompanied us down the slope through hundreds of yards of careful steps. Our snowshoes performed flawlessly, much more secure than I'd assumed. Eventually, the angle softened. We were both relieved to bottom out the drainage at Wallace Creek.

"We might be getting our feet wet," I said, half-joking. The water looked at least waist deep, and fairly swift.

Amped grimaced. "Let's head to the trail crossing. There could be logs or downstream snowbridges along the way."

We followed the winding creek, hopeful around every bend there would be some good news to avoid a testicle ice bath. But with a mile of disappointment behind us, we arrived at the trail crossing—which honestly seemed *kind of* reasonable. The large, summer stepping stones across Wallace were about knee-deep underwater. If we could resist the healthy current enough to stay balanced on top of the stones, we could avoid a deep wade. Of course, any slips would send us floating downstream…

I dropped my pack and sat to remove my snowshoes. "If wading through ice water is part of this game, we might as well get to it."

Amped wasn't going to give in that easily.

"I'll head downstream a bit, just to make sure."

I shrugged. "Knock yourself out, my man. I'll start poking around this crossing. Could be better than it looks."

Logically, the farther downstream you went, the more tributaries and snowmelt would be feeding the creek—therefore making it *larger*—and therefore less likely to have snowbridges. But two minutes later, while I was already halfway through kicking steps down the snowy riverbank and ready to get wet, Amped appeared on the opposite bank!

He yelled over to me, barely overpowering the rush of the creek, "It's sketchy as hell, but I think we can use it!"

"Sketchy" was a bit of an undersell.

I reversed back up the bank and headed downstream to see what Amped had found—*and crossed for some reason.* It was a decaying, dirty snowbridge over a whitewater restriction in the creek, maybe eight feet across, and appeared to be three sun rays from collapsing. It was U-shaped, and the pit of the U couldn't have been more than a foot thick. Splashing water had encased the entrance and exit of the bridge in thick, clear icicles.

I lifted my eyes to meet my partner's overjoyed, proud grin. With the same enthusiasm of a cat owner finding a crow on their pillow, I half-smiled back.

Does he really think this is the better option? Or is he trying to kill me and take my Snickers?

From Amped's journal:

Under the jagged edges of these kings thrusting sharply toward the sky, we come across a particularly proud river. Up and down its shores, it made itself present everywhere. Then we find it: a battered and beaten snowbridge holding on for dear life. Its top is dirty and its underside is ridden with icicles.

And it's thin. Scary thin. It's not much longer for this world.

We bet it'll hold out for one more set of outsiders—we hope.

Beta and I get to digging footholds into the bank. With the help of our ice axes the work progresses quickly. Slowly I cross the river raging below. The ice bridge strains under my weight. I make it.

I get to work digging a foothold on the far bank while Beta gathers the gear. We both take our positions and begin to hand gear over the river. The snowshoes first, then the trekking poles. We throw whatever we can, but then the real challenge: the packs.

Beta gets into position with my pack in his hand and reaches with all his might toward me. I do the same. Reaching, further and further. The snowbridge moans in complaint.

Got it!

One pack down, the other to follow. We both dig in. Reaching and stretching as long as our limbs will allow. Got it!!

Beta jumps the distance with ease. A small success on a single day.

How many, I wonder, will the kings let us get away with?

We stopped for lunch on the opposite bank of Wallace Creek under clear blue skies and a powerful sun. Both of us were silent, thankful for how our scenario played out—but contemplating what failure might've looked like.

Already mentally and physically taxed for the day, we kept pushing toward Forester Pass. The closer we camped, the easier our lives would be the next morning. Five miles from Forester was Tyndall Creek, where a three a.m. wakeup would get us up the steepest part of the pass while the snow was still bullet hard. If we camped earlier, we'd be waking earlier—and frankly, three in the morning was already too damn early.

Our minds were already looking forward to our sleeping bags, still many miles and two more notorious crossings away. We trudged into the afternoon toward Wright Creek, dreading what we'd find—but it never came. Climbing out of a shallow, snowed-over gully, I checked my GPS.

"Whoa, I think… that was it. That was Wright Creek."

Amped raised his eyebrows. "Damn, I hope the rest are that easy."

We stepped into the vast, treeless expanse of Bighorn Plateau. Sweeping hills of white ice stood in incredible contrast against a deep blue sky. Reveling in our surroundings, we were abruptly snapped back to reality by a sound I'd never experienced but recognized instantly.

WUMPH

The ice under both our feet settled simultaneously, even though we were twenty feet apart. This phenomenon had only been described to me, but the sound was exactly as I'd expected. It was a "wumph," the sound of the weak layer collapsing—the calling card of an avalanche.

Amped and I waited paralyzed, unsure what was next. We held perfectly still, scared to move, listening for more—but nothing came. The absolute silence in the blank landscape was replaced by a high-pitched ringing in my ears. On a sloped hillside with no trees, coupled with melting snow in the afternoon sun, we'd trudged right into potential avalanche territory. The angle of the snow was our only savior, pitched slightly milder than where slabs were most likely to detach and slide.

Amped traversed sideways toward a small patch of trees. I stayed still until he was safe, then followed exactly in his tracks, trying to avoid further disturbing the slab. Once in stable territory, we gave each other a what-the-hell-are-we-doing-with-our-lives look, but felt hesitant to talk. Speaking out loud felt dangerous, as if we were standing next to the ear of a sleeping ogre.

I broke out our topographic maps to chart the safest line through the plateau. Trees typically anchored avalanche slabs in place, so being above the treeline meant it was time to prioritize traveling on snow angles that minimized a slide threat, even if it meant some extra mileage. Saving a few steps by drawing a straight line through dangerous zones was a good way to get in trouble.

We departed our patch of trees into a sea of temperamental beauty, staying a hundred yards apart in case one of us got into trouble, the other would be able to at least *try* to help. We managed to stay on safe slopes for the rest of the Bighorn Plateau, but heading down into the Tyndall Creek drainage, we moved through almost a mile of unavoidable, thirty-five-degree snow. Perfect avalanche territory.

We were both beyond relieved to reach an anchoring grove of trees for the final mile. We'd expected to find another challenging creek to cross at Tyndall, but the trail gods extended us an olive branch after slapping us around for the day. The wide creek was ninety percent snowbridge, and the few exposed patches of Tyndall Creek—our water source for the evening—were guarded by six-foot, dead-vertical walls of snow.

I stopped over the creek, staring down to the whitewater below. "We're going to have to get creative if we don't want to melt snow."

We dropped our packs nearby and set up camp, then returned to Tyndall. I rigged a water bottle onto a string and lowered it off the upstream side of a snowbridge into the whitewater. The buoyant plastic bottle didn't want to submerge itself, but if I let it get sucked under the snowbridge, it had no choice but to fill with water. Bottle after bottle, we fished for snowmelt and dragged it back out from under the snowbridge against the pressure of the creek. Every batch was a gamble with my precious water bottle, a vital piece of gear I really couldn't afford to lose. Several times, the string and bottle became stuck, snagged on the icicle-lined roof of the bridge for minutes on end while I rhythmically tugged the evening away, whispering pleading requests to an inanimate string. Not unlike a lunatic, I suppose.

Each cast yielded about a half liter, which Amped would filter while I sent the bottle back down into the creek. It was tough going for him too; the freezing water moved through our squeeze filters like maple syrup. The feeling in our fingers faded until there was none left. There wasn't much of a choice though. We needed to not only relieve our immediate thirst, but also procure drinking and cooking water for the night, water for breakfast and coffee the next morning, *and* drinking water to get us up and over Forester Pass.

WUMPH

When we'd finally fished out enough water, we headed back to camp with stinging hands. Tyndall Creek was a popular camping spot in the summer. I'd actually camped in the exact same place several years earlier, and I got a kick out of knowing my tent was pitched somewhere around ten vertical feet above where I'd pitched it the last time.

Amped was hurting. His toe was still swollen, but snowshoes had been more tolerable than crampons. We retired to our tents and I set my alarm. Thoroughly exhausted, I fell asleep before I even had time to fret over the hell of a day we'd stumbled through.

13
FORESTER

MAY 21, 2017
TYNDALL CREEK

I half-opened one of my eyes at my alarm. It was 3 a.m., dark and way below freezing.

"Quiet, you," I mumbled to my phone.

I reset the alarm for an hour later, like a teenager putting off first period, and not like a grown ass man needing to wake up early to avoid dying in a wet-slab avalanche. I'd theorized high elevation would be hard on my ability to sleep, but after a day of creek crossings and unstable snow, I was, eh—*incorrect*.

In a surprising twist, it wasn't much easier to get up at the next alarm.

From Amped's journal:

The day starts before the sunrise. A crisp morning. I hear the alarm jingle on Beta's phone. He'll be up soon and I don't want him waiting on me. I make easy work of my bed and now it's time to boot up. They're frozen solid… I jam my double-layered socks into them and my toes go numb. This is going to be a long day.

We departed camp by headlamp, and conditions were about as perfect as we could ask for—but we needed to get to Forester before the sun. Amped and I marched side-by-side in silence, taking in the serenity around us. Our cramponed snowshoes bit into the hard ice, every step crisp and satisfying.

Crunch, crunch, crunch, crunch

At 13,200 feet, Forester Pass hung over the open landscape like a beacon. No navigation was required, just a general aim toward the obvious weakness in the jagged fortress ahead.

Crunch, crunch, crunch, crunch

Amped and I had been friends for over a *decade*. We'd certainly experienced a lot throughout our friendship, but this was on a whole new level. There wasn't a single person I would've rather had at my side. Even having Melanie out there wouldn't have worked. Knowing her precious life would be in any kind of danger would've stressed me out beyond my capacity.

And sure, *technically* I was putting her through some level of that same stress—but I'm all hairy and stuff. She's cute and smells nice. It's different.

Amped hadn't hesitated when I suggested he join me in the Sierra. He'd asked just one simple question.

"We'll be safe out there, right?"

We were tiny dots in a sweeping landscape of ice and rocks, its grand beauty matched only by its lifeless hostility. The truth was, I didn't know if we were safe. I'd done as much as I possibly could through training and research before we left to increase the *odds* of our safety, but it never felt like I'd successfully finished preparing. There was simply too much information, too much to study, too much to learn. I wasn't sure it was possible to *ever* feel finished.

Crunch, crunch, crunch, crunch

At 5 a.m., we arrived at the base of the behemoth ramp of smooth ice leading up to the pass, breathing heavily in the high altitude. In several summer trips, I'd climbed the impressive string of switchbacks blasted into the south face of the pass. It'd never been a *total* joke, seeing as how high elevation, poor cardio, and an unchecked affection for pastries rarely mesh well—but Forester was usually manageable with enough breaks to "appreciate the view."

This was a totally different pass.

Deep snow had filled in the switchbacks, leaving only a smooth sheet of ice behind. We stood at the base of a forty-five-degree slope that further steepened as it stretched for hundreds of yards above us.

Nervous to be standing in the presence of a giant, we flipped up our heel-lifters on our snowshoes and started up the slope. Those humble little U-shaped bars had long been my favorite part of alpine snowshoes. Essentially, they stop the heel from coming down as far, avoiding the intense calf burn and subsequent whining associated with snowshoeing up steep terrain.

The huge crampon points on the base of our snowshoes dug into the ice beautifully. The heel-lifters eased the burning, but nothing was going to outsmart the low oxygen and heavy packs. After a maximal effort hacking away at the slope, we slumped onto our ice axes, panting like dogs. I regretted every run I'd skipped, and every pastry I'd been unable to put down (so roughly—*all* of them).

Then I made the mistake of looking down. "Ohhh come on."

We'd made it barely a *fifth* of the way through the slope.

"Let's take small bites out of this elephant, twenty steps at a time, then rest and repeat," Amped suggested.

He mistook my fat panting for agreement and heartlessly ordered me off my ice axe.

"Let's go."

From his journal:

The air is thin and lays waste to our lungs with every step, twenty at a time. We count them out and rest. Twenty more. Up and up a sixty-degree incline. It seems that we're on an ice cliff. Beta keeps his cool, which calms my nerves.

This is no longer a hike. It's a mountaineering expedition.

The exposure worsened as we gained altitude up a steepening slope. We had no choice but to release increasing trust to the metal points under our feet. Being a lifelong climber, I'd never had a problem with heights, but I'd also typically had a rope to catch me if I fell. The unreal amount of air beneath our feet made my head swirl.

Truthfully, the idea of flying down a 700-foot slide seemed *almost* like a fun prospect, but I had seven different kinds of razor sharp gear strapped on and around me, and the slide was made out of refrozen snow, not slick ice. The surface felt more like rough concrete than a slip-and-slide—and it probably wouldn't be any fun arriving at the base as a stark naked, bloody mess for the under-compensated Search and Rescue folks to deal with.

Twenty steps at a time, we huffed and puffed up the ice. The last few switchbacks high on the pass were thankfully uncovered; an escape from the building exposure to aim for. The angle was so steep I could stand perfectly vertical and reach out to touch the slope. Our twenty steps dropped to ten. I felt like I was in decent cardio shape from hiking the southern 700 miles, but I could hear myself gasping for air like I was only in decent pie-eating shape.

I don't want this to come off as braggy, but "decent" is a bit of an undersell.

Finally, we put our gloves on bare rock and lifted ourselves up onto a foot-wide granite ledge, the outer lining of the first exposed switchback. We were perched above hundreds of feet of near-vertical ice, and it took a minute of panting in the low oxygen before our breathing calmed. We shifted into crampons on our tiny shelf, fighting against strong vertigo to maintain our balance.

"I'm bleeding," Amped said, shock in his voice.

He pulled back the leg of his pants to reveal blood smeared all over his calf. "I accidentally tapped my axe against my leg on the way up. It didn't really hurt, but the hole is a half-inch deep! These bastards are sharp."

Never one to make excuses, Amped rolled his pant leg down and cinched his crampon straps tight. A line of frozen depressions from the hikers ahead wound their way up the final switchbacks. We stepped from footprint to footprint with a dizzying amount of exposure nagging in our peripheral. In spite of my mind's favorite pastime of cooking up disastrous scenarios, a fall wasn't one my brain would entertain, and I remained focused on each individual step in front of me.

Amped and I arrived at the Forester ice chute, ready to tackle the notorious beast of the Sierra! The experienced guide who hadn't been able to make it over Forester typically arrived first and cut a flat sidewalk across the sixty-degree chute, to ensure safe passage for his clients, but also to help the approaching wave of PCT hikers. The chute had a partial path cut into it, but chipping twenty feet of ice was some Good Samaritan's limit before he'd realized his love for humanity only went so far. The other two-thirds were more ice depressions from footsteps.

Safely across the chute, a small headwall from a decayed cornice was the final obstacle. We planted our ice axes and hoisted ourselves up to stand on the cornice, arriving on top of the world.

Forester Pass. Almost two years after meeting Slim and Golden Girl in a mild snow year, when I'd marveled at the idea of Forester in the middle of May, I'd topped the infamous pass on May 21, after the most aggressive High Sierra winter in recent history.

I would be lying to say I felt like the heroic badass I'd envisioned. The Sierra had been tough, but hadn't been quite as difficult as I'd expected—and even so, I hadn't been able to execute it perfectly.

But I did feel a *little bit* cool.

Snowy, jagged peaks stretched in all directions. With not a single soul around for miles and miles, we stared in awe of our position. All low points between peaks were solid white. All lakes in the desolate landscape were still buried by twenty feet of snow. The morning was perfectly clear and we relaxed at the pass with our packs off, trying to convince our brains to believe our eyes. The forty-degree slope leaving the pass was in direct sun, and had been for close to a couple hours.

"We probably should've been up earlier," I said.

"Earlier than four a.m.? Screw that. We'll be fine."

A fresh layer of snow still clung to the mountain and there wasn't a tree in sight. If there was a perfect slope for committing suicide by avalanche, it was in front of us. Deep steps from those before us traversed the hillside, tattling on those who'd crossed the slope during the afternoon melt—the riskiest time of day—when the melting surface snow creates a lubricating layer of water between the old ice and the fresh snow. The tiniest disturbance can release a heavy slab of fluid concrete easily capable of carrying hikers hundreds of yards downslope to be hopelessly buried alive. It often took days, weeks, or even *months* before avalanche victims could be located. While it was good for us that the slab had been shock tested, I was disturbed by the likely unwitting danger those ahead had walked through. The cardinal sin of being the first to cross a potentially unstable slope had been violated to the extreme.

"You think these are from Fireball?" Amped asked.

"I hope he's at least one of these prints."

We spaced ourselves a hundred yards apart and headed out into the sun-baked snow. As we stepped into each haphazard footprint, the reality of the PCT in 2017 came into focus—people were going to get hurt. I'd felt unprepared to go into the Sierra after years in the backcountry, training in the Sierra winter, and doing as much homework as I could before leaving Kennedy Meadows. Following those deep steps I realized not everyone had done their due diligence—and the Sierra would eventually bite.

Throughout Southern California, I'd talked with hikers planning on heading into the snow with essentially *zero* preparation. Some were dead-set on heading into the Sierra but opted to skip the relatively tiny patches of snow on Fuller Ridge and Baden Powell because they *didn't want to hike through snow.*

Admittedly, information on early Sierra trekking was almost nothing outside of random Facebook forums and clunky, outdated trail journal websites. Those limited sources were difficult to sieve through and collect the nuggets of wisdom bobbing in a sea of outspoken armchair hikers. True wisdom from experienced outdoorsmen was greatly eclipsed by the muddled noise of the internet. I'd learned most outdoor wisdom resides in the minds of those who spend much more time outside than they do online.

Once safely on the far side of the slope, Amped and I were all smiles. The north side of Forester was a blast. We plunge-stepped off the sun-softened pass like two grown-up kids in the most grand, grown-up kid playground on the planet. We launched into massive, continuous glissades for hundreds of yards, stopping after each one to share a romantic moment inspecting each other's asses for torn pants.

My inReach beeped with some great news from Vagabond Runner.

"Looks like our pal Fireball is alive," I called over to Amped.

She'd seen Fireball standing on top of Forester in a post online, which meant he had cell service! So whether it was the advice I'd given him or something he'd figured out on his own, he'd exited the Sierra. He must've weathered the snowstorm in high altitude for *two days*, then pressed through a string of avalanche zones to exit the backcountry.

Amped smiled. "That's one tough bastard. Although, I wonder how many more Fireballs will enter the Sierra without being quite as lucky."

The angle off the pass eased, taking us below the treeline. Our progress slowed through the rolling snowdrifts along Bubbs Creek, although it took a few miles before the creek itself appeared from under the massive slab of snow in the canyon. We walked through a devastated clearing, then another. Pine trees of all sizes had been thrown around like match-sticks, the aftermath of large avalanches throughout the winter. The mess of fragmented pines was frozen into the mostly flat surface. I took a moment to appreciate having snow to walk over most of the mess. In a couple months, this would be a nightmare of obstacles once the debris had been laid across the trail.

"It's time to call it for the day," Amped called back. "There's a bear box!"

One of the large campgrounds along Bubbs Creek was underfoot and the first site had started to melt out. It was actual ground, the holy grail of snow camping. I managed to inflate my hopes as high as they could go before I took a step onto the spongy, sopping wet dirt.

We begrudgingly pitched our tents up on the snow overlooking the campsite, then gathered some firewood by snapping the low, dead branches off the pines around us. In high luxury, we enjoyed our civilized seat atop the rusty bear box, in front of a fire on our extra-fancy snowless ground. A light rain started up, but it wasn't enough to temper the fire, nor our spirits from the epic day behind us.

"We're going to remember today until the moment we die," Amped said with a big smile. He pulled his right boot off with a grimace to reveal an even *more* swollen big toe.

Melanie was resupplying us at Bullfrog Lake the next day, if she successfully made it up and over Kearsarge Pass. Kearsarge also happened to be the most convenient spot for an injured hiker to bail from the backcountry.

"I didn't want to say anything," Amped said, "But it's been hurting all day. It's the combination of my boots with these crampons. It puts such a bad pressure on my toe, and the multiple days of pain with the wet, frozen feet—it's just hard to handle."

I didn't know what I could offer to help. We stared into the campfire, lost in our own thoughts. His next words ran chills down my spine.

"I don't think I'll be able to keep going like this."

My eyes widened slightly. The thought of doing the rest of the Sierra alone was terrifying. Brazen at best, suicidal at worst. Being by myself through the many upcoming passes and river crossings was a line I wasn't ready to cross. I'd promised Melanie I would make good decisions out here, that I'd do everything in my power to mitigate risk. Proceeding forward without a partner was clearly a violation of that promise.

I sent Melanie a message letting her know Amped might be heading out Kearsarge with her. I needed to gauge her reaction. If she wasn't keen on the idea of me going ahead alone—well then, that would make two of us.

"My wife is crazy." I handed the inReach to Amped so he could read her reply.

What shoe size is he? I can pack a new pair of boots to you tomorrow with the resupplies. It's kind of a Hail Mary move and might not work, but it's better than nothing.

Melanie, at 115 pounds soaking-wet, along with the help of our good friend Steve, was already volunteering to carry twenty-four days of food and supplies up and over a 11,700 foot pass, alongside all the gear required to overnight in the snow with us. Adding four more pounds in boots—was simply too much.

"Maybe we should both exit at Kearsarge," I said. "You could actually try on some boots, rest a few days, then head back in?"

"We wouldn't make it to Mammoth before I'd need to be back to Vegas for work."

I'd forgotten one of the central ideas behind the angelic resupply was to save us the time of exiting and reentering at Kearsarge, to allow a sufficient window to reach Mammoth. If we exited the Sierra, Amped wouldn't be returning—which meant I'd either be returning alone, or not returning at all.

We sent our concerns to Mel, giving her a reasonable opportunity to denounce her marriage/friendship, but she immediately sent back:

It's just one other thing to bring, not a big deal. Heavy is heavy! I'm just excited to see you guys, and be a part of your journey.

I smiled. "Looks like you've got a fresh set of boots coming."

I probably knew better than to put limits on Mel.

In painful obligation, I sent a message suggesting she leave behind any luxury food supplies to save some weight for boots. I'd heard whispers of pancakes and bacon—and I instantly regretted hitting "send." If that message was flying off strapped to a carrier pigeon, I would've shot it out of the sky.

Her reply was quick.

"Not a chance. You need some actual nutrition, Danny."

My brow involuntarily furrowed. I knew what that meant.

She was bringing vegetables.

CRUNCH

It would be a borderline miracle if the boots fit Amped well enough without his ever trying them on. Turning in for the night, I can't say my hopes were high. I'd tried on shoes in stores only to realize they somehow didn't fit at home.

This hike might be over real soon.

The temps had plummeted, and my breath floated in a white plume over my pillow.

But I can see a few upsides to that.

14

THE RESUPPLY

I woke with my food-obsessed brain focused on one thing: polishing off every crumb in my bear canister.

Either Mel was coming with more food, or we'd be heading out to get food. Either way, I could officially let go of any self-control around my remaining rations. In such low temperatures and difficult terrain, our body's daily calorie needs were astronomical, estimated somewhere around 8,000. We'd tried our best to plan for it, but the physical strain had ramped up our hunger to an alarming ferocity.

Every meal was spent sifting through that translucent blue canister, inventorying the remaining provisions over and over, making one hundred percent sure every shred of food we could justify eating had been ingested. With such a short hike between us and Bullfrog Lake, we indulged in a late wakeup with plenty of coffee and pancreas-enfeebling breakfast foods.

There was something very satisfying about arriving at a resupply with a completely empty bear canister. It wasn't a feat I'd managed to pull off much before the PCT. Preparing for backpacking trips in past years, I would carefully schedule and measure out my calories for each day on the trail: my daily base 2,000 calories, plus another thousand to make up for the increased physical strain.

Tactfully prepared and ready to go, I'd set off into my hike, where the full breadth of my embarrassing cardiovascular shape would make itself known. My body would invariably react in a mortal panic by shutting down my digestive system in order to fight off the debilitating stress of walking outside.

After several days of a suppressed appetite, I'd arrive home to bitterly restock our cabinets with the freeloading Ziploc baggies of food after their scenic ride through the Sierra backcountry.

But with not a scrap of food between us, Amped and I began the 1,200 foot climb to reach Bullfrog Lake. The low elevation had certainly made for comfortable sleeping, but for the first time in the Sierra, the snow hadn't refrozen hard overnight. Soft snow was surprisingly taxing to hike uphill through. Every step was unpredictable. One would remain firmly planted, and the next would slide two damn feet back to where it started. The longer daggers along the underside of our crampons were the ideal weapon, but there was no way Amped was going to strap those torture chambers back onto his battered feet. I figured I'd stay in my snowshoes as well, in solidarity.

No, not laziness. *Solidarity.*

We stuck to the buried outlet creek of Bullfrog Lake, where deep snow had created a pleasant, gradual ramp resembling a snowed-over road. It was a gift to avoid the berms of rolling snow and tree wells. Even still, Amped struggled to keep up with the guy he'd spent the last seventy miles waiting for.

"Only a mile to go, bud," I called over my shoulder.

There was no reply, so I stopped to wait. A few minutes later, he appeared, trudging through the soft mess with his head down and a slight limp. Two hundred yards later, I'd lost him again. Five slow minutes went by, and right as I was about to backtrack downhill to check on him, Amped appeared from the snow-choked trees with a heavier limp, and an even heavier stare.

"How's that foot?" I asked, a growing pit sitting in my stomach.

He shook his head. "Not great."

"You want to hop on my back? We could probably make it to that next tree there before we'd have to call in the SAR team."

He smiled for a half-second and resumed his slow trudge.

I received a message from Melanie. She was on her way with the Hail Mary boots in tow. The pit in my stomach grew.

I'm going to lose my partner.

We were strolling toward the exit. We'd be camping eight measly miles from the parking lot at Onion Valley. We might as well have been camping in the parking lot of a hospital with Amped having a broken arm, and hoping to avoid going inside so we could go play tennis for the next two weeks. Amped was already hurting so bad, what were the odds that a pair of boots—in the off chance they even fit him—would be enough.

Bullfrog Lake was nothing more than a pristine white slab sitting under a royal blue sky. I slid off my pack and sat down, both to wait for my injured comrade and to enjoy the surreal display laid out before me. These spectacular 360-degree Sierra masterpieces were hard to fully grasp. I was standing six inches from a Da Vinci mural covering the entire side of a building.

I waited for a while, repeatedly reassuring myself Amped would appear any second—but the minutes kept flowing by. Eventually, my craning neck got tired of looking back in optimistic hope at the same three trees behind me, so I stood and picked up my pack to go find him. Naturally, he appeared the second I'd committed to a search and rescue, and the poor guy had a whole lot of misery in his eyes.

"Are you all right?"

"Yeah. Foot's just hurting."

Those were the words that came out of his mouth, but his eyes told me, "I can't wait to escape this hell."

From Amped's journal:

Something is wrong. Pain. Horrible pain on the top of my foot with every step I take. I try to bear it but end up stopping a lot. Every step is grimacing. What did I do? Did I break something and my feet were just too frozen to feel it? I mean, I did fall quite a bit yesterday...

*Then the thought hits me, **Is this injury enough to push me off the trail? To break my promise to my best friend and leave him to travel some of the most rugged terrain in America, all alone?***

There are few things I have quit in my life. I can name every one of them because they haunt me still. Will this be one of those?

Our only remaining objective for the day was to get to the other side of the frozen lake, which was as-the-crow-flies about 150 yards away but would take a half-mile to reach following the hilly shore. Circumnavigating the shore in sloppy snow was much less tempting than the flat slab of white concrete stretching out in front of us.

"Should we try—*walking across?*" I asked. "People do that with frozen lakes, right?"

"I don't know man, we're pretty heavy. I'm north of 240 pounds with this pack on."

Those words were in diametric opposition to the longing behind his eyes. I stabbed at the edge of the lake ice at a melting, blue crescent with my trekking pole, but it held solid. I stepped out onto the same thin ice with a snowshoe and shifted all my weight onto it. The surface groaned, and a few cracks splintered out from the metal spikes—but it didn't break.

I stepped out onto the lake until I was over water, but only a foot or two above the lakebed. With exaggerated force, I bounced my mass on one leg. It held without flinching.

"I'm gonna try it," I said.

With the evil grin of a six-year-old boy about to smack a hornet's nest, I set off in a straight line across the lake, taking steps as delicately as a

170-pound man with a forty-pound pack would allow. Amped hesitantly followed behind.

As two desert boys walked across a frozen lake for the first time in their lives, our apprehension gave way to giddy smiles and laughs. Most folks were certain to advise against crossing frozen lakes in May, but Amped and I weren't most folks. We were lazier, heavier, and of course: a bit more dim.

In no time, we stepped onto the east shore of Bullfrog Lake, where we'd agreed to meet up with Melanie and Steve. I stuck my bright orange snowshoes vertically in the snow as a fluorescent beacon, then found a spot to set up camp. Amped immediately sat down to remove his boots.

From Amped's journal:

Is it bruised? Swollen? Limited motion? Well, yes to all.

Hopefully the time off my feet today will help, as well as the new boots Melanie is packing in for me. Melanie the trail angel—no wait: trail archangel.

I headed down to the shore with our water bottles. Liquid water was visible through a large, melted hole twenty feet into the lake, but the thin ice surrounding the hole would only be useful for unplanned, miserable swims. About four feet from the edge of the hole, I stomped into the surface several times, breaking through into the lake below.

I filled our bottles from my boot-shaped well, then sat on the shore for a minute. Fish lazily swam under a white latex balloon sitting still in the water, a beautifully sad reminder of my species' impact, even in such a remote environment.

A surprising number of balloons littered the Sierra backcountry, typically the shiny Mylar balloons with fun things printed on them ranging from "Congratulations!" to "Happy Earth Day!" Who could blame those hapless litterers though? Everyone knows the boundless joy of watching balloons float away, right? Well, me neither—and it turns out the atmospheric air stream delivers them right to the Sierra, as far as possible from the nearest trash can.

So stop it.

I found Amped laid out in camp, resting and letting his feet dry in the warm sun. There was still no sign of Melanie and Steve. I checked the time.

Ten a.m.

The white saddle of the pass was a couple miles away, perched up on the horizon. There hadn't been any movement yet. It wasn't time to worry though. At least, that's what I tried to explain to the panicky wuss in my head, who was sure my wife and dear friend were already dead, and I'd have to live with killing them over a pair of boots and a shameful number of cherry Pop-Tarts.

The hours crept while we hung out on our small patch of bare earth. Noon came and went, and the daily snowmelt commenced, running small streams through our dry patch. We built a couple mini-dams to divert the streams and take our minds off Mel and Steve.

One o'clock passed.

Two o'clock passed.

Both of us were having an increasingly harder time relaxing.

Melanie had been adamant she'd wanted to conquer this alpine objective, and I was proud of her for it and wanted to give her all the support she needed—but my eyes couldn't leave the pass they *theoretically* should've already summited.

Did I put any undue pressure on her? Is she in danger? What if something happened? What if she needs help and I'm just sitting here watching snowflakes turn into water and complaining about balloons?

This internal dialogue wasn't exactly new. As a guy who loves a girl, my instinct had always been to keep Mel away from danger. I mean, there was an alarming amount at stake. I'd somehow tricked the world's coolest lady into being my life buddy, and I was certain the universe wasn't going to let that happen twice. The idea of Mel's life being at risk was unnerving for a guy who didn't want to spend the rest of his life eating corn flakes in his mother's basement, combing his rat tail, and telling strangers they were going to die on Facebook.

But I knew damn well and good my male instinct to protect had no place with Melanie (a clear exception I'll note: spiders). To assume she couldn't keep herself safe was baseless. She had a solid grasp on what she could handle, and what she couldn't. In climbing, she trended toward the high-stakes world of highball bouldering, where climbing took place twenty-five, thirty-five, even forty feet off the deck without a rope. She felt bizarrely comfortable in femur-shattering territory, relying only on her graceful balance, iron vice of a grip, and impressively cool head to keep herself safe. She'd often bent the limits of what I was even comfortable *watching*, much less climbing myself.

"Should we think about hiking in their direction?" Amped asked, his swollen foot resting on the slab.

If we put on our packs and start walking toward Kearsarge, our Sierra run is finished. My PCT run—will be finished.

I knew I wasn't strong enough to stop walking east once I started. If we left the Sierra, Amped wasn't returning. If Amped wasn't returning, odds were—neither was I.

"Let's hold off just a little longer. Mel can handle this. Maybe wait until four or five? The snow has to be in absolute garbage shape up there by now."

From Amped's journal:

More and more time—where are Mel and Steve? They had an eight-mile hike—what happened? No contact, nothing. We begin to worry. Did they make it? Was there an avalanche? Bears and lions are a for-real thing out here. An idle mind can play dangerous tricks. We started formulating a plan to go and search, then we heard voices!

They didn't belong to Mel and Steve. An odd sight appeared on the far side of the lake: other people! Four black silhouettes moved against the white shoreline. The sight of other humans was wildly comforting, and we called a greeting over to them.

Their individual loads varied across the spectrum. A German couple with tiny, ultralight backpacks introduced themselves as Arrow and

Navigator. They were clearly exhausted to the extreme, and had no interest in chit-chatting. Their two partners were middle-aged men wielding massive packs protruding from their backs like two hermit crabs living under comically oversized shells.

One man introduced himself as Medic, from Venezuela. Medic abruptly excused himself to follow Arrow and Navigator's lead, who already had their tent erected. The last hiker was a very friendly American named Candyman, who set his giant pack down to chat for a bit.

All of them were done, exiting at Kearsarge Pass to skip ahead of the Sierra, tired of the snow, tired of the cold, tired of the exhaustion, and tired of the postholing death-marches. Candyman told us about their group's doomed attack plan for the Sierra, which was a common one: keep packs light and the grit high (although it seemed only the German couple had implemented the "light pack" part). They'd come almost twenty miles that day, hiking what Amped and I had struggled to hike over the past *two* days.

The get-it-over-with, Band-Aid approach had merit, but not in the early season Sierra. 460 miles of snow wasn't a quick rip you could close your eyes and clench your teeth through; it was ripping an entire roll of duct tape off a gorilla.

Ten miles was tough in the snow, fifteen was a marathon day, and twenty miles was a record-shattering feat of human endurance. If you were the type who filled your non-hiking time with passions such as naked beekeeping, or handcrafting your own g-strings from sandpaper, *maybe* you'd be able to mentally withstand the torture of several back-to-back twenty-mile days—but even the most sadistic mutants would be brought to their knees well before they could withstand a month of it.

Candyman was a wonderful character, chipper and jovial, even through his exhaustion. I tried my best to be a good conversationalist, but my eyes involuntarily glanced up at the pass every few seconds, hoping for a glimpse of Melanie.

THE RESUPPLY

From Melanie's journal:

6:30 a.m. wasn't early enough.

Steve was up and ready with the sun, but neither of us had any idea how fast the snow would soften. By the time I had breakfast and my Husky, Storm, outfitted with his backpack and ready to go, the sun had already been up for a bit.

I figured we'd be fine. We'd spent the night in our vehicles at the Onion Valley trailhead at 9,600 feet and it was **COLD***. There was no way the snow would soften very quickly.*

Right?

As we started up the hillside from the parking lot, it was immediately apparent the snow conditions were going to fight us. Our backpacks were heavy. Thank God I had Steve with me to split the resupply weight. Together we had twenty-four days of food for Danny and Miguel, a new pair of boots for Miguel, and I was surprising them with everything to make veggie quesadillas, bacon, and pancakes. We also had our sleeping gear, so our packs were pushing fifty pounds to spend just one night. My ultralight summer setup was typically under twenty pounds for a five-day hike.

Fighting up Kearsarge was tough, but I was excited to see Danny. I hadn't seen much of him in the last couple months. We'd spent 24/7 together for almost four years in Bishop, climbing and doing homework side-by-side in our trailer. It's been weird, honestly.

At first, he wasn't excited about the idea of me trying to resupply him and Miguel, mainly because of the weight. Originally, I had four friends enlisted to help split the load, but those plans fell through once Danny and Miguel had to bail out of the snowstorm. Steve stayed on-board though. I'm fortunate to have such a good friend to help, because there's no way I would've been able to handle a load weighing as much as I do!

A lone hiker with a bulging pack was headed out of the backcountry. When I asked him if he'd seen Danny and Miguel down at Bullfrog Lake, he said, "I was trying to get in, not coming out! The pass is too gnarly to get over. The snow is **so** *bad."*

CRUNCH

The hiker told us he'd exited out Horseshoe Meadows Road to Lone Pine like Danny and Miguel had a week earlier, but was skipping a section and heading back over Kearsarge. Now, he was headed north to Oregon. He strongly suggested we also turn around…

Both Steve and I struggled under the weight. The last mile up to Kearsarge is a giant, steep snowfield. It's east facing, so it bakes in the sun the second it rises.

We only had five miles to reach the other side of the pass, but we were moving SO slow, less than one mile per hour. Storm was struggling along with us. Poor pup was punching through the snow with every step, postholing down to his chest. He kept trying to turn around, forcing me to keep him on a leash. We had no way to let the boys know we'd be much later than planned. Danny would be worried.

Two more PCT hikers appeared headed off the pass. It was a Swiss couple who'd also attempted to get over Kearsarge and gave up. I started to doubt our own chances of getting up and over the pass. All these PCT hikers were bailing, what chance did we have?

We stopped to discuss our options. If we didn't show up, Danny and Miguel would likely come find us. It wouldn't be the end of the world—but I wasn't ready to quit. We agreed to continue ahead, one foot at a time. If either of us felt unsafe and wanted to turn around, we would.

In the afternoon sun, every step was a posthole. The exposure was more than I was expecting. It seemed like if you lost your footing, you'd slide a thousand feet down to the frozen Big Pothole Lake. Storm continued trying to turn around. He seemed confused, almost like he wanted to ask, "Mom, it's way easier to walk the other way, what the hell are we doing??"

*Bullfrog Lake came into view as we summited Kearsarge Pass. It was tough, but not as impossible as the hikers we'd talked to had made it seem. I let Storm off his leash. He was so excited, running and bouncing around in the downhill snow. We were all exhausted. I can't believe Danny and Miguel are out here—**have been** out here—**are continuing** to be out here!*

From Amped's journal:

The chat with Candyman distracts us from the absence of Mel, but then she shows up! Her and Steve (and Storm).

They look beat. More than beat; emotional almost. You can tell right away Mel isn't her cheery self. She's exhausted, sweating, and overweighted with a larger-than-life sized load. I lift her pack. It had to weigh fifty pounds, and she only weighs ninety!! I don't think I could carry a pack more than half my weight. No wonder.

After the initial fuss, a dry pair of socks, and lots of water, the life comes back into her face. This woman is incredible. She immediately gets to work cooking some of the fresh food she packed in. Quesadillas to start; loaded with mushrooms, bell peppers, onions, cilantro, and cheese. She fries them in real salted butter so the tortilla gets that crunchy outer shell. They go down in seconds, faster than she can make them.

Round two is next—pancakes! With real maple syrup! And then OMG!!! Bacon!!!! As much as we could possibly eat. Round after round it goes down; the salty, savory crunch in your mouth with a little of the sweet syrup. I could die right now. But the best part are the boots. Steve gets credit for these because he picked them out and carried them. They fit perfectly.

It was so incredible to see Mel out there and share what I was doing with her, even for just a night. The 120-mile stretch of snow ahead of us was another looming unknown. I had confidence in my ability to manage risk and make good decisions, but the outcome of this trek was anything but certain.

Although my tent was technically too small for two people, I pitched it as high as I could to fit both Mel and me in for the night. For a nice surprise, I fired up the stove while Mel was distracted and threw some boiling water into my Nalgene. Then, I slid the bottle into a sock and tucked it into the foot of Mel's sleeping bag to give her some extra warmth to start the night off with. She slid into the tent first to get settled before I squeezed beside her. We just barely fit, like two peas in a... *single-pea* pod.

I loved having her there. She'd always been right next to me through our adventures, and being apart hadn't been easy. Amped was an incredible teammate, but it certainly was taking an adjustment being without my climbing/backpacking/life/donut partner.

Besides, Amped could take care of his own spiders and refused to kiss me goodnight.

From Amped's journal:

Today is like Christmas. I am recharged. The toe is feeling better. I also feel blessed. I am around a few truly good, honest, tough people. Their endeavors are inspirational. Their humility is incredible and their love for one another knows no bounds. Literal mountains can't stand in the way! I feel lucky to be a part of this human experience.

15
GLEN

At one in the morning, the neighborhood coyotes lit off an unnerving show, one of the most impressive displays of howling I'd ever experienced. Their shrill, piercing yips rang through the still night, echoing off the canyon walls around us in waves, as each coyote crew took their turn keeping the human visitors awake. They were close. Close enough for us to hear the light crunch of dozens of paws on the refrozen slush surrounding camp.

Storm was outside next to our bear canisters. Huskies can sleep down to fifty degrees *below zero* (!), so no matter what time of year we were camping, the pup's job had been to guard our food.

Melanie, like every ear-owning human within a mile radius, was awake and listening to the spaced yips and calls. "Storm is safe, right?"

I definitely didn't know how Storm would fare against a bunch of coyotes. He was a big, brute of a husky, but still only fifty-five pounds—and most of that mass was harmless fluff. Storm might've doubly outweighed a single coyote, but if a dozen of them wanted to get to our food, Storm would be in trouble. Melanie fell back asleep, but the soft crunching outside of camp kept me alert, waiting for the first sign of Storm needing help whoopin' some coyote ass!

Storm was disobedient as hell and some (for example: me) would say he was on the dim side, but Melanie loved that dog. Like, almost as much as me. So if it came down to karate choppin' 'yotes in the middle of the twenty-degree night barefoot in my underwear—that's what I'd do to keep that big, dumb, semi-lovable dog alive.

Everyone emerged from their tents at dawn, exhausted from the coyotes. We shook off the heavy frozen dew from our tents, packed everything up, and shouldered our reloaded packs.

"Holy God," I muttered under the weight of eleven days of food. I hadn't exactly noticed our pack weights gradually lowering over the previous few days.

The weight *increase* was a *bit* more noticeable.

Theoretically, our resupply would allow us a comfortable nine days to hike into Mammoth, with an extra couple of days of provisions, just in case we needed to bail. Not only was this stretch of the PCT one of the most rugged, it was also one of the most remote. Vermillion Valley Resort and Muir Trail Ranch were the typical resupply/bail points between Kearsarge and Mammoth, but both of those isolated Sierra outposts would remain closed long after we'd passed by. We'd be on our own.

We gave Melanie and Steve one last big hug before we said goodbye. Amped and I strapped on our snowshoes and headed back across Bullfrog Lake toward our next major objective: the 12,000-foot Glen Pass.

Recharged, we climbed out of the steep basin and into miles of side-hilling above Charlotte Lake with the dramatic, granite monolith of Charlotte Dome in the background. Under the increased load, our jacked-over ankles were soon pissed.

Amped came to an abrupt stop on the thirty-degree slope. "I can't do it. Now my snowshoes are pissing off my toe."

GLEN

He switched into crampons (a.k.a. the original offenders).

Please keep that toe from escalating, I begged the universe. *We're going to be in trouble if it flares up beyond Glen Pass.*

Amped led the way through some bizarrely bad snow as we climbed above the treeline. Yesterday's afternoon slush had a thin, hard layer of ice over the top, like the world's most evil crème brûlée. Random steps punched through the shell into the slush beneath, taking us down to our hands and knees repeatedly.

We spaced apart whenever the angle of the snow steepened into ideal avalanche territory, or at least what I suspected was "ideal." Accurately assessing our avalanche risk felt impossible, especially in the odd Sierra springtime when fresh snow falls onto essentially ice, and daytime temps are above freezing while nighttime temps are below freezing. The more experts I'd talked to, the more confused I'd become.

The bottom line seemed to be this: Avalanches aren't predictable.

But, BUT—there *was* a way you could suss out the terrain and learn a lot about the layers of ice and snow below you. It simply involved sawing blocks of ice out of the slope to study. Problem solved. Unless of course you're moving through fifteen miles of constantly changing terrain every day, don't have the time to devote to sawing, don't want to carry a saw, and/or don't have any measurable upper body strength from months of your thighs cannibalizing your biceps.

From all my research, I'd managed to scrape together three rules that seemed like foundational principles in any avalanche terrain:

1) Solid ice doesn't slide, so hiking through potential avalanche slopes while they were still frozen hard from the overnight lows was ideal.

2) Trees anchor slabs. So if we could aim for trees, we'd be safer.

3) Don't go first—unless your name is Amped.

I might've taken some liberties with rule three.

So anyways, Amped was about a hundred yards ahead of me on a footprint-free, sun-softened slope with nary a tree in sight—when an audible crack echoed off the canyon walls.

WUMPH

Amped froze like a deer in headlights. Fortunately, the snow stayed put.

"You should head downhill to that lake where it's flat, then hike back up!" he called back to me.

A frozen lake sat a hundred feet of elevation below us. In that moment, an avalanche felt preferable to the extra-credit thigh burning. I swallowed my irritation and headed down to the lake. Being buried alive was an uncomfortable thought, but dying with a bear can filled with uneaten Snickers was unbearable.

We were able to calm down much faster than after the previous wumph on the Bighorn Plateau. Maybe it was just a part of Sierra hiking, just another noise to get used to. It was well known most spring avalanches were preceded by a wumph—*but* how many wumphs were followed by an avalanche? Maybe it just wasn't that likely.

Amped shifted back into snowshoes for the steepening terrain. Glen Pass came into sight, but the path to the pass wasn't as straightforward as Forester. Random rock outcroppings jutted through a thick sheet of ice sweeping up to the high saddle we had to reach. We stopped to study the breathtaking terrain looming above us. It looked as if a fall wouldn't just be a thousand-foot slide—it would be a thousand-foot slide with rocks to pinball through.

"Doesn't this look just as steep as Forester?" Amped asked. "Glen wasn't supposed to be a hard one, right? Forester and Mather were the notorious passes?"

"Yup." I nodded. "I don't know, man. Maybe it just looks worse than it actually is."

We followed a pair of skiers' tracks along the side of a massive bowl, the sole sign of other people. The bowl steepened until we were walking with our ankles uncomfortably jacked over at forty-five degrees. For the last hundred yards, we faced the slope to sidestep into the final gully of snow and rock with a dizzying amount of exposure under our heels. Hundreds of feet of sheer ice—peppered with freshly melted out rocks—led down to a flat, white sheet in the distant bottom of the bowl. It was a lake in the summer, if I remembered correctly.

We hesitated there for a minute, trying to come to terms with feeling far more vulnerable than we'd expected. Glen was a thousand feet lower than Forester, and a moderate pass during summer hikes. We'd expected a step down in difficulty, but if Glen wasn't just as steep, it was *steeper*. The threatening rock outcroppings added a fear factor Forester didn't have. Falling wouldn't be a giant slide, it would be…

"No." I stopped myself under my breath. "Not the time to think about that."

I took my axe out and started to link short, steep sections of gully ice between protruding patches of rocks. On Forester, I was comforted knowing I could at least *try* to arrest a fall with my ice axe, but that wasn't going to happen here. Open space was needed to slide and arrest a fall, but any slips were going to result in a ricocheting impact before an axe could even start slowing me down. Amped chose to keep his trekking poles in his hands.

Shutting out the many jutting rocks below, waiting to deliver the consequences of a single careless step, was tough. From my vertigo-addled vantage point, I was attached to a straight vertical face, on the very edge of friction's ability to keep me from falling backwards. Bits of snow and ice tumbled down the rock-lined gully from Amped kicking each step into the slope above. I opted to side step to a patch of rocks to escape the raining debris, and set a diagonal course to the pass on mixed terrain of ice and loose talus.

We navigated our separate paths and rendezvoused at the saddle of the pass safely, albeit a bit shaken. Our initial reaction to a successful summit of Glen Pass was far from celebratory.

"Did that feel *harder* than Forester to you?" Amped asked.

I nodded. "Definitely scarier."

This was only the second of a dozen high mountain passes in the Sierra. Mather Pass was coming up in a couple days, and I'd been told repeatedly Forester and Mather were the two monsters in the early season Sierra. There had been no mention of Glen.

Amped and I stood in awe at the top of a thousand feet of sixty-degree snow flowing off the backside of the pass. The terrain north was absurdly beautiful, an ice world I never knew existed outside of Antarctica or the Himalaya, much less within fifty miles from home. The depth of the snowpack beyond Glen was a clear step up from where we'd come.

I'd suspected getting off this pass would be a challenge. Even in low-snow years, large patches of snow obscured the switchbacks late into summer. Getting down such a steep sheet of ice was an intimidating prospect. Soft snow was ideal for plunge-stepping down, but we'd summited too early for soft snow. We'd simultaneously arrived too late to walk down step-by-step with snowshoes. The ice had loosened just enough that there was a risk of our spikes sliding out from underneath us.

A butt glissade seemed like our safest bet, so we put our snowshoes on our backs and prepared our axes. Amped didn't hesitate to launch down the ice, screaming along at a speed that made me nervous just to watch. Amped hadn't died after a few minutes, so I launched into the slide behind him, immediately realizing Amped wasn't going fast for fun—it was the only option.

I flew down the slope in large sections, relief washing over me every time I managed to come to a stop. Within seconds of initiating each slide, I'd be a hundred more yards along, rolled over and digging my axehead into the ice again. Even when I was up on my toes, weighting the axe as much as possible, it took thirty yards of spraying ice to create enough drag to arrest my momentum.

Halfway down, we'd actually lost enough elevation that the air was substantially warmer, and the snow had softened. After the third or fourth heart-stopping glissade, I stopped for a minute to calm down. My hands shook from my adrenal glands working overtime—but I couldn't help but smile releasing my axe for one last, long glissade.

At the base, standing safely on the north side of Glen Pass, we took a second to celebrate another small victory, then continued our downhill run through a mix of snowshoe-skiing and glissading toward the Rae Lakes. Still a hundred yards above the closest lake, the skier's tracks we'd been following took a hard left across a blank, forty-five-degree slope.

"Let's head straight down to the lakes," I said. "Even if the skier got through all right, our steps are more likely to trigger a slide."

Turns out, the skier *hadn't* gotten through all right.

Hidden until we'd reached the lake, the ski tracks traversed into the top of a fresh avalanche scar, then departed the bottom—about sixty yards lower. Only ten percent of the hillside had slid, and the rest looked ready to let go. Amped looked at me with a bit of shock.

"Damn," I muttered, "we almost walked right into that."

We wound through the slushy shores of the Rae Lakes. The deserted ranger station there was buried up to its roof. The snow improved slightly on the west side of the canyon, and our spirits were high as we traversed under the magnificent Fin Dome. Glissading in snowshoes was possible in such sloppy conditions, and quite fun—similar to skiing with really short, fat skis. I hopped down one unassuming slope, leaning slightly back to disengage their aggressive bottom points, like I'd been doing all morning—but my lead snowshoe unexpectedly slammed forward, sinking all its points into hard ice.

I pitched forward down the slope, hitting the ground with a pained grunt—and a snap. The strap around my waist loosened and I slid to a stop in the bottom of the small gully. It took some effort to sit up against the awkward, unrestrained weight on my back.

"Well this isn't good," I whispered, holding the blown apart plastic and nylon remnants of my backpack's waist strap.

Amped came back over a small rise in the snow with a smirk on his face. "Heard that one from thirty feet away. You all right?"

I stood up, failing to find a smile to return. The fifty-pound load pulled stiffly against my shoulders. "My, eh, waist strap…"

His smile lowered.

There were a half-dozen more passes and over a hundred miles before Mammoth. A functional waist strap wasn't optional.

"I'm an idiot. I should've been moving slower."

Amped was silent for a second, not bothering to disagree. "Is it time to turn around?"

I didn't like that one bit.

"What?! No way. Screw that," I snapped back.

He shrugged. "You're not going to be able to carry fifty pounds through this mess without a waist strap. Some little things can turn into big things, and it needs to be asked: Is this one of those?"

He was right, but the idea of turning around—of getting *back up and over Glen*—was as detestable as it was terrifying. "Let's get down to Arrowhead Lake. I'll break out the sewing kit and see what I can do."

"Sewing kit" was a bit of a hyperbolic label for my two skinny needles and lightweight spool of thread. It was more suited to sew tags back on underwear than for heavy-duty pack repair.

Within a mile, my back and shoulders were already on fire. We stopped short of the lake next to an exposed section of creek. I broke the jagged plastic bits off of the nylon strap, then trimmed it to sew the remnants directly to my hip belt. It would no longer be adjustable, but it was better than nothing. Pushing the needle through thick nylon was hard work. The needle bent over and over, and without having a thimble to avoid stabbing myself, I utilized an old trick from back in my desert trailside sewing days: loud profanity.

Amped collected and filtered water for us, doing as much to help as he could, but spent most of the time waiting. Guilt hovered over me while he watched me sew. The snow was already in sloppy shape, and certainly not getting any better.

My battered needle looked like a witch's finger by the time I was done, but the strap was sewn back onto my pack. I crossed my fingers it could withstand more clumsy impacts, because there was no way that was the last one.

Fancy new hip belt in place, we continued into the afternoon, losing elevation through a sea of reflective, white slush. The sun—in spite of all of its warmth and life-affirming wonder—can be a real dick.

From Amped's journal:

The sun is hot today. I feel at home [Las Vegas]. The reflection from the snow is a little irritating though. I've never had to sunscreen the inside of my nostrils. I'm excited about sleeping warmer tonight.

All footprints from the hikers ahead had been erased. Heat radiated up from the snow, roasting us evenly on all sides. A healthy river cascading through my ass crack was a bizarre juxtaposition to the ice we were trudging through. At the beginning of an eighteen-day showerless stretch, it was probably the last thing we needed.

Leading was much more exhausting than following, as the follower was able to step inside compacted footprints, so we swapped leads every few hundred yards to even out the strain. When we dropped below 9,000 feet, ground appeared, but all of it was running with water. Bits and pieces of trail emerged, none of it usable, but any sign of the PCT was reassuring.

With plenty of daylight left, we reached the campground at Woods Creek. Not only were there several dry patches of dirt to pitch our tents, but there was easily accessible water, **and** a bear box stocked with amenities: a pair of dirty underwear and an old Bible (that no doubt smelled a bit like the underwear it had been entombed with for the last six months).

"That was a damn hard day," Amped said. "But God—what a *bad ass* day."

I wholeheartedly agreed. We were making progress, making miles, overcoming obstacles, all in the middle of an isolated wonderland we had to ourselves.

Bad ass, indeed.

Pinchot Pass was seven miles away, so we settled into our tents in the late afternoon to get an early start the next morning. We figured aiming to step out of camp right at dawn would be sufficient.

It absolutely, one hundred percent, was *not.*

16

PINCHOT

"Ouch," I whispered into my cup of coffee.

I touched my lip with a finger and winced. It was sunburned. I poked around and found other burns in the strangest places: earlobes, nostrils, the front of my neck. All had been roasted by the sun's reflection off the snow.

We took our sweet time sipping coffee by headlamp in the comfy elevation. I walked over to the creek to fill my water bottles and again, just like at Rock Creek, it had inexplicably *risen* overnight. A small island we'd stood on the night before was completely submerged. "Cross creeks in the morning" seemed to be such an inflexible, iron rule I'd come across many times in my preparation for the Sierra…

We clicked off our headlamps and stepped across the famous Woods Creek suspension bridge. Yet another rumor spreading like wildfire through the basements of the social media hiking community was that this bridge had been taken out by heavy winter storms. Many people had skipped the Sierra specifically because of that rumor. For a bridge that had been destroyed, it worked remarkably well.

I sent a message to Melanie to relay the news. On a stretch of dry trail, we walked up on stones arranged in three, large numbers. It was the 800-mile marker, signifying the 800th mile along the PCT.

It was a point of pride knowing that marker still meant something in my hike. Since most PCT hikers had either chosen to skip snowy and/or uncomfortable stretches in Southern California or diverted from the trail once they reached Kennedy Meadows, those twenty-six markers along the PCT had become effectively meaningless for almost everyone—but not me. Of course, walking around closures in Southern California and bailing in and out along Horseshoe Meadows Road meant 800 wasn't *exactly* accurate, but it was very satisfying to have hiked *at least* that many miles—not fewer.

A natural granite slide known as the Woods Creek Water Slide was roaring to our right. In summer, it seemed like a tempting feature to play on. But even at its weakest flow, all fun would almost certainly end with a helicopter transporting a corpse back to civilization. This version made the summer slide look like a suburban gutter being fed by a misaligned sprinkler. The rumble of the deluge ripping across the granite slabs vibrated our boots through the earth, even from a hundred yards away.

Snow returned and we strapped on our crampons. Six miles and 3,500 feet of elevation stood between us and the tame giant, Pinchot Pass. Pinchot had always been a bit of a joke in summer. It had a reputation for being one of the easiest passes in the High Sierra, with a gentle approach and descent. Neither of us was worried about it. The next real challenge would come tomorrow, on Mather Pass.

The canyon steepened until we were side-hilling along a constant forty-degree slope. Woods Creek maintained a thundering, nagging presence 500 feet downhill. The entire state of California was in the middle of a heat spike, and it had taken its toll on the Sierra. The snow hadn't refrozen overnight, and our pace was crippled before the sun even arrived. Stretches of loose scree and dirt punctuated the slope, and we flubbed our gear selection repeatedly. Our frustration grew, not at each other, but at our inability to maintain healthy progress. It seemed like every quarter-mile our packs were off to shift between crampons, snowshoes, and just boots.

Miles into the canyon, the snow inexplicably thinned to where the terrain was more talus than snow. Expecting snow to reappear around every turn, we kept our crampons on until the screech of metal points on rock drove us within three steps of fashioning straitjackets out of our sleeping bags. We stopped for the fifty-eighth time, hastily tearing the crampons off our feet. Again, we wrapped them up, strapped them to our packs, and hefted the weight back onto our shoulders. Not two minutes later, we were back on snow.

Between two small boulders, I stepped my left boot onto an innocent, three-foot-wide snow strip, and it didn't stop—as if I'd stepped onto a cloud. My foot, ankle, calf, knee, and thigh disappeared one by one, my momentum freely accelerating until my chest impacted the surface. The bear on my back pile-drove my face into the snow. I didn't recognize the grunt-whimper crushed out of me.

It took a second to summon the strength to sit up against the mass sitting on my head. I unclipped my ratty, doctored waist belt, grateful all the thread and blood had kept it together, then rolled my pack to the side. In a daze, I wiped the melting slush out of my eyebrows and surveyed my leg sprawled out awkwardly to the side. The other had been completely swallowed, all the way up to my crotch.

There was a half-suppressed chuckle behind me. "You all right?"

"My dick," I said, half to myself, "is *cold*. I *literally* just postholed down— *to my dick*."

It was funny. Objectively, I *knew* it was funny, but I couldn't smile. Amped offered me a hand and yanked me back up to the earth's surface. I brushed myself off and took a couple steps. The knee that'd stayed on top of the snow had twisted a bit weird, and it trembled under load, threatening to buckle. I took a short, unweighted lap to walk off some of the pain.

"We've got a problem," I said, pointing to the illuminated slope ahead.

The sun was up.

Our slow pace and posthole shenanigans was going to put us at the pass *way* too late.

CRUNCH

*It's **Pinchot**. How bad could it really be, even in slush?*

In the sparse clouds above, I could've *sworn* I heard deity-like snickering and—popcorn popping?

At ten a.m., *hours* after we should've been up and over Pinchot, the sun-soaked pass finally came into view. My back-sweat river had returned in full force, and I took out a little iPod Shuffle for some tunes to help me motivate, maybe some "Eye of the Tiger" or "Don't Stop Believin'" or "Fergalicious"—but a small, blinking red light crushed my hopes of shaking my ass up the pass. I hadn't even used the damn thing yet, but the cold had completely zapped the battery, leaving me with a tiny paperweight and a whole lot more silence to echo my whiny thoughts through.

"Well that figures," I muttered.

I'd left the charger at home to spare my back from that fraction of an ounce. A really, really, *really* smart move.

"Glad I'm giving this turd a ride through the Sierra."

Every fiber of my being wanted to chuck the little iPod out into the snow. Carrying those few bonus ounces all the way until Mammoth felt—insulting? But I tucked the metal joyrider back in my pocket and trudged on. The lousy Boy Scout inside me couldn't bear the thought of littering in my precious Sierra.

The awful, shelled-over snow we'd struggled with before Glen Pass had been amplified approaching Pinchot. Under the fragile shell was *two feet* of soft, loose slush. Amped and I fought with everything we had, but a half-mile took us an hour. Eventually, we reached the base of the final slope to the pass—but both of us were doubled over, out of breath and completely exhausted. I couldn't make sense of what had caused the abysmal snow conditions, beyond conspiracy theories involving God and that one time I farted in church.

Our snowshoes distributed our weight, keeping us *mostly* out of the slush, but every few steps a snowshoe would break through the hard crust. Snowshoes were glorious for keeping your feet above the snow, but if they ended up *below* the snow, they tried just as hard to stay there.

Removing them from the slush took an incredible amount of pulling force, enough that I worried about breaking something. It felt like they were submerged in wet concrete.

Amped headed higher up onto the slope, hoping to find better snow. He didn't. I stopped to switch into crampons, hoping that would help.

It didn't.

We were both getting nowhere, struggling inside our own little bubbles of hell, inventing new swear words for the English lexicon (I don't know what a "flucasshiticker" is—but it came from the heart). In desperation, I tried to establish back onto the crust, but every attempt snapped the shell, sending me sinking further into the subterranean slush pool.

Okay, fine! I farted *many* times in church.

"Which way?" Amped called down.

It seemed like an odd question, but there was a set of surprisingly fresh footprints that broke left, headed away from the saddle of the pass.

"Stay right," I shouted. "I have no idea what's over there."

The last 200 yards took almost an *hour*. That's sub-toddler-crawling-across-the-living-room speed. One by one, Amped compacted loose steps into the crust/slush mixture with the broad underside of his snowshoes. I waded through the slush, chipping my way through the crust with my axe like an Antarctic icebreaker ship. Within eyeshot of the saddle, I was soaking wet, sweating my ass off, and buried up to my chest in slush. We were actively being taught an important lesson about Sierra snow travel—perhaps *the* most important lesson—the hardest way possible.

You don't hike when it's light out; you hike when the snow is hard.

"Smug" would be the humiliating word to describe the satisfaction with our previous evening's plan to get up at 3:45 a.m., when we'd use head-lamps to get camp packed up, but then tuck them away to start hiking, thus saving the whole *minute* required to later stop and store them. Well thank the good Lord we'd waited until it was light out, because the shit-show we'd gifted ourselves was illuminated to *perfection*.

Every few yards, I had to stop to catch my breath and pray some energy would return to my burning legs. I dragged exhausted eyes down to my buried torso, then back along the pathetic hundred yards representing a half-hour of exertion. My arms limped to my side in a moment of complete defeat. The only sound was the furious groans of the warring man above me.

"*Why?*" I muttered to myself between uncontrollable gasps. Without any remaining energy or willpower, my subconscious had unrestricted use of my vocal cords. "Why are you out here? What could *possibly* be worth **this**?"

Pinchot Pass was impossible. It was *right there*—but we'd never summit. Amped was getting angrier, but getting about as far as I was just watching him. Every shred of me wanted to throw in the towel, but even quitting wasn't really an option. A helicopter wouldn't be able to land on this steep slope of slush. Did I really want a Search and Rescue team to land, fight through the terrain up onto the side of Pinchot just to find me… fine. Just tired and fussy?

My breathing eventually calmed, and my legs stopped trembling. With no way to turn back the clock, and no reset button to click, there was nothing to do but struggle forward. I resumed chipping away at the shell, literally inching my way up the pass.

After a hell-on-earth I didn't know existed, I crested the top of Pinchot and childishly threw my axe across the snow, then plopped down next to Amped. There was no celebration, just two shell-shocked suckers staring back over the terrain they'd voluntarily traversed—for reasons they couldn't remember.

We ate lunch in silence, simultaneously exhausted, soaked, frustrated, furious, relieved, and terrified. A lone marmot meandered among the snowy rock outcroppings we sat on. We'd hiked seven miles in five hours, our slowest pace so far. Inside both of us, unbeknownst to the other, our confidence had been absolutely mortared.

From Amped's journal:

Do you ever wonder what you've gotten yourself into? Question whether or not you're qualified to make big life decisions? Today I had one of those moments. When you posthole down to your knee in snow, with snowshoes on, you wonder what the hell you're doing. Today we climbed 3,500 feet over seven miles to top Pinchot Pass. It was the most difficult twelve miles I have ever hiked. Now, you may think I'm being dramatic, seeing how I've made these "hardest" statements before. But the reality is: this journey gets more difficult by the day.

"We're waking up at two a.m. tomorrow for Mather," Amped stated, more of a matter of informing me, not so much to discuss the pros and cons of such a ludicrous idea.

I was fully on the same page. I didn't say a word, just gave a silent nod. There wasn't anything to discuss. Hiking through such torturous conditions would *not* happen twice.

We departed the pass in snowshoes. The sun hadn't had as much time to bake the western aspect of the pass, so the fragile shell over the slush was stiffer—but not enough to change our mind about a two a.m. wakeup. In the lead, still within a pathetic hundred yards from the pass, my legs were back on fire. Nine out of ten steps broke through the shell, even with my weight broadly distributed. I'd yank my anchored snowshoe out of the slush, then single-leg squat back up onto the shell, my legs trembling under the 220-pound load. The follower could easily follow inside the leader's compacted steps, while the leader was in a torture chamber. We swapped leads every half mile or so, which was about the limit either of us could physically or mentally tolerate.

The struggle was beyond anything I'd ever experienced. If alone, I would've sat in that slush and bawled my eyes out in blinding frustration. But Amped was there, and since I didn't want to hear about the time I had a mental breakdown on Pinchot Pass every conversation we had for the rest of our lives, I crammed my emotions down into a deep, dark corner of my brain, where they were almost certain to surface on a therapist's couch one day.

We stayed outwardly positive and encouraging, mainly because there was a looming sense of being trapped, stuck in a situation with no easy way out. We were *so* far from help. Bailing would be just as horrific as continuing forward. Reversing back up and over Pinchot *and* Glen was an idea that made me want to curl up into the fetal position, and there were zero reasonable exits between Pinchot and Mather. The terrain standing between us and the Owens Valley was one of the most dramatic sections of the Eastern Sierra, where the desert floor went from 4,000 feet all the way up and over 14,000 feet in just a few rocky, cliff-bound miles.

We either stayed positive and kept moving, or—nothing. There was no other option.

Now off Pinchot, I'd be lying to say my thoughts weren't focused on the SOS button clipped to my chest. I'd joked many times about using it, but it was shifting into a serious consideration. I didn't know exactly how much a rescue cost, but I did know it was sufficient to destroy a bank account of which I wasn't the only owner. But aside from financially ruining my family with the tap of a button, I had a strong ethical rejection of the scenario where I would voluntarily walk into a mortally threatening environment, become mortally threatened (who could see *that* coming?), then call a group of people to come *threaten their lives* to get my doe-eyed, Gumby ass out of there. Having access to an SOS feature was objectively a good idea—but part of me doubted whether my pride would allow me to push the button before I froze to death trying to convince myself to actually do it.

We fought like hell to maintain a pathetic *quarter mile per hour* pace. My legs were comically exhausted. Moving down a steep, forested hillside, Amped tripped over his own snowshoe. With tangled legs too drained to react, he fell forward, lancing the soft snow with his arms, leaving his face to absorb the impact. His legs cartoonishly scorpioned above his head while the momentum of his pack shoved his undoubtedly frowning face deeper into the slush.

They say there are three levels of fun:

Type One: Something that's fun when you're going through it and fun to reflect on later.

Type Two: Something that's *not* fun to go through but is fun to reflect on.

Type Three: Something that's not fun to go through and not fun to reflect on.

Amped twisted out of the pretzel he'd been tossed into, then growled in frustration through scraping away the wet slush crammed into his eyebrows. It was a rare state to see him rattled. I *wanted* to say something encouraging, maybe even chuckle at his misfortune—but we were deep in Type Two fun, staring down the barrel of Type Three.

In the late afternoon, we reached the South Fork of the Kings River, a sizable challenge to cross, even in low snow years (sadly, it would take the life of a PCT hiker just weeks later). But this early in the season, a gigantic snowbridge still spanned the whitewater. A single track of footprints was stomped into the bridge—and they were fresh. R*eally* fresh.

We sat for an extended break next to the creek, longingly admiring the flat, potential tent sites around us. Mather Pass was four miles away still. We **had** to camp closer, but both of us were thoroughly done with the day.

With our last shred of motivation and strength, Amped and I packed up and resumed our pathetic trudge. Maybe Pinchot Pass was doable (and I use that word lightly) in the mush, but getting to Mather late would potentially be a mortal error. I'd read accounts of a massive cornice overhanging the lip of the high, steep pass—from which vehicle-sized chunks were actively *breaking off and rolling down the slope,* threatening to take out hikers like bowling pins. Reaching Mather long before the sun softened that cornice was an undeniable necessity—although the prospect of being crushed by a giant block of ice was still just *barely* enough to pull us back onto our feet.

We made it a whopping 0.8 miles. That was all we had left.

We set up our tents in silence and both disappeared into them. I took my boots off, then my sopping wet socks. My feet spent all day, every day pruned from their perpetually drenched home. I ran my fingers over cracks and inflamed lines I didn't recognize in the calloused undersides of my feet, resurging worries about the cumulative damage I was inflicting on my body.

My iron commitment had dissolved. I couldn't believe what I'd willingly gotten myself into. I'd stepped in a bear trap I wasn't going to be able to pry myself out of, and I'd convinced a friend to step in next to me!

Frustrated, ashamed, and confused, I sent Melanie a message:

Today was horrific. We're destroyed in every aspect. Might need to exit before Mammoth.

I instantly regretted sending it, while simultaneously yearning for the reply, an outside opinion, some direction on what to do—what to think—and from anywhere but inside my own doubting head.

She wasn't going to be much help.

Melanie wrote back:

A wise man once wrote: "I'm not satisfied living comfortably. Human's existence on this planet has always been in search of increasing safety, stability, and comfort. I don't want to be comfortable. I want to be uncomfortable. I want to push myself physically and mentally. I want to suffer with a smile on my face. I want a story to tell."

That was me. I'd written that foolish paragraph long before I knew about slush and frozen socks and Pinchot Pass. It had been an exercise to record my reasoning for wanting to hike the Pacific Crest Trail. I reread my own words several times, trying to recapture that drive I'd lost somewhere in the snow over Pinchot, trying to remind myself I was, indeed, uncomfortable; exactly where I'd wanted to be.

I lay down, closed my eyes, and slipped into a slumber just a half-notch up from death.

17
MATHER

My eyes shot open at the sound of the muffled alarm tucked next to me. I snatched my phone in a bit of groggy panic.

Two a.m.

I sighed in relief. "Oh thank God."

My near-coma sleep had changed once the sun went down. The paranoia of missing my alarm and ending up in another day of eggshell slush kept me tossing and turning. I woke countless times in the pitch black to search out my phone to check the time. It wasn't helping that I'd repeatedly found it smothered under me, where I definitely wouldn't be hearing any noise it made. Keeping my phone warm enough to keep the battery alive, yet still audible, was a tall order.

I sat up and clicked on my headlamp, illuminating the tent walls and the white column of breath drifting from my mouth and hanging in the freezing air above my sleeping bag. The lumpy, soft slush I'd pitched my tent over was now bullet-hard, in spite of the warm body lying over it.

"Ugh," I groaned, resisting the desire to roll back over my phone and recommence sleeping. "This is ridiculous."

Part of me doubted we'd actually do it. Certainly one of us would find a reason to weasel out of this early wake-up call. But Amped rustled inside his tent, clicked on his headlamp, and started shuffling gear around.

"Well... dammit," I muttered.

Stepping out of the tent was surreal. To be awake in the middle of the night, in the depths of the Sierra backcountry, with intentions to leave the security and warmth of our camp felt wrong. We gathered around billowing coffee and Ziploc bags of oats under headlamps, then broke down camp under the stars.

I'd gone to bed feeling quite hopeless and mentally stressed to my limit. But now, shouldering my pack at three a.m. in the freezing darkness, I felt strangely good. Invigorated. Hopeful.

Yesterday had taught us a borderline traumatic lesson: Do whatever it takes to walk on hard snow. We were doing it. Another full day of postholing through that sugar-and-dairy-free crème brûlée (a.k.a. Satan's brûlée) would break us. Luckily, it was incredibly cold. My little janky plastic thermometer only read down to twenty degrees, and it was pegged low.

"Ready?" I asked my bundled-up partner. He nodded and set off into the dark forest in the general direction of Mather Pass.

The teeth on the underside of our snowshoes bit into the bullet-hard crust. Our rhythmic steps were the only sound in the desolate, black landscape, each making a satisfyingly crisp *crunch*. Overhead, billions of stars hung over us, emitting enough light to illuminate the dramatic outline of the towering, 14,000-foot Palisade range ahead.

Crunch, crunch, crunch, crunch

I was beyond grateful to still have Amped there. Walking together in the midnight Sierra was a wonderful experience, but alone—the creepy factor would've been off the charts.

From Amped's journal:

Moving over snow and through pines in the middle of the night can let your imagination open up to very dark places. You have to keep a lock on it to stay sane. It's the only way to travel right now. Temperatures are rising and making travel more like a swim than a hike.

We were in the presence of a mind-altering level of beauty, immersed in a masterpiece beyond our ability to process. Warmed up, we stopped to take a couple layers off, Amped paused to stare up at the purple and yellow swirls throughout the Milky Way, spanning the sky from one jagged horizon to the other.

"*Unreal…*" he muttered into the universe.

The snow was a flat, hard sidewalk, and we made progress at a break-neck speed. Well, breakneck compared to the crippled snail pace we'd held the previous afternoon. The notorious cornice on Mather kept us moving. Both of us were anxious to hit the pass before the sun did. We marched above the treeline side by side, our snowshoes stepping in and out of sync.

Crunch, crunch, crunch, crunch

The first hint of dawn stretched across the sky, gently illuminating the behemoth Mather Pass—a thousand feet of steep, clean ice. The faded remnants of a single set of days-old footprints were pressed into the otherwise flawless surface. The fresh footprints we'd spotted the day before were nowhere in sight.

Winds had ramped up in the higher elevation, whipping the sub-freez-ing air around us. I dropped my pack on the only flat spot I could find, along the face of a short cliffline. Even though I was about to fight up a hundred flights of slippery stairs, I needed another layer on.

The dark cliffline had been absorbing the afternoon sun, forming a narrow crevice between the snow and the cliff. I took a curious second to peer down into the gap with my headlamp, but its beam wasn't strong enough to find the bottom.

Amped was already starting up the pass, so I hurried to take my fleece out of my pack. I zipped up the warm layer with a satisfied shudder, then threw my pack back onto my shoulder. An audible plastic ***click*** sent an object in my peripheral falling away from my chest.

The inReach.

In a horrific flash, the device hit the ice and slid into the black of the crevice, out of sight before I could even try to react. For a numb second, I stood still—staring at the crevice in the stiff alpine wind, waiting to wake up from the climax of a horrible dream.

I didn't.

"What," I muttered, panic building inside my chest, "did I just do?"

Losing access to the SOS feature was the least of our problems. People at home were watching us. Every ten minutes, our position was sent out, placing a line of dots on an online map so our friends and family could track our progress. Nobody knew the horrible thing I'd just done. I couldn't *tell* anyone the horrible thing I'd just done.

Everyone is going to see the GPS track hit the base of one of the most notorious passes in the Sierra—and then stop.

A hundred yards up the pass, Amped's silhouette was still, looking back at me, likely wondering what the delay was.

"Holy shit," I muttered.

"*SHIT!*" I repeated, in a more situation-appropriate volume and tone. "A rescue is going to be initiated."

There wasn't an exit for days in every direction, no way to even get into cell service (well, without just climbing random mountains searching for bars). It was *highly* likely a very expensive, very unnecessary helicopter would be coming for us before we'd be able to contact anyone.

I returned my pack to the snow and ripped the flashlight off my head, aiming the weak beam into the crevice. My heart jumped at the glimpse of orange plastic, but my relief stopped short. While the inReach was miraculously wedged, it was surrounded by a much wider gap on all sides. If I didn't tread carefully, it could easily be bumped deeper into the fissure.

I lay down on the snow, pressed my cheek into the ice, and reached as far as I could. My middle finger grazed plastic, but I couldn't get my hand around it.

The irony wasn't lost on me that the *inReach*—wasn't in reach.

With a growl, I grabbed my ice axe and started hacking away at the lip, attempting to chip away enough of a channel to reach further into the crevice, being careful not to let any chunks of ice fall down and knock the inReach. I glanced up at the pass, and a flood of white-hot guilt washed over me. Amped was making his way toward me, reversing the uphill progress he'd made.

The sun is coming, you moron. We woke up **so** *early to ascend Mather Pass on good snow and here you are, playing subterranean fetch with our most consequential piece of gear.*

With a renewed fury, I further chipped away at the ice, then dropped back down onto the snow, again pushing my cheek into the smooth, hard surface. I couldn't feel the low ambient temps and didn't notice the cold of the ice on my skin. I only cared about getting that stupid inReach back. With great care, I hovered each of my fingers in position around the device, then slowly closed my hand until I had it in a vice grip.

On my knees with the inReach in my lap, I closed my eyes in relief, taking a second to let my nerves calm. Amped appeared from around the side of the short cliff.

"What's the holdup, man?"

He spotted the obvious hole I'd dug before even finishing his question, then his eyes landed on the snow-covered inReach in my lap.

"Just thought I'd depth-test that crevice with our SOS device."

He froze, taking a second to process the nightmare I'd just dipped my toe in and out of.

"It's pretty deep."

I rigged a backup string and carabiner for the inReach before setting off, a chore I'd been putting off for arguably long enough. We exchanged our trekking poles for axes, flipped our heel-lifters up, and started up the pass. In the dim morning light, I couldn't make out the status of the death-cornice above, but we aimed to summit left of and above the pass, just in case a giant block did come rolling down.

The angle gradually pitched back to sixty degrees, similar to the climb on Forester. The points on our trusty snowshoes grabbed the ice beautifully, and we shifted back into our twenty-steps-at-a-time mode once burning legs and the high elevation got the best of us. Out loud, we counted out every step together, then paused to slump onto our axes and pant like dogs. The endless slide under our feet vied for our attention nearing the pass.

Mather was big—but simple. We summited just above the saddle of the pass with lungs and legs burning, but without issue. There *was* a cornice along the saddle, but it was tiny. Technically, almost not even an actual cornice.

"Another one down. That was easier than Glen **and** Pinchot!" Amped shouted through the heavy winds ripping over the pass.

My faith in just about everything I'd researched online was slipping. The early season Sierra I'd read about didn't match the one I was hiking through; the creek water levels, the cornices, the order of hardest passes. Here we were, done with both Forester and Mather, the beasts I'd been told to fear the most, and Pinchot had been the most difficult so far. Freakin' piddly, half-pass *Pinchot*.

Muir Pass was next, and touted as an easy ascent.

I found that oddly terrifying.

The sun still hadn't made an appearance. Even with me taking time to throw the inReach into a hole, we'd topped Mather just before six a.m. Our early start was paying dividends. Aside from the unreal beauty of hiking through dawn in the frosted Sierra backcountry, the snow itself remained in great condition with half of our day already behind us. We moved down the steep backside of the pass with fluid speed and zero concern of our feet slipping.

In the Palisade Lakes basin, a string of thirteen- and fourteen-thousand-foot peaks stood like a sawblade against the sky. Both Upper and Lower Palisade Lakes were still heavily snowed over, making for a perfectly flat, deserted highway. Several times, I'd walked the John Muir Trail perched above these big lakes on the east slope. Walking straight across them was certainly a first.

Our footprints were the only sign of life, aside from a lone set of mountain lion prints wandering across Lower Palisade Lake. I imagine nearing the end of May, the cat was wondering where all the food was.

"I'm right there with ya, buddy," I muttered to the cat's tracks, hoping it found a meal before it spotted my thick, juicy, cage-free hiker thighs.

Spring avalanche scars lined the western slope of the Palisade Lakes Basin. We stepped over huge, eerie cracks spanning the entire surface of the lake. The basin was otherworldly, gorgeous—truly indescribable. I stopped to take as many pictures as I could, desperately trying to preserve the breathtaking terrain for later. The Palisade Lakes were always a treat in the summer, but the snow had transformed them into something grander. My entire soul was grateful I was where I was, that I'd put in the effort and suffering it took to stand where I stood.

This—was worth it.

We maintained three mph off the pass, a normal, hiking on dirt pace! At the top of the famous Golden Staircase—a series of steep switchbacks blasted into a section of cliffs—we stalled out. The switchbacks were buried, leaving behind only dangerously steep, rocky gullies with no obvious way down. For some dimwitted reason, in spite of our snowshoes excelling on every bit of steep snow we'd come across, we figured switching to crampons would be our best bet.

That bet was on the racehorse with three legs, an eyepatch, and a dialysis machine cart in tow.

Forty yards later, halfway across a seventy-degree gully, we were stuck. A stretch of dry trail was just feet away, but our traction wasn't holding. I disengaged one set of crampon points and the other foot started to slide. I wobbled, and quickly reset all points into the ice, coming within a hair of tumbling into the narrow chute below. I wanted to go back, but couldn't. Vertigo was seeping in. Where snowshoes required facing uphill, crampons required the opposite—to face the dizzying exposure. I scanned the rocky chute, which was looking more vertical by the second, trying to envision a decent route that didn't involve any mangled rag-dolling.

"These things suck," Amped said. "Why did we take our snowshoes off?"

"Crampons are supposed to be better on the steepest terrain."

"Who told you that?"

My mind fluttered back across the litany of YouTube and Facebook forum "experts" I was likely referencing. "I don't want to talk about it."

My partner chuckled. "Well. Looks like we've only got one option here."

And then Amped—in classic Amped fashion—sat down, disengaged his crampon spikes, and launched into a slide. The crazy bastard accelerated out of control through the rocky, shaded chute, narrowly avoiding two protruding granite boulders. A hundred yards in, he turned over and dug his axe into the slope to arrest, but the axe tip was just scratching the surface of the hard ice. The drag allowed for Amped to check his speed, but stopping wasn't going to happen. I held my breath watching the fireworks display of snow and ice rooster-tailing behind him.

At the bottom of the chute, his whooping, celebratory cry echoed off the canyon walls. I was relieved—but in *no way* had I been convinced to follow. My climbing instincts told me to get to bare rock, so I took a series committing shuffles down into the chute toward the cliff lining its side, coming dangerously close to pin-balling behind my partner more than once. I slipped my gloves off and settled my hands on the cold, blocky granite. There were plenty of big handholds and foot ledges to use to work my way down. The crampon points firmly gripped the granite, but screeched like nails on a chalkboard. I slowly linked patches of bare rock until I was on an angle mellow enough to safely slide down to reunite with my insane buddy.

"My way was better," Amped said.

I laughed. "I'm not sure 'better' is the right word."

We assaulted our pancreas with a shared pound of peanut butter M&Ms and dropped back into the trees. Palisade Creek made a raging appearance from under the heavy snowpack. It escalated throughout the miles following the creek downstream, until the deafening rumble stood the hairs up on the back of my neck. I'd never heard water make such a violent sound.

Down and down and down we hiked, losing thousands of feet of elevation from our 12,000-foot perch on Mather that morning. Snow gave way to patches of exposed ground below 9,000 feet, although all of it was sopping wet. We entered a burned section where dozens of fallen trees littered the terrain. The confusing landscape resembled a giant, blackened game of pick-up-sticks. Broad, tempting patches of slush smoothed over sections of the jumbled matchsticks—but it was thin, soft, and no place for hikers to venture.

Is what we eventually learned.

Climbing up and over the chaotic piles of logs was awkward, slow work. We gravitated toward the siren song of the slush patches, which welcomed us with relentless postholing through the surface into boot-snaring branches, accompanied by the occasional sharp poke to the bum from an unlucky (for both parties) branch.

After the burn area, enough snow had melted away for us to stroll along dry trail (or whatever you call trail with six inches of water flowing along it). Slogging through the crystal-clear stream was a welcome relief. It was incredible how easy walking along open trail or hard snow was—but the soft, slushy, transitional terrain between the two was a nightmare. As May moved into June, an ever-increasing percentage of the Sierra would shift into that transitional terrain. Most people planning on hiking this section were waiting to enter until the middle of June. Leaving Kennedy Meadows, I'd thought moving into the Sierra on May 12 was foolishly early, but now—knowing the full extent of how punishing warm, slushy snow was—I would've pushed to enter the Sierra a week *earlier*. Creeks were swelling, snow was worsening, and there was no "waiting it out." In 2017, the snowpack wouldn't fade until the damn leaves started to change. Those June and July Sierra hikers were in for a real treat.

A drip ran out of my nose, which I wiped with the back of my glove, wincing through the sting. The sunburns on the underside of my nose had cracked open. In spite of ninety-five percent of my skin being covered by clothes and/or hair, the alpine sun reflecting off the snow had found every square millimeter I'd missed with sunscreen—and burned the absolute *piss* out of it. My upper lip, earlobes, and the *inside* of my nostrils kept crusting over in a vain attempt to heal, but would crack back open any time I ate, wiped my nose, took my shirt off, talked, existed, etc.

My nose ran constantly in the cold, whether or not I felt warm. My toilet paper supplies were limited, and using it for wiping my nose every three seconds would only get me a day or two before I'd run out. So, I used and reused the rough back of my glove—which was probably growing some new form of super-bacteria that I was repeatedly rubbing against my open face sores.

I had only a scant seven more days out there, possibly just enough time to arrive in Mammoth and die from my own booger-borne super virus. Being taken out by a nose blister wasn't exactly how I'd foreseen my death going. With any luck, a mountain lion would get me before my tombstone read:

Daniel Winsor. 1986-2017.

Battled valiantly against a runny nose—and lost.

Lunch was a tear-jerker. Every time I opened my mouth to take a bite out of my salty taco, my delicately healed lips would split back open to sample the salt first. The worst part was, I was *starving*. I'd packed a lot of food, knowing this was coming, and it still wasn't enough. I ate until my mouth was painfully raw, until I numbed to the sting of literal salt in my wounds—but I was unable to calm the hunger pangs. Amped was in the same boat. Lunch was followed by a longing stare into our bear cans.

Fifteen miles into our day, we arrived at Middle Fork Trail Junction at a balmy 8,000 feet, the low point before we'd have to start uphill toward the 12,000-foot Muir Pass.

"Camping here?" I asked.

"I can't believe that was fifteen miles," Amped said. "Yesterday took way more hours for way fewer miles—and honestly, I would've walked off the damn trail if it were possible."

I nodded in agreement.

"But today felt good. We figured something out. A key to this journey, ya know?"

We'd stayed on hard snow for the most part, and with our day's mileage already behind us, the afternoon sun hadn't even been given the *chance* to blister our blisters. We were drying clothes and charging electronics in the strongest sun of the day. Neither of us was exhausted, injured, or even in a bad mood!

It was a bit weird, to be honest. Unsettling, even.

A startling noise approached camp. Both of us stopped talking and went silent, our eyes widening.

Crunch, crunch, crunch, crunch

"You hear that? Or am I slipping a bit?"

Amped nodded, "I think it's a hiker."

We hadn't seen another human in days, but through the thick forest of pines emerged a towering man walking along the PCT. The impressive bulge of his pack was rivaled only by the tan on his exposed arms, neck, and face. Erratic lines of peeling skin along with red, cracked lips told a familiar tale of being torn apart by the elements.

"Ay, guys. You mind if I drop my pack 'ere for the night?" the stranger asked in a thick Australian accent. His soft tone didn't quite match his stature.

"Of course!" I answered, with an unrestrained enthusiasm I didn't recognize.

This new person instantly became part of our team before we even knew his name. While the Aussie set up his tent, we probed him with questions, trying to get to know our new friend—no wait, new *best* friend. His eyes shifted between his captive audience and his tent, answering our perky questions with minimal responses. Our best friend was a pretty introverted guy, but that didn't mean we were capable of leaving him alone, or that we didn't need to know when his birthday was, or how many balloons and strippers he wanted at the party (which we were definitely going to be planning—because best friends plan other best friends' birthday parties).

Many questions and shy answers later, I realized we'd skipped right over basic introductions. "Oh, I'm Danny, by the way, and this is Miguel—or eh, Beta and Amped, if we're doing the trail name thing."

The world we were in barely resembled the social, highly trafficked PCT. Using trail names felt more awkward by the day.

"Mark," he replied.

"No trail name, Mark?"

He broke eye contact and sheepishly replied, "It's Thor."

Ha. Of course it was.

Apparently, our Thor was in a bar with some fellow hikers and his Australian accent was attracting the ladies left and right. Introverted Thor wasn't exactly the kind of guy who'd spent a lot of time in bars, so this scene was fun for the other PCT hikers to spectate, no doubt looking on with equal parts amusement and jealousy.

As Thor's best friends, Amped and I certainly wished we could've been there.

From that bar, Thor's fellow hikers called him Chris Hemsworth, the devilishly good-looking Australian actor who played the lead role in the movie *Thor*. They shortened the nickname to just Thor and a trail name was born.

From Amped's journal:

When there is a lack of human presence, if you find another person you automatically gravitate toward them. They become part of your clan simply because they are human.

Thor told us about his hike, and mentioned going over the wrong pass at Pinchot, where we'd seen his footprints breaking away from the path of the PCT. He'd camped in the trees before Mather, where we must've passed his tent at some point during our night hike without noticing.

"You guys see the help message Breeze etched in the dirt?"

Amped and I looked confused enough for Thor to explain.

"I don't know what came of it, but a message in the dirt at Whitney Creek said, "Help. Hiker Breeze 1 mile," with an arrow pointed east. Was just curious if you'd come across him or not."

"Damn," I replied. "No, haven't seen him—or any signs of him."

Breeze was a monster. I'd met him in Southern California, and I really liked the guy. Our hiking ethics meshed pretty well, and I'd spent a whopping half-day hiking with him. That was the extent of my ability to keep up. He was a machine, and an experienced winter hiker on the East Coast, having completed a very impressive winter hike of the Appalachian Trail the previous year. It was hard to believe a guy like that could get into trouble in the Sierra.

We sat in silence for a minute, the heavy reality of our situation flowing through our minds. It was a reality all of us were more comfortable ignoring than pondering.

With the influence of best-selling books like *Wild* and *A Walk in the Woods*, not to mention the litany of YouTube and Instagram stars snapping jealousy-provoking selfies aggrandizing the thru-hiking lifestyle, people were flocking to the PCT in record numbers. Many wanted to be that person in their phone vlogging about how much they, *eh my goawd*, love nature and stuff. That wasn't inherently a bad thing. Why not have as many people as possible foster a love for nature? But many with little or no experience in the outdoors were attracted to big, romantic objectives like the Pacific Crest Trail. The grim reality was with more people, there'd be more accidents, and very likely—more fatalities.

Breeze was certainly not part of that trend, but what was worrying was if *he* could get into trouble—how was anyone else supposed to make it through the Sierra unscathed?

Including us.

Amped and I coaxed a couple small conversations out of Thor, enjoying the company of another human sure to join us for the rest of the Sierra. Our excitement was abated when we told him our plans to wake at three a.m.

"Uh, mates, I'm not doing that."

Coming from a best friend, it stung—but we kept the offer open, hoping he would change his mind. Waking early had produced such fantastic results, neither Amped nor I were willing to compromise waking any later. The three of us got along well, but we didn't want to force Thor into anything. He'd already made it that far by himself. Maybe he was better alone. Maybe he preferred it.

147

CRUNCH

Our small tribe settled into our sleeping bags with the sun still in the sky.

From Amped's journal:

Most importantly, our morale is high. Today is a day you truly understand the spirit of the trail. All the aches and blisters and the growling stomach noises subside because you are nourished by some of the most beautiful places the world has to offer. Yes, today was done right.

18

THE LION

Cold was an exposure without escape. There were no warm buildings or heated cars for days in every direction. Our only sustainable source of heat was our wool layers and driving legs. For the second morning in a row, we left the security of our warm sleeping bags and wind-blocking tents to step into the exposed, freezing darkness. Amped and I silently broke down camp while Thor's tent remained still. A part of me wished I could crawl right back into my sleeping bag, but a much larger part embraced the cold with open arms. More sleep wasn't worth the consequences.

Amped brought over a steaming cup filled with coffee. I opened a pack of Pop-Tarts and took a bite, wincing through my upper lip separating back open for the day. Weeping lip wounds would theoretically discourage eating, but I was deep in a calorie deficit, and any pain was far eclipsed by hunger. Eating just the one pack of processed pastry above my packed bear canister felt like licking a Tic Tac over a Thanksgiving dinner spread. I screwed the plastic lid back on, my stomach moaning in miserable protest.

Sitting with my legs crossed on the ground, I touched my stomach. The skin had been pulled tight against the muscle, even being hunched over. I didn't recognize the body I was touching, and I worried about the many weeks of snow I still had ahead. I'd run a pretty heavy calorie deficit even *before* I'd reached the snow. I couldn't imagine what it had swollen to since Kennedy Meadows.

Thor's dark tent bothered me. Just like with Fireball, why wouldn't a solo hiker jump at the chance to be part of a team? At Pinchot, Thor had stranded himself at the top of a small cliff. It required some down-climbing on exposed, icy rock with his eighty-pound pack on. Nobody was around to help him—or even notice if he fell.

I shouldered my pack. *That's not your responsibility. Fireball ended up fine. Thor will be fine too.*

We fired up the dry trail, gaining elevation through Le Conte Canyon where the snow soon reappeared. Navigation was difficult in the dark. We attempted to link sections of dry trail, but the huge snowdrifts mounded throughout the terrain thwarted our efforts.

The Middle Fork of the Kings River was to our left for most of the morning. The force of the water cascading down a series of short water-falls was sending a fine mist into the air, coating everything within fifty yards of the creek in a pristine, clear sheen of ice. It was like we had walked into a Sedona crystal shop, where everything was encapsulated in flawless glass.

Several yards ahead, Amped led the way over many thin snowbridges spanning tributary creeks feeding the river. Some creeks were small, but others were definitely large enough to sweep a hiker-sized object under the snowpack. The deafening roar of the Middle Fork eliminated the pos-sibility of chatting with Amped, so I decided to creep myself out instead.

If I broke through, would I be spit out into the Middle Fork? Or get stuck somewhere underground? Would I have time to cry out? Would Amped be able to hear? If he didn't, how long would it take before he noticed I was gone?

My partner hadn't taken a backward glance in a half-hour—which put a little more pep in my step.

I looked for opportunities to bounce test low snowbridges, which was increasingly reassuring. In fact, I had a hard time finding *any* bridge that would collapse under my weight, even extremely thin ones. The snow had frozen so hard overnight, even inch thick bridges spanning *several feet* wouldn't buckle!

We stopped to force ourselves to drink some ice water in the freezing morning. Staying hydrated was a persisting challenge, but it was like trying to drink coffee during a summer marathon through Death Valley. Just getting a few sips down took the same Herculean effort of swallowing discount multivitamins—you know, the ones sized somewhere between human and pony throats? With the comfy sandpaper texture to encourage lodging in your throat *juuust* long enough to catch a glimpse of that light at the end of the tunnel before progressing enough to unblock your windpipe?

Yeah, those ones.

Le Conte Canyon was lined with towering, sheer canyon walls, which had sloughed the historic snowfall in massive waves of devastation. The melting snow had only started to reveal the damage. Full-grown trees were bent over like an archer's bow, the upper branches upside-down, cemented in the ice, patiently waiting for enough warmth to spring back vertical.

The sky began to lighten when we reached the junction to Bishop Pass, one of the very few bail points from the backcountry, but a pretty lousy one. Twenty miles away, up and over a 12,000-foot pass, was a parking lot—seven miles up a closed road. My subconscious *insisted* a fifty-four-mile round trip detour to go to the donut shop was worth it.

The Panicky Pete inside me was offended we'd pass by the opportunity to escape. We might as well have been ignoring a fire exit in a building engulfed in flames.

Just exit, Pete whispered in my ear. *You've done more than most already. That's good enough. Nobody will fault you for quitting early. Let's get you out of here before you hurt yourself.*

Technically, everything was going well, so I cinched Pete's straitjacket straps a bit tighter and continued on. Fresh ski tracks appeared at the junction and we followed them uphill. Evidence of other humans was always a comfort, even if they were long gone.

Sunrise was spectacular. The tips of the dominant 13,000-foot peaks around us illuminated like rows of lit matches as the sun's rays crested the horizon. It was hard to believe several days ago, we'd stood above those towering peaks on Forester Pass. While the rising sun transformed our surroundings into a work of art, one thought shoved its way into the forefront of my mind.

*The snow starts softening **now**.*

We put our headlamps away, which made almost no difference with my sad excuse of an ultralight lamp. I could've strapped a damn pinecone to my forehead with similar results. That overpriced LED on a string was going in the trash the second I hit Mammoth, followed by a purchase of the brightest, heaviest headlamp I could find. My ultralight leanings were dying by the day out in the Sierra. I was all but sure to exit the snow with an assortment of cast iron Dutch ovens and all thirty-eight Harry Potter novels.

In the low morning light, something moving caught my eye—the unmistakable saunter of a cat. But not like the one chasing lasers and pooping in a box in your house. A *big* cat.

A mountain lion.

High on a ridge above us, about 200 yards away, the gray silhouette stood out against the white backdrop of the snow-covered mountainside. The lion's head was low, walking in the same direction we were—and at the same speed.

Is it, my heart spasmed into my throat, *tracking us?*

Chills crept up along my neck, making every hair I owned (and there's a lot of them, ask poor Melanie) stand on end. Amped hadn't noticed. I called out to him, but the sound of my voice instantly disappeared into the roar of the creek. I wasn't sure how loud to be. What if the sentence, "Hey, Amped, there's a mountain lion!" roughly translated in lion-speak to, "Hey, Cat, come nibble on my sweet, sweet liver and eyeballs!" I kept my eyes locked on the animal until it dropped out of sight—*right* into the small basin we were headed toward.

THE LION

I jogged into shouting distance of Amped and told him what I'd seen. By all available data and wisdom, we weren't in any danger. The odds of a mountain lion attack on the PCT were almost zero—the same as being attacked by a unicorn, or me stretching my feet each morning.

But the internet had been wrong about *plenty* so far, so statistics were of little comfort being isolated in such a vast wilderness with a 200-pound cat. Plus, there was still snow everywhere, with no signs of rabbits or squirrels or tuna or Friskies yet. What did that thing have to eat? Like, *other than* me and Amped?? Statistically, we were safe, but *also* statistically, all those non-attacks on the PCT happened when most people hiked the PCT: *in summer*. Amped and I weren't exactly in the same statistical field as the rest our attack-free peers. What if one hundred percent of the crusty dimwits who hiked the Sierra in the snow became lion food?!

We really didn't have much of a choice other than to keep moving forward. It was either that or turn back—and it was safe to say both of us preferred being ripped apart by a mountain lion to reversing the snowy canyon we'd worked so hard to get up. In the low dawn light, branches moving against the white background played tricks on my mind, creating movement where there likely was none.

While I stumbled over my snowshoes staring into the trees, I tried to come up with a defense plan. When it attacked Amped (because my mind preferred it not attack me first) would my little three-inch knife hanging on my pocket be of any utility? Could I stab it with a trekking pole? Karate chop to the neck? A squirt with a spray bottle?? Did rape whistles work with mountain lions?

We entered a dense forest where I could no longer see far enough to invent movement to panic about. I had to accept the reality that if a cat wanted to stalk us—or even attack—there was nothing we could do about it.

The snowpack thickened until the Middle Fork disappeared underneath it, finally muffling the chaos that had accompanied us the entire morning. There was 4,000 feet of elevation gain between us and Muir Pass. Sections of steep snow were separated by milder stretches. Each time the angle passed fifty degrees, we'd flip up our heel-lifters and mechanically shift into our twenty-steps-at-a-time system. Our team was becoming a well-oiled machine, and the budding sense of mastery over our terrain felt incredible. The sun was now fully baking the east-facing slopes we were climbing, but the low overnight temps were helping the ice resist turning to slush.

At ten a.m., we launched into another steep sun-facing hillside, only this time our snowshoes were sliding. Each step required a forceful kick to push the softening layer out of the way, to sink the crampon points into the underlying firm snow.

Cresting the hillside, out of breath and sweating, Amped turn to me. "Is it time to stop?"

We were within a few miles of the pass, and the idea of stopping so early was instinctually ridiculous—but we had indeed completed our goal for the day, if that was to hike as far as possible on hard snow. The hard snow was done; therefore, it was time to stop.

"Yeah, I guess it is," I said. "Let's start looking for a spot."

Sure, we could've kept struggling our way up the pass in the afternoon sun, having to kick every single miserable step through the deepening slush. We were certainly *capable* of death-marching uphill. We could've slipped and slid around on steep snow, accompanied by a raging case of swamp-ass under the intense sun, whilst further blistering our blistered bits. Amped and I were *one hundred percent* capable of getting up and over Muir Pass that afternoon.

We could've also had a testicle-flicking competition with each other.

No thank you. To *all* of it.

From a high perch over a sweeping bowl of snow, we spotted what looked like exposed, flat rock slabs. What were the chances we'd find a dry spot to camp at 11,000 feet?

Not zero, apparently.

A sizable, flattish slab jutted out from the snow, overlooking the frozen lake in the bowl below. It was perfect. A dry room-with-a-view in a sea of white. Our mission was complete. We were within three miles of the pass, with only 1,000 vertical feet left to go, a piece of cake back on hard snow in the morning. We stepped out of our snowshoes and retired them for the afternoon. Amped went to town rigging his rain fly as a sun shelter, using rocks and trekking poles to hold the fabric taut overhead. I gathered some snow and threw it into a gallon Ziploc bag, setting it on the warm slab to melt water for us.

Sitting under our shelter, I stuffed my face with every scrap of food I could afford to take out of my bear canister, which came nowhere close to satisfying the vicious hunger inside me. I shuffled my rations around, hoping I'd somehow conclude I could eat something else. *Anything else*—but it was all accounted for. Everything had a time and a place to be eaten, and all of those times and places were in the future.

My thoughts refused to leave that blue canister, begging me to eat more. With not much else to do waiting for the afternoon to pass, I reorganized my food over and over again like a heroin addict organizing a bucket of loaded needles. It was a miserable exercise in self-control.

"Here, bud," Amped snapped me out of my food-fixated trance, again handing me the other half of one of his snack waffles.

His hunger was likely similar to mine, and if I had any shred of pride capable of standing up against my brain stem, I would've at least tried to turn down his offer. But I didn't, and thankfully inhaled that euphoric mouthful of sugary ecstasy, savoring every millisecond.

We kicked off our boots and reclined under our bright green shelter. Even under the shade, our sunglasses remained on to protect against the white, reflective world around us. Sunglasses were an absolute must to have on for every minute the sun was up. Sunburnt eyes were a real threat, and a much worse issue than sunburnt nostrils. I'd learned this particular lesson the hard way, on a snowy overnight where I'd forgot my sunglasses and figured I'd "man-up" and whatnot. I would've been better off shielding my retinas with jalapeno slices.

Under the direct noon sun, our clothes quickly dried and Amped's solar panel easily recharged our electronics. Our efforts to wake early and walk on hard snow were paying off. The day had been almost too easy. It seemed we'd found a way to flip the script, to use the brightest time of day to our advantage, rather than using it to formulate new swearwords, further bake our already-crisped nostrils, and to sweat another crust layer into our *already* sufficiently crusted underwear.

Speaking of crisped, swearing PCT hikers, movement on the far side of the bowl caught my eye.

"Thor!"

Thor spotted our tent and beelined toward us, wading through the slush. Without any communication beyond a nod behind exhausted eyes, he dropped his pack and joined us on our rock shelf.

From Amped's journal:

Thor strolled upon our rock island in the middle of the sea of snow. No invitation was needed. He would share our island simply because we are all human.

A lone marmot wandered around, transporting grass in its mouth with a springtime purpose.

Where is that little guy finding grass?

Three backcountry skiers appeared, the first other humans we'd seen since Mel and Steve at Kearsarge Pass. They cut off the path of the PCT and disappeared over a nearby high ridge, returning the landscape to the still, lifeless white we'd become accustomed to.

The rock slab was too small for all three of our tents, so we decided to cowboy camp side-by-side for the night. Most other PCT hikers were fine sleeping without a shelter over them, but I'd always set up my tent, rain or shine. I found no pleasure in ants exploring my hair while I slept, or offering myself up as an easy mosquito buffet. This was different. At 11,000 feet in May, we'd have zero bugs to deal with.

Why *wouldn't* we sleep under the stars?

19
MUIR

Praying for time to show me mercy, I shivered in my sleeping bag, staring impatiently at my phone.

Twelve thirty a.m.

Night was usually when I was able to forget about food for eight hours, but being kept awake by the cold allowed for plenty of time to focus on my growling stomach—the one I was powerless to help. I kept my eyes bitterly locked on my phone, resenting every minute crawling by with excruciating resistance.

1:58

1:59

2:00

My alarm sounded, but it wasn't needed. Instantly, all members of our trio stood up.

"Ugh, finally," I grumbled. My frozen partners grunted in agreement.

Our afternoon sleep had only lasted as long as the sunshine. Once that ball of heat had ducked, a steady breeze replaced it. At first, it wasn't a big deal. Beanies were donned and we wrapped up in our sleeping bags a little tighter. But the temperature plummeted into the thirties, then into the twenties—and that breeze grew into a stiff wind.

Without any shelter from our tents, the wind crept through our sleeping bags and layers, leeching our precious warmth. We all took turns shuffling our packs and ground sheets around, attempting to block the wind, but it was too much. We'd made another mistake, and Mother Nature was glad to teach us the lesson.

Nobody bothered making breakfast or coffee. We were all on the same page—no conversation necessary. Warmth was our only goal, and warmth meant hiking. Within twenty minutes of my alarm, we departed camp within the bubbles of our headlamps.

Thankfully, hiking uphill under three jackets and fifty pounds is a fantastic recipe for warmth. Three points of light moving across the starlit Sierra, we traced the frozen shoreline of Helen Lake and headed into the last big uphill to Muir Pass.

Thor didn't have alpine snowshoes, only crampons that were on the less aggressive end of the spectrum, so his capabilities on steep snow weren't quite the same as ours. I did my best to find the mildest angles up through the snowdrifts.

The final headwall leading to the pass was steep enough to introduce Thor to our twenty-steps game. Our friendship grew gasping for oxygen and offering encouragement together. We topped the pass and our headlamps illuminated an iconic stone building in the middle of the desolate wilderness—the Muir Hut. The structure had absorbed warmth from the sun throughout the days, sufficient to clear the snow around it in a perfect circle. It was a six-foot drop to get off the snowpack to reach the hut.

The massive Wanda Lake was beyond the north side of Muir Pass, and one of my favorite lakes in the entire range. I was excited to see it in the snow, and maybe use the frozen surface to make strong headway. Coming off the pass, I beelined straight down the moderate slope, figuring we'd walk downhill until we found the shore of the frozen lake.

Wanda Lake was about a mile from the pass, but after walking well over a mile, we were still standing on angled snow, without any sign of flat terrain ahead.

A gut wrenching thought crept into the back of my mind. *Did I somehow lead everyone down the wrong drainage? One we'll have to reverse to get back on track? Amped might kill you.*

I stopped to check the GPS, then rechecked our position several times. I couldn't believe what it was telling me.

"We're standing in the middle of the lake right now."

Standing on a slope in the middle of a lake didn't make sense, but the absurd volume of snow dumped in the Wanda Lake basin had masked the shoreline. Giant ramps of snow from all sides of the basin converged into a "V" on top of the east end of the lake. The depth of the snow had to be astronomical to morph the landscape around a lake that size—fifty feet? Seventy feet? A hundred??

This area was known for continuous winter storms dumping many feet of snow at a time. At the Mammoth ski resort, the crazy 2017 winter had dumped over six hundred inches of snow, over *fifty feet*. Where we stood, in the unmeasured backcountry, it had reportedly snowed *even more*—and we were standing on it.

The basin widened enough for us to finally step onto the surface of Wanda Lake, somewhere in the middle of the lake. We enjoyed a *mile* of flat ice as the low, blue light of dawn flooded the basin. The unbelievable beauty unfolding in front of our eyes literally stopped us in our tracks. For a moment, we forgot about capitalizing on hard snow and simply watched, lost in collective awe.

"You don't get to see this unless you put in the work," Amped mumbled.

We hiked past Sapphire Lake, another large lake buried under the snow-pack. Our Ziploc bag water from the previous afternoon was running out, so we took the opportunity to gather from a short, exposed section of the Sapphire Lake outlet. The Arctic creek was filled with huge, broken, slanted chunks of ice, and guarded by vertical snow walls. Thor led the way, hopping from iceberg to iceberg until we found a spot to reach down into the sluggish, *extremely* cold water.

I submerged my water bottle, grimacing through the cold sucking the heat from my hands. I hopped back across the icebergs, threw my pack on, opened my water bottle, tilted it back for a drink—but nothing came out. In disbelief, I pulled the bottle away from my lips. The same water that had been a flowing liquid two minutes prior was a hard slug of ice!

Evolution Basin had always been one of my favorite places in the Sierra. This was my third time hiking through it, but instead of green meadows and turquoise lakes surrounded by majestic peaks, we were treated to a landscape just as beautiful, but 1,000% different. We strolled across a snowed-over lake, the three of us looking around in a reverent awe.

We took pictures by the dozens, but they weren't doing it justice. They couldn't. The freezing wind, fresh air, deathly silence, and burning legs were all part of it. It was almost sad knowing we would only be able to experience that magnificent show in person, right then. Whatever memories we left with would be our only accurate souvenirs. Pictures would remind us of those memories, but would be far from able to put us back in our boots, standing on top of Evolution Lake.

My nerves turned on as we dropped down the steep hillside toward Evolution Creek, a notorious river crossing. The waist-deep summer wade was usually the way across, but it was likely to be deeper and swifter for us—a full-on *swim* even. The only other crossing I was aware of was usually off limits until deep into August. It was a bit shallower than the wade, and just ten or fifteen feet across—but very swift, and just upstream of a series of big waterfalls. I was all but sure for us, the second option was only an efficient way to die.

So essentially, our options were an ice bath—or death.

I couldn't decide which was scarier.

Our only hope of maintaining a positive relationship with our sensitive bits was a snowbridge, but the only parts of Evolution Creek I was familiar with were quite wide. We purposefully broke away from the path of the PCT to walk along the bank of the creek to start looking for alternative crossings as far upstream as we could. We wanted to know every one of our options before deciding which ice water bath was, eh—*best*. I prayed for any signs of a crossing not involving submerging our entire bodies into the same water that'd frozen solid in my water bottle two miles upstream.

The trail gods were having a gracious morning, and within a half-mile of tracing the bank, we found a restriction in the creek with a beautiful, thick snowbridge spanning the torrent of water rushing beneath it. All fifteen of us (I'm including testicles and nips here) emitted a collective sigh of relief.

Being so easily on the other side of the notorious Evolution Creek was surreal. My food demon had been subdued by nerves, but with the morning crossing in the rearview, it clawed its way back into my brain for the day.

You haven't eaten anything yet.

As soon as that realization popped into my head, my hands began to tremble. I had to immediately drop my pack to dig a breakfast out of my bear canister. I figured the impressive nutrition of a couple packs of Pop-Tarts would do the trick, but my stomach growled right on through 800 calories of pastry, begging for more. Eating over 3,000 calories each day, I was starving. My inability to keep up with my hunger was alarming—and a bit embarrassing. I seemed to be the only one of our team struggling with it.

Once the sun had peaked into the canyon, we stopped for a quick break. Like a junkie digging for his stash, my hands shook retrieving the half-pound bag of dried fruit and nuts I had allotted for the day's snack. My instinctual hunger had a vice grip on my brain stem. Five minutes later, packed full of trail mix, I felt the obnoxious twinge of hunger return.

"What's wrong with you?" I muttered to myself.

Amped and Thor were quickly ready to continue, to capitalize on hard snow—but I had one more thing to attend to. I apologized and took off into the woods with my faithful baggie of butt wipes.

This was my first poop in *three days*, which wouldn't be too alarming in my day-to-day life, but I'd been ingesting a *massive* quantity of dried, fibrous food. I had no idea where all of it was going. After an extended struggle, I worked *something* out—but it was far from the record-shattering log I'd been expecting.

"There's *no way* that's all of it," I whispered to my unimpressive poopette.

Whispering to a tiny poop in the middle of the woods with my pants around my ankles kind of felt like a new low.

I hurried to wrap up my stop, even more guilty that I'd made my buddies wait for roughly an ounce more than no reason. Amped and Thor didn't seem irritated in the slightest, but were happy to start moving again.

Progress along Evolution Creek slowed through tiring ups and downs of rolling snowdrifts below the trees. I struggled to keep a strong pace, fighting to ignore the ever-present growling in my gut. Not ten minutes later, my hands trembled under a tanking blood sugar. I kept pushing, lost inside my head.

*There's **no way** you can really be this hungry!*

My addled cloud was infiltrated by a thought that stopped me in my tracks.

Your gloves.

I patted vacant pockets and the blood drained from my face.

"Dammit. Guys, I forgot my gloves at the last stop."

Amped turned and cocked his head curiously, with a hint of irritation. Being so careless wasn't like me. "Well… go get them."

We'd made it more than a half-mile through difficult terrain. A gigantic part of me wanted to leave my gloves behind—but in the cold nights and mornings, those two pieces of gear weren't optional.

I dropped my pack and sprinted back through the snowdrifts, cursing my lapse in attention. Forgetting something in this environment wasn't acceptable. We were fighting for every inch of progress, and adding an additional mile to my day was a sizable error—especially when I *barely* had the food to fuel the day's mileage as it was!

I found my truant gloves loafing around on the boulder some idiot had set them on. I shoved them into their designated pocket, audibly placed the blame on my subterranean turd, and jogged back toward my team. I pushed until I was out of breath and my legs were on fire. Amped and Thor were pacing when I returned, anxious to get moving, freezing out in the cold morning. They still weren't outwardly impatient or angry—but Amped was clearly ready to go.

"You good?" he asked, although it sounded more like, "Can we please get this shit moving again?"

I wasn't good. Aside from burning muscles and panting like a dog from power walking up and down a thousand snowdrifts, my hands were vibrating from the tantrum being thrown by my incessant stomach. Hot guilt flooded the back of my skull.

"Yeah man, let's get moving."

I took the lead. My stomach churned, making noises like I hadn't eaten in days. My hunger flared up to an intensity I couldn't make sense of. All of the food I'd rationed for myself until lunch was already inside me, and we weren't planning on stopping for food again until we'd reached camp, which was still *seven* miles away. I kept putting one snowshoe in front of the other, battling against myself in an all-consuming turmoil unbeknownst to my teammates. It certainly didn't match the serene hiking alongside the meandering, turquoise creek. Every bit of my base urges demanded I stop and eat, but the cold reality was—I didn't *have* the food to eat. My logical thoughts were backed against a wall, desperately trying to remind my pitchfork-wielding, mutinous crowd of instincts *just* how terrible an idea it was to eat ahead into my rations.

Three miles of internal hell later, we arrived at the summer crossing for Evolution Creek and were all immediately grateful we'd crossed early. Steep snow guarded both banks, and the water was moving faster and deeper than I'd figured—at minimum a chest-deep wade, likely a swim.

Gross.

I put my pack down in the sunny clearing, worn down by the relentless fighting inside me. The last hour had felt like twenty miles. My pride faltered enough for me to ask, "You mind if we stop for lunch?"

Amped gave me a puzzled look. "Nah, let's get to camp. It's only four more miles. We should keep going while the snow is still hard."

He was right, and I certainly didn't want to be the reason we had to finish our day on slush, but I was also way past hungry. If I put my foot down and got my lunch out anyway, they wouldn't leave me behind—but I'd be the cause of a third extended stop in five miles.

I hefted my pack back up through a wave of suppressed frustration and anger. My thoughts pinged from fury to desperation to misery—then to just a *smidgen* of optimism I'd survive—but then quickly back to fury.

We're all going through the same ordeal, carrying the same load. Thor is carrying damn near twice the weight. What is going on with me?

I took off in front of Amped and Thor, ready to be done for the day. If four miles stood between me and food, I was going to put those four miles behind me as fast as possible. My adrenaline spiked, as if Amped had suggested we wade into a shark tank wearing meat dresses, and not that we simply walk a bit further before lunch. I marched ahead at a feverish pace, as if I could outrun my stomach, making big strides and running the downhill slopes in my snowshoes.

My teammates drifted further and further behind me, completely against my own prescribed behavior in the Sierra—but I didn't want teammates anymore. I wanted to be alone. I wanted to be able to stop as much as I desired without anyone there to see I wasn't capable of keeping up. I didn't want to be the group weakling holding the team back. I wanted the freedom to choose whether to walk for twenty miles straight, or collapse in the snow and spoon my bear canister until my $35,000 ride came to airlift me to Pizza Hut.

A sensible voice inside me suggested I slow down to keep our team together, but it was eclipsed by the all-consuming, primal instincts with a death grip on my thoughts. My entire world had narrowed to only two goals: food and moving forward. Since food couldn't happen, I could only focus on driving my legs toward the finish line.

I marched and slid through the tough terrain, holding a furious pace. On the south-facing slope dropping down to the South Fork of the San Joaquin River, the sun had worn through the snow to reveal massive slabs of shale and granite. Too impatient to stop and remove my snowshoes, I clacked down steep rock slabs between snow patches. The metal points on the bottom of my snowshoes screeched in protest. Eventually the snow ended entirely, giving way to loose, black shale and the Pacific Crest Trail.

Highly irritated at—well, *everything*, I set my pack down, sat on a black shale ledge and ripped open my snowshoe bindings. I reattached my snowshoes to my pack while avoiding eye contact with the blue plastic canister filled with individually packaged heroin. A distinct sound floated above the rush of Evolution Creek, the characteristic chirp of the Mountain Chickadee. That familiar three-part "Deeee dee-dee" was Melanie's favorite—and just the thought of Mel, and how much I missed having her by my side, and how little she'd approve of my behavior, was enough to snap out of my hungry rage.

Amped and Thor weren't far behind, both appearing within five minutes, out of breath and flustered. I wanted to explain myself, but I honestly didn't quite understand what was happening well enough to verbalize it. I was terrified of how weak and worn-down I felt, of how my hunger seemed to have a boot firmly planted on my skull, pinning me into submission, no matter how much food I ate.

"I snapped my damn trekking pole back there trying to keep up with you." Amped held up one of his poles. The top half of the handle hung limply to the side.

Another wave of hot guilt arrived. Amped wasn't the type to blame others for his problems, but I was at least partly responsible. I'd convinced him to join me on this trek. The Sierra wasn't a place I could afford to let my hunger get in the way of our safety. In misery from many angles, I watched Amped fiddle with the droopy half of his handle.

Without two sturdy trekking poles to descend the wet, slick shale along the trail, it didn't take long until Amped slipped and went down hard. Growling in anger, it took a fight to rise against his heavy pack. Two switchbacks later, his feet slipped out from under him *again*. All of us were getting further and further from a good mood.

At only eleven a.m., after sixteen miles on hard snow, I threw my pack on the dirt bank of the South Fork of the San Joaquin River and immediately retrieved my bear canister. With hands trembling in excitement, I slid an envelope-shaped brick of salmon onto a smashed, hole-ridden tortilla, then covered that mess in Arby's Horsey sauce and Fritos dust.

And I'd never tasted anything so orgasmic.

I made my three allotted tacos and savored every last bite in an absolute state of bliss. My two partners also dug into their lunch. It was good to see they were at least a little hungry. The life surged back into all of us resting next to the sturdy bridge spanning the roiling San Joaquin.

"Those sixteen miles felt like thirty dry trail miles," I said.

"I can't believe sixteen miles before noon is possible out here," Thor said. "And with zero slush. That's incredible."

The snow blanket on the canyon floor was honeycombed with dry patches. Each of us chose a patch to pitch our tents, and spent the afternoon digging small trenches to divert the intensifying snowmelt. It would've been far easier to pitch our tents on top of the snow—but we were going to sleep on dry dirt, dammit.

Warm afternoon naps were broken up by long conversations about the food we would eat when we reached Mammoth.

From Amped's journal:

Punctuality can mean the difference between a successful day and a failed day. As is in life, if you procrastinate, you increase your chances of failure at the endeavor at hand.

The benefits of punctuality in the early season Sierra are very straightforward. The snow is easily traversed in the morning while it's still frozen. River crossings are often lower because the snowmelt has yet to feed them. Most importantly, the High Sierra sun is avoided, which can take a toll on your body. You prepare for cold, but the heat ends up exhausting you and your morale.

We get up between two and three a.m. every morning to beat these elements. The momentary suffering of leaving your warm sleeping bag to dress and pack is well worth avoiding the prolonged harassment of the other weapons of the Sierra. Today, our punctuality lands us sixteen miles farther and in camp before noon, plenty of time to tape up the trekking pole handle I snapped on the way down.

I love early camp. It gives you a chance to enjoy your surroundings. It also gives you ample time to tend to wounds, repair clothing, and plan for the next day.

How you hike can teach you many things about how you live life. Just make the effort to find the lessons. Have a detailed plan. Think about the future but be flexible. Don't procrastinate. This is only my interpretation of these "wild" classroom lessons, and I will make my best effort to become a better human when I get back to civilization with what I've learned.

20
THE DARK

MAY 28, 2017
SAN JOAQUIN RIVER

"Just sit up and put your fleece on," I ordered myself, like I'd done a dozen times already. But again, I stubbornly resisted with my eyes pinned shut, wide awake, trying to ignore the mild bouts of shivering.

At eleven p.m., I'd woken *just* over the line of too cold to sleep but warm enough to not be an emergency. To sit up and put on my fleece and down hood meant I'd be puffing out all my hard-earned sleeping bag warmth.

After two hours of my nonsensical struggle, I finally sat up and grumbled my way through puffing out my remaining bit of warmth, then shivering through donning my icy fleece and down hood. It was a fleeting moment of misery, but within minutes of being back in my sleeping bag, I was dead asleep.

In what felt like the blink of an eye, my alarm was nagging at me from its claustrophobic stink dungeon, located somewhere between my sleeping pad, sleeping bag, and left ass cheek.

If I were the phone, I'd be nagging to get the hell out of there too.

I clicked on my headlamp, which was *barely* able to illuminate the inside of my tent. I'd planned on switching out the battery the afternoon before but had completely forgotten about it—and it was time to get up and get moving.

Standing out of my tent, my boots sent white splinters of ice stretching out from each footstep, shattering the frozen mud I'd shaped into snow-melt diversion dams the previous afternoon. It seemed the only place the mud was still unfrozen was where it was mushed into the netting lining the underside of my tent.

Goody.

I crammed the mud pile into my backpack and threw down a quick breakfast. I intentionally only ate half of my meal, wrapping up the other half for later. My hunger was *kind of* subdued in the morning, so strictly rationing then would—in theory—give me more to eat later in the day. Amped led the way into the darkness and I was grateful to have his strong headlamp in front of me.

The trail soon disappeared under snow. Within the first mile, we stopped in the middle of an icy swamp, lost and with no idea where the trail was. Marshy, frozen islands of grass were separated by deep pockets of brown water. We took turns groaning in offense as the freezing, dirty water filled our boots and extracted the feeling from our feet.

The roar of an unmapped creek appeared ahead. The swollen, seasonal waterway cut through the swamp to contribute to the mighty San Joaquin, which was just a short distance through the trees to our right. We split up to search for any reasonable ways across the swamp creek, which took some time.

"Beta, Thor! Over here!" Amped shouted downhill.

He was thirty yards away, at most, but his words were barely audible over the combined rumble of the creek and the river.

Under my fading headlamp, I stumbled uphill through thick reeds and surprise boot-dunks. I reached the log Amped had found, which he was already two-thirds of the way across. The narrow timber wasn't perfect, but it was enough, and more reasonable than anything I'd found. My light was barely able to illuminate the surface of the log, but Amped's headlamp lit the crossing well enough, even being near the end. Without hesitation, I balanced onto the timber and started my way across. In unfortunate sync, Amped hopped off the end of the log, out of sight— right as my headlamp died.

I paused, frozen in the incredible darkness. The deluge of water flowing under me disappeared, only remaining in my world as a deafening roar.

"Amped!" I called out, with a concerted attempt to keep my tone out of needy wuss territory—and failing.

Amped didn't hear. My voice was easily overpowered by the creek. I could barely hear *myself.*

"Thor!"

The Aussie was somewhere behind me but nowhere in sight. My legs wobbled as vertigo started taking over. The odds of avoiding all icy, involuntary swims on this trek weren't great. Really, I'd accepted an icy dunk or two would be part and parcel of this adventure—but this wasn't the place to do it. Falling into whitewater just upstream of the sea of snowmelt roaring through the San Joaquin wouldn't be just an embarrassing dunk—it would be a death sentence.

I wobbled again, narrowly maintaining my balance. I couldn't convince myself to try another step forward. I couldn't convince myself to try a step back. A sobering thought crossed through my mind.

Is this it?

Amped appeared back at the edge of the creek, illuminating my world and instantly lifting my vertigo. Relief flooded through me, and I balanced across the rest of the log with vibrating legs. My adrenaline pegged to a ten while we waited for Thor. I'd never felt my mortality so acutely threatened, even through all my years of climbing. If Amped hadn't turned around, that could've been the end of—*everything.* No more hiking, no more Sierra, no more friends, no more family, no more Melanie.

Everything.

Thor appeared and followed us across the log. I stayed a half-step behind Amped until the sky began lightening. In the early dawn, we crossed a steel bridge back to the north side of the San Joaquin drainage to traverse the south-facing hillside where the snow disappeared.

Well, kind of.

The trail was blasted into cliffs lining the river, where the aftermath of winter avalanches lingered, leaving some sections of trail frozen over with near-vertical sheets of ice. Our progress ground to a halt while we carefully climbed and traversed the loose rock above the ice slides, doing our best not to look down.

The trail veered away from the river and we settled into a strong pace along a mucky but essentially snow-free trail for eight glorious miles. Packs were heavy with both crampons and snowshoes on our backs, but that wasn't enough to spoil the foreign gift of both navigating and walking on manicured, flat trail.

We walked past the junction for Muir Trail Ranch, still weeks away from opening. This part of the John Muir Trail was normally a bustling intersection. Strolling through the peaceful pines, I soaked in the stillness and isolation along one of the busiest trails on the planet.

Our team paused for a quick breather before a long uphill section, where I finally allowed myself the rest of my breakfast, followed by the uncontrolled inhalation of every last crumb of my snacks for the day. A lone, sleepy mosquito bumbled through the air, making no attempt to land on anyone.

"Whoa," I said. "That's the first mosquito I've seen, and we've been in the Sierra for *weeks.*"

Thor hadn't spent any time in the Sierra hiking, so Amped and I explained to him how horrific the mosquito hatch could be. I'd spent entire *days* being death-marched forward in these mountains, literally fearful of stopping. One year, my parents had joined Mel and me on a seven-day hike where we'd unwittingly strolled into the thick of the hatch, armed only with natural oils to deal with mosquitoes. We'd watched enough YouTube to smugly turn our noses up at DEET.

DEET, you see—was *poison*. It melted *plastic*, for God's sake! Who would be stupid enough to voluntarily lather that stuff all over their body?

You know what else is stupid? Dying at the lips of weightless bugs.

They were voracious, bloodthirsty monsters biting indiscriminately through bare skin, hair, and clothing. Just stopping for a procrastinated pee was enough of an opportunity for dozens to latch on. Holding still through the prickling along shoulders and arms was maddening. I can't imagine what it must've been like for Mel and my mother, who couldn't just expose the last .03-percent of their pee stick like a turtle peeking to see if the coyotes had lost interest yet.

If given the opportunity to attack, the war wasn't winnable. Dozens would latch in seconds, and in the time it took to convert those dozens of asshole bugs into dozens of blood streaks on one arm, another dozen had latched onto the other arm! If you didn't run, that ridiculous slaughter would continue endlessly, until you either ran out of blood or went insane.

My poor parents, who'd probably hoped to *enjoy* their vacation, ended up in an obligatory march ahead of a cloud of mosquitoes drifting behind us like tiny zombies, patiently awaiting any breaks. Word of our delicious, peppermint-infused blood must've spread throughout the mosquito community, because we started every day in the swarm, and ended every day diving into our tents, zipping ourselves inside, then killing the fifty bloodsuckers that had followed us in for the night. The onslaught forced us to pull a couple marathon days to reach Muir Trail Ranch, where we bought every drop of DEET in the house. At that point, I would've happily chugged the stuff to keep the mosquitoes at bay.

All this snow business had some serious challenges but also afforded some equal advantages. A bug-free Sierra was a big one.

The 3,000-foot, typically dry ascent to Selden Pass was filled with water running along and across the trail. In past years, there had been a (get ready to gasp) *six-mile* stretch without water here, the longest along the whole John Muir Trail. Dramatic notes had been tacked to trail signs, warning hikers of the desolate, barren expanse before them.

I'll be the first to admit career Sierra hikers are a *bit* spoiled. My eyes had been opened through a couple thirty-plus-mile dry stretches in Southern California.

Snow returned, and I led the way across a snowbridge spanning the gushing Senger Creek. In a past June hike, Melanie and my parents had taken a long nap alongside the west bank of that creek, stretched out in the warm sun without a snowflake in sight. I'd spent the afternoon chatting with PCT hikers, in awe of the incredible feat they were tackling.

My hunger pangs had caught up and the fight to keep them from affecting my mood was taking every bit of my focus. We broke through the thick forest onto the shore of one of the Sallie Keyes Lakes. I stopped, staring out over the lake. It was the most melted-out of any we'd seen. Thin, light-blue crescents lined the white blanket in several spots. It was strange, almost *offensive* to not be able to walk straight across. It didn't seem *fair* to actually have to stay above solid ground to get to the other shore.

Although—that could've just been the cheeseburger-lust talking.

I needed to simply choose whether to hike around the left or right shoreline to reach camp—an inconsequential decision if there ever was one.

But after a minute of fruitless internal debate, Amped sensed I was struggling with the world's easiest decision. "Um… That way?"

Oh thank God.

"Perfect."

We passed a half-buried ranger cabin and balanced across the outlet of the lake on a jammed collection of thin logs. Thor and I crossed without issue, but Amped slipped off a log and went for a shallow, potty-mouthed dip. Luckily, the water was only knee deep, so there wasn't much harm done, other than gifting me with something to remind him of for the next, eh—forever.

At 10:30 a.m., we called it a day, just a mile from the mellow Selden Pass. The elevated platform had a fantastic overlook of the Sallie Keyes lakes and plenty of flat spots for our tents. Under the bluebird sky, we lounged under the sun and attacked our bear canisters.

After our three p.m. dinner—or perhaps more appropriately "supper," since we were scheduling meals like ninety-year-olds—it was time to go drop my base weight. Back the ol' motorhome out of the garage. Negotiate the release of some hostages…

Poop. I'm talking about poop here.

I took off from camp to find a private fortress of solitude, and was delighted to find (keeping in mind we were the only sign of life in the area) a *perfect* set of footprints leading away from camp!

How convenient! I thought.

I'm an idiot.

Those footprints led me directly to a hunched over Thor, who'd *also* left camp to drop *his* base weight. I hadn't made eye contact with a grown man taking a dump since my boot camp days.

Can't say I missed it much.

Figuring my friendship with the introverted Aussie couldn't handle pulling up a snow stool and throwing an arm around him to share the moment, I took a sharp left and postholed further from camp to leave Thor to his business.

We retreated to our tents to prepare for our next two a.m. start. I laid my head on my pillow, relieved to be horizontal.

Headlamp!

I stayed still, unable to find the will to sit up.

Maybe *I can make it without light for one more…*

"NO," I dragged myself back into the seated position by the metaphorical ear and swapped the batteries out of my headlamp.

My thoughts drifted back to those fair-weather PCT hikers along Senger Creek. They'd been able to stroll through the backcountry on dirt, making twenty to thirty miles per day, finishing the High Sierra in a matter of *weeks*, not months. That evoked a twisted feeling of jealousy—and pride. This long-distance mountaineering chapter of my

CRUNCH

PCT hike had been incredible beyond words, but the last 160 miles of snow had also resulted in a withered, food-obsessed maniac. I couldn't help but wonder if I had enough left in me to see anymore of the PCT beyond the Sierra. Just assuming I'd actually see a successful end of the Sierra felt preposterous.

Everything was improving, though, especially since Pinchot. Amped hadn't mentioned his foot in two days, which was a good sign. I was starving but still moving forward, and we'd successfully stayed on hard snow for four consecutive mornings.

Maybe this will all just keep feeling easier.

I closed my eyes and almost instantly fell into a deep sleep.

Atop Dick Peak, a devilish smile spread across the trail god's faces.

21

BEAR CREEK

I sat up in a groggy fog, clicking my light on to illuminate a frost-lined tent. My stomach growled at me as I struggled to get moving and organized, stumbling through my morning routine. My mind felt slow, like it was locked halfway in a dream. I was more tired than sleep could fix, more hungry than food could fix.

In the twenty-degree dark, we started up the final uphill stretch to Selden Pass. The absolute silence was interrupted only by the rhythmic sound of our metal points penetrating the hard snow.

Crunch, crunch, crunch, crunch

I loved this part of each morning. Brilliant stars illuminated the peaks around us, again challenging our senses to grasp the beauty. A series of short, safe ramps of snow guided us up the bottlenecking canyon. Before long, we stood atop Selden at 10,900 feet.

"Holy God, was that it?" I hesitantly asked, as if the question itself would reveal a surprise final headwall of icy cliffs covered in lions.

Amped checked and double-checked our GPS location. "That might've been the easiest pass so far."

Forty yards from the crest of the pass, we came face to face with our deserved karma. The ground just—disappeared. We inched closer to survey beyond what looked like a cliff, until we stood in a row, shining our headlamps down a seventy-degree ice face, maybe even a bit steeper, with no bottom in sight.

We paced the cliffline but found nothing better. Without being able to see the end of the slope, we couldn't know whether a slip would result in an exciting, but safe, slide into low-angled snow—or off the edge of a cliff.

"I'm *ninety-percent* sure there aren't cliffs on this side of Selden," Amped said.

I agreed—*however*, that other ten percent wasn't exactly comforting.

Maybe we're up too early. Maybe this is where night hikes don't work.

Right before I was about to suggest we setup our tents to wait until dawn arrived, Amped stepped up to the rim of darkness and turned around. "Our snowshoes have handled everything we've thrown at them so far. Why wouldn't they work here?"

In his true cowboy style, Amped flipped his heel-lifters up and stepped backwards over the edge of the precipice. Our bullish friend worked down the near-vertical face, truly pushing the capabilities of his snowshoes—and just plain *physics*, at that.

Fifteen feet down the slide, Amped called up with obvious relief, "There's a bottom!"

Thor went next, slowly chipping in shallow steps with the edge of his crampons. To avoid becoming the bowling ball responsible for three helicopter rescues (fingers crossed for a buy-two-get-one-free special), I waited until Amped and Thor were safe before turning around and stepping down along Amped's tracks.

We headed back into the night across the Marie Lakes Basin, all of us silent, unable to put our unsettled thoughts into words. Selden, the weenie ass, barely-worth-a-mention pass, had presented us with the steepest slope we'd had to navigate so far. Not Forester, not Mather, not Glen—but *Selden*.

A giant obstacle was only a few miles away: Bear Creek. It was the second of the two notorious crossings along the John Muir Trail. Even in low snow years, it had a reputation of sweeping hikers off their feet.

We intersected the West Fork of Bear Creek, a major tributary feeding Bear Creek, and found just snow, no sign of an actual creek. I'd done my homework and was aware of an alternate route to get on the far side of Bear Creek by *not* crossing the West Fork—instead following it downstream and crossing the individual tributaries of Bear Creek before they converged into the notorious powerhouse at the PCT crossing.

But—up until this point, I hadn't needed to use any of the alternates I'd cooked up at home. Every major creek had still been snowbridged. That included the West Fork, just a mile shy of Bear Creek itself.

I led the way over the West Fork, angling sharply in the direction of Bear Creek, hoping to intercept it a ways upstream from the trail crossing to theoretically cross the first stable snowbridge we found.

For *surely,* there would be plenty to choose from.

Just as the sky started to brighten, we found our crossing. A steep, thirty-yard embankment led down to a section of creek where several snowbridged tributaries were convening, an easy path across Bear Creek—once we got down. The angle of the embankment rivaled what we'd down-climbed to get off of Selden.

Amped turned around, again leading the way backwards off the edge. I followed, staying several yards above him. With aggressive kicks, we slapped each snowshoe into the ice, driving the metal points as deep as possible.

Thor took out his Whippet (basically an ice axe fixed to the top of a trekking pole) and started inching down the slope toward a large boulder protruding from the snow partway down the embankment, aiming to pause there before tackling the rest. With his toes facing downhill, his ankles were torqued in an extreme angle. One shuffle at a time, the lumbering Aussie forced as much of his crampon points into the snow as he possibly could—but it wasn't enough.

A panicked grunt snapped me out of my focused steps. Thor's right foot slid out from under him, taking him down sideways, and our new friend started *rolling down the slope*. Amped and I froze in shock as Thor rag-dolled end over end, desperately trying to insert his Whippet into the ice, but his eighty-pound pack was calling the shots.

He collided with the boulder he'd been aiming for, but his momentum rolled him across the flat top of the granite stone—and off the ten-foot drop on the other side. As with many pieces of rock in the Sierra, the warm afternoons had melted the snowpack away from the sides of the boulder, forming a dramatic knife's edge of ice on the downhill side of the rock.

In a flash of brilliant luck and pain, 250 pounds of Thor spun over and landed—*crotch first*—directly onto the knife's edge. The poor bastard came to an abrupt rest straddling the spine of ice. Both Amped and I released breaths we didn't know we were holding. Thor let out a heavy groan and sat up, adjusting his position on the ice blade to remove the pressure off his testicles.

Amped's face was stuck in a horrified, sympathetic grimace. "**Dude**. Are you all right?"

Thor didn't respond but looked halfway back at us to give a weak nod, then returned to coping with the shock and pain. We down-stepped to the slope adjacent to Thor and waited in silence until he finally stood back up. Without a word, he shouldered his pack and resumed down-climbing the rest of the embankment, obviously embarrassed at being the focus of our attention. At the base, Thor assured us he was "fine."

That word was almost certainly used incorrectly.

We crossed the first snowbridge, then moved across rolling drifts bridging the other small tributaries. Amped turned a shallow corner to cross the last bridge we'd spotted—or at least what we thought was a bridge.

"Ohhh *crap*," he called back. "It doesn't connect."

What we'd seen had the *illusion* of being a snowbridge in the rolling drifts, but it wasn't. The last channel of water separating us from the north side of Bear Creek was swift whitewater too deep to even consider trying to wade. Even worse, there were no other options in the ravine we'd descended into. Short clifflines prevented us from being able to move up or downstream. We had to reverse back the way we came—which included the slope Thor had just liquefied his taint descending.

"Sorry, Thor," I said. "This was a mistake."

"I'm good, mate. I promise."

Thor led the way back up the slope, which thankfully went much better than going down had gone. Successfully out of the ravine, we continued further downstream.

Amped stopped at a solitary log spanning a narrow, rapid section of the creek. The pathetic, sagging pine hung at least a dozen feet above the surface of the torrent, and looked like a great option for hikers who preferred death to eating another packet of cold tuna.

Amped looked back at me with a bit of hesitant optimism.

I returned it with a less optimistic, are-you-out-of-your-damn-mind look.

We reached the Pacific Crest Trail crossing at dawn. The sky had lightened enough to illuminate the roiling, black water. I'd crossed here several times, as had Amped, but our summertime memory of a twenty-five-foot-wide, knee-deep creek didn't match what was in front of us. The banks had been overflowed by several yards, and the creek looked at least three feet deeper.

"Let's drop our packs and keep looking," I suggested, unwilling to dive right into a testis-torturing ice-water bath at six a.m.

We continued downstream, weighing our options, but nothing was safe or simple enough, especially not in a twenty-five-degree morning. There were risky jumps across raging water, full body dunks in wide, ten-foot-deep, sluggish sections, but not a single one of us could mentally brace for even the *idea* of hopping in for a swim.

"So, the trail crossing?" Thor asked.

The cold was adding an urgent pressure. My fingers and toes were numbing just from standing still and trying to decide, before I'd even touched the creek.

I nodded. "Yeah—I guess. Let's get to it."

Back at the PCT crossing, I stalled at the edge of the intimidating mass, trying to convince myself it was possible.

*How deep is it in the middle? The current **almost** looks slow enough—but is this it? Our best option? Should I demand we all backtrack uphill to attempt the alternate instead?*

I was lost. The alternate seemed like the more responsible route, but it was also reversing a steep uphill mile through tough terrain, and it was theoretical. There was no guarantee we'd find anything better.

A confident Australian accent snapped me out of my dilemma. "I'll go first."

Amped and I raised a couple of eyebrows—but we didn't know Thor super well. It was possible he'd done a lot of creek crossings back home. Maybe he wanted to help the group with something he was proficient in. Perhaps he'd simply tired of watching me stare at a creek while freezing his ass off.

Thor took off his boots and started preparing his gear to wade across, and that settled it. We were going to wade Bear Creek at the trail.

With his bare feet slipped inside clunky camp shoes, and hiking boots perched high on his pack, Thor stepped up to the edge of the black water. Amped and I shivered our way through stripping down and compressing all our hiking clothes into a dry bag, to give us clothing to change into once we'd crossed. Our slick, lightweight rain gear went on, which wouldn't absorb any water in the creek, but also offered next to zero warmth. We slipped bare feet back into our boots and Amped handed me his electronics to tuck into another dry bag. Our plan was for the first crosser to be electronics free, just in case the creek took them for a ride. Once there was a proven way across, the second would follow with the most sensitive gear.

I cinched the cord to the electronics dry bag just as Thor stepped off the bank, about thirty feet downstream of the trail crossing.

What is he doing stepping in there? I dismissed the thought. *Maybe he found something I didn't see.*

Within feet from the bank, the rapid current rolled past his waist.

Amped chose to lower in at the typical summer crossing. He easily waded into the middle, pausing to probe the deepest part of the channel with his trekking pole. I snapped out of my spectator's trance to finish shoving my various dry bags into my pack. When I looked up again, Amped was still in the same place, probing the depth around him. He was typically quite brave when it came to charging through obstacles, but his three-foot-long pole was under water—along with half his arm. The turbulent creek rolled over his shoulder as he probed again and again. Thor was making progress, but very slowly, one hesitant step at a time.

With trembling fingers, I threw my backpack on and extended my trekking poles. Amped turned into the flow and lowered into the deepest part of the creek, staggering sideways, fighting against the stiff, waist-deep current rolling snowmelt all the way up to his chest.

Thor stalled about a third of the way across in waist-deep current, probing the deep water ahead with a visibly tremoring trekking pole. He'd been in freezing water for several minutes, an eternity for a warm body trying to maintain feeling in its extremities.

A lump formed in my throat, and an ominous thought appeared.

This can't end well.

Although clearly with his own crossing to worry about, Amped noticed Thor had stopped. He turned his torso slightly to yell, "Thor, come up here! It's not as deep!"

For the second time that morning, poor Thor slipped, wobbled—and went down.

"NOOOOOO!!!" Amped yelled in dismay. "SWIM, THOR, SWIM!"

The distraction was enough to cause Amped to *also* wobble, and he came dangerously close to joining Thor.

My mouth slacked open in disbelief.

The freezing current tossed and turned Thor, pushing him further and further downstream.

Amped faced back to lock horns with the creek and released a hair-raising growl; a primal concoction of frustration, anger, and terror. He clicked into fight-or-flight mode and bulled his way across the last twenty feet.

From Amped's journal:

In the frantic moment of the situation, I feel myself about to plunge. I scream out with shock and adrenaline running through my veins. I'm waist deep now. Thor is tumbling end over end fighting to keep his head above the frigid current. I fight with all my might to stay up. I only have one hope as to not suffer the same fate as my hiking brother. I have to make it.

Amped emerged on the other side of Bear Creek as Thor stumbled into the shallows of the bank he'd departed from with empty hands. The creek had stripped him of his trekking poles, which included his Whippet.

Both were soaking wet, looking toward me in shock. None of us were close enough to communicate, but we all knew we were in trouble. It was 6:30 a.m., below-freezing, and the sun's warmth was still hours away. Two of the three of us were soaking wet, standing on opposite banks of a dangerous obstacle.

"This… is a *nightmare*," I muttered.

Thor staggered up to me from the bank of Bear Creek, his sopping wet t-shirt clinging to his torso. With an unsettling calm, he said, "I lost my trekking poles."

Incredibly, he wasn't shivering.

"Jesus, Thor. This is insane. We need to get you warm!"

"My clothes are wet," Thor looked at the ground in front of him with glazed-over eyes. "I'll just wait here until the sun comes. You guys keep going."

I stared back at him for a moment in silence. "Thor—that'll be *hours* from now. You've got to get warm before then. We can hike back upstream to get your blood moving and find some snowbridges. There has to be some within a couple miles."

His snow-burned face still void of expression, he lowered to sit on the snow and offered another matter-of-fact statement.

"My boots are wet."

Amped had changed into dry clothes but was pacing back and forth on the other bank, pausing every few laps to stare back across at us. I couldn't tell him what was going on across the sound-swallowing creek, and had no idea what to do. Our teammate sat frozen on the snow, blankly staring at the bank in front of him. Steady streams of water dripped from his chin and elbows onto the ice.

Just leave him, a dark voice inside me suggested with cruel indifference. *He's not your responsibility. You're Amped's partner, and Amped is freezing his ass off every second you put off crossing.*

I can't leave Thor, I pushed against my dark thoughts. *What if he doesn't pull out of this state on his own? What if we move on and find out later he froze to death?*

*Then Thor freezes to death. Again: not your responsibility. You didn't invite him out here; he came into the Sierra on his own. That choice will play out however it's going to play out. However, it **was** you who convinced Amped to be here.*

I shivered in the stiff, dawn breeze. My reptilian instincts had a point, and I was losing my capacity for empathy the colder I got, especially knowing Amped was many times colder. After Thor's fall down the embankment and overconfident entry into Bear Creek, I couldn't help but wonder if Amped and I were risking the success of our own trek by teaming up with the accident-prone Aussie.

I stood up and marched toward the PCT crossing. If the path Amped had taken was safe enough for me, then maybe I could encourage Thor to try again—but that rationale was pure nonsense. Thor no longer had trekking poles, and crossing Bear Creek without trekking poles would be like crossing a busy highway without legs.

Guilt enveloped me walking away from Thor, but I didn't know what else to do. My only other options were to either stay there and let Amped freeze, or throw 300 pounds of sopping wet, paralyzed Thor onto my back to hike him upstream—a questionable proposition for a guy finding ever-increasing challenge opening ramen salt packets.

With quivering legs, I lowered into the creek and waded into the chaos, gasping in discomfort as the water filled my boots and flowed up my pant legs. Halfway across, I reached the edge of the swiftest channel. Just like Amped, I probed my extended trekking pole into the water and found the exact reason why bullheaded Amped had hesitated. The current was too swift to even drag my trekking pole against. To probe upstream, I had to remove the pole entirely from the water first. The black creek swirled around my thighs, removing every shred of warmth from under my useless rain pants. I attempted to curl my toes inside my boots, but my feet had already gone completely numb.

No wonder Thor fell in after being out here for five minutes.

Simply staying balanced was difficult without feeling in my feet—and my next step was to dip down beyond my waist, into an even more aggressive current.

Amped stared at me with arms crossed tightly across his chest.

"Dammit," I muttered. "This was a huge mistake."

Being just close enough for Amped to hear, I shouted, "I'm not going to try it! We'll head upstream to find a different crossing!"

Amped nodded and returned to pacing back and forth. I turned around to wade back to the bank.

If I'd just gone first, I could've called this crossing off for all of us. The hell was I thinking? This is such a mess.

Thor was still sitting on the snow in his sopping wet t-shirt. His lips had blued, and he was shivering. All thoughts of leaving him behind vanished. There never should've been a suggestion to try wading Bear Creek, and a large chunk of that fault settled squarely on me. Instead of stepping up to lead our team—to either first sample the crossing myself or demand we backtrack to find a dry, safe way to cross—I'd allowed my teammates to take risks I would've backed away from.

"Get your boots back on, Thor. We're going to hike upstream."

His shock seemed to be slightly worn off, and one of his boots was resting in his lap. "I can't get my feet in these."

Thor gave the boot a hard twist, which cracked and splintered, showing me the saturated boot had been encased in a clear layer of ice! Solidified creek water flaked off in chunks as he flexed the leather with red hands, trying to return it to a malleable material a foot could get inside of.

I went to put my socks and actual pants back on but found my boots were already in the same boat as Thor's! The laces were encased, as if they'd been dipped into a vat of clear epoxy. I didn't have enough feeling in my fingers or the patience to figure out how to break into my shoes.

I shouldered my pack. "Guess I'm hiking sockless—in rain pants."

Thor was looking more alive by the minute, albeit in increasing misery as he *felt* his reality.

"While you change into dry clothes and work on your boots, I'm going to go scout upstream. If you see me next to Amped, I found a knee-deep or lower crossing, and you need to follow my footprints. If I don't find anything safe enough, I'll be back within the hour, and we'll go down to the slow, deep part of the creek and swim across. We're already wet; another dip wouldn't be so bad, right?"

Of course, that was a joke. I was only wet from the thighs down. Thor had icicles clinging to his damn eyebrows. His mouth momentarily lifted into a smile, and he gave me a nod.

"You've got to get out of your wet clothes. Stand up and get that done first."

He nodded again and stood, then groaned through peeling off his drenched shirt and exposing his wet skin. White wisps of body heat drifted off his pale torso.

I stomped my two blocks of ice into snowshoes and took off back along Bear Creek in a fury. I had at least a mile to hike with two freezing teammates waiting on me. My frustration and disappointment fueled my numb legs to charge up the drainage almost in a run. With two torched legs and wheezing like a pie-eating contestant shuffling between booths, I backtracked over the snowbridged West Fork of Bear Creek and turned north along the alternate.

At a second tributary of Bear Creek, I found a steep, heavily snow-bridged ravine. The third and fourth major tributaries were the same: large, infuriatingly solid snowbridges. Water running below the bridges was heavily muffled, floating me peacefully above what was sure to melt into a deafening monster in the coming weeks. With next to zero effort, I was running back downhill on the north side of Bear Creek—ecstatic but stinging with regret.

Two rules cemented in my mind while I sprinted downhill to find Amped:

I would ALWAYS go first across future obstacles. Amped had made it across, but largely because he trusted my judgment, and I'd been complicit in attempting to cross Bear Creek at the trail. If I'd gone first, I could've turned the team around.

I would NEVER attempt a crossing without verifying there wasn't a safer one upstream.

Amped was snapping low, dead branches off nearby trees to start a fire when I found him. A huge smile spread across his face. He was shivering but in good spirits.

"Damn, it's good to see you over here. I was getting a fire going so once Thor crosses he'll be able to warm up. How is he?"

"I'm not sure. His boots froze solid on his pack after he went in. He couldn't get his feet into them."

Across the creek, Thor was still sitting on the snow fiddling with a boot in his lap. Amped brought two fingers up to his peeling lips and delivered an ear-piercing whistle. Thor's head shot up, his body straightening as he realized I'd made it to the other side of the creek.

We went to work on starting the fire. Amped assembled the wood we'd collected into a log cabin while I dug out my Vaseline-soaked cotton balls I always kept in my pack as emergency fire-starters. With numb fingers, I pulled apart the gummy cotton fibers and ignited it with a single strike of my fire-steel. The external warmth was an unbelievable, alien gift from the universe in our time of need. I'd been in the presence of a *lot* of campfires in my life—but I'd never quite literally *needed* one.

My shivering calmed and feeling slowly returned to my extremities.

"What the…" I muttered.

My eyebrows furrowed at Thor, who was standing on the far bank, forty feet away—holding a boot in his right hand. He yelled something, but his small voice was no match for the boisterous creek between us. The Aussie repeated a throwing arm motion, pointing toward us.

Amped's eyes widened. "He wants to throw his boot over here."

"What?!" I asked, taken aback. "No, that doesn't… I mean, why would he…" but Thor continued to repeat the throwing motion.

"I think he wants us to thaw his boots on the fire," Amped said, stunned.

I huffed. "I can think of one forty-foot, boot-swallowing problem with that."

Clearly, he still wasn't thinking completely straight. One botched throw—from either side of the creek—would spell doom for Thor. If he thought losing his trekking poles was bad, he would soon figure out just how much worse his life could get if one of his boots went for a dip.

Both Amped and I shook our heads in extreme exaggeration, made giant X's with our arms—everything we could to discourage any throwing of vital gear in our direction.

Thankfully, Thor turned around and lumbered back up to his pack. He began violently stomping his right foot down into its boot, over and over. We could feel the frustration from across the water.

"Come on, Thor," Amped muttered. "You can do this."

Thor stomped with enough force to the point I was concerned he'd snap his own ankle trying to get a boot on—but then, it worked. His right foot slid into place.

He looked up at us with pure joy spread across his face, then moved on to the next. With Thor's hammer of a leg, he stomped over and over, crushing his left foot into its rigid cage. Boots on, Thor disappeared upstream. Amped and I stayed by the fire, hoping and praying enough shock had worn off for Thor to make good decisions on his own. The snow was still quite hard, so my footprints wouldn't be as easy to follow as I'd hoped. There were plenty of good snowbridges where I'd crossed—but there were just as many dangerous ones. An anxious silence sat between me and Amped while we fed the fire in anticipation of Thor's arrival.

"You think we'd see his body float by if…?" Amped stopped, unable to speak the last few words.

"I honestly don't know." I refused to believe dealing with a dead friend would even be a remote possibility, but my eyes diligently searched the black creek anyway. "Maybe."

After a tense half-hour, Thor appeared from the forest. Our team reunited around the fire, drying clothes and silently mulling over what we'd just gone through. To me, Bear Creek wasn't a victory.

This crossing had turned into an epic we would never, *ever* forget—but unnecessary, one that would've been completely avoided with better decisions. Just two days ago at Evolution Creek—Bear Creek's equally feared sibling—we'd easily crossed with a deliberate, upstream search. We clearly hadn't appreciated the potential nightmare we'd avoided in doing so.

We gathered our belongings and drowned the embers of our fire, spreading the ashes to minimize the evidence of our morning there. Humility reset, we set off on the trail again, dropping elevation following the creek along exposed, south-facing rock slabs.

The trail gods weren't quite done with us yet, though.

Dozens of streams intersected the slabs, where the alpine sun had accelerated the erasure of any snowbridges. The tricky crossings wouldn't let up. None was overly serious, but every one took extra time for poor Thor.

To avoid the sloppy conditions on the rock slabs, we moved under the trees, sticking to the firm, six-foot cliff of snow lining Bear Creek. Progress went well until a loud rumble underfoot ripped a crack through the ice, separating us from the stable forest snow. The crack widened as the huge platform we were on began to list into the creek.

Amped reflexively jumped over the crack to safety, but Thor and I were further away—too far to react. Thankfully, the crack widening slowed at just a few inches, giving us time to step across to stable snow. The huge block slumped steadily into the creek underneath, like a flooded ship sinking into the ocean.

Adrenaline pumping, we continued on. Dry lengths of the PCT started appearing and we stopped for lunch along the trail. The stress and strain of the morning hadn't done my hunger any favors, aside from some temporary appetite suppression when I thought I'd be cryogenically preserving all my unspeakables in Bear Creek. My planned lunch disappeared in a flash, and my emergency rations taunted me from my open bear canister.

I'm not the type to take any shit from dehydrated potatoes—so I ate them.

Stinging regret accompanied the last spoonful of goop. Those potatoes were meant for a worst-case-scenario bail over the long, complicated passes and untraveled terrain we'd potentially have to navigate. I couldn't help it though. I needed food. I had an insatiable demon on my shoulder, *constantly* reminding me of all the unwrapped, sugary fixes I had in my bear canister. To add a little salt to the wound, even after two large lunches—and *maybe* that night's dessert—I was still *starving*. My stomach was distended, objectively packed to capacity, but my primal hunger cared little for objective truth. I was capable of eating every damn crumb of everyone's food supply right then and there.

While my partners finished their lunch, I rearranged my dwindling provisions, taking inventory of what was left and praying for a sudden realization I'd somehow overpacked a blue cheese, bacon cheeseburger with endless fries and a milkshake. Amped caught me slumped over my bear canister, once again in mid-staring contest with my remaining Pop-Tarts.

For what felt like the dozenth time, he opened a packaged waffle, broke off a small piece for himself, and handed me the rest. I had no capacity for polite refusal. I'd lost my pride a hundred miles back.

After lunch, we set off to tackle the last objective of the day: Bear Ridge. A thousand-foot climb would take us to the crest, followed by a 2,000-foot descent to camp near the Vermilion Valley Resort Junction. Short pieces of soft, muddy trail were punctuated with mounds of slush. We briefly lost the PCT at one point, resulting in a miserable bushwhack through mud and thorns to find it. Joking stopped. Conversations died shortly after. Smiles were incompatible with afternoon snow.

We were relieved to summit the ridge, assuming the remaining downhill to camp would be a breeze.

It wasn't.

The snow's consistency was impossible to read on the steep descent off Bear Ridge. The shifting shade from large trees throughout the day left some snow patches bullet hard, and others complete mush. It all looked the same though. Whatever gear we needed on our feet, we chose wrong, and we took our turns being involuntarily deposited into tree wells. With only moderate crampons and no trekking poles, Thor was getting the worst of it.

Every battered soul on that mountainside wanted nothing more than to fly down the hill to reach camp at the base. But rather than being able to utilize gravity to speed up our descent, we spent a cruel amount of time tenuously tiptoeing across the hillside—*perpendicular* to the slope—trying to scout a safe path down.

The three of us split up, individually finding our way through the forest, searching for the optimal path for our chosen traction. Through the trees to my right, I heard Thor go for another slide—but this one ended in pain.

"FuuuuuUGH!"

"Thor?" I called out.

No reply.

"Thor, buddy—you okay?"

Still nothing.

I made my way toward the sound and found Thor sitting up in a tree well, holding his left shoulder. He looked up at me with drooping, red eyes.

"My shoulder dislocated." He let out a long sigh. "I put it back in though. My, uh—*ass* hurts."

I chuckled, like any good friend would—until I traced his slide mark uphill. The smile wiped from my face the moment I locked eyes on a hefty, two-foot long, broken branch jutting up from the snow—a veritable *spear*. Thor's slide mark originated about twenty feet above it, and *disappeared* for several feet after, where Thor had slid up and over the groin-destroyer and gone airborne.

"No, Thor, no! Is your dick still there?!"

A smile briefly lifted on Thor's face but dropped back down into a defeated stare. "Today's just not my day."

I took out my ice axe and handed it to him. "Here. I've been managing all right with just my trekking poles. I'm not sure how much more of a beating you can take. We've got to get you to Mammoth so we can laugh about all this eventually."

"Thanks, mate." Thor took the axe and stood, groaning through full-body pain.

A shout echoed through the trees, undoubtedly Amped wondering where his team had disappeared to. I set off to get him up to speed on Thor's newest pains, then hung back to keep an eye on our battered comrade, trying to maintain a bridge between the bull and the beaten.

The end of the downhill snow deposited us into a marsh. Our pace ground to a crawl through thickets of ten-foot-tall stubborn reeds. We answered the beckoning call of a stretch of solid snow laid over the reeds—making it clear we'd learned nothing from the burned section at the base of the Golden Staircase.

Amped wasn't in a good mood, and when Amped was pissed, he became even more bullish. He pushed ahead, charging over the flat snow, clearly annoyed with our creeping progress. In a flash, one of his boots punched through the surface and the lower half of Amped disappeared.

"OOMPH!"

His stomach collided with the rim of the hole he'd made, and the heft of his backpack made sure it hurt. It turned out our "solid snow" was a thin shell with an incredible volume of water flowing through reeds underneath.

Amped slumped onto the rim of ice, gasping for breath. I felt for him, but wasn't sure what to say. I can only imagine how uncomfortable it must've been for Thor to be watching pain happen to someone who wasn't him. With a growl, Amped pushed himself back to remove the ice from his abdomen.

Through clenched teeth, he muttered, "I think my diaphragm might be bruised."

Thankfully, we soon stumbled upon a length of exposed PCT. The path was littered with evidence of a harsh winter. Branches and needles were everywhere, and fallen pines created sticky obstacles for us to work around. It wasn't perfect, but it was a trail we simply had to follow—and *damn* if I hadn't gained a renewed appreciation for established trails. In all honesty, I'd finished the Southern California PCT a bit mentally worn down. Not from the physical pain or exhaustion, but from monotony: wake up, pack up, follow a clean, easy trail, set up camp, and repeat. Ad nauseam. The Sierra had certainly broken up that monotony, and I'd never take an established trail for granted again. Any trail crew members I came across would be getting an indiscriminate smooch and a pinch to the bum—for sexual assault could be the *only* way to translate my gratitude and respect.

"Unnn," Amped moaned through the trees ahead. "Another one?"

Standing between us and camp, an unmarked stream stood savagely overflowing its banks with brown, muddy water. It was only eight feet wide, but the current was incredibly swift. Amped moved a bit downstream to some small, bobbing logs and bulled his way onto them. He quickly lost his balance and went for a dip. Once he'd paddled to the far bank, the sourpuss look on his face made his feelings clear about being soaked less than a mile from camp.

Knowing a fire was in our immediate future to dry Amped off, but mostly just tired of the endless effort to stay dry, I turned to face upstream and walked straight through at the trail crossing. The current rolled the cold, dirty water almost up to my chest.

Thor was frozen, still clutching my glossy, red ice axe, staring at the water with red drooping eyes. He hadn't moved since watching Amped fall in. This little stream was in his head, a bad sign for the major crossings heading up to Silver Pass the next day.

Unwilling to wade, Thor chose a small-diameter log spanning the banks just upstream from the trail. Amped threw his trekking poles over to him to help balance, and we called encouragement over the rush of the water. With darting eyes, Thor hesitantly placed one vibrating foot in front of the next.

A fall into the stream wouldn't have been a big deal, aside from some wet clothes and a hit to the ego, but Thor looked like he was balancing across the precipice of death. Amped reached out from the shore and offered Thor a hand to pull him to safety once he could reach.

We crossed the raging Mono Creek on a steel bridge, finally arriving at the trail junction hikers typically used to reach their resupply at Vermilion Valley Resort (VVR). There was still snow everywhere—except for on the trail itself. We hadn't seen another person in days, so it was a safe bet we wouldn't be inconveniencing anyone by camping on the trail. VVR was still closed and wouldn't open for another few weeks, their latest opening date in decades. On one of the most trafficked junctions in the entire Sierra, we pitched our three tents in a neat row blocking the trail.

After over twelve hours of brutal hiking, mishaps, and lessons learned, we relaxed by the fire, drying clothes and recapping the day. Although bruised and beaten (some more than others), we were grateful to have all members of our team alive and relatively uninjured.

The major crossings the next day were looming, but I did my best to shut my brain down. The only option we had was to take it one day at a time, one foot in front of the other.

CRUNCH

From Amped's journal:

The plunge Thor took would have been enough to make anyone turn around. The rest of the day the Sierra threw everything they had at Thor—the kid kept going. He slogged with us despite his injuries and lack of trekking poles and still managed to make it to camp. He was soaked, bruised, and thousands of miles away from his home in Sidney, but around the campfire, he was able to laugh and look forward to the next day. I respect this man for having the perseverance to continue and the attitude to laugh it off. [Thor] is an extremely tough individual.

22

THE WATERFALL

MAY 30, 2017
VVR JUNCTION

Packing up under headlamps after a perfect night's sleep, I was nervous.

We were all nervous.

Silver Creek's waterfall was just a few miles away, and it had a nasty reputation.

Dawn revealed the outline of the peaks above just as we arrived at our warmup crossing for the day, the North Fork of Mono Creek. The darkness hid the water from view, but the impressive roar made its presence known. A massive tree spanned the creek. Protruding branches created handholds, which made walking across a breeze—for two of us.

It took Thor a minute to collect himself. One hesitant foot in front of the other, he stepped along the log with the eyes of a man delicately tightrope walking above a den of lions. He stepped onto the far bank with a forced smile and a pent-up, stuttering sigh of relief.

A dull roar in the distance grew until it drowned out all competing noise. At a break in the trees, we got a view of the approaching wall of towering granite cliffs and it dawned on me.

That's the waterfall.

A series of forty-five degree pristine granite slabs set our calves on fire, and delivered us back onto a thick snowpack—and into the mist billowing off the cascading Silver Creek.

During summer months, the "waterfall" label was nonsensical. I'd never seen the creek any more aggressive than serene babbling over polished stones. Past accounts were almost hard to believe. They described the waterfall as a jet power-washing a flooded trail, a crossing requiring full rain gear.

Honestly, that description didn't sound so bad to me. Sure to be less than comfortable in below-freezing temps, but more intimidating than dangerous, like walking through a flooded, drive-thru car wash in January—only with fewer suds.

Well, depending on who'd been camping upstream, fewer suds.

The snowpack persisted right up until the powerful cascade came into view. The ambient temperature took a sharp dive in the mist. Winds tugged at our jackets and pack straps.

Nearing the waterfall, a surge of hope rushed through me.

"Is it—*snowbridged?*" I muttered.

The snowpack appeared to stretch across the creek, a potential skywalk *above* the jets of the waterfall! I tucked my head into the mist and onto the snow platform above the most forceful jet—and any shreds of optimism vanished.

The snowbridge was an optical illusion. I peered down the vertical face of what definitely *used* to be a bridge—but the middle was gone, eaten away by the waterfall, leaving a clean, twelve-foot face of ice behind with no obvious way down to the flooded trail.

Thor had stopped twenty yards shy of the falls. I leaned in to Amped, who already had a line of frozen droplets clinging to his eyebrows. "THOR'S GOING TO HATE THIS."

Despite making borderline-sensual contact with Amped's ear, my voice barely made it through the clamor of the falls.

THE WATERFALL

"I'LL GO LOOK AROUND AS FAR UP AND DOWNSTREAM AS I CAN," he shouted back.

It was the *right* move—but upstream was a sheer cliff. Downstream, the creek was cascading down the steep slabs we'd just climbed. Crossing the waterfall outlet over wet, slippery granite with a thousand feet to tumble down wasn't going to happen.

I wandered closer to the waterfall, wincing through sporadic spits to search along all edges of the platform. Any lingering hope of finding an easy way down to the trail was soon gone. But I did find one, eh—option.

If one could summon the bold-faced recklessness to call it that.

There was a boulder. It sat four feet below the platform's edge, directly in the path of the strongest jet of water firing off the cliff above. That jet had excavated the boulder from the snowpack, and continued on to tunnel a dark forty-five-degree hole into the heart of the platform, which left a prow of ice resembling a diving board stretched out toward the falls—and its tip hung four feet over the boulder.

I tried to calmly assess the situation over the panicked tantrum my brain stem was throwing. Walking the plank to lower down to the boulder wasn't a *great* option—but it was an option. It was *the* option, really, unless we wanted to turn around.

The thought of quitting was the only thing that gave my internal tantrum pause.

Safely lowering off the prow and into the jet would be tough, not to mention uncomfortable. The stream was power-washing the boulder—and the space above—with the force of an open fire hydrant. The stability of the prow was also a big unknown. Would it even *try* to stay intact with up to 250 pounds of hiker sliding off its tip? The consequence of overestimating the strength of the svelte prow was horrific, at best. Any breaks or falls would deposit us right into the dark chute under the platform. That hole was a thing of nightmares.

If I end up in there, would I be able to escape? Would I be spit out the other side to tumble down the slabs? If not, could I reverse back out of the chute, against the force of the water? Or would I be trapped in the bottom, being power washed by snowmelt until—

Amped appeared back onto the platform, snapping me out of my thoughts. "THERE'S NOTHING."

I swallowed against the hard lump rising in my throat and glanced back at Thor, who hadn't moved. I was suddenly envious of those past accounts where they'd put on rain gear to stroll through a knee-deep car wash. That sounded downright lovely.

"Oh no," I muttered under my breath, then pointed to the diving board over the boulder. "I THINK THAT'S OUR WAY DOWN."

Amped's eyes widened and his eyebrows furrowed into a clear "absolutely not" position. He paced around the platform, peering off all sides, just like I'd done. He stopped right where I had, staring at the side profile of the prow-o'-doom with suspicion.

We stepped away from the overbearing noise of the falls to discuss our only absurd option, and to hopefully brainstorm a second, much better one—but the steep granite cliffs up and downstream were inflexible roadblocks. Frankly, we were lucky to have the one option.

The only thought more torturous than lowering down to that boulder was turning around. Maybe this wasn't in line with my typical standards for acceptable risk, but we stood in front of the last major obstacle before Mammoth—death seemed preferable to throwing in the towel.

I was scared, but I found that fear almost irritating. Logically, our one and only option had a high chance of success, maybe not one hundred percent, but probably eighty or ninety. My thoughts were recoiling like there was a hundred percent chance I'd be sliding into that chute, and that mismatch felt—annoying, unnecessary, illogical. More than I wanted guaranteed safety, I wanted to know I was capable of pushing through fear, that I could entrust my mortality to sound reason.

"I'll try it," I said. "If it doesn't go well, we can turn around."

I didn't want to go first. I didn't want to test my theory of just how uncomfortable the inside of that chute was. But worse than being power-washed by snowmelt in a slippery, dark hole was the thought of watching that happen to Amped, someone I'd dragged into this trek—or Thor. A terrible vision flashed across my mind of Thor disappearing into the ice chute, then listening to him scream for help, unable to do a damn thing but wait until the screaming stopped.

I shuddered, shaking my head as if I could physically shepherd my thoughts away from the darkest corners of my brain. I dropped my pack and took out my rain pants and jacket with numb hands. Holding still in the wind and mist had already stripped much of my warmth. Intentionally without my pack on, I inched onto the diving board to test its stability unweighted. I bounced on each step nearing the edge of the prow until I stood at its tip, staring down into the mouth of the chute. The boulder was set back further that I'd thought. I bounced one last time, intentionally hard—but the prow stayed put.

Both of my partners' unblinking eyes were locked on me. I returned to them with hands trembling. I went to hoist my pack but paused.

Amped would go first if you suggested it.

I shook off the thought and gave Amped my trekking poles. "Hand these to me when I reach the boulder. It's probably best to stay back until then, so there's only one of us stressing the snow."

I knew damn well Amped trusted me enough to go first if I asked him to, but I didn't know how this was going to end, and I wasn't going to watch him suffer again. If this was a poor choice, *I* was going to feel it.

You can still quit! Turn around. Who would blame you for quitting??

Fully loaded, I cautiously retraced my steps back onto the prow. I stomped on the snow ahead, hoping to find any weaknesses before I found them under full load. Although every bit of me wanted to be a courageous, unflinching leader both inside and out—I wasn't.

***Please**, don't pioneer this sketchy idea. Let Amped go first, or at least go back to think about it longer!*

I drove the handle of my axe deep into the snow about a foot back from the edge. Perforating the prow was nowhere near ideal, but with just snow around, I needed some kind of handle to help lower out over the lip. I took a deep breath, turned around, and stepped backwards into the waterfall.

Inconsistent spats of water slapped at my back, legs, and head on the other side of my thin rain jacket, as if a blindfolded child was attacking me with a fire hose from ten yards away. I grabbed the embedded axe with both hands and slid further down, dangling in space above the dark chute.

I straightened my arms past the point of no return. My biceps hadn't had much of a job in the last two months, and definitely weren't going to be able to reverse my mass back up onto the snow. My dangling feet found nothing but open air.

With every ounce of my flailing weight hanging off the edge of the prow I'd just punctured, I reluctantly extended my arms even more, begging my foot to find the rock before anything snapped. My face pushed awkwardly against the ice, preventing me from seeing where my feet were.

Still nothing.

Now in the direct line of fire from the main jet, the blindfold was off. I took another deep breath and extended my arms until they were locked out.

Still nothing.

Panic flooded my brain. *It's not there.*

I'd miscalculated. There was no boulder. I'd committed too far over the edge to get back onto the prow, and now I had nothing to step down onto.

I flexed my toe downward and back, trying to get as long as I could. *Did I underestimate the distance? Am I going to have to **let go**, and just hope I make it out of this alive?*

The boulder was set slightly back from the tip of the prow. It was pretty clear a fall would take me straight down into the chute. All the theoretical consequences of slipping into that black hole flashed through my mind again. The burn in my shoulders, biceps, and forearms escalated, and my numb grip involuntarily loosened. My upper body had been in retirement for the last ten weeks, and I was suddenly asking a lot from it.

I let out a desperate, strained, "***Shit.***"

Without hesitation, Amped stepped out onto the prow, risking it collapsing under our combined weight. He extended his hand and gripped my right wrist. Trusting his vice-like grip, I relaxed my own on the axe enough to lower a *hair* further—and my boot contacted granite.

I settled onto the boulder with sewing machine legs. The jet had forced water into my sleeves and around my waist and neck, but I couldn't feel the cold. Amped handed me my trekking poles, and I sidestepped onto exposed stones protruding through the whitewater rushing across the trail. A dead, fallen pine tree was suspended above the creek. All of its branches had rotted away, but the spindly trunk stretched toward me from the other bank, a helping hand extended to a tired, wet traveler.

From Amped's journal:

Beta makes it across and I don't like to think about the insane things I'm getting ready to do, so I move quickly. I drop down to the starting stone and the noise is deafening. I have a death grip on the ice axe and will my already frozen fingers to release. I utilize one trekking pole for stability and traverse across the rocks. The glacial cold fills my boots and soaks my legs. I'm being pelted in the back and neck by arctic bullets. I step across slowly and make it to the other side. Now I have to crawl under the helping hand tree with my fifty-pound pack on, hoping it will have enough clearance. I get on my hands and knees, water running down my sleeves.

With both teammates a good bit taller than me, lowering down to the boulder wasn't as much of an issue. Thor's overall weight was thirty or forty pounds higher, though. With surprisingly little hesitation, like a fighter entering a cage, the Aussie stepped up to the planted axe, turned around, and lowered himself off the edge.

"Please stay put," I muttered to the inanimate diving board. Thor stalled over the chute, not committing to fully extending his arms. "Don't let Thor be the one…"

Thor released his arms and one foot made contact with the boulder. A jubilant, relieved smile spread across his face. He dislodged my axe from the snow and set off across the stepping stones. With no trekking poles for support, he took a bit more time balancing across with a thousand feet of granite slabs lurking in his peripheral. Amped and I shouted encouragement, attempting to out-roar the waterfall power-washing our best friend.

With shaking hands, Thor reached out in a bit of desperation to grasp the helping hand tree. With one hand tasting the sweet promise of safety, he hastily went to get his other hand on the tree, the hand holding the ice axe—specifically, the hand holding *my* ice axe. My precious (not to mention expensive) self-arrest device fumbled through Thor's fingers and dropped into the whitewater. Before anyone could react, it disappeared over the falls.

Thor snapped his head up to meet my eyes, his face twisted in pure, apologetic horror. Watching my axe go for a ride down Silver Creek with more steep snow ahead of us was clearly a problem—but Thor didn't need anything else to worry about.

I shrugged in feigned ambivalence. "It's not a big deal! Keep going!"

We arrived safely on the other side of the waterfall, alive but cold. *Really cold.* The freezing water had drenched all of us, despite our rain gear, and multi-directional gusts worked to remove any remaining shreds of warmth the jets had missed.

Switchbacks used to access the top of the cliffs were still deeply snowed over. Although mostly shaded, the snow was in bizarrely poor shape. We all warmed up fighting for elevation in the loose, exhausting slush. There was now only one axe among the three of us, and working up the side of a sixty-degree slope over ballooning exposure, it was hard to ignore the risk.

We emerged above the cliffs onto low-angle terrain, and into the glorious embrace of the morning sun. Without any discussion necessary, we collapsed in the snow to soak in the life-affirming rays and to celebrate another small victory.

We'd made it. Our team had conquered the last big obstacle before resupplying at Mammoth. Thor was still alive, among others.

"Hey mate, I'm sorry about the axe. I was trying, eh… to hold the—and…"

I held up my hand. "Don't stress it, bud. This happens. In the climbing world, we're constantly dropping or losing other people's expensive gear when we're at the crags. At the end of the day, we go to the local climbing shop on what we like to call an 'apology tour.' Whoever fumbled the gear re-buys those pieces. It's just part of the game."

"We'll get to the gear shop in Mammoth, then," Thor promised.

He dug into his bear canister, which was approximately ninety percent oatmeal packets—and wet inside. *Really* wet.

"What's up with your food, Thor?"

He cocked a half-smile, glancing up at me and back down to his canister. "From falling in at Bear Creek. I guess bear canisters aren't waterproof. Some of my food was plastic wrapped, but my oatmeal wasn't."

A big smile spread across his sun-abused face. "I've got a ton of soggy oats to eat."

The terrain opened up into the vast snowbowl under Silver Pass. The blue sky above the perfectly white ice was a feast for the eyes, but it came with a rather irritating feature common in Sierra spring snow: the suncup. Suncups are dishes that bake into the surface, stemming from a humble bit of dirt or debris absorbing warmth from the sun and melting out a bowl around it. The snowpack is filled with bits and pieces of debris, so as it melts, the flat surface is transformed into a million ankle-wrenching dishes. The suncups had been mild for us earlybirds, only a few inches deep, but in a couple weeks they would grow until the peaks and valleys were one to two *feet* from each other—forming a hellish terrain of rounded dunce caps, sure to inflict emotional scars to last a lifetime.

In snowshoes, suncups were almost negated, as the broad surface area spanned several peaks at once, making it not much different than walking on flat snow. With only crampons, Thor fell behind while he wrenched and rolled his ankles through miles of innocent, baby suncups, cultivating material for a future $200-an-hour, brown leather couch. We walked by Silver Lake, which had no sign of melting out yet. Eleven months prior, Amped and I had gone *swimming* in the lake. Voluntarily.

"Should we go for a quick anniversary dip?" I asked.

He smiled. "As long as it's you first."

CRUNCH

We reached the base of the final slope leading to the crest of Silver Pass and flipped up our heel-lifters. Counting to twenty together over and over, we hacked away at the remaining elevation.

With no issues beyond shameful panting, we arrived atop the last pass before Mammoth. We were treated to a sweeping view of Mammoth Mountain to the north and the jagged peaks behind us. It was surreal seeing how much of the Sierra we'd worked through. There was still plenty of serious terrain to navigate between Mammoth Mountain and us, but it felt amazing to be done with the last major obstacle separating me from *pizza*.

Also: Melanie.

The vast majority of our conversations were consumed by food. What we were going to eat when we got to town, what backpacking food we'd never touch again, the unspeakable sexual acts we'd be willing to perform for a cheeseburger, and so on. Unlimited food was nearing. Our eyes could actually look at Mammoth Mountain, and at the base of that world-class resort was an absolute *sea* of overpriced, impressively okay options of tourist trap cuisine.

Mammoth felt like a finish line, simply because I didn't have the mental capacity to think beyond it. Amped had to leave to go back home when we arrived. Thor had had enough of the High Sierra creeks. Odds were, he wouldn't be proceeding into North Yosemite, home to the most dangerous water crossings in the early season Sierra. A major chapter in my hike was closing. Moving on from Mammoth would be much different.

Staring into the endless expanse of iced-over mountains beyond Mammoth was overwhelming. I'd hiked *so far* in the snow. *So much* had happened, both good and bad.

*What else do these mountains have in store for me? Can I handle a few more Bear Creeks or Silver Creek waterfalls? Do I **want** to handle a few more of those? How exactly am I going to tear myself away from endless food and warmth in Mammoth?*

A thousand-foot glissade on perfect snow interspersed with buttery plunge-stepping put the pass quickly behind us. After a couple miles following a prominent gully, we paused for some lunch at the first section

206

of creek flowing from under giant, broken chunks of snow, allowing us access to some much-needed liquid water.

I dug a quick snow-chair into a sunny drift and sat to assemble my lunch. I'd been eating the same thing for weeks, but *damn* if it wasn't getting more and more delicious as my hunger escalated. While I was falling in hot-and-steamy love with a smashed tortilla filled with cold salmon, a message came in from Mel.

I saw a group of hikers walking north along the 395 today. Stopped to see if they wanted a ride, and one was Fireball! They all were adamant about walking though. Said they were connecting steps... Just like you.

Those last words had some snark behind them, if I knew my Melanie.

My gut reaction was respect. I'd gotten used to being the *only* hiker dim enough to put miles on asphalt in order to stick to my goals. So hearing of fellow sufferfesting souls felt like something to cheer on. But calling what they were doing "connected steps?"

Yeah.

No.

I mean, sure, *technically*, they could literally walk from Mexico to Canada along a combination of PCT and highways. But if they had no qualms about bypassing open sections of trail—such as, say, the Sierra—why hike along the PCT at all? The PCT is kind of... hard. Why not just head over to the western flanks of the Sierra and hop on Interstate-5? It's pretty flat, not to mention their connected steps would only cost them 1,400 miles instead of 2,650!

I didn't understand their logic, but honestly, I found their dedication inspiring—because I would've rather packed snow in my underwear until I died of hypothermia before roadwalking along a desert highway for hundreds of miles.

We wrapped up lunch and headed down to a steel bridge crossing the raging Fish Creek. Snow banks were four feet tall at the entrance and exit to the bridge, with the middle completely melted out. Awkwardly lowering onto the alien wood planks and shuffling across in our snowshoes and crampons, I wondered—of the hundreds of thousands of hikers who had crossed that bridge—how many had crossed in *snowshoes*?

I'm guessing we were in the minority.

After an uncomfortable mile of sidehilling upstream with our ankles jacked over to the side, we found a wonderful campsite right next to a lazy section of the creek. We spent the rest of the afternoon largely in silence, lost in our thoughts. Everyone's level of exhaustion had amplified throughout the trek, and we were close to the end. Tomorrow, we'd hike thirteen miles to camp near Mammoth Pass junction, Thor and Amped's planned exit off the PCT. The next day, I'd spend a solo day hiking twelve more miles to reach my optimal exit at Agnew Meadows. Mammoth Pass was a fourteen-mile roundtrip entry/exit, whereas Agnew Meadows was only eight. Amped and Thor weren't continuing on with me into Yosemite, so it made sense for them to prioritize hiking into Mammoth at an earlier, more convenient escape. With most of my pack weight eaten, I'd theoretically float the miles to Agnew Meadows, hike out the easy four miles to the resort, ransack the town's women and pizza supplies (well, wom**A**n, and pizza supplies), rest a few days, then return the four miles to Agnew Meadows to pick up where I left off.

Another message came in from Mel.

It looks like you guys will have weather tomorrow. Be careful.

The thought of being snowed or rained on was quite demoralizing at the end of a hard day. Figuring we were within safe striking distance of civilization, I helped myself to a post-dinner treat of two giant servings of emergency mashed potatoes with summer sausage, all soaked in olive oil, over 2,000 calories in one sitting, while Thor treated himself to another oatmeal eating contest. *Logically,* we should've been full—but mere logic knows nothing of hiker hunger.

I hadn't been satiated. I could feel the heavy mass of potatoes and impatiently hydrated, semi-crunchy pasta sitting inside me, but I could've eaten the same mass again. Reason was my only tool to assure myself I wasn't going to die of starvation. We settled in for the night dreaming of Mammoth, of warm food, beautiful wom**A**n, cold beer, and dry feet.

Thor was almost certainly not dreaming of oats.

23

THE STORM II

I opened a groggy eye and shut off my three a.m. alarm, then groaned into the sitting position. I stopped mid-yawn and cocked my head. Something felt off.

"It's... *warm*," I croaked.

Rolling up camp without numb fingers and frozen boots was a wonderful gift, but warm nights meant slushy snow. They were also a preamble to bad weather.

"We're in for it today," Amped said, pushing some of the unfrozen mush around with his boot.

Ten minutes later, I cinched my last snowshoe strap and went to hoist my pack, but paused. Amped was speedwalking into the dark forest with TP and his axe.

"Damn, already?" I called after him.

"It's all the food we've been packing in!" Amped called over his shoulder.

Thor was packed up and ready to go until he saw Amped taking care of business. Without a second thought, he dropped his load of wet oatmeal to go drop his load of—well, wet oatmeal. Thor's mission to get through his soggy rations meant he'd been eating like a king, but you can't take in eight packets of oats at every meal and not expect your digestive system to be working overtime.

My lack of desire to join my teammates in defiling the morning forest was bizarre. My system seemed to be the most stressed for food. I'd been eating more than either of my taller, heavier teammates, but poops only came along every two or three days. It wasn't like I was giving birth to record-shattering turds, either. Pretty much every snowy bowel movement concluded with a disappointed scowl.

Once my teammates had returned, we set off on slushy drifts toward the thousand vertical feet of switchbacks crawling out of Tully Hole. This section of trail was usually a dry-and-hot experience.

Not this time.

A garbage combination of slush and mud fought us the whole way up. Without any hard ice to bite into, our crampon points only served as resistance to the loose mixture, like forks dragging through mashed potatoes. But not just *any* mashed potatoes; chunky, roasted garlic potatoes with thick, gooey bands of Gouda cheese—maybe some peppered gravy on top…

Mmm.

My legs were on fire halfway out of Tully Hole, not even an hour into our day. The ambient temperature was just above freezing, but sweat still burned my eyes.

"Ughhh," Amped growled at the slurry under his feet and inside his boots, a sensation we'd all been enjoying together. "Why isn't it colder?"

We crested above 10,000 feet, fighting to smile through the collective collapse in our love for life. With exhausted, wobbling legs, we savored a short stretch of flat hiking across a saddle leading to Virginia Lake. The sky began to lighten, illuminating Melanie's forecast setting in. Gusting, multi-directional winds stirred dark clouds hovering what seemed like just a few dozen feet overhead.

"I don't think we're going to get out of being rained on today, fellas," I said.

There were no replies, just two sighs from a crew done being at the whims of Mother Nature.

Virginia Lake came into view, a spectacular scene that made us all but forget about the muck in our boots. The sky had turned pink, which colored the gorgeous, sparkling surface of the frozen lake. Amped and I had camped here many times, and it was one of the most picturesque spots along the John Muir Trail. But the hostile, redressed beauty in front of us was on a new level.

Small patches of sun broke through the stirring sky, igniting revolving groups of clouds into bright pinks, reds, and purples that reflected off the surface of the ice. The colors and patterns in the sky shifted quickly from one mind-blowing display to the next, again challenging our capability to process such incredible beauty.

We were wary of the stability of the ice in the warm morning, but the lake felt secure under our boots. Our eyes had spent the morning locked on the next three feet of slush, but the obstacle-free lake let us stroll ahead with our eyes on the heavenly display over us.

Amped took off in a jog. His heavy pack bounced around as he awkwardly shuffled along until he made it onto the far bank.

He turned and shouted, "I just ran across Virginia Lake!"

I chuckled and continued to enjoy the beautiful morning at an adult's pace. It definitely wasn't that I had neither the energy, nor cooperating tendons to go for a weighted jog almost 900 miles into this hike. Finding a quicker pace would've taken a ravenous mountain lion approaching at a full sprint, and even then I'd potentially remain "too mature" to run.

Brilliant reds and purples faded into a thick, black blanket overhead as we departed the lake. Uncomfortably close thunder chased us below 10,000 feet to Purple Lake, where snow conditions weirdly improved.

Our ankles were in for a nightmare. The summertime section of trail between Purple Lake and Mammoth Pass was an easy, flat trail dug into a forty-degree hillside. With the trail smoothed over by ice, only the ankle-hating slope remained. *Ten miles* of it.

A fresh set of mountain lion tracks joined the buried trail, soon followed by small bear prints the size of my fist alongside much bigger prints the size of my *head*—Mama Bear prints.

Within a mile of torqued ankles, I was already wavering in my conviction to spend an extra, solo day beyond Mammoth Pass to reach Agnew Meadows when a message came in from Mel.

There's a couple Facebook posts from the crew ahead of you guys. Looks like they exited Duck Pass with plans to reenter at Agnew Meadows. Why didn't you think of that?

I chuckled. "She thinks she's *sooo* funny."

Duck Pass was the earliest route into Mammoth, Agnew Meadows was the furthest (and shortest) exit out of Mammoth. That itinerary also happened to skip twenty miles of the PCT. With rain clouds overhead, twenty fewer snow miles sure sounded nice—but it also sounded an awful lot like *not* hiking the PCT.

It was hard to keep the bitter feelings back at Duck Pass junction. Every single set of footprints we'd been following broke off the PCT and headed toward the pass. Every one of them knew what they were doing. They'd made a conscious decision to skip many miles of snow *again* (this was much of the same crew that skipped up to Whitney Portal after the storm), which not only eased the difficulty of their hike, but also helped to maintain their respected position as the first hikers to push through the Sierra—the collective "Tip of the Spear."

For a guy hiking all the miles, Duck Pass didn't make sense to both exit *and* reenter the backcountry through. It was one of the longest trails in and out of Mammoth. It only made sense as a one-way exit. My exhausted, snow-sick brain struggled to cling to my convictions, to push aside the lure of an early escape.

*You're not out here to hike **most** of the PCT; you're out here to hike **the** PCT.*

After all the effort and extra miles, I couldn't give up on my connected steps just to get to pizza twenty-four hours earlier.

Could I?

My convictions felt suddenly hollow. I took a lingering moment to stare at the footprints headed away from the ankle-wrenching terrain and toward the pizza-and-beer terrain. We stood eleven miles from rest, eleven miles from warmth, eleven miles from endless food, eleven miles from Melanie. We could be sitting down in a heated truck in *six hours*.

Every shred of resolve I held for an efficient entrance into Mammoth was buckling. It was almost guaranteed if I suggested we exit through Duck Pass, Amped and Thor would jump at the opportunity.

Rebelling against every shred of base instinct screaming at me, I turned to face the long hillside ahead and stepped past the junction for Duck Pass. My trail-devil popped up onto my shoulder.

What are you doing?! the red, pointy-horned little guy demanded. *Almost guaranteed, if you skipped this next section along with everyone else, you'd be able to still tell everybody you "hiked the Sierra." Who's going to know the difference? Get out of the weather, hike twenty fewer miles, and re-enter the backcountry at an easier trailhead. Don't be so stubborn. Nobody would know!*

"I'd know," I responded to my cartoonish hallucinations (an activity I hoped wouldn't become too regular).

Seven miles of sidehilling were between us and camp. The rumbling clouds above us sank into the canyon, swallowing the peaks around us. Salt was sprinkled into the wound as raindrops began to tap our shoulders with Duck Pass still in sight.

"Faaantastic," I muttered, flipping my hood up.

Amped and Thor had the option of hiking out at Duck Pass. I was the only one in the group concerned with exiting to Mammoth efficiently because I was the only one coming back to pick up where I left off. But these two were teammates to the bitter end, stoically turning their backs to Duck Pass in solidarity with their stubborn buddy.

Our uncomfortable hillside traverse shifted into a confusing, broken cliffline. We kept being pushed downhill under a growing cliff, with no options to regain our lost elevation. I finally stopped to force a GPS location through the spotty storm.

"Dang. We're way below the trail," I said, annoyed with the objective information when it finally appeared on my inReach.

Getting back above the cliffline should've been simple. All we had to do was reverse the half-mile or so until we could correct our course—but backtracking any ground this close to Mammoth felt too insulting to handle. So we continued on as the raindrops picked up. A weakness in the cliff appeared, and we climbed between ledges, hoping to connect runnels of snow to the top. At the very end of the climb, feet away from being back on track, another dark, bottomless gap appeared in a solid band separating us from the top of the cliffs. I peered down into the crevice with one reflexive hand on my inReach.

Amped wandered around the corner and shouted, "Over here!"

Thor and I followed his voice to where he'd found a thin snowbridge spanning the gap. We were wary of snow next to sun-soaked granite. We knew it meant trouble. Unfortunately, by this point we were also too soggy, tired, and burger-deprived to remember what we knew.

Amped stepped out onto the snowbridge with his huge, right snowshoe, which seemed solid until he went to move the other foot. In a flash, Amped's right leg—snowshoe and all—vanished under the bridge. His mass came to a jarring halt once his groin made contact with the ice.

Judging from the "Uu-UHNN" noise—which took a painful uptick the moment his testicular air bags absorbed 230 pounds of free-falling force—Amped was going to need a minute.

A minute is a *really* long time to not make any smashed teste jokes.

Amped lay still long enough to reflect back on better times—such as when he'd voluntarily passed the junction to Duck Pass—then braced to excavate himself. But one hand punctured right through the snowbridge with little to no resistance, followed by the next. My instincts were to move in and help, but I didn't dare walk out onto the fragile bridge with him. All three of us froze, unsure what to do. The depth of the void under Amped was a big unknown.

Amped extracted his arms and sat up, which was apparently the last straw for that tired bridge. Time slowed to a crawl as the entire snowbridge shifted and began collapsing with our teammate entangled in its surface. In an adrenaline-fueled snap, Amped bunched up his left leg, settled his snowshoe points on a patch of adjacent rock, and stallion-kicked with all of his might. The snow crumbled away from his trapped leg and Amped came to rest with his torso over the cliff's edge, his legs dangling in space. Against the flopping weight on his back and long snowshoes, he awkwardly fought to get his lower half on top of the cliffline.

With wide eyes and hammering breathes, Amped stood and peered down to where the collapsed snowbridge had fallen.

"Jesus. There's a cavern under there!"

Rumors of room-sized voids under the snow were common, but that was the first time we'd actually *seen* one, and they'd likely become more prevalent as the days progressed into summer. Thor and I decided to head around one more corner, where we found a very stable snowbridge insultingly close to where Amped had almost been swallowed.

Summit fever was setting in. That soft snowbridge shouldn't have been trusted. Mammoth was our summit, and Amped pushing onto that sketchy bridge was a poor choice—one neither Thor nor I had attempted to stop.

Rain intensified, saturating the snow and turning our acceptable slush into loose garbage. Our morale tanked, taking our pace with it. In a sub-one-mph crawl, we kicked one torqued-sideways set of metal points into the slush after the other.

The swirling gray ceiling lowered until we were also enshrouded in the storm. Temps dropped back into the thirties and kept lowering. Fully sheathed in rain gear, we marched in a silent row through the fog, staring at the slush in front of us. My warmth was slipping, even while I was actively moving—one of the telltale signs of freezing rain.

Freezing rain is rain at or near thirty-two degrees, and is one of the more sinister arrows in Mother Nature's quiver. A little colder, and the rain turns to snow, which glances right off jackets. A little warmer, and it's easy enough to stay warm while moving. It's a tough foe, no matter how much experience in the outdoors you have.

Amped and I had been chased out of the Sierra by freezing rain on a training hike before I'd started the PCT. We'd stubbornly pushed into a winter storm, heading into the backcountry. We were determined to suffer, to learn every hard lesson there was to learn in that hellish class-room—but we'd found ourselves unable to stop, for *anything*. Pausing to add layers or eat a snack was too much. The evaporative cooling from our body's moisture coupled with the cold rainwater and sleet stripped our body heat with alarming speed. Our expensive, top-of-the-line gear couldn't stop it. Ten miles in, our resolve buckled, forcing us to turn around and deathmarch back through the two feet of accumulated slush to a road where Melanie could get to us.

When we'd reached the truck, neither of us had feeling in our extremities. My hands were completely inoperable. Melanie literally had to walk around the truck and open the passenger door for me.

"You think we could've set up camp like this? If we would've stayed out?" I'd asked Amped, sitting in the backseat of our truck.

He'd scoffed. "*Hell* no."

Even with all their layers on, Amped's and Thor's lips were pale and shivering. Thankfully the rain came and went in pulses, giving us some relief between downpours, but the wet cold continued to work its way in. I could *swear* water was getting through my fancy DWR jacket. I brushed the thought off as baseless paranoia. It was a rain jacket, after all. Rain couldn't get through a jacket *specifically designed* to keep rain *out*.

Mmhm.

Through the peripheral outline of my cinched hood, I stared numbly at my repetitive, snowshoed steps. I had nothing else to think about aside from food. There was trail mix in my waist belt pocket, but I didn't dare stop to pull it out. I had to keep moving. This wasn't a training hike. We were still at least twelve hours from reaching help. Even a helicopter was unlikely to get there in time if any of us slipped into hypothermia. Starting a fire in such soggy conditions would be damn near impossible.

In exquisite detail, I daydreamed about the food I would conquer in Mammoth. I could almost taste the warm, savory juices of my future bacon avocado cheeseburger—the crisp, slightly charred pizza crust under stringy, melted cheese, pepperoni, mushrooms...

My stomach growled in extended rumbles while I tormented myself, but I couldn't help it. The idea that tomorrow we'd not be walking, but *driving* through an endless supply of delicious food was impossible to ignore. Really, there was nothing better suited to distract me from the cold.

We crossed the 900-mile marker. Rather, we *walked above* the buried marker. I figured it would be a good spot to stop, maybe build my own "900" out of sticks and pine cones to celebrate 200 miles in the snow—but nobody was going to stop, including myself. The faint heat we were producing from hiking was just *barely* enough. The consequence of stopping wasn't one we felt at liberty to explore.

The sidehilling finally relented, and the trail cut through thick forests where bear prints criss-crossed our path. To zero fanfare, we arrived at the junction for Mammoth Pass, where we'd agreed to camp for the night. Rain continued to fall in sporadic intensity, never stopping, but never fully opening up past a mild downpour. The temps had settled right at freezing.

"It doesn't look like we're going to be fortunate enough to get snowed on," I said, fighting to keep my tone cheery. "Just cold rain, at least until we get camp set up. Maybe our last tent stakes will usher in the snowflakes."

I gave my partners a weak smile that wasn't returned.

On auto-pilot, we found the biggest tree in the area to temporarily shelter under. Less rain was coming through the tree's branches, but the drops collecting on the pine needles were much bigger, falling down onto the trio of hikers below with loud taps on stiff jackets and backpacks.

I pulled my jacket zipper down to have a peek inside. I felt *drenched*. A billow of moist steam—my precious body heat—rolled out and dissipated. I poked a finger into my soggy thermal.

Yep. Drenched.

Trapped body moisture could theoretically drench you from the inside, but that wasn't this. My jacket had failed, even after renewing its DWR waterproofing before Kennedy Meadows. The aggressively helpful, ultralight zealots online had ensured me *repeatedly* that was all the jacket needed. Of course, it had long since been made clear the advice I'd found online had been spotty, at best. But I found something potentially even *more* irritating than how poor the advice had been: how damn *confidently* it had been given.

These weren't people offering humble advice with asterisks of potential shortcomings; these were people who would swear on their mother's graves their words were the guaranteed path to success. In this particular instance, many had been one *hundred* percent on team-DWR, positive that one of their ultralight jackets would **only** fail if the water-proofing had worn out, or if the hiker drenched themselves in sweat.

In their defense, I'm sure they'd never experienced their jackets failing while dangling on a dusty hanger in their basement. And sure, those helpful chaps could've actually gone out to gain knowledge from actual experience, but where was one supposed to find time to test out gear with so many people seeking advice on the internet?

Without options, I zipped my sopping layers back up. My stomach overruled my shivering, and I pulled out my bear canister along with Thor and Amped to shuffle through the unappealing, strictly rationed contents. I was so tired. Even the effort to open my last salmon packet seemed unbearable. We all remained silent, staring at our last bits of food.

Amped broke the silence. "You really want to continue on from here?"

Both of their faces told me they were done, over the cold and snow. Ready to go home.

I took a second to reply. "I absolutely *don't* want to continue—who in their right mind would? But if I don't push out to Agnew Meadows, and instead we all exit right now, I'll pay for it later."

My teammates didn't reply.

The tapping on our packs picked up. Mammoth was still a disappointing seven slushy miles away. We were all already exhausted from the relentless sidehilling. Everything was wet. Everyone was cold. Setting up camp would be a monumental task with slippery, numb fingers.

"Screw it," I said. "Let's get out of here."

Morale instantly skyrocketed. Amped lit off his Jetboil, serving up cup after cup of boiling water for our various Ziploc bags. Exiting that night meant we could eat the rest of our food in our bear canisters, which was dinner, dessert, *and* all the next day's food!

In our soggy snow pit, we feasted, finally relaxing our willpower to eat every last calorie we had. We socked away all the coffee, soup, and—of course—oatmeal, we could handle.

In a perpendicular vector to the PCT, we marched toward Mammoth Pass with a renewed vigor I didn't think we had left inside of us. Before we'd made it a half-mile, Thor dropped his pack in a clenched rush.

"I gotta stop, guys," he said, digging the trowel from his backpack in a bit of a panic. For the second time that day, the giant Aussie shuffled into the woods, cursing into the forest.

"Damn oats!"

We followed bright blue cross-country ski markers through the forest, a welcome break from navigating with GPS. We topped Mammoth Pass and headed downhill toward Mammoth Lakes Basin, an extremely popular and busy cluster of lakes—typically.

Tomorrow was June, but Horseshoe Lake and its large parking lot were still under six feet of snow. The signs of civilization sent a flood of relief through me. I could've kissed the mostly buried, graffitied, heavily trafficked pit toilets—but I figured I'd save those kisses for Mel.

Aw.

We walked along the snowy road, enjoying ski markers, traffic signs, and tourist marquees. Loud, heavy-metal music emanated from a cabin with an open cooler sitting on the porch. The music, the warm light, the sighting of beer—all of it felt so alien, so exciting.

The road transitioned from snow to asphalt. We'd done it. The High Sierra were done. And Thor—well Thor was still alive; alive and heart-healthy, if oatmeal marketing had taught me anything.

We stopped next to a cabin to remove our crampons for one last time as a team. A couple bundled up in the gray afternoon noticed the plethora of metal points protruding from the outside of our packs.

"Hey guys, enjoy your hike?" the man asked.

In unison, all three of us burst into an involuntary laugh. That was a tough question.

"It was, eh—great," I replied.

The man lifted a curious eyebrow. "Where'd you hike out of?"

"Kennedy Meadows."

He scrunched his face, probably expecting to hear a location nearby in the Mammoth Lakes Basin. "I'm not familiar. Where's Kennedy Meadows?"

Amped pointed back into the jagged, white backcountry. "About 200 miles that way."

The man was blown away. He congratulated us, shook all three of our hands, then handed his phone to his girlfriend, demanding he get a picture with us. We enjoyed our minute of celebrity status. Even if it was just one tourist in Mammoth, we were a pretty big deal now. Fighting through the paparazzi to get to Melanie was certain to be a challenge.

In a plowed lot just before the locked gate leading up to the Mammoth Lakes Basin, our lone silver truck came into view, no paparazzi in sight. Our trail angel appeared from the driver's side with her big, beautiful smile. An equally big (but debatably as beautiful) smile spread across my face. Seeing her smile again was never guaranteed, and as long as I live, I'll never forget it.

Armed with donuts and hot chocolate, Mel rushed us into the warm truck. "So? How're you guys feeling?"

With three dumb smiles, we sat in silence, unsure where to begin.

"Well," I said. "Thor's still alive."

We unleashed an onslaught of stories, telling Mel all the details of our trip. In the warm security of civilization, the endless snow and raging creeks already seemed absurd.

THE STORM II

At Zpizza in Mammoth, we arrived ready to consume every calorie in the establishment. Amped ordered two pitchers of beer and two gigantic, extra-large pizzas piled with various meats and crisp, real vegetables that had never seen the inside of a dehydrator. All conversation halted when those heavenly circles were slid under our noses. They didn't last long. Not wanting to get in the way, Mel ordered a separate, small pizza.

We ate that too. (Well, the part she let us eat. I'm not crazy.)

With our bellies full for the first time in weeks, Mel drove us to the BLM campground in Crowley Lake, our usual home for the summers. I caught Amped's eyes in the rearview mirror and smiled.

From Amped's journal:

An overwhelming feeling of accomplishment begins to fill my worn body. We did it. Seventeen full hiking days and 240 miles through the snow-covered cold of the beautiful Sierra mountains has me rendered full. Full of life, and humility. It'll be a story I one day may tell my grandchildren. How their old grandpa braved one of the highest snow years on record and came out weary, but successful.

Being inside felt almost strange. I stepped out of the trailer to sit on the concrete picnic table and gaze into the towering mountains.

Amped and Thor were done with the Sierra, and truthfully, I—was jealous. I wanted it to be over. I was tired, drained, and sore. I was done, too!

But smoldering under that exhaustion-fueled jealousy was a renewed fire. I'd learned *so much* in the High Sierra. My confidence in the snow had grown twenty-fold since Kennedy Meadows. Part of me was excited for the next challenge, ready to pit my refined skills against the notorious rivers in Tuolumne.

Although I was losing my teammates, I wouldn't be alone. Steve, the same friend who'd helped resupply us at Kearsarge Pass, was joining me for North Yosemite. He didn't have much snow experience but was a lifelong rock climber with a level head and an unrelenting positivity.

My mind drifted forward beyond Mammoth, impatient to know what I needed to prepare for. The unfeeling granitic peaks lining the flank of the

CRUNCH

Eastern Sierra stood in front of me like a fortress. Being *outside* of the range felt almost more intimidating than hiking *through* it.

"How much more are you going to let me get away with?" I muttered into the fading dusk light.

24
REST...ISH

JUNE 1-3, 2017
CROWLEY LAKE BLM CAMPGROUND

Two thirty a.m.

I finally gave up, got out of bed, and wandered to the back of the trailer where my fellow insomniacs were already sitting up. Our bodies were ready to go, ready to tear down camp, ready for some billowing coffee, ready to move over hard ice to the next pass—but there was nothing to do but relax, something we couldn't seem to indulge in.

I flicked on the light in our minuscule bathroom, and it took a second to recognize the man in the mirror. I hadn't seen myself in weeks. My beard had grown into a new unwieldy stage, but the most shocking sight was my torso. Two branching veins protruded from the skin on either side of my abdomen, erratically crawling toward my chest. I traced the foreign blue lines with my fingers in amazement—and fear.

Because of my undying affection for donuts and cheeseburgers, I'd never had much of a six-pack. My upper two abs were usually there, maybe upper three if I blurred my eyes and flex-grunted to within a hair of unconsciousness. After over 200 miles through the backcountry, eight distinct ab muscles were in the mirror, which would've been neat if my sunken chest and arms didn't look like I'd stumbled out of Auschwitz. I slid a small scale out of its stowed slot.

One hundred and fifty-five pounds, a solid twenty lighter than when I'd left Kennedy Meadows.

I poured myself a Nalgene full of water and wandered outside to sit back on the concrete picnic table under the stars. The cold breeze coming off the mountains was oddly pleasant.

The next section was the supposed "dangerous" part. During past high snow years, the few accounts I could find had actually mentioned little about the High Sierra, focusing more on the creek crossings north of Mammoth. I'd gained a healthy skepticism of the stories and information online, but that didn't mean I could forget stories of quarter-mile-long wades, leaping from logs to shorelines over fatal rapids, and swimming through channels of snowmelt. My mind had created palpable scenes I'd never actually experienced, and played them in my head on a permanent loop.

For the first twenty-four hours Amped, Thor, and I were back in civilization, we ate. We ate *a ton*. When we weren't actively eating, we were brainstorming where to eat next. While we *were* actively eating, we'd *also* be thinking of where we'd eat next. We were an unstoppable trio of food-destroying machines.

Thor ordered zero bowls of oatmeal.

The second day, Amped returned to Vegas, proud of a successful completion of his longest, most difficult hike yet. It was bittersweet to watch him drive off into the desert. He'd been a great partner. I was nervous about heading back into the mountains without him.

Thor had decided to stick around Mammoth for an extended rest period. His rough plan was to skip about 120 miles ahead to Sonora Pass, which was still heavily snowed in, but beyond the dangerous North Yosemite crossings.

For three days, I rested in Mammoth, as much as a guy about to voluntarily stroll into a lion's den could rest. Unknown to Thor and Amped, or even Mel, conflict was raging inside me. I'd set a goal. I was going to bring myself up to this challenge, not water it down until it suited my tastes. I wouldn't be satisfied until I either succeeded or failed in the process.

But.

The next challenge was big, possibly *too* big, and whatever "failed in the process" looked like kept my mind uncomfortably churning, demanding I reexamine my plans—and my motivations.

Three days was too much time to think, while nowhere *near* enough to recover physically. My soreness rose exponentially through all three days. Each morning I woke more sore than when I'd gone to bed. W*eeks* of rest might've been necessary to find the apex of my soreness, and possibly weeks more to completely heal, but time wasn't a luxury I had. Days were getting longer and warmer. Snowmelt was accelerating, feeding creeks that were getting more dangerous by the hour.

Three days would have to do.

The rumor mill was churning online and in the Eastern Sierra hostels. Hikers continued to pool in Kennedy Meadows, Bishop, and Mammoth. Most were busing or hitchhiking north in search of dry trail. Like Fireball, some had talked themselves into walking hundreds of miles along the highway to bypass the Sierra, God bless 'em. Many had outright quit, tired of the snow interfering with their romantic idea of a PCT hike.

Returning to the twisted world of social media wasn't pleasant. While the handful of early-season hikers slowly chipped away at the backcountry miles, those who'd given up or experienced accidents took to the internet. Post after post from the weakest and least prepared among us broadcasted harrowing stories and doomsayer proclamations, assuring all aspiring Sierra hikers they were guaranteed a cold, snowy death. I wasn't brazen enough to proclaim the Sierra had been a happy-fun-joyland of rainbows and unicorns, but the objective reality was no one had died (even with Thor trying his damnedest).

Very few had ventured into the Sierra behind us. I read bizarre attempts to *shame* those like myself, who had entered or planned to enter the Sierra. Our example, you see, was *hurtful* for those who were unprepared and/or unmotivated to attempt the snow. Our successful completion of the stretch between Kennedy Meadows and Mammoth was an *attack* on those who had made the devastating decision to skip ahead.

Please.

I wasn't going to launch an online crusade in defense of what I'd done, because—aside from the pure idiocy of the grievances—arguing online is about as effective as arguing with the driver next to you in traffic. Instead, I organized my photos and videos of what we'd experienced and posted them on my website.

The *nerve*, I know.

Cheeto-stained, basement enthusiasts united to accuse me of encouraging *everyone* to head into the Sierra. By virtue of posting those photos and videos online, I was coercing hikers who otherwise would've skipped the Sierra to head on into the backcountry where they would surely parish. I was a *murderer*—or something.

But my goal was far from convincing people to attempt or not attempt the Sierra, rather to simply build a resource. Hikers could ignore all the fear mongering and look at the conditions with their own eyes, then make an informed decision to skip or not skip the snow. It was a collection of information I would've killed for a month prior. I felt I owed it to the thru-hiking community. Those who would venture into the snow would be safer because of it, and those who skipped ahead could do so with absolute certainty they'd made the right decision for themselves.

Just as we'd come into Mammoth, Breeze and Monster—the towering, ex-military German—had left to push ahead into North Yosemite. Through conversations with hikers in the hostels, we pieced together what had happened to Breeze on the backside of Mount Whitney, where he'd left the help message etched into the bank of Whitney Creek. He'd pushed into the High Sierra solo almost a week before our team, but hadn't prepared for the severe cold. His phone and battery packs had rapidly drained, and had no method of recharging them. Alone, days into the snow, and with no trail to follow, his sole method of navigation and SOS was dead. He'd sought shelter at the Crabtree Meadows ranger station, approximately one mile east of his ominous message, in hopes other hikers would see it before he ran out of food.

Nobody did.

Fortunately, the same group he'd separated from passed through Crabtree Meadows after hiking up and over Mt. Whitney, but they walked right by the ranger station without any idea Breeze was inside. A *day* later, Breeze found their faded footsteps in the snow—and *took off after them*—moving further into the backcountry in a Hail Mary move to catch up to the owners of those footsteps. That maniac managed to reach the group, and joined them over Forester Pass.

That leading crew had splintered along the way to Mammoth. Some had bailed out of the High Sierra via an assortment of passes. The remaining members had fractured in the harsh environment. We heard stories of the "team" camping up to a mile away from one another due to disagreements about mileage, pace, and creek crossings. One pair went far down off the PCT into the Fish Creek Valley, attempting to navigate around the big river crossings only to find even more water, causing them to split, as well. The team members had trickled into Mammoth effectively solo.

Amped, Thor, and I had our disagreements, but we'd been able to stick it out together. I was glad we'd made it to Mammoth without losing our camaraderie and friendship. It wasn't even like we'd been on the verge of tolerance with each other. If I could've had both Thor and Amped by my side heading into North Yosemite, I would've leapt at the chance.

Of the ten to fifteen hikers who had left Kennedy Meadows ahead of me, there were five left: Sneaky—a mellow friend I'd spent some time with in Southern California—Breeze, Monster, Roadrunner, and Longstride. I'd camped with Roadrunner once in Southern California. He was perfectly nice, but I'd never been in the presence of such a radiating ego. He was running marathons *on the side* of twenty-five mile days along the PCT—objectively badass, and he clearly knew it.

As for Longstride, well, I'd spent an entire day death-marching through the desert to get away from Longstride. The braggadocious beanpole had graced me with her presence one night, pitching her tent an inch from mine in a wide open clearing. I spent that evening listening to her boast about her daily mileage and connecting her steps with absolute purity—which included hiking through every illegal and officially closed section.

It was an illuminating one-way discussion. I, for one, had always been puzzled why anyone with strong legs would bother with integrity.

There was comfort having Monster and Breeze leading the charge into North Yosemite. Having the two strongest bulls sampling the terrain was a good test for the rest of us. If they couldn't do it, common sense would suggest no one else try.

During my three days in Mammoth, I sorted through my gear, removing the few items I hadn't used while supplementing my pack with items I sorely needed. Amped was leaving his Jetboil stove behind for me to use through North Yosemite. It wasn't the lightest stove option, but it was quick, easy, and had performed flawlessly through the High Sierra. A heavier but much better headlamp was added to my kit (right after I dropped my ultralight headlamp in the trash—and maybe spit on it a little). My heavy snowshoes were staying with me. I was tempted to leave my crampons at home to save a few pounds but decided against it.

Despite my respectable winter-gear base weight of twenty pounds, my pack inflated into the low-fifties, by far the heaviest pack I'd ever carried while backpacking. Most of the additional weight was food, so it was easy to rationalize a rough first week in exchange for a heavenly pile to eat at each meal.

Aside from the terrain, the next biggest unknown was my new partner. Steve had expressed a desire to do a stretch of the snow with me, and I took him up on the offer. We'd been good climbing friends for a long while in Bishop but had never undertaken any hard objectives in the backcountry together.

Why not start with the hardest section of the PCT in a record snow year?

Mel and I had met the reserved Englishman years back. As we'd traveled around the Southwest to different climbing areas, we kept running into Steve in his restored Westfalia van. He was always good, positive company, and we climbed more and more together, but getting to know him was difficult. Questions about him or his past were always answered as shortly as possible, without much detail.

REST...ISH

For years, we knew Steve was a strong, quiet, amiable guy, and well—that was about it. But with enough prodding, we learned some surprising things. You know those smartphone cameras we all have? And how incredible the pictures turn out with zero editing? He was part of a small team who developed that technology. His team was later acquired by a struggling company expanding into the smartphone market: Apple.

Steve's full-on life of high education and high-earning jobs eventually led to an unshackling from the American Dream to regain his time and recenter his life around climbing. I was taking Steve into the unknown territory of long-distance mountaineering, but with his sharp mind and calm personality, I was sure he'd be able to handle whatever we came across.

We dropped Thor off at the Mammoth hostel for the last night before I headed back into the snow. It was no problem having Thor camped out with us in our trailer, but there was a certain need for Melanie and me to spend a night alone.

You know, so we could, eh—play checkers.

Nothing gets me in the mood for sex like checkers.

25

RED'S MEADOW

My heart leapt at the sound of my alarm, tearing me out of a fitful sleep haunted with scenes of Thor rolling in Bear Creek and dangling above dark ice chutes. Against the resistance of a billion(ish) sore muscles, I groaned into the seated position and lowered my head into my hands while my heart rate slowed.

It was three a.m. on the 4th. That's when I was heading back into the Sierra. At least that's what I'd committed myself to the hundred times I'd been asked.

With much more grace, Mel sat up next to me and put her hand on my back. "Are you ready for this?"

"You think it's too late to just be, like—a *really* dedicated knitter?"

I stood up in the dark trailer and flipped on the light to reveal the organized pile of snow gear and technical layers I'd set out the night before. My sweet wife had a big breakfast and coffee ready for me by the time I had all of my alpine gear on. The heavy weight of my boots and constricting warmth of my thermals was oddly comforting. I strapped all of my sharp metal gear onto my backpack, including a shiny new axe from Thor, and hefted the oppressive weight onto my shoulder—and it almost felt *good*.

I can do this. I've already done 200 miles of it. Remember, this isn't exactly the cutting edge of alpinism.

Those last words had come from Steve's mouth about six months earlier. We'd met at the local coffee shop to chat about my concerns revolving around hiking the Sierra section so early. Steve was a level-headed guy with extreme intelligence, so I respected his perspective.

"Not that the snow travel won't be difficult," Steve had said in his heavy British accent. "But you won't be summiting any peaks. You'll essentially be just—*walking*, right? This isn't the Himalaya at 25,000 feet. You'll be at worst what? 13,000?"

I'd nodded with a contemplative frown.

"Again, I don't want to diminish your trek, it will obviously be hard—but it's not exactly the cutting edge of alpinism."

I found comfort in those words; if nothing else they served as a mental trick to knock down the intimidation a peg or two. He was also objectively correct. Hiking through the snowy Sierra was far from the biggest challenge ever undertaken in the alpine. But I was also just a donut-enthusiast/climber from Bishop, not freakin' Ueli Steck soloing up the vertical north face of the Eiger.

Steve pulled up to our dark campsite in his van. An hour later, we clicked on our headlamps, said goodbye to Melanie, and walked past the reflective orange gate into the waiting darkness.

The snowy road Amped, Thor, and I had hiked out several days earlier was now mostly plowed, a sign of the town's valiant battle against the snowpack. Mammoth's economy revolved around tourism, especially in the summer when the ski resort slowed down. But most of the summer attractions were still inaccessible, blocked by iced-over roads that had to be chipped out before tourists could visit. Mammoth would be lucky to have their summer attractions up and running for two months before the snow returned for the winter.

The night had been relatively warm. Expansive, thin sheets of water silently trickled across the road. After crossing through the fourth or fifth sheet, Steve looked over at me with a cheeky smile. "It's a relief to get the scary ones behind us."

When the asphalt ended, we strapped on our snowshoes and slogged past the buried pit toilets at Horseshoe Lake. The snow hadn't come anywhere close to refreezing overnight. This was the warmest morning I'd hiked through so far, and more warmth was in the forecast. At first glance, all those full suns and comfy conditions on my phone's weather app were a welcome sight. What could be better for an outdoor romp in the Sierra? But those sunny, warm days were a wolf in sheep's clothing.

A beautiful alpenglow illuminated the Mammoth Crest just before we disappeared into the trees. Steve's only experience with snowshoes had been with the standard, tube-framed style, which had about as much prowess on angled snow as greased-up dinner plates. He'd borrowed Amped's alpine snowshoes, and I spent some time coaching him how to use the new weapons on his feet. Of course, on sloppy snow, we weren't in an ideal classroom. Learning to trust snowshoes on steep slush was like taking trust falls at a cannabis convention.

Four exhausting, sloppy miles later, we reached the buried PCT. The snow pit Amped, Thor, and I had been sheltering in several days ago looked much more pleasant under a bluebird sky. That miserable moment felt like a thousand years ago.

Making forward progress along the PCT again felt good. Snow miles were hard miles, so every foot spent getting to and from the trail was irking, although a necessary evil for rest and resupply. We had twelve days of food on our backs, theoretically enough to make it 121 miles to the mythical Sonora Pass, just beyond the northern boundary of Yosemite National Park. If we made it to Sonora in one piece, we'd be past the major creeks and past the most dangerous section of the Pacific Crest Trail.

Steve and I headed back into the ankle-wrenching territory my team had been dealing with the last day before pulling into Mammoth—only this time, our traction wasn't biting. It was a brutal training ground for Steve. The slush was working in direct opposition to my encouragement to trust his gear.

I'd spent the morning praying the switchbacks leading down into Red's Meadow would be dry enough to make some quick miles—and I'm sure the trail gods got a kick out of that. Steve quickly learned of yard-saling after we both took turns demonstrating the proper technique. The slushy mountainside was peppered with mud patches, rocks, branches, and other ass-jabbing obstacles for us to sample.

What I'd hoped would be several easy miles into Red's Meadow turned into a messy stretch of digging muddy ice sticks out of our waistbands. Several gushing creeks stopped us in our tracks and took some time to cross safely. This part of the John Muir Trail was typically very dry. I'd never seen a *drop* of water along these switchbacks, much less struggled to cross any full-blown creeks!

A strong sun welcomed us into the open valley floor nearing Red's Meadow Resort. Blackened totem poles stretched out for miles in every direction, remnants of the 1992 Rainbow Fire. The cafe at Red's had always been a favorite place to satisfy some hiker hunger and trim a few tear-jerking ounces from the wallet. But the resort was still lifeless, closed until the plows succeeded in clearing the access road.

We paused at the junction to the resort to hold a moment of silence to process my grief. Daydreams of bacon and pancakes got my appetite going. I made it roughly thirty steps beyond the Red's junction before I had to stop for lunch. In old-man-grunt harmony, we landed our packs alongside the Middle Fork of the San Joaquin River with two semi-controlled thuds.

"I can't wait for the day I've eaten the weight out of this monster," I said.

Steve wasn't smiling. Our pack weights were similar, but Steve was a small guy. His body weight was closer to Melanie's than mine. Fifty pounds on him was probably analogous to seventy on me.

"What've we gone so far today?" Steve asked. "Seven or Eight miles?"

"Seven, yeah."

He nodded. "Just a few more for the day then. I feel worked already."

Ten miles? We're doing more than that before camp.

I nodded but didn't reply.

With Sonora Pass being 121 miles from us, and those miles divided by our twelve days of food, Steve was *technically* right to be aiming for ten miles—but the math was fuzzier than that. It was 121 **PCT** miles to Sonora Pass, but the actual distance we'd have to hike was a looming unknown.

Most of the creeks in North Yosemite were going to be too dangerous to cross where the PCT did. An unknowable number of upstream miles would be required to find safe crossings, followed by backtracking those miles to rejoin the trail. So making it across a twenty-foot-wide creek could take miles. Ten miles along the PCT could be ten miles, or it could be thirty. Those 121 miles to Sonora could be 122, or they could turn into 200. A daily mileage goal was almost impossible to calculate—but it was definitely greater than ten.

"Let's shoot for an above-average day while we've got dry trail."

Steve nodded.

Our lunch concluded with another round of elderly groans to shoulder our packs. Minutes later, the trail disappeared under a lovely mix of gigantic treefalls and patchy, postholing ice. Our pace ground to a near halt through the mess. Trail crews were still months away from clearing the debris, and after an hour bushwhacking through downed pines, I was sticky enough to ensure I'd kiss the damn feet of every trail crew member I would ever come across, on every trail I would ever hike—for**ever**.

My hopes of knocking the day's mileage out of the park faded around every bend, where another fallen tree obstacle course was invariably waiting. The "smartest" move was always to leave the trail, where we'd find even *more* fallen trees, with even *sketchier* snow to posthole through. I cursed the dry ground and uncovered trees, longing for the flat, hard, midnight ice in the High Sierra.

Yeah okay, Universe. You win.

We pushed deeper into the mess, reaching a section where several ancient pines had fallen into a cliff-lined corridor. One half-hour string of expletives later, we'd made it only a couple hundred yards. I stopped to check our GPS track.

"Steve—we're not on the trail."

His face sank. "What? Where is it?"

I pointed a sap-stained finger up the steep hillside to our left. "It's been climbing that bank this whole time."

We stared numbly at the GPS screen, unwilling to accept our options were to either reverse the sticky nonsense we'd just pushed through, or find a way up the near-vertical dirt hillside, which could very well include impassible clifflines or steep ice. My irritation was building. We were still well under ten miles into a day I was hoping would be close to twenty.

"Well we're not going back through that garbage," Steve said.

I agreed, and we begrudgingly set off up the loose dirt, beelining for the trail somewhere above. Every step slid back six inches, progressively depositing rocks and silt into my boots until a substantial percentage of the hillside was in there. My legs were on fire squatting my weight up the unstable hillside one leg at a time. My pack was getting heavier by the minute.

At lunch, we'd felt relatively good about our progress. Just two hours later, we stumbled back onto the hard-packed PCT with burning lungs and trembling legs. I'd been used to the wrong turns and tough terrain over the past few weeks, but this was on a new level.

Trying to catch his breath, Steve didn't say anything at first, but behind his eyes was a clear, *What the hell was that?!*

"How far have we gone?" Steve gasped between heavy breaths. "Since lunch?"

"One whole mile."

He scoffed, glanced down at the trail, then met my eyes again. "And that makes what for the day?"

"Nine miles."

"And you wanted to do fifteen or twenty today? We'll be lucky to get to ten."

I cringed. He wasn't wrong though.

As we followed the PCT along the hillside, the treefalls thinned—but our pace was dragging. Both of us were already beyond exhausted. We made it a few more miles until a snowed-over section of the trail stopped us. The angled ice was on the verge of being too steep to cross without crampons. The snow had cleared off the crumbly hillside below the trail, which was tempting—but it was very steep, and of the loose, PTSD-inducing variety.

While I was scanning the hillside, trying to assure myself dirt couldn't fit into boots already full of dirt, Steve made a decision.

"I'm sticking to the trail."

"All right," I replied, happy to get out of sliding down and trudging back up the dirt.

Oops.

Invisible to us, a tiny stream of water had melted out a hollow beneath the surface of the ice on the trail. A loud crack sent Steve's right foot through the shell. The surprise drop was less than a foot, but it sent the inertia of his huge pack toward the dirt hillside we'd *just* decided—quite firmly—we wanted no part of. Steve couldn't stop it. He wobbled, involuntarily pivoted to face uphill, and backpack first—fell *backwards* off the trail.

Steve impacted the hillside with a sharp grunt. I stood wide-eyed and helpless while my friend somersaulted end over end, violently tumbling backwards down the dirt. A few tumbles in, he managed to roll onto his stomach to claw his fingers into the hillside, eventually coming to a rest.

For a tense few seconds, he stayed still with his forehead pressed into the dirt, possibly trying to sort out what had just happened, or maybe taking some time to recall a single reason to remain friends with me.

Still standing up on the trail, now with a clear demonstration of where *not* to step, I locked my face in an empathetic grimace, figuring that was about all I could do to help. I certainly wasn't going to grab my first aid kit and go for a swan dive after him.

"You all right, Steve?" I called down.

He kicked his boots into the hillside and groaned, finally separating his face from the dirt. He unbuckled his pack and rolled it off to the side to get back onto his feet.

"Yeah. I'm good."

Those words sounded more like, "No, of course not, dumbass."

I took a few careful steps, avoiding the thin snow Steve had found (thanks, Steve!). A wave of guilt came for a visit while my partner hoisted his pack onto his shoulders and staggered back up toward the trail.

I should've been first. We've been over this, Danny.

Truthfully, I hadn't expected to find any dangerous situations moving through Red's Meadow, so I hadn't been forcibly assuming the lead. With dirt still adhered to his face, Steve trudged up through the sliding mud. One of his fingers had been ripped open in the fall, and the grip of his left trekking pole was mottled with fresh blood.

While I rested, and, in a feat of super-human restraint, made *no* jokes—not even one about yard saling being typically reserved for snow—Steve regained the trail. He was understandably pissed, and his tone was more curt than I'd ever heard from the mild-mannered Englishman.

"We need to find a place to camp sooner rather than later."

I didn't like that. We were only twelve miles in, which technically *was* over what we needed to average each day—but I wanted more. At the same time, I needed to avoid running Steve into the ground before we even reached North Yosemite.

A mile later, we dropped our packs in a perfect clearing. A message came in from Melanie:

A flood of PCTers came into Bishop from Kennedy Meadows today. Supposedly, a mountain guide with experience on K2 was turned around at the second North Fork of Mono Creek crossing, just a couple days after you guys were there. He bailed to VVR, then hurried to proclaim Mono and Bear Creek impassible.

I was skeptical. The snow was obviously melting, but how could the upstream snowbridges on Bear Creek totally vanish in two kind-of-warm days? As for the second North Fork of Mono Creek crossing, it took a minute searching my maps to even recall which crossing that was. A *massive* snowbridge had made it all but invisible to us, shortly before the slabs climbing up to the Silver Creek waterfall. There was zero chance that behemoth ice slab had melted completely through.

I'd learned to distrust people quick to brandish their resume on the internet. The few bad ass, highly experienced mountain guides I personally knew struggled to remember what their phone looked like, much less remember how to log into their social media accounts. Their lives were consumed by gritty decisions in very real, very consequential environments—and they didn't seem to concern themselves with giving unsolicited advice on Facebook.

It was frustrating to be in the backcountry, unable to contribute to the conversation. I prayed anyone who was prepared and looking forward to tackling the Sierra would find the information I'd put online to see it with their own eyes, preferably before they abandoned their plans because an "experienced" mountain guide didn't know to look upstream.

Once my tent was pitched, I pulled out my bear canister to retrieve my most unnecessary but highly prized luxury item: a small water bottle filled with real half-and-half for coffee. I dug out a little snow cave for it to chill after a day spent sloshing around in a warm pack.

Lounging around camp, Steve's mood lifted and we enjoyed a warm evening hanging out, bandaging wounds, and eating some of the weight out of our packs.

"Tomorrow looks like smooth sailing up to Agnew Meadows, which is about six miles from here." I scrolled my phone screen around, following the red line cutting through topographic lines.

"We should aim for lunch there. Should be an easy day to get ahead in our mileage."

I had the trail gods chucklin'.

26

MINARET FALLS

I pried one eye open to my three a.m. alarm buzzing away somewhere underneath my chest. It felt like a lifetime ago when I'd last woken to an early morning Sierra alarm, even though it had only been five or six days.

I was doubtful waking so early would be worth the effort. It was warm. The four a.m. slush probably wasn't going to be much different than the ten a.m. slush. I peeked outside and a bobbing headlamp inside Steve's tent got me moving anyway.

With a warm coffee in my lap, I enjoyed a calm slice of bliss before what I figured would be a mildly challenging bit of trail.

In my journal that night, I would write: "Miserably hard, slow day."

We set off into the night, guided by our small, bobbing bubbles of light six feet ahead. We'd started hiking a little later than I'd wanted, but that was understandable. The learning curve for our new partnership would be steep, and it would take some repetition to iron out the kinks.

Navigation was tough in the dense forest. Small creeks were everywhere. With our limited light, it was tough to judge the stability of snowbridges. The snowpack wasn't anywhere near frozen, and we took turns having

CRUNCH

our legs swallowed. My trust in the bridges spanning the bigger creeks in North Yosemite was already wavering. Those creeks were capable of swallowing a lot more than just a leg.

A distant roar reverberated through the trees, gaining in intensity until the dim dawn light illuminated a fantastic display of whitewater.

Minaret Falls. It took a bit of purposeful effort to reclose our dropped jaws.

"Holy God," I muttered under my breath.

I hadn't been expecting Minaret Falls to be an issue. There hadn't been a single mention of it in past journals.

Steve leaned in toward my ear. "We're supposed to cross this *here?*"

"THERE'S NOWHERE ELSE TO REALLY TRY," I shouted, struggling to push my words through the roar of the falls, "UNLESS WE WANTED TO REVERSE THROUGH THE MUSH WE JUST CROSSED TO FIND THE TOP OF THE FALLS."

Steve didn't reply, just stood staring across the flooded terrain.

"MAYBE IT'S MORE INTIMIDATING THAN HARD TO CROSS."

The outlet of the falls had swollen far above its typical banks. The PCT was visible, but submerged for hundreds of yards. It took a minute staring into the chaotic puzzle of fallen logs, rushing water, and slush just to decide where to start. We split up, slowly forging our own paths into the maze. We both kept our boots dry through ninety percent of the crossing—and then we arrived at the final, main channel of water.

Most of the waterfall's volume was collecting in a course of steep whitewater, which widened into a swift, eight-foot-deep, twenty-foot-wide section at the PCT. I'd crossed this outlet years earlier. It was hardly remarkable then, just a babbling stream trickling under a couple of modest wooden footbridges. Those footbridges were long gone, swept away by the river that had subsumed the humble stream.

Well this isn't good.

Steve and I scanned up and down the outlet for a viable crossing that didn't involve swimming across whitewater. But upstream progress was limited by cliffs, and downstream was a flooded swamp emptying into

242

the San Joaquin River. Twenty minutes later we stood back at the trail crossing, trying to wrap our heads around our one horrific option. Windy mist billowed off the base of the falls, sending shivers throughout my body.

"YOUR FIRST BIG CREEK MIGHT BE A FULL-ON SWIM," I joke-yelled, unable to keep the apologetic grimace off my face.

Steve glared back at me with ninety percent, *Absolutely not, you psychopathic asshat I should've never befriended,* and ten percent, *Okay, I trust you.*

Although my partner was probably going to be easier to convince than my internal wuss, who refused to entertain the idea that had just slipped out of my mouth. With most hikers skipping to Agnew Meadows, it was possible we were Minaret Falls' first suitors. That was unnerving.

Steve and I split up again. I set off into the swamp, hopping between fallen timbers and wading shallow water to scout another path across the main channel. I spent fifteen minutes stringing together bobbing and unstable logs only to arrive at a dead end, forcing me to reverse back to where I'd started. Then, I put a half-hour into *another* web of logs, just to locate *another* dead end. But on the third attempt—I found something.

A tree rooted in the middle of the deep channel had fallen in our direction and spanned the bulk of the creek. Beyond its upended root cluster out in the creek was more flowing water, but the current looked reasonable. The tree wasn't *entirely* compelling—other than the root cluster, it was fully under water, but a collection of smaller logs had been dammed up by the tree's branches. A couple pokes with a trekking pole didn't exactly shore up my confidence. Every bobbing log spun easily to reveal their sopping wet underbellies. Nothing was anchored, and definitely wouldn't be safe to tightrope across. But it wasn't like this was one of a few choices. This was it—and one bobbing log *did* stretch all the way to the root cluster.

Maybe if we sat down into the water and straddled it, we could scoot across without it spinning, I hypothesized, trying to come up with an optimistic angle to sell to Steve. *Getting just our lower half wet would be a hell of a lot better than an all-out swim.*

From the general vicinity of my underwear, I could've sworn I heard, "For the love of God, keep looking!"

Enough dehydrated potatoes and *anyone's* mental state would decline into some degree of underwear-schizophrenia. All something to worry about if/when I emerged from the PCT alive, where I could kick the trail cold turkey and white-knuckle my way through the potato shakes until my testicles stopped yelling at me.

I wandered back toward Steve, hoping he'd found something less—nippy?

"THERE'S NOTHING," he said, struggling to sufficiently amplify his quiet voice. "WHAT NOW?"

I groaned under my breath. Our morning was about to take an uncomfortable turn.

"FOLLOW ME."

I led my partner across the string of logs until we stood at the edge of our one and only option—or at least the one option that wouldn't involve muttering a soft "goodbye, cruel world" before attempting. Steve also prodded the floating log, spinning it in its place. He wasn't impressed.

"We're crossing here?"

My voice mirrored his doubt, "Um... yes."

"And if we actually get to those roots in the middle? What then?"

I couldn't tell if beyond the cluster was knee-deep or forehead-deep, but I figured it didn't matter. If we still had to submerge ourselves to swim some part of this crossing, at least this would be a milder, shorter swim.

"I'll figure it out if I make it there. This looks like our one option if we aren't turning around," I said.

Steve stared at the bobbing log, not stepping forward—but also not turning around. This was the first major obstacle of our new partnership, and I think deep down, neither of us wanted to be turned around by it.

"All right then," he said, "let's go."

I took a hard swallow and rolled the log with my trekking pole until the most comfortable sliding surface was facing upward. My breath was stolen lowering to straddle the unstable, slippery pole. Snowmelt rolled up my pant legs and into my lap, fully realizing my quarrelsome testes' worst fears. I inched toward the root cluster one wobbly scoot at a time, trying to control involuntary shivers. I'd already been chilled from the slow navigating through the swamp, and now my thighs were submerged in ice water.

Coupled to my pack, I was obviously top heavy, and the log wanted nothing more than to relocate my weight to its underside. It shifted and twitched from side to side, threatening to spin. The stiff current pulled my legs to the side, and strengthened the further I scooted into the creek. A dense jam of logs bobbed on the surface just downstream, nagging in my peripheral. Falling in and being swept under it would be a big problem.

Still a scoot or two away from the most intense current, my ability to maintain my balance was slipping—but the next scoot sank the sharp crampon points on my right foot into something solid.

"Oh, hell yeah!" I called out. "I can reach the main log here!"

With the additional point of stability, I could stop the log between my legs (insert classy joke here) from wobbling, and easily scooted the rest of the way across onto the woven structure of the upended root island.

After an awkward climb up and over the roots (picture a bear giving a whale a piggyback ride while sneaking over the fence to use the neighbor's pool) (or whatever bears and whales do when they hang out), I dipped down into the final channel, which was thankfully just a quick dunk down to my thighs. I gave Steve a thumbs-up and a smile. He returned a stare of pure friendship-regret, shook his head, and lowered his legs into the snowmelt.

Safely on the far side of the main channel, we were all smiles, smug in our victory. The Middle Fork of the San Joaquin was swollen multiple feet above its normal banks, and the end of the shin-deep swamp wasn't in sight.

A hundred yards of slow, northward slogging led us to a dry island, where we caught an elevated view of the incredible flooding, but saw no end to the swamp. The whole meadow under the falls was flooded.

It took a solid quarter-mile of wading to finally step onto sweet, sweet dry… slush. The sun had risen above the trees and we stopped to empty some of the water out of our boots in a patch of light making its way into the pine tree bayou. My drenched crampons were strangled in seaweed-looking grasses, as if I'd gone scuba diving in mountaineering gear.

I checked the time. Nine thirty a.m. We'd made it two miles in over *five* hours. That was Grandma-shuffling-around-the-mall speed—but only if Grandma had lost all her limbs in 'nam and refused to use a wheelchair.

"We're going to have to haul ass from here on out to make our miles."

Steve didn't reply but nodded.

The next single, piddly mile took *two hours*. There wasn't a specific reason or excuse, just tough navigation through loose slush.

We angled toward the raging San Joaquin and found the manmade bridge we needed to gain the far bank. Bridge or no bridge, the rumble of a large river always stood the hairs on the back of my neck up. For Steve, this was a first time being in the presence of that power.

We followed the river downstream, cutting across the steep, mashed-potato slope that led down into the whitewater. The slope's angle worsened, so I slowed my pace to focus on each step, figuring Steve would be close behind, utilizing my compacted footprints. It was a challenge to keep the consequences of a slide from creeping in.

The angle softened a hundred yards later. I called over my shoulder, "Here's to hoping that's as bad as it gets, eh?"

No answer. I turned around—and Steve wasn't there.

He'd stopped, just before the angle steepened. He took a trepid step forward, then reversed it. An inch forward, then back; over and over again, unable to commit to following my footprints across the slope. He wasn't trusting his crampons in the slightest. Unable to do much to help, I waited while Steve eventually moved into the slope but made painfully slow progress. I yearned to keep moving, to settle into a respectable pace, but stayed put until my partner made it to me.

Be patient. He'll gain trust and speed with time.

A quarter-mile later, Steve was still trailing by a healthy margin, even on milder snow. He was rattled. I entered an even *worse* section of the hillside, where the snow was a few degrees steeper than we'd seen, and the San Joaquin was even closer—and louder.

"Steve's going to love this," I muttered.

Even *my* brain stem felt the need to inject a shot of adrenaline venturing above the turbulent river. My body buzzed needlessly while I snailed my way across the slope. Where the snow would allow, I took the time to kick deep, flat platforms, hoping Steve would find some comfort in them.

An ice axe probably should've been in my hands, but trekking poles provided a great amount of stability. They'd be worthless if I needed to arrest a slide, but in the short distance to the river, the odds of arresting a fall were slim, even with an axe. This terrain wasn't going to be forgiving of *any* slip, so trekking poles were preferable to sliding into the whitewater with an axe to kiss goodbye.

I reached milder snow and took a dread-filled second before turning around. Sure enough, Steve had stalled out again.

We were in trouble. This was the second of two days I'd banked on putting a hefty chunk of mileage behind us, and that obviously wasn't happening. We only had so much food to make it to Sonora, with very limited bail options. Moving slow enough to stay safe was obviously important, but we wouldn't exactly be safe anymore if we ran out of food in the middle of Yosemite.

I wanted to shout something back at Steve but didn't know whether the appropriate words were "Hurry the hell up," or "Take your time, buddy. We've got all summer!"

For minutes, Steve made zero progress. I begged the universe he'd sort it out and commit to stepping through my compacted footprints. But instead, he stopped moving and just stared back at me.

"Ughh… Steve."

I started back toward my partner. Crossing the same sketchy slope a second time—and then a subsequent third—wasn't exactly the smartest move, but I didn't know what else to do. No progress was being made staring at each other

But what exactly am I supposed to do when I reach him? Strap him to my pack? Heat the tip of my trekking pole for an impromptu cattle prod?

I planted my crampons in the mush a few yards from my wide-eyed compadre. "How're you doin', bud?"

"I'm sorry. I don't know what it is. I just can't trust my feet. Everything is sliding!"

"This is just like climbing in a dangerous spot where you can't fall. Shut out the environment and focus only on placing each step perfectly."

He shook his head. "This is **not** the same. There's no rope, no pad—nothing to save your damn life if you slip!"

I figured there were better venues for a debate about the similarities between climbing and snow travel, so I dropped it. Our sluggish progress was irritating, but his frazzled state was quite satisfying coming from the guy who'd assured me this—and I'll quote—"wasn't exactly the cutting edge of alpinism."

And I'd gone through terrain a hell of a lot more intense than this.

Steve had a long history of exposure in bouldering, as well as inside the nerve-wracking world of trad climbing. In fact, Steve had climbed many things far above my ability to stay calm through. I'd assumed any exposure we'd come across would pale in comparison, but exposure is tough to handle when you don't trust your gear. New climbers often become gripped when they're first introduced to exposure high off the ground. It's not because they're not safe, their equipment could support a VW Bug without flinching; it's because they haven't yet learned to trust their gear.

I spent a few minutes reiterating crampon techniques I'd honed over the last month, trying to divert Steve's attention from worst-case scenarios.

"Your crampons can handle this, I promise. They could handle snow twenty degrees steeper. I know it feels crazy, but we *have* to move forward. You literally just watched me cross this twice. We're just walking here. Stick right behind me, don't look down, and focus on each step."

He didn't reply—but he also didn't refuse.

"Unless you want to go cross back over Minaret Falls, you have to trust your gear. I *promise*, everything will hold. I wouldn't lead you across anything beyond the capabilities of your traction."

I stayed one step ahead to keep an eye on his crampon placements and to offer encouragement and small critiques. The taunting river never stopped reminding us what an unforgiving classroom we were in.

After one and a quarter eternities, we made it beyond the steepest slope but were far from out of the proverbial woods. There was nowhere to hike but alongside the river, and the angle of the snow shifted between terrifying and slightly less-terrifying for over a mile. Every couple hundred yards, I took a break so he could catch up. As the hours progressed, my frustration began being overtaken by worry.

Is he going to get the hang of this in time? Is all this stress going to erase his psych for being out here? What if he has to bail?

The ever-present roar of the river offered no answers. It simply continued to indulge itself in torturing my teammate.

The miles crept while the minutes flew. The end of the riverside slope came, but messy terrain followed it. Many small, but serious, creeks took time to scan for crossings. Some had beautiful logs spanning the torrents; others were bushwhacks through submerged reed patches cultivated by Satan himself.

Perhaps too hastily, I pushed forward into one thicket—until I couldn't.

"Don't come across just yet," I called over my shoulder. "I think I'm stuck."

Stubborn, elastic branches had wound though my pack straps and clothes. Water of unknown depth flowed under my boots, which were awkwardly jammed sideways between reed crotches. I tried reversing my course but couldn't. I'd never dealt with claustrophobia, but being unable to move in any direction brought up a surge of panic. I pushed with an adrenaline-fueled growl, unleashing all my force to snap whatever reeds were stopping me—and went nowhere.

My manliest moment of manly moments.

I pushed one more time, and while I didn't move forward, I *did* manage some progress in the only direction I *didn't* want to move. My right foot shot out of its jam and into to the marsh underfoot. Thankfully, it wasn't too deep, but now with one leg submerged, and the other still lodged between dry reeds at my waist, I was officially in a tangled mess. One particularly awful branch pressed between my legs, squeezing against parts I typically preferred, shall we say—*unsquozen.*

I wriggled out of my pack, which hovered in place, suspended by the seventeen branches threaded through it. That gave me enough room to shimmy out of my reed prison and rejam my boots above water. I untangled my pack, but couldn't put it back on, so six frustrating inches at a time, I rejammed my feet between the next set of crotches, then reached back to scoot my pack behind me.

Steve was smiling on the other side.

"What?" I asked, likely more curt than I meant.

He shrugged. "Feels good to see you struggle a bit."

All laughed out for the day, the trail gods gifted us with a dry stretch of PCT switchbacking up to Agnew Meadows. We were finally moving at a respectable pace. Twelve hours and a pathetic *five* miles ago, my doe-eyed goal had been to skip our way past Agnew Meadows by lunch, aiming for a fourteen-mile day to end near Thousand Island Lake.

Ha.

But dry trail rekindled my optimism. The day wasn't over. Maybe Steve and I could still put our heads down and crank out an evening chock-FULL of miles. Maybe we'd blow right past Agnew Meadows. Maybe with a pair of heroic scoffs! It would simply take a smidgen of good luck, just enough to keep the trail free from slush for just a few more miles.

One whole smidgen was clearly too much to hope for. Within a half-mile, the snow returned. Ten minutes after that, we were trudging up steep, muddy slush with no idea where the trail had gone.

Morale had officially flatlined. My pack was getting heavier by the step, and we stopped to rest after summiting a rocky ridgeline, panting like dogs. To add to the fun, my GPS signal was struggling to find our location.

"Is that the trail?" Steve pointed to, sure enough, the Pacific Crest Trail—200 *mother f^%$in'* yards down the awful mess we'd just trudged up.

One of my eyelids slid half-closed and froze there.

"Do we—*go back down* to it?" Steve asked between pants.

In a stroke of pure, potato-inspired genius, I shook my head. "No way. We're going to let the *trail...*" an eyebrow flicker here emphasized my strategic brilliance, "come to *us.*"

I led the way, paralleling the PCT along the ridgeline, attempting to neither gain nor lose any elevation while the trail snaked its way uphill toward us. Feeling smug in my superior Sierra navigation skills, we promptly dead-ended at a series of overgrown ledges. Turning around was the prudent move, but instead, I pushed us forward through ledge after ledge of limb-trapping, hiker-stabbing brush.

By the time I figured out we'd made the wrong choice, there was just as much hiker-stabbing behind us as there was in front of us. The lazily winding trail remained visible on the slopes below, taking its sweet ass time gaining elevation to rescue us from my dumbass plan.

We stepped back onto the PCT adorned with leafy branches protruding from our packs, and covered in fresh, red scratches.

Morale had not been improved.

After the longest mile of my life, we arrived in the suncupped fields of Agnew Meadows. My snowshoes riding on the top of my pack were the theoretical weapon of choice. But through my utter exhaustion, I couldn't bring myself to drop my pack to change into them. Instead, I slipped and staggered through the suncups, staring forward toward the campground with the tunnel vision of a bereft man in the Sahara, closing in on a squiggly vending machine.

Buildings in the popular Agnew Meadows campground came into view through the trees. It was a snowy ghost town. A dry patch of gravel adjacent to an unlocked pit toilet needed no further introduction as our camp for the night. Amusingly, the well-worn PCT was our closest water source. It was no trail in these conditions, but a healthy stream almost a foot deep.

Steve and I plopped down our fat, freeloading backpacks next to a couple parking barrier logs and collapsed against them with no remaining willpower to pitch our tents.

It was done—the official shortest and possibly most difficult full day of hiking I'd ever put myself through.

Steve gave me a weak half-smile. "Well shit. That went poorly."

I let out an exasperated laugh.

There was a bit of daylight left, but we weren't going anywhere. Both of us were physically and mentally destroyed. I'd underestimated Red's Meadow to an embarrassing degree.

In the warm sun, Steve dozed off against his pack. I stared at an exposed bit of road, lost in thought, mesmerized by the sheeting water running over the clean, black asphalt.

*Mammoth is only four miles away, by **far** our easiest escape in the next hundred miles.*

My stomach cringed in response.

Going into North Yosemite demanded having Steve with me, but having Steve with me demanded he gain immediate proficiency in snow travel. As if he'd been listening to my internal conversation, Steve turned to readjust against his pack. "Even though today wasn't great, I think we'll be fine. I haven't been hungry at all yet, so my food can easily be stretched a day or two to make up for being slow."

Steve's optimism was heartening, but effectively one day of travel had just taken two. I could stretch my food, but not as far as my partner could. Our individual hunger levels were very different. My partner probably wasn't starting to wonder what his shoelaces tasted like.

A part of me felt obligated to hike with Steve as far as possible, whether or not we made it to Sonora Pass. After all, I'd invited him along and he *had* invested his time and money into this trip. But the other, much louder part of me was desperate to avoid any more extra snow miles. Bailing from somewhere before Sonora was a big unknown, but sure to involve many miles through unfamiliar, dangerous terrain.

My inReach beeped, bringing two messages in.

Apparently, a female hiker was swept away in Horseshoe Creek and narrowly survived. Spent the night without her pack and swam across the Tuolumne to get to the visitor's center. Didn't say the name, but the only female ahead of you is Longstride, right?

Also, a Yosemite ranger posted that the bridge at Glen Aulin is washed out. The one that crosses after Tuolumne Falls, I'm pretty sure.

The Tuolumne River was a big one, even in summer. We'd be facing it, as well as Horseshoe Creek, within the next few days. I took out my phone to check for service, and sure enough, our proximity to Mammoth gave me a connection to the internet.

That was a mistake. Bad news and pessimistic forecasting wasn't in any short supply. It was unsettling that *any* of the hikers ahead could've been taken out. Every one of them were powerhouses, and all more experienced and confident on long trails than I. My whole focus was absorbed into my screen, and I snapped out of it to realize my phone was shaking in my hands. I reinstated Airplane Mode and tucked that black brick of bad news back into its pocket and sat silent. There was so much I needed to talk through, but I didn't exactly want to jump right in and tell Steve how thoroughly screwed we were. He had enough on his plate.

Is it time to get out of here while we're only four miles from safety? Before we become the second and third victim of North Yosemite?'

"A hiker ahead almost died," I said, studying Steve's reaction.

He raised his eyebrows. "Where we're going?"

I nodded. "A few days from here. She got swept away in Horseshoe Creek, supposedly ditched her pack with all her gear. Had no navigation, lost the trail, and swam across the Tuolumne River to get to help."

Steve was very familiar with Tuolumne. In a lower tone, he muttered, "That's a rather large river."

"And it's probably a lot bigger than we've seen before. I'm guessing a tad colder, too."

We both sat still for a minute, quietly pondering the horrors of swimming across a swift, thirty-foot-wide river of snowmelt.

I pointed to the asphalt. "Mammoth is four miles up this road. I obviously don't want to quit, but the reality is we're heading into unsure terrain, and I'm stressed about our pace. You might be able to stretch your food supply for multiple extra days, but my hunger isn't going to allow it. I'm not sure where your thoughts are on adjusting to the snow travel, on figuring out how to trust your traction—but this is the time to bail if that's what needs to happen. If we maintain this same pace through North Yosemite, we're going to be in for some pain when we run out of food and have to find a way to bail there instead."

I took a hard swallow against the words I'd allowed to leave my mouth. Brutal honesty wasn't exactly a wise tactic to keep a partner around. But even more than I wanted a partner, I wanted neither of us to get hurt, at least not without being fully aware of the risks.

"If I can keep up, I'll keep going."

Part of me couldn't believe Steve wasn't going to jump at the chance to get away from me and my absurd trek. I had a great amount of respect for that, especially after such a miserable day.

"All right then," I said.

My inReach beeped again, a once-joyous sound that was starting to grate on my nerves. More bad news. Initial reports had come in about *another* accident in North Yosemite. I groaned and slipped my phone back out of its pocket, almost irritated having such easy access to the horror stories hikers ahead were crafting for us.

Roadrunner was the victim this time, but there wasn't much more information.

This meant two hikers had been involved in accidents in the hundred miles ahead. Two—out of *five*.

I wasn't excited about those odds.

"You ready for some more bad news, Steve?"

27

ISLAND

Two thirty a.m. wasn't exactly an ideal time to crawl out of our warm cocoons into the night. We didn't have a particular pass or crossing to be up early for, no hard snow to capitalize on. What we needed was simple: time.

Our slow pace was going to get us in trouble, and since I'd left my cracking whip at home, more hours to slog was our sole option. The early morning had been Steve's call, and while evening-me had been impressed by his motivation and initiative, 2:30 a.m.-me brooded over the perky, energetic packing noises coming from the other side of camp.

Groaning my way to the sitting position against the resistance of a hundred different sore muscles, I clicked on my headlamp and opened my standard pack of Pop-Tarts. I inhaled the first of the two identical pastries but stopped there for a longing stare at the other half of my breakfast.

If your food has to stretch further, you have to start now.

Stretching eleven days into fifteen would be much easier than waiting until I had one day of food left to last four or five. I'd only eaten half of my mushroom and pepper pasta the night before, even managed to find the self-control to save my dessert Snickers and hot chocolate.

My stomach growled angrily, as if it had a mind of its own—and knew what I was up to. My hiker hunger was definitely back, and I feared it almost to a greater degree than the creeks ahead. Food had become more than just sustenance; it was a euphoric escape five or six times each day, where I could indulge the insatiable, impatient addict inside me. The idea of swimming through ice water was something I could handle. I could *not* handle the idea of starving while being days of hard hiking away from food.

We packed up camp, then set a few minutes aside for one last dignified poop in the campground facilities before reconvening at the edge of the black forest. I paused to take one last affectionate look back at the luxurious pit toilet, which would always hold a piece of my heart.

My ramping affection toward stainy toilets was probably going to be an expensive issue to sort out later.

We headed straight uphill through the snowy forest rising out of Agnew Meadows. Within a mile of camp, the trees ended and the snow disappeared. My heart rejoiced at the sight of dry trail. Trail we were neither above, nor below—but standing *directly on*.

Traversing the hillside, rabbit and squirrel prints crisscrossed through the muddy PCT. A lifeless landscape had become the new normal, and there was comfort in seeing signs of other living things.

Although the damn *grouse*...

With my head down in the dark, dead silence of the early morning Sierra, an innocent bush three inches from my leading foot exploded into a frenzy of flapping wings, feathers, and squawking.

It happened again. Then a third time. Then a fourth.

Every bush explosion challenged my heart's ability to beat fast enough—not to mention my colon's ability to resist its contents from relocating to the suburbs. My pace actually slowed from my increasing suspicion of trailside shrubbery, as if I was walking room to room through a haunted house.

The ninja chickens only gave it a rest when our gained elevation reintroduced snow into our morning and reburied all the brush. The snow was in decent shape, and we spotted footprints from the hikers who'd come back in through Agnew Meadows. The lucky bastards had no idea the torturous joy they'd avoided by skipping Red's Meadow and Minaret Creek.

It was mildly irking that hiking every mile had set me so far back from the lead. I'm not denying there were major benefits to *not* being the first to test out obstacles—but I would've liked to be in Monster and Breeze's lauded position as the "Tip of the Spear." Although, through no effort of my own, I'd gone from sixth to fourth as the Sierra thinned her suitors. Maybe Tip of the Spear was closer than I thought.

Steve and I maintained 1.5 mph through the easy, early morning miles. Not record breaking, but closer to a normal snow pace. Creeks cascading down into the canyon appeared by the dozens, requiring precious time to find ways to cross. The canyon walls steadily steepened until our easy, flat snow became couloirs of steep ice and whitewater. Around every corner was a new, more intimidating snowfield being split by an even angrier creek. Two miles of forty-degree couloirs took us over two hours, but we were moving forward. Flat snowfields came into view as we approached the final couloir, and relief washed over me—until we finished turning the blind corner. A fifty-degree slope of ice smoothed over the trail for hundreds of yards up and downhill.

"Come on," I muttered.

Steve visibly tensed sizing up ice flowing down thousands of feet into the canyon below. Our equipment was absolutely capable of crossing this, and much steeper—but Steve didn't share my confidence.

I set my pack down. "Let's change into snowshoes and take our axes out. There's plenty of self-arresting area below the trail."

"I'd rather have my trekking poles for stability. I don't think my axe would help."

I eyed the slope again. An unarrested slide wouldn't be *guaranteed* deadly—but sure to be long and uncomfortable. I shrugged and sat to strap into my snowshoes. I couldn't force Steve to follow my suggestions. If he didn't trust himself to use his axe, maybe it really wasn't worth being in his hands.

I put up my heel-lifters and side-stepped into the couloir, which was indeed steep, but a far cry from the steepest angle I'd tested my snowshoes on. The shaded gully had kept the snow bullet-hard, so every step was secure. After negotiating a small stream, I stepped onto a patch of exposed trail, successfully on the other side of the couloir with easy snow ahead, as far as the eye could see.

"That wasn't so bad," I muttered to myself. "Steve'll be fine."

That opinion lingered about as long as a fart in a tornado.

My partner hesitantly stepped forward, then back. Up, then down. He was gripped, and trying his damnedest to avoid cutting directly across the couloir. From a hundred yards away, I silently cheered him on—but a half-hour slowly slid by, and my mood slid with it. Steve eventually stopped moving. He'd made no progress, and stood staring across the slope in my direction.

He's... frozen. We don't have time to be frozen.

The brief break from hiking sent my stomach churning. Aside from sleep, physical exertion was the only other activity that somewhat tempered my appetite. An extended break was the last thing I needed if I was going to be able to stick to rationing my calories for the day.

"*Come on*, bud. Just try it," I grumbled through another bout of stomach growls.

With exaggerated arm motions, I pointed along the middle of the path where I'd come across. "YOU HAVE TO TRUST YOUR FEET!"

Steve stood silent for a few seconds, shook his head, then returned to shuffling back and forth, up then down. He climbed to a dry patch higher on the slope and paused at the edge of the ice, trying to find the nerve to step out onto an even *steeper*, even *higher* section than I'd crossed.

Minutes later, my willpower buckled. I put my pack down, ashamedly inhaled the second half of my breakfast, and pulled my layers back out to block the consistent breeze rushing through the gully. My hunger demon wasn't about to be satiated by a single Pop-Tart, so against all of my better judgment, I opened my bear canister and devoured the Snickers I'd saved from the night before—then a second.

With the shame of a recovering alcoholic waking up in a pile of tequila bottles, I tucked my canister deep into my pack and pushed it all away from me. Steve was still standing in the same spot higher on the slope, so I searched around for somewhere to sit until I found the most luxurious sitting rock the screefield had to offer: a wobbly, lopsided number that might've been just a big, sharp clump of dirt. Anxiety welled as the minutes continued to flow by.

It didn't take long until I'd lost feeling in half my ass meat, so I stood back up and began pacing along the trail to get my blood flowing. Steve was slowly reversing back down from the higher patch, back to where he'd started.

"I shouldn't have dragged him into this," I muttered.

It's only been three days for him, you've had almost a month. You be patient, I internally scolded myself.

Right, the other side of me rebutted, *but how many days do we have for him to learn?*

I paced back and forth, giving random butt hemispheres test pinches to see if feeling had returned (it's not as sexy as it sounds). My hunger ramped higher, and waves of shivers strengthened as my warm muscles cooled and stiffened. North Yosemite alone was a bad idea. I knew that—but it seemed like a growing possibility.

Is going ahead solo anywhere near reasonable though? Would it be a logical move, or an insane one driven by overblown ambition? Most importantly—would it be fair to Melanie?

The many creeks had already swallowed a hefty percentage of the hikers ahead. Hell, it was possible *all* of them had been taken out, and the outside world had only heard from the luckiest two. Leaving my wife to deal with losing me was the absolute last outcome I wanted from this trek—but a deep, pessimistic, curious part of me doubted the notoriety of Yosemite.

Clearly, the hikers ahead were being whittled down, but I'd also been watching their footprints for hundreds of miles. They'd painted a picture of *disastrous* risk management in the mountains. The people being taken out were the same folks who'd crossed over Forester and the backside of Glen in the most avalanche-prone time of day, the same people who wandered *downstream* into Fish Creek Canyon to look for better crossings—and were surprised to find more water. Prior to the PCT, what was their experience in the mountains? In the Sierra? How much had they really prepared for this? I'd seen and heard a half-dozen horror stories about the High Sierra before we'd left Kennedy Meadows, but it had been totally manageable. Hard, yes—but manageable.

What were the odds I'd find North Yosemite the same?

Forty-five minutes after we'd arrived at the couloir, Steve committed to link the few dry patches higher up on the slope. Once he finally started, he made slow progress, but crossed without a hitch. I fought to remain patient as he forded the small stream to join me—almost an *hour* after I'd crossed. Conflicting emotions clashed inside me.

YOU asked him to come out here! I scolded myself. *It was a damn miracle he agreed to try this ridiculous trek. What could you possibly be angry about, you ungrateful ass? Who else would even* **consider** *doing this with you?*

Hot guilt tightened the back of my skull right alongside the anger, impatience, frustration, and panic. I struggled to sort out the mess flying through my head. One clear thought emerged through the haze.

He deserves to hear the full ramifications of moving slow, absent of any petty emotions.

"Steve… what was that?" I asked. "We've been here for *way* too long. We don't have the time or food margin to move this slow."

"I know that! I just can't… I don't know what's *wrong* with me. I can't trust my feet!"

I'd never seen Steve so rattled. My frustration evaporated. He obviously cared about trying to move fast. It just wasn't happening. He was clearly more frustrated with himself than I was. It wasn't necessary to further dig at him to drive the point home.

"I'm not sure what change we need to make—but something does need to change. Either your speed needs to increase, or we need to find a way," I paused, hesitant to end the sentence, "for you to exit."

That stung, for both us. It was one of the most difficult things I'd ever had to say to a dear friend. Steve nodded and broke eye contact, looking down at the ground. A heavy lump lodged in my throat while I removed my extra layers and threw my pack back on. I didn't feel the need for further discussion. The ball was in Steve's court. He could either keep up or take himself off the trail. I trusted he'd make the right choice.

We maintained a decent pace through large, sun-cupped snowfields, but it didn't take long before my stomach demanded we stop for lunch. We paused in the shade of some pines to get out of the harsh sun. I put half of a peanut butter packet on one tortilla and took intentionally small bites, trying to savor every calorie. With irrational misery, I tucked away the rest of the packet and my other two tortillas I'd planned for lunch. My stomach made sure to list its grievances.

Heading to Thousand Island Lake, we reached a junction where we needed to head either uphill or downhill. Relying solely on my mountain-seasoned instinct, I consulted nothing and tromped confidently downhill. It took a half-mile to realize I'd chosen incorrectly.

I executed a bitter, humiliating 180 and headed back uphill to wrap up our bonus mile.

"Sorry, man."

Steve didn't say a word to Mr. "We don't have the margin."

We emerged at the outlet of Thousand Island Lake, which had a mild slope to traverse which led down to a cliff's edge over the beautiful, blue water. It was close to noon, and the sun had already baked the snow into a soft, slippery mush. Once again, Steve slowed with the exposure under him.

Uncovered rock slabs perched above the outlet had a couple of perfect sittin' rocks, so I set my pack down to wait for Steve while he was busy having his trust further eroded. I took out the trail mix I'd allotted for the day, picked out four whole cashews, savored every last second of them, and tucked the snack back in my waist pocket.

I wandered down to the outlet to fill my bottles. Island Pass, a small saddle above Thousand Island Lake, was our next objective. The warm alpine sun reflected off the water's surface, a wonderful slice of serenity before the impending torture of trudging up slush in the middle of the afternoon.

Alone, I would've stopped right there for the night. Hiking up passes in the afternoon was anathema to my strategy in the Sierra. But more than I needed ideal snow, I needed Steve to understand firsthand why moving quickly was so crucial. Hopefully experiencing an afternoon pass would nudge him to accelerate his gear trust. We were at a junction where we needed to decide whether Steve was going to stay with me or exit. A bit of willful suffering on my end was necessary.

The completely snowbound Thousand Island Lake was a wonderland. Banner Peak lorded over the immaculate landscape, dominating the horizon. This beautiful lake, peppered with small islands (although not nearly 1,000 of them) had always been a favorite spot along the John Muir Trail. The snowy version was quite literally hard to stop staring at.

At just a hair over 10,000 feet, Island Pass had always been a bit of a joke. I was on the record suggesting "Island Hill" would be more appropriate. The pass remembered those hurtful words—and was excited to get even.

Knee-deep slush covered the entire two miles and 1,500 vertical feet to the pass. We did our best to link shaded patches of firm snow, but shade was sparse on Island Lump, leaving us with a sea of hot slush to wade through.

Steve pushed his hardest to keep up with me, but I still found myself waiting in the spaced shadows of wind-sculpted, towering pines. Under the afternoon sun beating down on the reflective environment, we were in an oven climbing a StairMaster made of Jell-O. Both of us were drenched in sweat and snowmelt.

My impatience had oddly vanished. This wasn't fair. I'd spent the last two months hiking, building my leg muscles up through Southern California. Then I'd tuned my snow skills and endurance through 200 miles in the snow with a full load. At times, it felt like my body was falling apart faster than it was building any strength or fitness—but that couldn't be completely true. I'd invited Steve into an unforgiving environment where we'd both underestimated how difficult it was going to be to get him up to speed. To his credit, every time that sweaty, panting Brit reached me, he'd give a slight smile and a nod, signaling he was ready for more.

The summit eventually came, and on the north side of the pass the snow firmed up to a perfect consistency for fast, fluid snowshoeing down toward a potentially difficult crossing at Davis Creek. Past journals had stories of sketchy wades through a torrent, but the sluggish creek was still under a generous selection of snowbridges. At a flat creekside clearing, we called it for the day. After pitching our tents, we reconvened with our bear canisters to prepare dinner.

"How'd you feel about today?" I asked.

"I think it went all right," his eyes lowered, "after the couloir. Probably still slower than we needed to move, though."

I nodded. He wasn't wrong. We'd averaged a hair over one mph, which was *better*—but still insufficient to get us to Sonora Pass safely.

"I really don't want to hike through North Yosemite alone, but we've got to be honest about our odds of making it through together. We're going to run out of food at our current pace. I've been trying my damnedest to save calories for later, but I'm right on track," and with some Snickers shame added, "maybe even a hair behind."

Morose, Steve nodded but didn't reply. I felt like a total dick, but this wasn't an avoidable conversation.

"I'm most nervous about North Yosemite. It's guaranteed to get *more* difficult. We've been hiking the 'easy' part, the part barely mentioned in past accounts of early season Sierra trekking. By far, the most notorious section starts the day after tomorrow, once we hit Tuolumne."

Steve again only nodded.

"You're capable of figuring this out. I *know* you are—but maybe just not in time. I've been doing this weird, long-distance mountaineering thing for a month now. If you'd been with me since Kennedy Meadows, I doubt you'd have issues with the exposure or the mileage. This just—isn't the time to learn. I'd love for nothing more than to execute all the challenges in North Yosemite with a great friend by my side, but I'm genuinely worried about one or both of us getting hurt by putting our blinders up and continuing on."

More silence—but I'd said my piece. I felt like a bully. I didn't want to hurt the guy. I respected him in a hundred different ways.

"I'm really not trying to be a dick. I just want to keep both of us safe."

"I know, I know," Steve finally answered. "Just a lot to process. I honestly don't think I'll be able to figure out snow travel fast enough. I'll find a way to exit the backcountry. I can also hand over whatever food I have to make up for our pace, so you can have enough to make it to Sonora."

With that familiar hard lump returning to my throat, I nodded, trying to process the new flood of thoughts, worries, and logistics revolving around a split.

"This is *your* trip," Steve said. "The priority is to support *you* getting through your PCT hike. I came out here to see the snow, to see what you've been dealing with—but I'm mainly out here to help you. If I'm not helping your chances, and especially if I'm hurting them, I don't have a problem getting off the trail."

I was silent for a second, unsure what to say. "Thanks, Steve."

We returned to camp chores, our dissolving team lost in thought. Splitting was going to involve some careful logistics. Steve couldn't just call an Uber and hop in.

Where is he actually going to exit the backcountry? And can he navigate his way out without me?

There was a trail heading directly east from us, past Waugh Lake and out to the small mountain town of June Lake—but there was no actual trail to follow yet, only snow.

If I don't want to go with him, does that mean I have to hand over my inReach? My backup maps and compass?

Steve had a navigation app installed on his phone, but he had very limited experience using it. I'd been the sole navigator while Steve was behind me focusing on not dying, and maybe how to best sneak a fart into my water bottle. I couldn't just send him off into the snow to learn how to use his app.

What if he doesn't make it out?

That was the haunting question. If something terrible happened to him just so I could save hiking ten miles, I'd lose my damn sanity to the guilt.

The next option was twenty miles away in Tuolumne, where the closed Highway 120 passed through. It wouldn't take any navigation skills to follow the road to the east gate where Mel could reach him. Problem was, Tuolumne was still over a day away, up and over Donahue Pass.

"I'll leave from here in the morning and head toward June Lake," Steve said.

My stomach clenched. I couldn't sacrifice one of my methods of navigation. That meant I needed to escort him out.

*But **also***, I thought, *I'd rather suffocate myself with my own sweat-starched underwear.*

"What do you think about continuing up and over Donahue, then exiting from Tuolumne?" I asked.

"I don't know, that's still far. I'll be all right finding my way out from here. That will let you move as fast as you need."

"I can't let you wander off into the snow on your own. You're only out here because of me, so I either need to hike with you out to June and add miles there, or we can have a leisurely hike up and over Donahue together. If you're going to leave me with your extra food anyways, then a slow pace matters much less."

Steve hesitated for a few seconds. "All right," he replied. I hated the hurt in his voice. "Let's do that."

I settled into my tent for the night with nerves worn thin. Yosemite was tomorrow. North Yosemite, the battleground of the PCT, was the day after—and I'd be alone.

More information about Roadrunner's accident came in from Mel. It had happened in Bolton Creek—a notorious one. I'd read about many harrowing crossings involving that creek in past journals.

It was hard to believe. Both Longstride and Roadrunner were objectively strong hikers, but they also carried heavy egos—and egos are dangerous.

Of course, the ego isn't a total negative. It's actually quite necessary in the mountains. Mountaineers and climbers need *enough* ego to push themselves into uncomfortable, demanding situations. But *successful* mountaineers check their ego at the door. The mountains are truly heartless. They're big, beautiful, and care absolutely nothing about whether you're strolling along in a forest or dead in a ravine. That places a mountaineer's health and safety within their own decisions, and egos get in the way of good decisions.

I didn't know Longstride or Roadrunner beyond passing observations, which certainly could've been off base. But I wondered if either of them had the humility to say, "I'm awesome, but I'm not awesome enough to cross this creek *here*."

Sleep wasn't going to come easy. I couldn't stop running through the litany of fears and worries of what lay ahead, of going on alone, of negotiating creeks alone, of the buckled Glen Aulin bridge.

If I get swept away—will I also be lucky enough to walk out of there?

Is all this really worth the risk?

And again, the most constant and pressing question: *Is any of this fair to Melanie?*

28

DONAHUE

Two a.m. arrived quickly. A bit too quickly.

Every sore, resistant fiber in my body begged to remain lying down—for the next two months straight. I was pleasantly surprised I'd slept so well. All those relentless, unanswerable questions appeared to be no match against my exhaustion.

I clicked on my headlamp and was also surprised by a strong cloud of my own breath drifting toward the foot of my sleeping bag. It was cold. Not just chilly, but *way* below freezing. This was great news for Donahue Pass—and not so great news for the soaked boots I'd neglected to dry before bed. I leaned out of my tent and picked one up.

"*Crap,*" I muttered.

Ice. My boots were blocks of ice. I rotated my left boot around, momentarily mesmerized by the stiff, white laces no longer abiding by the rule of gravity.

"That's going to be fun to put on."

After a delightful breakfast, I enjoyed a solid ten minutes of hammering my feet into two inflexible, frozen bricks. Hiking out of camp, my laces remained loosely woven through the eyelets, every strand in the exact same position from when I'd taken my boots off ten hours earlier. Tying them wasn't an option.

We weaved through giant trees by headlamp. We'd packed up and started hiking quickly. Very quickly. *Impressively* quickly.

Crunch, crunch, crunch, crunch

I loved that sound. It was the sound of good conditions, of forward progress, of adventure. Breaks in the trees revealed a sky with an impossible number of stars. Mel and I had pretty much always parked our home right up against the mountains, but I'd *never* experienced such stillness, such incredible skies clouded with purple and yellow galaxies.

Crunch, crunch, crunch, crunch

We closed in on Rush Creek, where past accounts told tales of a raging deluge forcing *miles* of upstream hiking to ford a wide, deep, slower section. The reroute was so long, it drastically changed the approach to Donahue, requiring the summit of a rarely traveled pass. The idea of navigating not only off the PCT, but in the dark over an obscure pass, had my stomach in knots. But marching along inside the bubble of our headlamps, the torrential rage of Rush Creek appeared—*behind* us.

"What creek was that?" Steve asked.

I took out my GPS. "Well, damn. That was it. Rush Creek."

We'd crossed over what must've been a *massively* thick snowbridge, massive enough to mask the sound of cascading whitewater.

"Let's hope there's that much snow over the rest of 'em," I half-joked, but Rush Creek at 10,000 feet was sure to look different from Horseshoe or Bolton Creek below 8,000. With those creeks already swallowing hikers, it was probably safe to assume they weren't going to have great snowbridge options.

Huge ramps of gently sloped ice led us above the treeline into the soft blue light of dawn and wide-open views of Donahue Peak and the sawtooth ridge on Koip Crest. The snow was in exceptional shape, with temps low enough to keep it that way, and we maintained an incredible pace toward the pass—which was kind of irritating. I almost preferred the day went poorly, just to solidify Steve and I were making the right decision to split.

Deep rabbit prints had been cemented into the shallow suncups by the cold. The landscape illuminated as we worked our way up the gigantic bowl of snow. A mere four miles into our day, the warmth from my feet thawed my laces enough to actually tie my boots.

The sun ignited the peaks around us as we reached Donahue Pass—winded but without much fuss. It was only 5:30 a.m., which meant we'd smashed through five miles in 2.5 hours. All uphill! Even hiking on flat ground, that was a *great* pace. Two days ago, we'd taken the entire, miserable day to eek out six miles.

"Man. This is going too well," I muttered to myself. Steve cruised the remaining hundred yards toward me in good spirits.

"This is unreal!" he shouted through the stiff morning breeze. "*Unbelievable.*"

I smiled, happy he'd been able to experience an early morning Sierra pass—but a knot sat in my stomach.

Am I giving up on him too early? Did I fail in my attempt to remain patient long enough for Steve to get his bearings out here?'

Donahue Pass was usually a bustling summit with groups of fair-weather hikers enjoying lunch. It was the dramatic, perched entrance to Yosemite National Park, where backpackers took in the big views while fending off aggressive marmots trying to snag their food. Other hikers enjoyed feeding the fat alpine critters (who are the largest member of the squirrel family), unwittingly further habituating them into annoying little thieves.

Today was different. No people, no marmots, just peaceful snow glowing golden in the alpine sunrise while we snowshoed across the saddle. The big sign welcoming us to Yosemite National Park wasn't there, still entombed somewhere in the ice below.

Yosemite.

My heart involuntarily stuttered, and not just from the steady diet of M&M's and Pop-Tarts. In twenty-four hours, I'd officially step into the hiker-swallowing minefield of North Yosemite. Horseshoe Creek would likely be the day after next. Bolton was within the next week.

"Give me a minute," Steve called over. He slumped his pack into the snow and rolled his shoulders around. "I think this thing got heavier last night."

The north side of Donahue was steeper, with many cliffs to navigate down through, but how hard could a bunch of downhill snow be?

The gentle slope pitched down until we were on a featureless, sweeping sheet of forty-degree ice flowing thousands of feet into Lyell Canyon below. It was incredible. We hiked down and down—and down. Steve increasingly pumped the brakes until I was on my own, inching down fifty-degree ice, facing a dizzying amount of exposure.

"Come on," I pleaded with the no-doubt-grinning trail gods. "Don't turn this into an epic."

Steve was out of sight, but I kept going. I figured I'd scout ahead before stranding us both a mile down the slope at the edge of a cliff. I reached a sharp downturn and stopped. I couldn't tell whether the next twenty yards were more angled snow or a sheer drop-off. My knees trembled inching closer, and I stopped again, hesitant to go any further. I was pushing down a slope Steve was all but guaranteed to refuse.

I might've reversed back up if I had any respectable amount of faith we'd find a safer path down elsewhere, but I had a pretty jaw-dropping view of the terrain all around me. This was it.

I inched a few more yards forward to peer beyond the edge of the downturn. Some small rock outcroppings protruded from the slope. I moved further down toward them. Even for me, the exposure was tapping on my nerves. One hundred percent of my weight, and my existence itself, was entrusted to the metal points under my feet.

"Steve isn't going to like this," I whispered to myself.

His silhouette appeared above me. Surprisingly, he'd still been moving forward but came to a halt right where I had, on the edge of the downturn.

"THAT'S NOT IT, IS IT?" he shouted down.

It was. I already knew it was. But I gave another look around to make sure I hadn't missed a milder slope, or a dry patch of rock to downclimb, or any misplaced mall escalators.

"I THINK IT MIGHT BE!" I shouted back.

Perched dizzyingly high above the canyon floor, I flipped up my heel-lifters and downclimbed through a hundred feet of sixty-degree ice to reach the rock outcroppings. They were the top of a squatty, exposed cliffband. A knife's-edge lip of ice lined the face of the cliff, and it looked like we could use the lip to traverse off the steepest snow to reach a series of milder ramps. *But*—a few short feet below the ice lip, the snow's angle pitched past seventy degrees. A slip would be an unarrestable good time.

It was an *acceptable* option—or, more accurately, it *had* to be an acceptable option.

"THIS IS IT! SHOULDN'T BE TOO BAD!"

I'm not sure I'd ever lied that loudly before.

"Our friendship isn't going to survive this," I added, only loud enough for my pack straps to hear.

But again, with surprising little hesitation, Steve committed down the slope. He progressively slowed but never completely stopped moving. He arrived at the cliffband and eyed what his dickhead-excuse-for-a-friend had found.

"Well… damn," he muttered.

"We can do this, just one step in front of the other. We've simply got to shut our brains up and execute."

And one more time, Steve caught me off guard when he immediately nodded in agreement. I moved out along the lip, one lateral step at a time. Soft impressions, the initial stages of suncups, had formed just below the knife's edge. I forgot about the stomach-churning exposure at my heels and focused all my energy on planting each step with surgical precision, aligning my most aggressive, longest snowshoe points perfectly inside the impressions. Steve stuck right behind me, following me across the precipice of some of the worst exposure I'd experienced in the Sierra so far.

He joined me on the milder ramps with a proud smile. But at the first available flattish patch of snow, Steve grimaced through dropping his pack again.

"Give me another minute, this thing is killing me."

Steve's confidence on snowshoes was clearly improving, but reaching the floor of Lyell Canyon still took an extended chunk of the morning. I would scout a zig-zagging path downward along the lightest angle I could find, periodically pausing on flatter areas to throw on another layer or pick at a handful of trail mix while I waited. We weren't setting any speed records, but he did keep moving forward.

At the bottom of a thousand feet of switchbacking ramps of snow, we reached the southern tip of Lyell Canyon, the ten-mile-long riverway that would take us north into Tuolumne Meadows. The higher elevation and shade from the dense forest had kept the snow in perfect condition. At a major footbridge over the Lyell Fork, there was no sign of an actual wooden bridge, just a suspiciously long and stable snowbridge.

The conditions deteriorated as we lost elevation. The forest thinned, spitting us out into a sunny field of baby pine trees peeking out from snow that had already been baked into a miserable slop. From almost a mile away, it was clear the Lyell River was insanely swollen. Most of the canyon floor was under water.

Patches of muddy trail began to appear as we plunged down the soft slope. At the canyon floor, we stepped off of the snow and into a marshland. At an impeccably clear stream crossing the trail, Steve dropped his pack again. This time, his mood had lowered, and he pulled his shirt up to examine red, raw bands along his shoulder and waist. I could feel the same sores forming. Our packs spent a lot of time slipping and shifting around through the uneven, slippery terrain, but I had more to cushion the wear than Steve. His sores were deep, like we'd been out there for weeks. He didn't complain, just took a minute to decompress before hoisting his pack back onto the sores.

The Lyell River was a nondescript channel under the surface of a moving *lake*. The sheer volume of water was unbelievable. Snowmelt rushed into the canyon from all angles, maintaining the river swollen many feet above its summer banks.

We stumbled upon enough dry ground to sit for some lunch and soak in the humbling scene. A waterfall cascading down the canyon's east wall was creating a reverberation I could feel through the *ground*.

"What are you walking into?" I quietly asked myself.

The PCT was mostly flooded from the river, but was still easy to follow. The lazily snaking Lyell River had always been a gorgeous blue/green channel. Seeing the popular canyon overtaken by snowmelt was surreal, almost as surreal as Lyell Canyon *void of people*—and we definitely had the whole mess to ourselves.

The trail moved away from the river and we were gifted a long stretch of easy, dry trail. Our packs were a few pounds heavier with all of our snow gear riding on our backs, but we were grateful for some simple hiking.

A few miles later, we were caught off guard by a wide, swift creek with no obvious way across. The next major crossing I had on my radar was the Tuolumne River the next day, so I was a bit confused. I'd hiked this canyon several times and didn't recall crossing any notable creeks.

"What the hell is this?" I asked. "Are we lost?"

Steve shrugged, welcoming another opportunity to set his pack down, to give it a rest from all its hard work rubbing him raw. I pulled out my GPS, which took a minute to locate us through the dense forest. We were dead on the PCT—at the *seasonal* Ireland Creek.

It only took a hundred feet of hiking upstream before we found a cluster of logs spanning the creek. I followed Steve across the impressive mass in complete disbelief something that size could ever dry up completely.

We called it a day when we hit snow again, just a couple miles from Tuolumne. In a perfectly flat, snow-free meadow, we threw down our packs for the last time and went to work setting up camp after thirteen miles, our longest yet, and an above-average day!

The haunting thought crept back in, *Should Steve really leave? Are we calling this too soon?*

But Steve was already winding down, looking forward to being back in civilization, not waking in the middle of the night, not having his pack's straps dig into his sores, not having to wade any more icy creeks, but most importantly—not feeling like an anchor.

Both of us were exhausted from the day. My raging hunger made its presence known, and I abandoned a slumping, partially erected tent to plop down and start working on dinner with shaking hands. Still unsure about the miles ahead and the food we had between us, I pulled out my planned dinner for the night, red beans and rice, and dumped about a third of the dehydrated contents into a hodgepodge bag containing portions of other dehydrated dinners I'd been rationing.

Effectively planning and rationing food felt damn near impossible. In the seventy-five miles and dozens of creeks between me and Sonora, I'd be walking as far upstream as I needed until I was one hundred percent comfortable with a crossing. Without anyone's help or gear, one slip could turn into a horrific epic to extract myself from the backcountry. My greatest chance to make it through North Yosemite alive was patience—but patience required time, and time required food.

I had more than a good reason to walk away from the PCT with Steve, but I couldn't. I wasn't sure why I needed to see North Yosemite. I certainly held no delusions of this trek being anything but an arbitrary, selfish mission—but I needed to tackle it. I needed to push myself past my comfort levels, even if it threatened so many important things: my health, Mel's future, my... existence.

I poured the boiling water from my Jetboil into the rest of my red beans and rice, setting it aside for the requisite thirty minutes it needed to rehydrate.

Yeah, right.

I lasted five whole minutes before I was inhaling the glorious bag of mush, crunching through uncooked rice and mealy beans with a big, dumb smile, ecstatic with the magnificent feast I was scooping out of a Ziploc. I took out my dessert, a Snickers bar I'd been borderline-sexually undressing in my mind all day, but stopped short of opening it.

*Every calorie counts. I can do without it—can't I? Maybe just eat half. No, I don't need it. Put it away. **Damn** it looks good though, with its tight little brown ensemble… But what about the weight?? There would be a few less ounces to carry in the morning if I just ate it now!*

From across camp, I emerged from my daydream and caught Steve's eye. I'm sure it was a bit unsettling for him to watch me having a staring contest with a Snickers bar. I took a brave breath and slipped the bar back into my bear canister.

After dinner, we settled into our tents for a much needed rest.

Tomorrow was the day. North Yosemite. Alone.

What the hell are you thinking? my mind demanded, panicked. *If you called it now, you could head out with Steve. No more snow, no more ice water, no more discomfort, no more danger, all the food!*

"Not now, brain," I grumbled, rapidly slipping out of consciousness.

29

TUOLUMNE: PART I

Snowmelt gushed around me, filling my clothes and pack, rapidly stripping any shred of warmth from my skin. I tried to yell for help, but couldn't get my head above water long enough. I tumbled end over end, being pushed and pulled by a force many, many times stronger than I. In the dark chaos, I couldn't find which way was up, couldn't get a breath of air, couldn't get my bearings.

Suddenly, I was airborne. I shook enough water out of my eyes to see I was falling alongside–sheets of water? My brain couldn't think fast enough.

A waterfall? Did I go over a waterfall?

I was falling forever, enough time to look around and take a breath. I couldn't remember how I got there. I'd obviously fallen in a creek, but which creek? What had I been trying to cross? What mistake had I made? I'd promised Melanie I wasn't going to toe the line close enough to get anywhere near allowing this to happen.

Oh no. Melanie.

My panic shifted to numbness as the gravity of the situation settled in.

What have I done? Why did I try North Yosemite alone? Was it worth losing everything I have? Just to hike some stupid trail in the most dangerous way I could concoct for myself?

I was lost in misery but bizarrely comfortable free falling through whipping winds and freezing water. I looked around, where the same suspended sheets of water were still being pulled downward by the same force I was. When I finally looked down, my eyes widened at the sight of wet, jagged rocks rapidly accelerating toward me. My heart raced, attempting to beat itself out of my chest.

This was it. I'd failed. I'd sacrificed everything for this ridiculous trek.

I closed my eyes tight and covered my face with my hands, bracing for the impact.

"SHHIIII," I gasped through an invisible force yanking me into the sitting position.

My breaths fired moonlit plumes across the top of my sleeping bag in tight succession. It took a minute to fully convince myself I'd been dreaming. My heart was jackhammering, unwilling to accept we weren't dead.

"Jesus," I whispered to myself, slumping my head into trembling hands, "that was so real."

I checked my phone. 2:45 a.m., fifteen minutes before my alarm. There was no way I was going to fall back asleep, so I grabbed my half-and-half, coffee, and Pop-Tarts from my bear canister, then slid back into my sleeping bag to enjoy an extra long breakfast.

I couldn't pry my mind away from the dream. My hands shook through my mundane morning routine while the adrenaline reluctantly faded from my system.

Was that a premonition of some sort?

Mystic phenomena weren't exactly my thing, but I'd barely dreamt the entire trail. Why now? Why that dream? Was I just stressed about the creeks, or was the universe trying to send me a message?

It's not going to happen. You'll turn around before you put yourself in that kind of danger. You can always turn around.

The hike into Tuolumne Meadows was half snow berms, half marshland. Crampons were needed for the small, steep berms, and we stopped to remove them to cross the marshy fields—the *first* dozen times. But once that got old, we resigned to staying in crampons through the tan, dormant fields.

"We doing this right?" Steve asked with a half-smile, holding up a crampon interwoven with long strands of grass and mud.

The trees all but vanished in the wide open fields in Tuolumne Meadows. Under a gray sky, we had a clear view of the needle-topped Cathedral Peak and Tuolumne's signature granite domes. We crossed the swollen end of the Lyell River over two manmade bridges. Trees lining the river had their trunks submerged by several feet. The earth-rumbling volume of water moving under the bridges was uncomfortable even to walk above.

This wasn't the big one though. In six miles, I would have to cross the product of this and several other large tributaries combining to form the Tuolumne River. If the Glen Aulin bridge was indeed out, there was no way a crossing was possible without a swim. I gave myself a physical head shake to see if I could slap my remaining brain cells around enough to temper my escalating stress.

"You can always turn around," I repeated under my breath. "You can always turn around."

Like a lit match, the sun ignited the sharp tip of Cathedral just as we stepped into the Tuolumne ghost town. Shacks for housing the summer employees sat eerily quiet. Heavy winter snowfall had caved in several roofs, but the shacks sat unattended, in ruins while Yosemite National Park battled against the snowpack on the roads leading into Tuolumne. Most buildings were unlocked, but I felt weird about welcoming ourselves inside. We found the one picnic table outside without a mound of snow on it, and threw our packs down.

It was time.

We emptied our bear canisters and food bags onto the table, laying out every scrap we had between us.

"Take anything and everything you could use," Steve said, adding with his cheeky smile, "just leave me enough for a snack on the way out of this hell."

I organized and sorted the food supply while Steve whipped up some coffee with a small pour-over filter, filling my Jetboil to the brim. I'd missed actual coffee so much on the trail. The instant stuff was *almost* satisfying enough—for a guy whose options were instant coffee or pine needle tea.

"If there's one thing going with me, it's the rest of your coffee. I'll leave my damn underwear with you before the coffee."

Steve laughed. "I'm not hiking out with your underwear. Whatever you want, take it. There's lots of coffee where I'm headed."

Just his mention of civilization brought up a surge of panic. I paused the shuffle of processed food packages while another flood of fussy questions marched through my mind.

What are you doing? Going ahead alone isn't safe. Escape now, while you still can, you idiot. Why not quit while you're ahead? What are you trying to prove?

I shook my head again, trying to physically erase the doubts, as if my brain was nothing more than a '93 Etch A Sketch. Steve noticed I'd disappeared into my thoughts, once again having a stare-off with food.

"You all right?"

I nodded. "Yeah, just thinking."

I set a day's worth of rations aside for Steve, just in case. He was following a snowy asphalt road out, so odds were he wouldn't be getting lost. But if anything did happen, and he starved to death after I'd hoarded all but a handful of peanuts—boy would my face be red.

In organized rows spread across the table were thirteen days of food. Thirteen days to make it seventy-five miles. That meant I needed to only average six miles along the PCT every day. I had no idea if that was overkill or underkill with the additional crossing mileage, but six miles felt reasonable. It was almost guaranteed I'd be able to push more than that, but I wasn't about to send Steve off with any extra food. Every possible scrap was coming with me. I was always starving. If I ended up moving faster, I'd just get to eat more.

God, my stomach churned while I stared over the sea of food. *It would feel great to eat more.*

Again teetering on the verge of sexual arousal by the lusty spread of packaged foods (sample thought: If a Pop-Tart didn't want to get eaten, it wouldn't dress like that), I was pulled back to reality by an alien sound rushing through the trees above the abandoned camp.

"Is that…?" I muttered, listening intently as the sound grew louder.

"Oh my—it's a truck!" Steve stood up from the table as a huge plow drove by.

We hadn't been able to see any roads yet and weren't sure how much snow was still blocking them. A plow moving along at highway speed was certainly a good sign for Steve.

I carefully packed the precious thirteen days of food, puzzling together as much I could in my bear can. I slipped everything into my backpack, cinched the top cord, went to pick it up off the picnic table bench—and it didn't budge.

Ding, ding! Round two.

With all the strength I could pull out of my emaciated, exhausted, cold body, I bent down and squatted the pack up off of the bench with a groan.

"How's it feel?" Steve asked, picking up his unweighted pack with one arm and slipping it onto his shoulder like a school bag.

"Well," I fought to adjust the straps to make the weight more comfortable. "It's heavy. Pretty sure this is my heaviest so far on the PCT."

That wasn't an exaggeration. It was easily over fifty pounds, likely closing in on sixty. Panicked thoughts reminded me of the rivers and logs I'd have to cross, certain to be more difficult with such a huge weight strapped to me. Other thoughts were celebrating. There were thirty *freaking* pounds of food on my back—and all of it was going to go into my mouth over the next week.

Hell ya.

"I'm not sure what you're complaining about." Steve's smart ass, half-smile spread across his face. "Mine feels just fine."

We relaxed for a minute in the deserted Sierra camp, enjoying each other's company before the next leg of the journey. Everything ahead was so unknown—and so intimidating. I enjoyed simply sitting there with a friend, having a light conversation, momentarily forgetting about all the things to stress over. The conversation took a serious turn when Steve surprised me with a tough question.

"Something I can't quite wrap my head around—why is this trek so important to you?"

It was a loaded question, one I hadn't really been able to answer the billion times I'd asked it myself.

"I mean, I can see why the whole hike is important," Steve continued. "But why hike this section now? People are skipping the Sierra but coming back later for it, right?"

I nodded.

"And at the end of all this, those hikers will call themselves PCT hikers?"

I nodded again.

"Just like you'll call *yourself* a PCT hiker?"

"That's right."

After a silent pause, Steve shook his head. "I don't know, maybe I just don't get it, but it seems like you're putting yourself through a much more difficult hike than most, for really no more of an achievement. It seems like suffering for the sake of suffering."

I smiled. It was a blunt assessment, one only Steve could deliver. He wasn't off-base.

* * *

February 2003. Mesa, Arizona.

After a day of classes, my best friend Seth walked in to find me lying on the strip of carpet between the wall and the far side of his bed. It was where I'd been living, my "bed" where I spent a solid bit of my time mulling through the various dark chambers of teenage angst. He had some exciting news to share.

"Did you hear Chris is getting a brand new truck when he gets off his mission?" he asked with a headshake. "I need to get me some rich Mormon parents."

I forced out a pained laugh. "This is the same guy drinking, doing drugs, and bangin' his gorgeous, *also-theoretically*-Mormon girlfriend every night, right?"

"Ha! Yup, that guy."

"Perfect," I muttered, laying my head back down on the carpet.

Chris was a popular guy at my high school, but he wasn't a friend. Face to face, Chris and I were just fine, similar to my relationship with most of the Mormon kids I'd grown up alongside. But internally, I despised Chris and everyone like him.

I'd never quite fit into place in the religion I was raised in. I liked music and bands I wasn't allowed to like. I enjoyed violent video games, skate-boarding on Sundays, spiking my hair—all things that rubbed my fellow Mormons the wrong way. I never quite bought in to what I was being taught, and certainly couldn't stomach the thought of continuing toward the compulsory two-year mission at the age of nineteen to go proselytize and baptize people into that faith. Since I wasn't on the same page as the church, I figured I had no choice but to be honest about my intentions.

But through a blur of immature words, painful arguments, and angry moves, my clumsy attempt to be honest had resulted in my rehoming with Seth. His family was one of the few non-Mormon families I knew. My relationship with my parents froze over, both of them ashamed and disappointed with their wayward son. My relationship with my Mormon friends at school disintegrated into judging looks at best, and outright shunning at worst. Whether it was true or not, every room began to feel like people had just been gossiping about the prodigal Winsor kid.

Not a minute went by where I didn't question if I'd made the wrong choice. That sliver of carpet between Seth's bed and the wall became an invisible space to retreat to, to hide from all the confusion and embarrassment, and to think. Hearing the news of how excellent Chris' life was moving along, compared to the dumpster fire my senior year had collapsed into, brought up thoughts I'd already cycled through a thousand times

I could've just pretended. I could've just gone on a mission. I could've still had parents who were proud of me. I could've played the Mormon game for as long as I could. I could be like Chris—still have my family, eventually marry a nice Mormon girl and have a few Mormon kids.

In spite of how cookie-cutter nice it *should've* sounded—that wasn't a person I could face in the mirror.

I was friendly with all the people at school, but they thought little of me, and the feeling was mutual. I couldn't stand Chris and his many clones. I hated that I felt like the only one who was being honest, who wasn't okay living a double life. Of the Mormon group of kids I hung out with, I was far from the worst among them. I sampled a bit of alcohol, like any curious teen, but never touched marijuana or anything harder. I minimized sexual exploits, not wanting to be a complete dog for a future wife to find a way to accept—a stark contrast to the revolving door of ladies my Mormon pals bragged about flowing through.

On Sunday, those same pals would smile and nod along, give two-faced sermons about chastity and the evils of drugs and alcohol, and straight-faced lie to their bishop in order to maintain their sacred ascension toward a mission, to keep face with their community. I didn't believe a lot of it but still tried my best to keep my behavior somewhere in the realm of my parents' expectations, to be responsible about my future.

I was in a dark place for my last year in Arizona. It truly felt like being honest had about ruined my life. I couldn't stomach watching my amoral, integrity-free classmates living their depraved under-lives, then reaping the benefits from adoring parents who were none the wiser.

Two years later, after another intense day in the Navy's nuclear training pipeline, a letter came in the mail from Chris. He was in Ecuador on his mission, halfway toward that truck. We'd exchanged a letter or two but hadn't spoken much. Admittedly, I'd been desperate for friendship, and still had people like him from high school I kept in touch with, simply because I had no one else aside from Seth. All of my "good" Mormon friends had progressively quit responding to my texts, calls, and letters.

As I read Chris' letter, my lips curled in disgust before I finished the first sentence.

*What up my brother [*There was a racial slur here I'll spare you from]*? It's a little difficult here in Ecuador. They sell beer for like, thirty-three cents! You can get wasted off your butt for like a buck. But I haven't received a companion that will join me. My current companion is so annoying. I want to kick the crap out of him. Women are so hot and horny here, especially for North Americans. Almost every day in my mission I have heard girls whistling and saying, "When are you going to come teach me?" Dan, it's very hard. I could get laid every day by a different girl if I wanted. Dan, I want to hear about every prostitute—I mean prospect—that you conquer in your room. It's okay if you send some pictures without clothes too. Keep being you and win them women.*

 -Elder Chris.

I put the letter down and caught myself in the mirror. I was a totally different person from that kid lying next to Seth's bed, in much deeper ways than the buzzed hair on the sides of my head, and the crisp, ironed lines pressed through my uniform. Chris and I had set out on wildly diverging paths, and my contempt for him had shifted into feeling— *sorry* for him.

I was proud of that man in the mirror. He was exactly who he said he was. Sure, Chris was going to have a truck and would return home to the adoration of his family and congregation—but it was all veneered, a reality out of sync with his true self. It was tragically fake. I wouldn't want to be walled inside that life, a life of burying my actual self for the sake of impressing others. Not for one truck, not for a *dozen* trucks.

I slipped the letter into a folder of memorabilia, vowing to hold on to it as a reminder. The image of success was far less valuable to me than maintaining an honorable path.

*　*　*

A rush of wind pulsed through Tuolumne, rustling the pines over me and Steve.

"Ya know, I'm *more* than fully aware I'll be just another PCT hiker if I make it to Canada, but I need to do it in a way that feels honest to me—and that's uninterrupted. I don't see a successful PCT hike as anything confusing or up for interpretation. No matter how many people call themselves PCT hikers, *actually* hiking this trail from border to border is still a rare and difficult achievement—and one I'll continue searching for ways to complete, and not finding reasons to take credit for. If I decided to flip-flop around to find the most comfortable weather or skip hard sections entirely, I wouldn't call myself a PCT hiker. I realize others have taken full credit for partial hikes in the past, with friends and family who will never know the difference, and it's guaranteed they will this year too—but that's just not me."

It was time to go. Glen Aulin was six miles away. If a washed-out bridge was going to end my PCT hike, I was going to see it with my own eyes.

I could always turn around.

I said goodbye to Steve, thanked him for being there for me, for letting me torture him for a few days. While it was not the original plan, he'd ended up essentially carrying a full resupply for me. If I ended up eating all the food on my back enroute to Sonora Pass, Steve would be the reason I made it.

I forced a big hug on my partner (Brits love hugs about as much as cats do).

"Good luck, buddy," Steve said.

I turned north and headed off through the worn wooden structures in the employee camp. The buildings creaked and groaned in the wind. Abandoned clotheslines clinked metal clips together. Wind chimes rang above picnic tables with mounds of dirty, melting snow still sitting on top.

I was alone.

TUOLUMNE: PART I

My heart was needlessly hammering. I started muttering encouraging, positive things to myself, but my subconscious wasn't onboard. My evolutionary instincts to seek warmth, safety, and comfort were in full protest, kicking and screaming more with every step I took in the opposite direction of all those things.

A contrarian smile crept across my face. In spite of my fear, I felt—ready. Excited to step into the arena.

"This is it, Danny." I stepped onto Highway 120, the last easy exit to safety. "This is what you were looking for."

I stopped on the two painted yellow lines in the middle of the deserted road. Overcast clouds were churning, sending cold gusts through the trees to tug at the dangling straps on my pack. Safety was right there. A few miles on pavement and I could be next to Melanie, watching a movie in our comfy trailer in a matter of *hours*. All this would be over. No more cold. No more water. No more hunger. No more pain.

Strangely, none of that sounded appealing.

From the time I'd joined the Navy, I'd followed the path I assumed was the preferred way to be an adult. Jobs kept paying more while getting easier and less engaging. My couches got bigger, my cars got nicer, and my houses had an increasing number of unnecessary bedrooms filled with unnecessary furniture. Comfort increased, stability increased, and safety increased—but I was bored. Unchallenged. In a competitive race toward mediocrity.

In jobs after the Navy, that race seemed fine with everyone around me. I'd actually been envious of their contentment to play Doodle Jump on their phones for eight hours in front of a control room screen until the next year's promotions were announced, but I needed more. I had limits, and I had an intrinsic need to explore them.

The obstacles ahead were unknown, but not impossible. They *couldn't* be impossible. And if I truly found I couldn't safely move forward, then I would safely move backward. The opportunity to do something great was in front of me, maybe not on the cutting edge of alpinism, or even the cutting edge of thru-hiking (if there is such a thing), but it *was* on the cutting edge of—me.

I turned to face the roadside Lambert Dome, where the PCT headed into the waiting chaos of the North Yosemite backcountry, took a breath, and stepped off the asphalt.

30

TUOLUMNE: PART II

JUNE 8, 2017
TUOLUMNE MEADOWS

Lambert Dome is a madhouse in the summer. The massive mound of glacier-polished granite is a popular attraction in the heart of Tuolumne. Visitors looking to experience a slice of the pristine beauty of Yosemite National Park's high country could usually be seen fifty yards from the highway scaling the slabs, taking selfies, and eating overpriced concessionaire's sandwiches.

Not today though.

The typically bustling parking lot was still half snow, without a car in sight, lined by rows and rows of empty bear-proof trash cans and storage lockers. The granite dome towering above the lot stood bare, majestic, and more intimidating than I remembered.

The PCT followed a dirt road that served as parking overflow for the dome. Vehicles belonging to the summertime hoards would normally line both sides for hundreds of yards. Loud, cooler-wielding tourists would waddle along the road after releasing their cooped-up children from the long drive up into the mountains. The hyper little-ones darted in and out of the woods, enjoying the pure air and warm alpine sunshine like kids should, while desperate orders and pleas followed behind them.

Today, the only sounds were the cold breeze rustling the pines, the occasional flapping of my jacket hood against my pack, and the steady crunch under my boots. Another sound soon joined the party: water.

Water *everywhere*.

One section of dirt road was straight up gone, replaced by a healthy creek where Mother Nature had reclaimed the surface for herself. I splashed on through, only half-trying to keep water out of my boots. A rusty, laser-cut sign marked where the PCT split from the road. I stared at the sign for a moment, shoulders already burning from the absurd weight pulling at them. A thousand doubts flooded my mind.

"You can always turn around."

I took another deep breath, and stepped into the backcountry.

The trail was half-snow, half-rock, and similar to the morning coming into Tuolumne, where the right traction choice was hard to nail down. In front of significant stretches of snow, I begrudgingly slid off my lead pack, put my crampons on, then twitched and struggled to get that monster powerlifted back up into its freeloading position on my shoulders. Too many damn times, often just a fraction of a mile later, I was back on my butt to shift traction again.

Being alone carried new risk I needed to mitigate, and having the proper traction on snow was uncompromisable. A mundane rolled ankle could turn into an epic to extract myself to safety. Not having a partner in a deserted backcountry meant every precaution I could take needed to be strictly followed—regardless of how repetitive or annoying.

While my inReach *did* have the SOS feature, I still wasn't sure what horrific circumstances it would take for me to swallow my pride enough to use it. I was willingly putting myself into a dangerous position, and I felt my only acceptable option would be to get myself out. Aside from destroying my/Melanie's bank account, pressing that button would be a grand admission that what I was attempting was, indeed, terribly stupid.

At every family event, party, or dinner for the rest of my life, I'd have to tell the story of the time I heroically walked into a dangerous backcountry, found out it was dangerous, called some real heroes to come save me, then came groveling home to zero dollars and a promise to do the dishes for the next 700 years in exchange for Melanie staying married to me.

All that compared to death? I have to say, death was more intriguing.

Dishes—are the *worst*.

I walked into a huge herd of deer near Soda Springs, a cool little attraction where natural carbonated water bubbles out of the ground. There were dozens of deer, and most were human habituated, a hallmark trait of animals in Yosemite. Like lazy cattle, some were letting me get just feet away before I'd have to stop and shoo them off the trail with my trekking poles.

Near the end of the herd, one large buck stood in the trail, staring at me. I made loud noises and waved my trekking poles around, but the buck stood his ground. I came to a slow stop just feet away. I could've tapped on its antlers with a Slim Jim if I wanted to, but its black, soulless eyes encouraged me to think twice before assaulting the buck with any flimsy meat products. I awkwardly shuffled around him, making soothing noises and no quick movements. The muscular creature kept those eyes locked on me, tracking his head and neck to follow my path, but holding his body perfectly still. When I stepped back onto the trail, I became suddenly aware of the dozens of still, black eyes watching me.

I'd witnessed many slack-jawed tourists in Yosemite petting highly habituated deer, even feeding squirrels Cheetos in their lap, sometimes adjacent to the many "DO NOT FEED WILD ANIMALS" signs. It was weirdly part of the zoo-like Yosemite experience many city folk looked forward to.

In the early season, alone and way outnumbered—it was creepy as shit.

I spent the next twenty minutes glancing over my shoulder, waiting for Bambi's dad to come run me down, lusting after the Fritos in my backpack after a prolonged, Fritoless winter.

For the second day in a row, a loud rush of a creek moving through the trees ahead surprised me. The next big creek crossing on my radar was at the Tuolumne River still miles away, but my progress was halted by a knee-deep creek flowing over a solid slab of granite. GPS told me I'd found Delaney Creek. I wasn't looking forward to wading a creek already, and truth be told, I had no idea what wades I could trust. These weren't the lazy summer creeks I was used to charging right through. If I lost my balance, it wasn't going to result in just a couple blushed cheeks and a soggy shirt. I'd be forced to spend hours building a fire and drying off.

Of course, that was **if** I was allowed to walk away.

The main threat of swollen creeks wasn't the cold or drowning, but trauma. Especially in swift, relatively shallow water, a loss of footing is all it would take to commence a rag-dolling ride where a quick whack to the head would be all but inevitable. Even if a shot to the head didn't kill me, only knocked me out, the freezing and drowning would promptly finish the job.

I couldn't afford to underestimate the wrong creek.

I headed upstream to scout my options. Within a hundred yards, I came across a steep snow bulge leading down to a log spanning the creek. Just downstream was a slower, deep section, ideal to reduce the risk of trauma if I somehow ended up in the water. But getting off the bulge and onto the log would take some work. The angle of the bulge just above the log pitched to near vertical, too steep for crampons or even snowshoes to stick to reliably.

I dropped my pack, took out my axe and began downclimbing the slope, cutting stairs along the way using the aggressive front points on my crampons. I kept my ice axe's handle planted deep in the snow above me as a backup to hold on to while I forged a row of steps down the bulge. After I'd finished compacting each step, I'd bounce up and down with as much force as I could to ensure it wasn't going anywhere. I'd be fifty-something pounds heavier the next time around.

Once the snow turned vertical, I formed a series of laddered, foot-sized pockets by kicking straight into the compacted snow. The snow ran out a bit above the log though. Leaning back on my axe, I could see a two-foot gap between the end of the snow and the top of the log, where the creek had eroded the underside of the bulge to form an overhang.

Just above the lip of the overhang, I kicked in the last and most important step. The snow compacted more than I would've liked. I stomped and stomped, bouncing up and down, trying to convince myself the thin shelf would hold my weight once I came back. If it broke, I'd likely be pinballing off the log and going for a chilly dip.

Quasi-confident in my ice step craftsmanship, I extended my right leg toward the log, which took a bit more of a stretch than I was hoping, but the bottom points of my crampons eventually sank into the soft, wet wood.

I stood there for a minute evaluating the path I'd made, spending the majority of that minute with a suspicious frown directed at that last step.

Am I rushing this? Is this a smart crossing? Would wading across at the trail be better? Should I hike upstream farther to find something different? Maybe just turn around? WE COULD HAVE PIZZA TONIGHT, YOU FOOL!

My own wussy thoughts annoyed me. I stepped back up onto the last step and performed roughly 763 more test bounces. It wasn't going anywhere.

"It's time to cross," I said out loud, more as a command to myself than anything.

I returned to my pack and assembled what I'd affectionately labeled my "doodie-hit-the-fan bag." In a small, waterproof compression sack, I stuffed my down jacket, compass, map, fire starter, inReach, phone, and a day's worth of food inside. I tucked the bag inside my rain jacket, zipped it up, and cinched the waist cord tight.

In the scenario where I actually fell into a creek—and managed to refrain from headbutting any river rocks—I'd likely have to ditch my pack in order to escape the current, just like Longstride had done. The odds of retrieving the pack would be grim, at best, leaving me standing on the side of the creek with only the clothes on my back to extract my soggy butt from the backcountry. That bag was the solution, a collection of essentials to give me a fighting chance if doodie did indeed strike the proverbial fan; to give me navigation, warmth, and a bit of food to get me back into the loving embrace of cheeseburgers.

MELANIE. I meant Melanie.

With my DHTF bag tucked into place and my giant pack shouldered, I headed down through my formed steps. I weighted the last one as delicately as a guy giving a whale a piggyback ride could. I maintained a death grip on the axe, ready to pull myself back up if the step collapsed—or at least hang there like a cat on a wire to see if my grip could last until the firefighters came. My biceps had long ago been cannibalized by my thighs, so doing a pull-up with 220 pounds of resistance wasn't going to happen.

I wasted no time lowering my other foot down toward the log. The clamor of the creek was a never-ending reminder of what awaited any mistakes. My foot lowered into space further than I'd remembered. I blindly hunted around for the log while the dead weight of my pack pulled back on my shoulders, as if it were looking to go for a swim.

I released my locked-off arms to sag down past the point of no return, and finally felt the bottom points of my crampon sink into the log. I stepped off the thin last step and breathed a sigh of relief, then dislodged my axe and slid it into the side of my pack, turned to face the creek, and unbuckled my chest strap.

Common advice was to unbuckle *all* straps, including your waist strap, before a crossing, the idea being you'd be able to escape your pack easier if you did fall in. It was an internet idea that works beautifully in basement theory, but one I didn't trust in actual practice. From my perspective, the only thing less fortunate than falling into a creek would be setting myself up to be awkwardly pulled off-balance *into* a creek by a flopping, unstable mass on my back—one I'd *voluntarily* unsecured from my torso.

I preferred the added stability the waist strap provided to the whole second I'd save unbuckling it once I was in the water. I could handle unbuckling one buckle in a creek if it meant my pack wasn't going to deposit me there in the first place. My goal was to increase the odds of *not* going for a swim, not to set myself up for smooth sailing once I was floating downriver.

That wasn't going to happen. That couldn't happen.

I placed one careful foot in front of the other, letting the metal points under each boot sink securely into the wood. Crossing the wet, slippery, rounded log in just boots would've been a harrowing experience, but crampons were masterful tools for the job. Each step surgically attached to the log like a magnet.

The fast-flowing water through the middle of the creek created a dizzying vertigo effect, challenging my ability to keep ahold of my balance. But I kept it together and stepped onto the damp ground on the far bank.

"YEAAAHHH!" I called out.

It was involuntary. A victorious war cry. A release of the stress I'd been suppressing.

The roar of the creek immediately swallowed my yell and I stood staring back along the log, breathing heavily, my entire body trembling with tardy adrenaline.

"I did it," I whispered, almost surprised. "I can do this."

I tucked my emergency bag away and resumed hiking. Delaney Creek was a small one, but I navigated a safe and successful crossing all alone. I could do that again. I could do that as many times as I needed to.

"If I keep this up, I might hold on to semi-dry feet today!" I chirped to myself as the roar of Delaney Creek settled into the background. Things were lookin' up.

Ten minutes later, I was up to my knees in dirty, cold swamp water, already in my fourth or fifth unavoidable wade. The terrain was a mess. The lower elevation meant higher temps, and the snowpack was melting off quickly, leaving mounds of dirty slush with innumerous creeks running under, over, and through them. I caught sporadic glimpses of the trail, but it was submerged or too muddy to actually use.

This was textbook posthole territory, and leg-swallowing voids hid every-where around me under the innocent, rolling mounds. I weaved my way through the forest on high alert, constantly scanning for signs of thin snow. Postholing itself wasn't life threatening, but with so much weight on my back, the possibility of spraining a knee or ankle was high. Reversing back across Delaney Creek with anything sprained or broken would be borderline impossible.

I emerged from the forest onto giant granite slabs that flowed downhill into a rolling monster of a river, the Tuolumne. There were two crossings of that behemoth I had to get past. The first consisted of two bridges, which during past high snow years had been reported chest-deep *under water*! The second was the bridge that had been reportedly washed out at Glen Aulin. My confidence in making it beyond the Tuolumne River wasn't exactly great, and any remaining shreds evaporated when I reached the bank of the river.

"No. Way," I mumbled.

The forty-foot-wide, seething torrent was unlike anything I'd seen in person. The unbelievable volume of water barraging by was deafening. The sheer power sent nonstop reverberations through the earth, like standing feet from of an endless freight train.

I have to get to the other side of this?

Twice?

My blood ran cold and my heart rate escalated into hummingbird mode.

TURN AROUND. You're making a mistake! What are you doing out here alone?! GO BACK!

The amazing force of nature in front of me was mesmerizing. I stood there for several awestruck minutes. It was *beautiful*. Not in the classic sense of delicate, flawless beauty—but like a Cheetah in a full run. A beauty to admire from a distance. Untouchable. Dangerous. One not to be messed with.

Any confidence I'd gathered crossing Delaney Creek was clearly not applicable to this monster. Unsure what my next move was, I wandered upstream until I found the two bridges, which were nowhere *near* submerged chest-deep. In fact, they were still several feet out of the water. Perfectly safe.

If this wasn't as high as the Tuolumne was capable of getting, it was damn close. Chest deep water over the bridge would mean the already-swollen river would have to swell a dozen more feet. *Highly* unlikely, and not to mention an impossible force for the bridges to stay intact under.

That's, eh—*quite* the exaggeration, internet.

A reflexive thought popped into my head, *What are the chances the Glen Aulin report is also overblown?*

I wandered onto the two end-to-end bridges. They were solid and spanned the most aggressive current about three-quarters of the way across, but dead-ended at a stone spillway under a strong, knee-deep current. Downstream of the spillway was a nightmare. It fed immediately into the river, which turned into rapids and waterfalls within a hundred yards.

I put my pack down on the first bridge to think, and force down some lunch. My nerves had been on edge since leaving Steve, so my appetite was weirdly absent. The familiar lunch ritual was comforting, but when I finished preparing my signature fish taco, I didn't really want it. My mind darted back and forth through my skull like a freshly caged wild animal, desperate to sort out my options, with little to no interest in eating. I forced down a few bites, watching the edge of the river flow around the trunks of nearby pines.

I can still go back. Crossing back through Delaney Creek would be possible.

I stared across the bridges and the spillway. Knee-deep, swift water wasn't *ideal*—but it wasn't unsafe, per se. The odds of staying on my feet were good, maybe not one hundred percent, but close to it. The consequences of the one or two percent worst case scenario though…

"I should probably explore the alternate," I muttered.

Just like with Bear Creek, I'd spent time at home mapping out a potential alternate to avoid the Tuolumne. Since I had to cross the river twice, *tech-*

nically, I was already on the right side. The terrain along the alternate was a big unknown though.

Not having to cross the Tuolumne was too enticing an idea to ignore, so I finished my lunch with a final, forced swallow, and headed downstream without my pack for a scouting mission. Downhill slabs quickly ran into ledges. I downclimbed a couple of tricky, fourth-class sections before I lost all optimism. The steep granite slabs had a lot of snow still, and the resulting snowmelt would make staying on dry rock next to impossible. Ending up on steep, wet, slippery granite wasn't less dangerous than a knee-deep wade. A fall down the slabs would be just as deadly as a fall into the Tuolumne.

I scrambled back up to my pack and power-cleaned it back onto my shoulders. I couldn't stomach quitting. That left the spillway as my best/only choice.

"If it ends up being deeper than mid-thigh," I muttered while extending my trekking poles, "I'll turn around."

I didn't bother assembling my emergency dry bag. There was no point. If this went wrong, I'd soon be a spirit floating directly upward (or plummeting downward, depending on how many dick jokes the big man upstairs had overheard).

I walked back across the bridges, thankful for every last weathered plank allowing me to bypass the swiftest channel of the rumbling mega-mass. I arrived at the edge of the spillway and sat to strap on my crampons. The bare rock under the water was clean-cut blocks of smooth granite. The sharp metal points on my crampons were machines on ice, but they grabbed equally well on rock. If there was any slippery moss or algae, the points would dig right through and grip the underlying granite. Plus, the added inch or two of height would bring my legs a bit more out of the water, reducing at least some of the fluid force trying to drag me off the back of the spillway.

I took a breath and stepped into the water. I felt oddly calm.

My subconscious was on a whole separate page though.

Instinctively, my brain dumped as much adrenaline into my bloodstream as it could, which was really not helpful. I needed to be still, precise, and balanced—and vibrating legs were working against that. I faced upstream and leaned slightly forward, forming a solid base with my two trekking poles. Water drove higher onto my legs with each step, the strong current rolling up to my mid-thigh. The straining pressure on my legs built, but my crampons kept a secure grip on the spillway stones.

GET OUT OF HERE!

My eyes darted to a fallen log on the other side of the spillway, almost within panic-dive reach. My subconscious wanted an option to fast-forward to safety, rationality be damned. I focused back on my trekking poles and feet, making one careful move at a time. Years of rock climbing had made me somewhat proficient at ignoring my reptilian brain. Although I always used gear and tactics to stay as safe as possible on the rocks, unavoidable situations would arise where a fall on lead or off a tall boulder would result in broken limbs—or worse. I'd been in many situations where my safety was solely dependent on my ability to stay calm. This was a familiar headspace.

Humans' instinctive fight-or-flight reaction is an incredible mechanism and was a vital survival tool throughout the vast majority of our evolution. Now fast forward to 2017, where our safety and security has become *so* solid, *so* guaranteed, and that foundational reaction has little utility outside of risking our lives during leisure activities like climbing, mountaineering, skydiving, and taking selfies at the Grand Canyon.

Interesting, isn't it?

Our adrenal glands are still trying to keep us safe by delivering super-human bouts of energy when we're at the greatest risk, but climbing and crossing rivers are examples of dangerous situations where adrenaline works in direct *opposition* to staying safe. Fight-or-flight assumes in the face of danger, you need to move fast. Whether it's to fight off an attacker or sprint in the opposite direction, the ancient response can't fathom an inverse situation in which you'd actually need to stay still and calm in order to stay alive.

My limbs vibrated, impatiently waiting to fly. Through steady, deep breaths, I fought to harness my thoughts, suppressing every instinct to panic-flail my way across the channel like a water-winged toddler at swim practice.

In the deepest part of the spillway, it took a surprising amount of force just to move my feet forward against the current. Every time I unweighted a crampon to shuffle it further sideways, I felt the chilling sensation of the spikes losing their grip and being dragged back along the granite, toward a drop I couldn't afford my mind to ponder. Each step took all the force my trail-muscled legs could muster to pull forward against the flow, and replant a tiny bit further along the spillway.

After a few hour-long minutes, I waded into shallower water toward the far bank of the flooded river, where my mind exited the state of calm focus. Whatever stress I'd been suppressing came up in a surge, like it was surfacing for a breath after being held underwater. My heart rate exploded and my body shivered uncontrollably. Involuntary tears blurred my vision, forcing me to stop in shin-deep ice water until I got a grip on myself.

I was scared. More scared than I realized before I'd started the crossing— and a part of me felt trapped.

What did I just do? What if I have to cross back over that spillway again if the Glen Aulin bridge is actually gone?

My "You can always turn around" mantra was quickly losing traction.

I climbed out of the water onto a steep snow berm, officially on the far bank of the Tuolumne River.

"There's two," I whispered, looking back along the spillway. "I really hope I'm not digging myself into a hole I won't be able to get back out of."

Sweeping views opened up across the canyon on the rocky mountainside headed down to Glen Aulin. My pack was heavy enough to convince me to take frequent breaks on the myriad natural, chair-height, granite marbles to take in the glacier-carved beauty of the Tuolumne domes. Patches of blue sky kept threatening to break through the low, gray overcast. I begged the trail gods for some sun. Not only to help warm and dry my soaked lower half, but to lift the doom-and-gloom feeling of the day.

The snow was in terrible, mashed-potato shape. My crampons could only do so much to maintain traction, and more times than I'd like to admit, my downhill progress was in the form of sideways yard-saling until a helpful exposed rock or tree stopped me. The momentum of my pack was too much to fight, so every time a foot would slip, I would surrender my dignity and just go with it, almost grateful for the break from being on my feet. I stopped to rest repeatedly, exhausted to a degree I couldn't justify. As the crow flies, Tuolumne Meadows was barely in the rearview, but I was already *very* done for the day.

"I'll see what's going on at Glen Aulin and camp there," I strategized with myself, alone on another granite marble. "If there really is a destroyed bridge, maybe that'll be it. Maybe rest will come sooner than I think."

Having a valid reason to turn around, to head toward safety, was comforting. My eyes drooped. My face felt heavy.

"How am I so tired?" I growled, forcing myself to stand back up before I spent the night growing a drool icicle right there on that marble.

As I continued on, the angle of the slope eased. But before I could start celebrating, one step onto an innocent patch of snow punctured through the surface into a hidden void—and didn't stop.

I pitched forward while my leg free-fell into space. Thankfully, my crotch was there to arrest the fall. I came to a jarring halt when the rest of me wouldn't fit into the hole my leg had made. The merciless fatty on my back pile-drove my face flat into the snow.

All the violence was over in a snap. My right foot never came into contact with anything solid, just hung dangling in a void. My left leg was sprawled awkwardly to the side, still on top of the snow. All remaining traces of air in my lungs had been forcefully evicted, so I stayed there for a pathetic, wheezing second trying to reintroduce oxygen to my respiratory system, all while my freeloading pack sat high on my back, holding my face pressed against the slush.

I eventually scraped the energy together to push myself up to shake the slush out of my eyelashes. Random twinges of pain shot through my left knee. I attempted to extract my right leg, but between the weight of my pack and my tanked energy, I didn't get anywhere. I unbuckled my chest and waist strap, rolled my pack to the side, then braced to hoist my leg back to the overworld. I stalled for a numb second to stare at my red, stinging hands pressed into the slush.

Even without my pack, standing took exaggerated effort. After a few shaky, unloaded steps, it was clear I'd just toed a line. Faint pains shot through my left knee. It had twisted weird, but wasn't serious—good enough to walk on, at least. Before I picked up my pack, I slipped into another few seconds of numb staring, wondering if I could just spend the night on it, like an alcoholic bum draped over a trash can.

A soft hiss was drifting through the trees. Adrenaline kicked my grogginess aside as the narrow, rock-lined gully I was in led me right toward the building sound until I could feel it through my boots. Swirling plumes of mist floated through the trees, and I stepped into the spray to witness a spectacular display of nature's power.

"Holy God," I muttered, the sound of my voice inaudible against the violent cascading of millions of gallons.

Tuolumne Falls. The same Tuolumne Falls that had washed away the bridge I needed to cross at Glen Aulin. There was no fighting the instant decision to cancel any attempt of a downstream wade. It would be a guaranteed swim across a huge channel of swift whitewater, and something clearly not worth risking.

But a pivot of my head was all it took for my internal panic to shut up.

I squinted through the mist of the falls. "Is that—a *bridge*?"

My heartbeat ratcheted up in excitement, and I hurried away from the falls along the drenched trail and back into the trees.

The bridge at Glen Aulin is washed out, confirmed by Yosemite rangers. So what did I just see?

If it was possible to safely get across the Tuolumne, that would be a game changer. Against the wishes of my left knee, my stride lengthened until I was almost in a run when I emerged from the trees.

There it was. The Glen Aulin bridge.

The *perfectly intact* Glen Aulin bridge, *perfectly spanning* the Tuolumne River.

I shook my head in complete disbelief and happiness—peppered with a bit of irritation. "Washed out, my ass," I muttered. "Glad I spent so much energy worrying about this."

I caught something in the corner of my eye. It was *another* bridge in the distance, which was definitely buckled.

"Uh oh. I might've spoken too soon."

I crossed over the bridge, which ended at a heavily flooded area, under about four feet of water. There was little to no current, just a lazy pool lapping the granite walls along the trail, evidence the Tuolumne River had swollen close to *eight feet* higher under the falls!

I balanced along a bobbing log to gain a clean granite ledge above the PCT. The crippled bridge came into view, but it was branching off the trail, not something I needed to cross. A quick check of my maps told me it was a bridge leading across Conness Creek to *Glen Aulin Sierra Camp*. So the social media fear machine had transformed a report of this inconsequential bridge, on a side trail *off* the PCT, into a rumor the PCT bridge across the Tuolumne River was out.

Little bit of a difference, there.

Even the buckled bridge wouldn't stop a motivated hiker. There was still plenty of wood above water to monkey across. The report from a

Yosemite ranger was likely just an innocuous condition report of a winter infrastructure casualty. It probably wasn't them coming forward to declare guaranteed death to all who attempted to hike through the section. That job had been hijacked by a bunch of armchair internet hikers who hadn't seen the outside of their mother's house in a month, much less laid eyes on the Tuolumne River.

Bad information spread like wildfire online. I couldn't understand it. Why did ignorant bystanders feel the need to jump in to parrot rumors until the telephone game had finished morphing inconsequential information into real fear? Strong hikers had skipped ahead or even *quit the PCT* because of this twisted report. I'd certainly been scared. This "crossing" had been a looming monster in my mind for a damn week! The crossing of a solid bridge!

While the repeated failure of online information was irritating, I also found a certain amount of comfort there. If the Tuolumne River wasn't chest-deep over the first crossing, and definitely didn't have bridges washed away across the second, there was a chance the other looming monsters ahead weren't going to be what I feared. Horseshoe Creek, Bolton Creek—maybe they weren't worth fearing until I actually saw them for myself.

Sure, there had been accidents, but it was possible humans could've been the problem. The obstacles were what they were. Varied and complex, sure, but was every creek *really* that unavoidably dangerous? Or were flawed and/or inexperienced hikers throwing themselves into scenarios they shouldn't? Flawed humans had warped and spread misinformation about the Tuolumne River. Why couldn't every other notorious creek be a pleasant surprise?

Not having to swim across the Tuolumne, nor reverse back across the upper spillway crossing and Delaney Creek, was invigorating. Three major crossings were officially done, and it was only the first day in North Yosemite. I headed away from the Tuolumne with a smile.

"I can do this."

A big, flat, snow-free campsite called my name minutes later. I set my pack down against a tree, wincing in a bit of pain as the straps slid off my torso. I touched under my shirt to find raised, oozing welts along both shoulders and my waist. The heavy pack coupled with the constant falls and postholes had rubbed me raw throughout the day.

I began the ritual process of boiling water to rehydrate food while I set up my tent and attended to camp chores. I unfolded my solar panel across the middle of the trail, where the most sunlight was making it through the pines above. In the summer, I wouldn't even consider leaving gear on the trail. But this isolated hike felt light-years away from summer hiking. I could've stripped down naked and snoozed next to my solar panel, if I really wanted to.

Several unexpected raindrops tapped on the surface of the panel. I sent out a weather request, but the clouds and trees were interfering with the satellite signal. Rain hadn't been in the forecast, but Sierra weather had always been far from predictable.

The mighty Conness Creek flowing by camp was swift but much calmer compared to the torrent I'd been hiking alongside all afternoon. I filled my water bottles full for dinner and breakfast the next morning, then removed my socks to slip my feet into the ice water. My planter fasciitis had been much better in the supportive boots and lower miles through the Sierra, but my heels still ached at the end of long days. Icing my feet brought me back to summer hikes with my mother, who always looked forward to a good foot soak. I gritted my teeth and lowered further into the creek until my left leg was submerged past the knee to soothe the twinged joint.

"I suppose being surrounded by ice water has certain fringe benefits." I smirked.

Lost in my thoughts, I relaxed on the bank, reflecting on the creeks I'd crossed. I took my phone out to plan the next day. In step with my food supply, I only needed to make my six miles along the PCT, and the next major crossing at McCabe Creek was still eight miles away.

"I'll probably shoot for camping just before McCabe. Maybe cross it the next morning."

There was a strange comfort in hearing a voice, even if it was just my own.

"Maybe I'll even try to cross the creek tomorrow. That would be some *great* progress for one day."

I tucked my phone away and sat back, enjoying the constant white noise of the creek and the beauty of the swollen volume of flowing glass in front of me. The raindrops started tapping a bit quicker, so I plucked my numb legs out of the water and slipped my wet socks back on. I tied my boots and awkwardly stood up, chuckling at how bizarre it felt without feeling in my feet.

I turned around to head back up to my tent and froze. A large silhouette appeared in my peripheral. My heart jumped.

"What the hell?" I muttered, not believing my eyes.

It was a person.

31

HORSESHOE CREEK

I opened my eyes to the soft patter of raindrops on the walls of my tent.

"Fantastic."

I turned on my phone. Three twenty-five a.m., a whopping five minutes before my alarm was set to go off.

"I wonder if Pete and Nick are still going to get moving this early in the rain."

Nearby sleeping bag and tent zippers answered that question.

The duo been following my footprints since Mammoth. When Pete had first spotted me the night before, he'd called out in a jolly, Eastern European accent, "Ha! We found you! And…" he paused to look around. "Where's the woman?"

That brought an eyebrow up. "What?"

"There were two sets of footprints. One smaller set. You're with a woman, no?"

I laughed. "Those were a man's feet, my buddy Steve. He's a smaller buddy, I guess. The guy only outweighs my ex-ballerina wife by a hearty meal."

Nick promptly came along on the trail. I'd met him once or twice in Southern California but just in passing. I remembered walking by his lunch spot within the first week on trail, and the guy took lunch seriously. He had his groundsheet setup under a shady tree, his Jetboil firing, and a spread of ingredients in his lap, whipping up some delicious warm food for lunch—and making my cold tuna look like a pouch of lukewarm cat food.

Nick was a beefy fella. Burly, blond-haired, and farm raised from rural California. His blue/green eyes were striking, and he had a reserved demeanor that stood testament to a religious upbringing. Nick was an obvious introvert, and his calm, confident presence was a comfort to be around—and not just because those dreamy eyes made it hard to remember my wife's name (Mike, was it? Billanie?).

In stark contrast, Pete was a smiling, friendly extrovert. The thickly bearded Bulgarian was a longtime friend before we'd exchanged a single word. After a day where I could barely find the energy to stay standing while peeing (only a thousand miles of walking could make a man ponder the logistics of peeing while lying down)(Aim downhill, I reckon), Pete had gone to work setting up a campfire. While we dried our wet gear, he enthusiastically recounted their path through the Sierra, which was just a few days behind Amped, Thor, and me.

If successful, Pete would actually be the first Bulgarian to ever thru-hike the PCT, and he had connected steps the entire way as well. I asked him a few questions, curious if we were both talking about the same thing, but he had, in fact, hiked every step from the Mexican border! Our idea of a thru-hike was identical, to hike through the hard, the easy, the uncomfortable, the comfortable, the scary, the boring—*everything*, from point A to point B.

Needless to say, I instantly respected him, and I envied his energy. I ended each day feeling like I'd been run over by a herd of semi-trucks, where Pete seemed like he had enough left over to go for an evening jog. I was overly engaged in our conversation, and my excitement had replaced my ability to remember I was drying my expensive wool socks next to open flames. I burned a hole right through one of the toes.

They'd set up their tents next to mine and tacitly absorbed me into their team, just like Amped and I had done with Thor, although a nagging thought in the back of my mind wasn't sure that's what I wanted. I'd braced myself for a certain challenge: me against North Yosemite—solo. Adding teammates almost felt like I was cheating myself out of it.

With my headlamp on in the dark, rainy morning, I flaked away the crispy edges of the hole in my burned sock and slid it on over my outer sock. The sorry sight of having to stack socks to come up with one layer of wool made me feel suddenly very homeless—and I couldn't help but wonder if Pete had any spare change.

I removed my sleeping thermal, wincing in pain as the fabric separated from the sticky welts on my waist and shoulders. Even being shirtless in the near freezing morning, I hesitated before sliding my tight-fitting hiking thermal back on.

After popping my morning vitamins, I whipped up a standard Pop-Tart and some real coffee and half-and-half for breakfast, a meal I always looked forward to. But my beloved cherry pastry didn't taste right. I searched out the expiration date, but it was still way far in the future.

I emerged from my tent into the dark, wet morning and quickly packed up, not wanting to be a burden on my new team. I shouldered my pack with a grimace, but the surface pain thankfully dulled under the pressure of pack straps. We convened in the middle of camp, exchanged short greetings and headed out by headlamp. A rare gift of open, dry trail climbed away from the Tuolumne River toward McCabe Creek, but the steep grade right out of camp rapidly uncovered my stacked exhaustion.

My left knee didn't want to warm up, still sore and stiff from when I'd tried to find the center of the earth with my right boot. Pete and Nick pulled ahead, which I'd expected. Having both snowshoes and crampons, along with a food supply sufficient for a worrywart with a history of hangry afternoons, I was going to be slower.

The rain scaled back into a light mist. When the sky lightened, I paused on the rocky trail to remove a couple layers and put my headlamp away. I was sweating trying to keep up with my new team, and I didn't want to drench my fleece in case I needed it to stay warm later. Sliding my pack off across my shoulder welts was a bit miserable, but I savored the momentary break from my semi-portable torture device. I figured my teammates would keep moving along the trail and we'd meet up later.

I squinted into the dim, hazy morning light. Several hundred yards ahead, my teammates had also stopped.

Are they—waiting for me?

I threw my pack on with a groan and hustled up the trail, catching up to them by expending all the energy I'd recovered from my small rest. Neither looked irritated or annoyed.

"You all right?" asked Pete.

"Yeah. You guys don't have to wait for me. I'll be able to track you down from your footprints. Worst-case scenario, I'm geared up to be alone. I don't want to hold you back if you're set up for higher mileage."

Pete shook his head. "It's no problem. We'll stick together."

I took the lead, trying to shake off a nagging worry in the back of my mind. Luckily, we hit snow, allowing me to remove four pounds of snowshoes off my back and more closely match the pace of my cramponed teammates. That pace wasn't exactly stellar. The morning rain had softened the snow into an unpleasant slush.

The stress of being alone had vanished, so my temporary lapse in hunger had come to an end. A sharp end. My stomach *begged* me to stop barely two miles out of camp. I ignored the many, rumbling requests and continued to push ahead. I couldn't be the slowest guy, and also the guy who needed a thousand breaks—even if I technically *was* the slow guy who needed a thousand breaks. I didn't want to make my new team regret their addition within the first hour. But charging uphill through slush was hard work, and my hunger escalated until my legs trembled under a tanking blood sugar. Eventually, stopping wasn't optional.

"Sorry, guys, you go on ahead."

Out of breath, sweating, and already exhausted, I took out a snack as quickly as I could while Pete and Nick strolled into an open, suncupped meadow.

"These guys are *machines*." I pushed through record-shattering handfuls of trail mix being crammed into my face. "How do they feel so good?"

I stopped to look down with suspicion at my standard bag of trail mix (if a rehomed, raging-fatty-sized bag of peanut butter M&M's could be considered trail mix). It didn't taste right. It was—*faded*, a duller version. Just like my breakfast.

The meadow stretched out under swirling, dark clouds was beautiful. I briefly considered taking out my phone to snap a picture but rejected the thought. I needed to get moving.

A visible front of weather caught up to us, and the light morning mist was exchanged for wind and heavy, spitting rain. We worked our way across the meadow over a series of snowbridges spanning the lazy, wide creek. Pete and Nick were quite a ways ahead, but their bright red and orange pack covers made them easy to keep track of. My food-obsessed brain affectionately labeled them Skittles. If there was anything capable of picking up my pace, it was the prospect of catching gigantic pieces of candy.

I was moving as quickly as I could, but getting quite chilled. The wind tore right through my layers. As testament to my iron memory, I'd forgotten to switch out my failing rain jacket in Mammoth. There hadn't been even the slightest chance of weather in the Sierra forecast, so I'd slid upgrading my dumpster-ready rain jacket to the bottom of my list of priorities. The wearable turd that was supposed to keep me dry was quickly wet though, somehow directing cold rainwater straight through to soak my clothes— while *simultaneously* locking my body's moisture against my skin.

A tip of the hat to the sadistic bastard who thought DWR jackets were a good idea.

It was forty degrees, windy, raining, and I was soaked—and unlike the last two times I'd been failed by my rain jacket, there was no death-marching to safety. Chasing Skittles generated *just* enough heat to keep mild shivers from escalating. Stopping would be a problem though. Fortunately for me, if there was anything my mind was proficient in, it was coming up with reasons to take a break.

My pack straps wouldn't stop digging into my raw skin. I adjusted and readjusted them, trying to relocate the pressure points, but my waist had shrunk beyond the ability of my main belt to cinch tight enough. The pain begged me to stop and unload for a bit. I was hungry. I needed to change out layers. My knee hurt. I suddenly wanted to build a snowman—*endless* solid reasons for an extended rest popped up.

I managed to ignore my brain long enough to catch up to my fruit-flavored friends. They'd paused to check the GPS track, so I embraced the opportunity to stop with them. But within thirty seconds, my shivering ramped into tremors standing still in the spitting wind. I dropped my pack and put my damp fleece back on, praying it would help.

I set off ahead, moving out of the meadow and uphill into a forest. Even damp, the addition of the fleece did the trick, although soon, the trick was going a bit too well. Pete and Nick caught up behind me, and I found myself sweating inside of my rain jacket, but unwilling to pull over to remove layers.

The sun broke through the swirling clouds above, lifting our environment from doom-and-gloom to bright and comfortable. I finally started to feel like my pace had found a rhythm. We marched into a peaceful, sheltered area where a few small patches of sun were shining through the pine canopy.

Pete stopped on top of a flat slab of granite. "Breakfast?"

"You guys didn't eat breakfast already?" I asked.

"Nope," Pete replied in his heavy Bulgarian accent. "We don't eat breakfast right when we wake up."

I wanted to press forward while I felt good, a condition sure to be fleeting, but I also couldn't resist the excuse to get my pack off my shoulders. I was warm, but my wet clothes were going to be a problem sitting still in forty degrees. I found a small square of intermittent sun to sit in while Pete and Nick rolled out their cooking gear.

Sliding my pack back off my shoulders was a moment of painful ecstasy. My clammy skin under damp layers had split into bleeding lines surrounded by white, puffed up skin. The welts had grown, just in the last few hours, and it was no wonder. The pruned skin shed under the light scrape of a fingernail. I had no idea how I was going to heal the welts with no escape from my pack for most of my waking hours. I had a collection of Band-Aids, but nothing near big enough to cover so much surface area.

Part of the problem was my clothes no longer fit. My windproof alpine pants were a surprise gift from Melanie before I'd entered the Sierra. They'd originally fit perfectly, but were now cinched down as tight as the belt would allow, causing the waist fabric to bunch and fold up on itself. Those folds formed hard knots under my pack's hip belt, which were the main source of the waist welts.

My shoulder welts were the fault of my Sierra-thrashed pack. My sewing job after exploding my waist strap under Glen Pass had been sized for my waist then. Almost 200 miles later, the waist adjustment needed to be able to be cinched tighter to both secure the load, and transfer more of the weight to my hip belt—and off my shoulders—but I didn't have the guts to risk cutting it back apart to resow in the middle of North Yosemite.

My sunken waist was a pathetic sight. The daily calorie deficit had continued to take its toll. At least now, for the first time in the Sierra, I had plenty of food to eat. Maybe it wasn't enough to satisfy my hunger—because I'd need a full husky team to be following me, dragging 900 pounds of pizza behind them—but it was enough to hopefully keep my weight in check long enough to reach Sonora Pass.

I jammed a handful of trail mix into my mouth, and *again*—the taste was faded. I pulled the Ziploc away, assuming to find I'd accidentally pulled out my bag of dehydrated baby wipes to snack on, but there was just my standard bag of M&M's, with the rare, offending cashew.

Sure hope this body can keep it together for another 2,000 miles.

That number was almost comical. Every hiker's starry-eyed goal was to make it to Canada, but if my senses were going to start failing within 1,000 miles, I had my doubts.

Pete and Nick were serious about their breakfast. Forty-five minutes after we'd stopped, they were still eating, and the cold ambient air had progressively sapped my body heat. I got up to try engineering a solution to take some of the pressure off my welts. I took out my foam sit pad, a small square I used to put a waterproof barrier between my butt and the snow, my butt and sharp rocks, my butt and my bear canister; really anything uncomfortable my butt came in contact with. I folded it over on itself several times and slid the accordioned foam into the inside of my waistband to give me some extra girth to cinch my belt against.

Having a giant piece of foam shoved into my pants wouldn't go down as my *coolest* moment, but it worked. I hefted my backpack on and made a few small adjustments while my partners wrapped up their breakfast.

Closing in on McCabe Creek, my new hip belt padding felt amazing! The load between my shoulders and waist was actually balanced, which relieved the harsh rubbing that was tearing up my skin. I trucked uphill through the trees with the smugness that's part and parcel of a superior pants-engineering mind.

Ten minutes later, the foam had rotated ninety degrees to cup my moist ass crack like a diaper. I waddled stubbornly along with my pack again sitting right back on my angry welts, now with the bonus of an awkward load in the back of my pants.

Did I mention I sleep with my face on that piece of foam?

While pondering the odds of contracting pink-eye from my diaper, we broke through the trees at McCabe Creek about a half-mile upstream of the PCT crossing. We'd purposely angled upstream along the hillside leading to the creek, keeping our fingers crossed for snowbridges. McCabe wasn't supposed to be a very hard creek to cross, but scanning up and downstream the powerful whitewater, we didn't see a single reasonable crossing.

I set my pack down to remove my diaper and strap the emotionally scarred piece of foam back to the outside of my backpack to eh, *air out.*

Through brutally steep, soft snow, we trudged further upstream. Nick was in front, compressing steps for Pete and me. The angle was exhausting. In ten minutes, we'd barely gained a hundred yards, but hope arrived when a log came into view spanning the cascading whitewater.

That was the good news. The bad news was it would be a thirty-foot-long balancing act—and falling in would be almost *guaranteed* fatal. There was no room downstream of the log to swim to a bank.

"What do you think? The log looks good, no?" Pete asked rather—nonchalantly. Nick and I exchanged a hesitant glance.

It certainly looked *possible*. It was wide enough, with few branches to get in the way, but the consequences of a slip were hard to ignore. It was also *barely* attached to the bank. Most of the tree had cleanly snapped whenever it fell over, and only a few remaining strands of bark and sapwood anchored it on our side. I wouldn't put money on it holding three 200-plus-pound hikers.

Worst-case scenarios of the log detaching with one of us crossing danced through my mind. It would be a long balancing act, and the whitewater under the log would be vertigo-inducing for me.

"Not sure I'd be able to confidently tightrope across, but if it's sturdy, I'll just sit and scoot my way over," I said.

Pete smiled behind his burly, thick beard. "All right then."

Nick shrugged in agreement, absent of much reaction. He dropped his pack and started compacting a path down to a small boulder where we'd be able to step out onto the log. Similar to Delaney Creek, we were standing on an overhanging snow platform where the underside had been eroded away. Nick moved methodically down the bulge, cutting in wide, flat steps while prodding the lip with his trekking poles, searching for any thin or weak spots.

Pete stepped up to go first, moving off the hanging snow platform onto the rock. Placing a cramponed foot on the splintered base of the log, he gave a hearty kick to see if it would stay anchored. The gigantic timber actually swayed under Pete's force—an alarming sight my subconscious didn't like one bit—but it held. If I was still on my own, that would've stamped a big ol' fat NOPE on this crossing, but it didn't seem to rattle Pete.

He called something back to us, but we couldn't hear him over the raging creek. With an impressive amount of confidence, Pete stepped up onto the log and strolled across with careful, precise crampon placements. He made it look easy—maybe a little *too* easy.

Man, maybe if it's that simple, I'll stay on my feet instead of scooting across.

But then Nick went.

He also opted to stay on his feet, but his progress slowed over the turbulent middle channel. His steps turned into jittery shuffles, his body wobbling as he fought to retain his balance over the disorienting flow beneath him.

It dawned on me how close I was to witnessing someone lose their life, and I had to turn my head through a couple big wobbles. Standing on opposite banks, Pete and I inaudibly cheered Nick on, making no attempt to vocally compete with the deafening creek. In the time it took Pete to finish crossing, Nick had barely reached the middle of the log. His legs were *trembling*—which in turn sent my legs trembling.

"Yeah, I'm definitely sitting down," I muttered into the noise while my heart tried to beat itself out of my chest.

Part of me was almost disturbed by how easily Pete had strolled across such an intimidating obstacle. I didn't know much about Bulgaria, but was death-log-tightrope-walking a favorite Bulgarian pastime? Maybe the stereotypical jokes about how absurdly tough people were from the Eastern Europe/Russia corner of the globe were true—and maybe I needed to keep that in mind before following Pete across any more creeks.

Nick took a long time to cross the log, and a big part of me wished I'd gone before him. But he made it past the most rapid channel, where he paused for a few seconds to collect himself before stepping across the rest of the log to join Pete on the far bank.

I took a deep, stuttering breath. "Guess that means it's my turn."

Is this safe? Would there be something better upstream? Are you letting other people dictate where you're crossing? If Melanie were standing here, would she be happy about this?

The only question I confidently knew the answer to was the last one—but through all the nerves and mental images of glaring Mel, I felt confident enough in my ability. Maybe I wouldn't be able to Cossack across like freakin' Pete, but I'd never met a log I couldn't conquer with the tried-and-true butt scoot method.

I stretched out my right leg and placed the sharp metal points of my crampon onto the end of the tree, giving it a hard kick, and then another. Again, it wobbled but stayed put. A log that size able to be moved by little-ol' me released enough adrenaline to ensure I wouldn't be able to sleep for the next twenty-four damn hours.

"Oh boy."

I tugged the steel crampon points out of the soggy wood, then stepped my left foot up and braced my hands on the log to steady the awkward load on my back. I lowered my left leg over the downstream side until I was in the straddle position. Within a few scoots, I was over whitewater. Powerful slaps on the inside of my left leg jerked my foot to the side with enough force to make one thing very clear: This was a zero-error arena.

Staying in control of every movement, every shred of momentum, I inched my way across. The slick surface was a bit unnerving, but the low friction ensured little resistance to forward scoots. My center of gravity had to remain directly above the log, because I wasn't going to be able to do much to resist spinning around to the underside if my pack ended up too far from centerline. Hanging upside-down, clinging to a slippery log with my pack prying my arms apart seemed—less than ideal.

Although I'm sure my ass-sweat englazened sit pad would welcome the end.

Scoot by scoot, I settled my hands a foot in front of me, then slid my butt forward. All the danger and intimidating noise faded into the background as my mind shifted into that beautiful state of focus, one only accessible by a mind whose existence is at stake. My eyes remained locked onto the wood immediately in front of me, analyzing every bump, split, and texture to choose the optimal place to settle my fingers before each slide. All fear vanished, bizarrely twisting into joy.

Climbers, especially those involved in the more dangerous disciplines where ropes aren't used, or the protection is sparse, are often labeled as "adrenaline junkies," but that's incorrect. Adrenaline is the enemy. It makes your hands shake and sweat while encouraging desperate, quick, panicked decisions. Adrenaline shakes climbers off the wall. It also shakes hikers into creeks (I'm assuming). High-stakes climbing wasn't in search of adrenaline, and neither was this. Quite the opposite, the goal was to find calm and focus in an arena where instinctually, adrenaline is the answer.

Strengthening slaps against my boots convinced me to tuck my feet up onto the log behind me, which felt oddly secure with the front points of my crampons daggered into the wood. I moved confidently through the middle of the creek and past the main channel of whitewater.

Near the end of the log, a few stumps remained from branches that had mostly broken away. The small spears halted my scooting, no longer possible without risking my pants (and/or reproductive capabilities). I gave one of the spears a surprisingly light twist, and it crumbled into dust in my hand.

Hm. I sure hope the log itself is sturdier than that.

I let the crumbles of rotted wood slide out of my fingers and disappear into the swift water below. The sight brought the suppressed adrenaline-monster inside of me straining against its straightjacket.

I stalled out, merely to consider my options. I needed to be on my feet, but I'd kept my trekking poles awkwardly threaded through my fingers, hoping they'd be of some use during the crossing, but now they were in the way. If I got standing, I could easily walk the rest of the log.

I was worrying my teammates. Pete yelled out my name to ask if I needed help, but I didn't hear it. The roar of the creek was absolutely overwhelming. I tossed my poles the rest of the way across, then gave a couple of the branches a hearty tug. Both remained sturdy, but I was skeptical they'd stay put once I had my full weight on them. If they broke, I'd be in the creek.

I gripped as close to the base of the branches as possible to minimize the torque I was able to put on them. Tucking my left leg all the way up under my body, I settled the points of my crampon into the wood, and carefully stood, doing my best to keep most of the lifting in my leg.

Out of the corner of my eye, Nick stood at the shore just feet away with a strained expression. I smiled, finding amusement in returning the favor. His lips moved, asking me an inaudible question.

"I'm good!" I shouted in his direction, but I could barely even hear myself.

I returned focus on the log and easily reached the sweet, sweet bare rock on the far side of McCabe Creek. A big grin spread across my face. Both of my teammates were also smiling.

We did it. McCabe Creek. Check.

Just like after Delaney Creek and the Tuolumne spillway, a powerful rush of emotion and adrenaline came storming out of the cage I'd locked my subconscious in. As we moved back into the trees, my limbs and lips trembled while the same relief, elation, and fear all surfaced together. Embarrassed, I kept my head down, converting my trembling energy into physical work to practically run down the steep snow.

I didn't want Pete and Nick to think anything was wrong, because there absolutely wasn't. I felt amazing. However intense, I was in the middle of living my life to the level I wanted to, finding challenges and solving problems in a beautiful, isolated, and complex environment. The few humans I had next to me were impressive and motivated. I was right where I wanted to be.

This—was why I was on the Pacific Crest Trail.

The next creek was a looming one: Horseshoe Creek, where Longstride had been swept away just a few days ago. It only took fifteen minutes after crossing McCabe Creek to arrive at the PCT crossing of Horseshoe—and it was a waist-deep, swift nightmare.

Nope. Not here.

Without any need for discussion, Pete and Nick were on the same page. We dropped our gear to explore upstream. With our packs still in sight, the rolling, clear creek narrowed into whitewater tearing through hallways of granite. At the tightest constriction, maybe ten feet across, Pete walked over to the edge of the granite to peer into the channel.

"Right here. I could jump."

Both Nick and I chuckled, but Pete didn't join in. He scanned the gap with pensive, curious eyes. Pete's English was pretty damn good, but there was still a slight language—and obviously a huge cultural—barrier between us. Nick and I exchanged a confused glance before Pete left the granite ledge to continue upstream with us, where we'd hopefully find options more ideal than an Evel Knievel stunt.

Just around the corner, a beautiful sight came into view. Horseshoe Creek broadened into a fifty-foot-wide, shallow creek. A swift, knee-deep section would be the crux of the crossing, but that was only ten feet long, right off the bank.

"That didn't take long at all," I said. "And we only had to walk a couple hundred yards. But um, this kind of begs the question: Why didn't Longstride cross here? Are we missing something?"

Nick shrugged. "No idea."

Heading back toward our packs, Pete again stopped to scan the narrowest gap in the granite hallways.

With dead serious eyes, he asked, "We could jump across. You'd jump with me?"

Once again, I chuckled. I couldn't read the stoic Bulgarian, and had no idea whether he was kidding or not.

"Sure, Pete. I'll be right behind you," I said, with all the sarcasm I could muster.

With our packs retrieved, Pete led the way back upstream and once again, when we reached the granite channels, Pete stopped.

"Will you throw my bag?" he asked.

I cocked my head and glanced over at Nick, then looked back at Pete. He wasn't smiling.

"What? Are you serious?"

"My bag—I'll jump here. Will you throw it to me if I jump without it?"

The man was 103 percent serious. "Jesus, Pete. I mean… I'll throw your bag, but I can't promise it'll make it to you! What about the crossing we found? You'd rather cross *here*? By jumping??"

A mischievous smile spread behind his beard, and he gave me one, strong nod in the affirmative.

The granite ledge we stood on was about four feet higher than the far bank. The gap Pete would have to clear was at least ten feet wide, the landing slab was angled, and—as a fun bonus—wet. I was stunned, unwilling to accept anyone would think this was a better idea than a knee-deep wade, especially being so far from help if anything went south.

Still looking at me, Pete asked, "You'll jump if I jump?"

A reflexive scoff puffed out of me. "What? *Hell*, no!"

Nick joined in. "Yeah, buddy. You're on your own with this one."

"This is okay, I don't want to pressure. I'll meet you where you cross. I'm confident to do this. You'll throw my pack?"

Nick and I glanced at each other. "Yeah, man. We'll throw it."

I was in a mild state of shock. Thoughts of intervening and demanding Pete wade with us came to mind.

What if he falls in? What if we don't throw his pack well enough? What if all his belongings end up floating away downstream? That would screw over our whole team! All three of us would have to exit to get Pete out safely.

None of those thoughts made it to my mouth, probably because the beer-hatted, giant-foam-handed spectator inside me was very curious to see this play out. Besides, Pete could do what he felt comfortable with. This was his hike, and I hadn't the faintest idea what crazy activities they were into over there in Bulgaria. He'd made shockingly simple work of the last crossing. Maybe jumping over dangerous whitewater was another favorite Bulgarian pastime my soft, apple-pie-lovin' American brain couldn't wrap itself around.

Pete handed his pack to me. Expecting to support a similar weight to the one on my back, I braced for a fifty-pound curl—but it wasn't anywhere *near* that heavy.

"Pete—this thing weighs *half* of what mine does."

He smiled and shrugged. "I travel light, you know?"

Pete inched over the edge of the gap, peering down to the whitewater tearing through the channel. After sizing it up, he stepped about fifteen feet away and turned to face the creek. He split his stance, took a few deep breaths, and stared out over the gap.

This was the most nervous version of Pete I'd seen, but it wasn't in the same realm of nervous I would've been. It was more of a supermarket, I-hope-I-buy-the-right-kind-of-cheese nervous. If it were *me* about to huck *my* life over a raging creek in the middle of the backcountry, my nerves would've been more in the my-boots-are-brimming-with-doodie realm. Pete stared forward, rocked up onto his toes and heels, and stepped from side to side.

I was sure he wasn't going to try it. This was clearly insane.

Anything less than full commitment would end up with us having a soggy, beaten-up Pete on our hands. Downstream, the creek *did* eventually open up into a relatively sluggish, deep section—but it would take a massive stroke of luck for his head to miss all the rocks along the way.

He'll chicken out.

But Pete didn't chicken out. He chickened in.

That psycho suddenly launched forward, sprinting toward the edge of the rock at full steam—and jumped.

I couldn't believe my eyes. Time slowed while Pete hung in the air, ten feet above the roaring channel. The angled landing slab Pete was flying toward was *mostly* running with water, but on the far right side, it was dry where the granite rose out of the creek. I assumed he would aim for the dry patch, but his trajectory placed him squarely on the *wettest* part of the slab.

He planted on the slippery granite and stumbled past it onto dry rock where he caught his balance, safely on the other side of Horseshoe Creek.

While Pete engaged in a short victory dance, Nick and I released the breaths we'd been holding. I picked up Pete's pack and walked over to the edge of the granite. We hashed out a coordinated plan to swing the pack and release on the count of three, hopefully with enough force to err on the upstream, far side of Pete. We figured throwing the pack into the bushes *behind* Pete was a much better scenario than the throw coming up short.

His pack's weight was still blowing my mind. I'd always been a fan of carrying ultralight, but to feel prepared and safe in the Sierra, my pack weight had easily doubled. Pete's pack felt like he'd tossed in crampons and an extra sandwich and called it good. It was maddening, and brought up irrational levels of jealousy. I *hated* how much my pack weighed. And with every mile it opened my waist and shoulder welts up further, I hated it even more. How was he getting away with it? Was Pete just able to eat less? Was he not as prone to getting cold at night? How in the hell could a full mountaineering setup weigh thirty pounds?

Grabbing opposite straps, Nick and I swung the bag back and forth, counting up and releasing on "three." We put as much force behind the pack as possible. Time slowed again while it flew through the air, straps violently flapping about.

Pete caught his pack, which made it official: It actually worked. He'd jumped across Horseshoe Creek. He'd completed one of the most notorious crossings in North Yosemite *without wetting his feet*. He signaled through the roar he would hike upstream to meet us at our soft American crossing.

We reached the wide, slow spot in the creek and both of us dropped our backpacks to get dressed and prepped. While I was still putting electronics in dry bags, an upward glance spread a grin across my face. Nick already had his pack shouldered—with no pants on. Wetting as little as possible through a crossing to have dry clothes to wear on the other side was a smart strategy, but I couldn't help but chuckle at my burly teammate stepping into the creek with his jackets and bulky pack on his upper half, but just underwear and water shoes below the equator.

This guy knew how to party.

Though clearly not as risky as Pete's choice of crossing, staying on our feet through the short, swift channel was crucial. The granite corridors Pete had hopped across were just a few dozen yards downstream, and being rag-dolled through them wouldn't be survivable.

Nick stepped his UV-neglected thighs down into the dark stream and I gave my sunglasses an appreciative pat. The swift current rolled the water almost up to his waist. He wobbled a bit but moved through the channel without issue.

I focused my attention back on my bag and finished waterproofing all of my important gear. I had a much different strategy for crossing creeks. For more grip, I left my crampons on. I also basically wore everything I normally wore: boots, socks, and *definitely* pants. Our team didn't need the raw, aggressive sexuality of my bare thighs distracting us from the task at hand.

I took my time, settling back into that beautiful, calm headspace sidestepping through snowmelt. My crampon points scraped against the smooth, unstable river rocks while I hunted for solid foot placements, securely settling each foot in the creek bed before moving the other. Even at just knee-deep, the force pushing against my legs was humbling.

I stepped up onto the dry island in the middle of the swollen creek and slowly made my way across the rest. Having Pete and Nick's eyes on me was a great comfort, even if realistically there was little to nothing they'd be able to do if I was swept downstream

The sun moved out from behind the clouds just in time for a celebration lunch. We'd successfully crossed two major creeks before noon! We rolled out our wet gear, removed our boots, insoles, and socks, and laid it all out to dry on the warm rock.

A couple messages came in from Melanie—and I instantly felt like an ass. She was worried, asking for a confirmation we were safe. She'd likely spent her morning watching my GPS track moving up and down the same creek Longstride had been swept away in, and the GPS wasn't accurate enough to pinpoint which side of the creek I was on.

Mel was never the type to nag or demand too much. She usually kept messages to a minimum, and even avoided sending them until the end of the day to allow me to focus on the hike. It broke my heart a bit to read the series of apologetic, worried messages simply requesting to know whether I was still alive—and there I was, feet up, sunbathing on the far side of Horseshoe Creek with a mouth crammed full of Sriracha almonds.

Husband of the year, right there.

Guilt for my carelessness stuck with me, and I vowed after every future crossing to let Mel know I was safe before even dropping my pack. Melanie didn't deserve any more stress than she was already putting up with.

"It's hard to believe this creek took Longstride out," Nick said. "Must've waded right across at the trail."

Indeed, one of the most notorious creeks in North Yosemite was behind us, dare I say—*easily*?

Our team was working well. All three of us were fine with extra miles hiking upstream to stay safe, we'd discussed every crossing so far, and I'd felt zero pressure to attempt anything I wasn't comfortable with. Sure, occasionally one of the foreigners among us (not going to name names here) would choose to *jump* across whitewater—but to his credit, he made sure we were okay with it. I was certain if either Nick or I had clearly said, "No, you're not jumping because we don't want to deal with the consequences of you potentially screwing it up," Pete (oops) would've waded with us.

But it *had* only been a day—and in the back of my mind, I was concerned about the discrepancy between our loads. Now knowing the light weight Pete was carrying, I knew *exactly* why I'd been having a hell of a time keeping up. Nick's pack looked heavier than Pete's, but that green-eyed, creamy-thighed beefcake would've probably been able to throw my pack on top of his and still out-hike me. Deep down, I was sure I'd be holding these guys back in the miles ahead.

I needed to average six miles of progress and one creek crossing each day to stay within my rations, and we were wrapping up lunch with *nine* miles and *two* big creeks behind us! At this rate, I'd arrive at Sonora Pass with hamburger meat for shoulders, tear-stained jackets, and a week of food still in my bear canister!

I really wasn't sure what I preferred, to traverse the dangerous North Yosemite section alone at my own pace, or safely death-march behind teammates.

The decision is going to make itself. I'll either be able to keep up—or I won't.

Clouds moved back over the sun, and a stiff wind picked up, blowing our belongings around on the rock slabs. One particularly strong gust sent my sit pad flying toward the creek, and Pete made a heroic dash to snatch it before it went for a Longstride.

…

Too soon?

Pete returned the pad to me with a smile. I didn't have the heart to tell him where that chunk of foam had been, but I promised myself to give him a call after the trail to advise he go visit the doctor to get checked for… all of it.

We packed up our gear and I took a minute to shove the sit pad back inside my pants, adjusting it a bit higher than before in an attempt to keep it from reconnecting with my eh, *well-seasoned* underwear. My teammates patiently waited as I slid my pack's straps back over my raw shoulders, trying not to wince too obviously.

Inside, I wanted to be done for the day. My preferred schedule had firmly settled on waking up early and finishing around noon, like I'd done successfully throughout the High Sierra. But schedules aside, I was just tired. My waist and shoulders hurt like hell, and my motivation to keep moving was next to nothing. I wanted to lie down on those warm slabs all afternoon and enjoy the soft rush of the creek. Heck, maybe even tend to my wounds in a more appropriate manner than just crushing more sweaty shirt into them.

We reversed back downstream along Horseshoe Creek, where we picked up the PCT and continued toward Spiller Creek just a mile away. It was yet another iffy crossing we'd have to figure out. These creeks were stacked almost on top of each other, *dozens* within the seventy-five miles between Tuolumne and Sonora Pass.

We intersected the gushing creek a quarter-mile downstream of the trail crossing, and headed upstream with our eyes scanning the cascades for snowbridges or fallen logs. Our forward progress turned into a crawl as the slope pitched steeply uphill through warm afternoon slush.

Sweating and winded, we found the trail crossing for Spiller Creek, which looked *doable*—but around thigh-deep and very swift. All three of us wanted nothing more than to have this obstacle behind us. I felt an alarming temptation to just try it—to roll the dice and hope for the best. But after a discussion, we put our heads down and continued our afternoon, upstream slog.

Lubricated by a fresh film of butt sweat, my foam pad greased out of its place, periscoping out of my pants this time. For its own sake, it was no doubt better off rising than lowering, but that stupid pad was the only way to relieve some of the pressure from my shoulders. When I couldn't take the tip of the pad tickling the back of my neck anymore, I dropped my backpack to rip the vertical foam the rest of the way out of my pants and strap it to my pack. It would only take a minute to reset it, but I was already lagging behind, and the guilt of being the team anchor out-weighed the desire to relieve pain. Every second I stood still, Pete and

Nick pulled further ahead. I rushed to throw my pack back on, gritting my teeth through again dragging the weight of the bag across my sores. I cinched my waist strap and belt as tight as they would go, but it wasn't enough to remove the pressure. I was too skinny.

"I wonder if a rescue chopper could just drop a crate of cheeseburgers. $35,000 sounds about worth it," I joked; accidentally saying the word cheeseburger, thereby removing my ability to think of anything else for the remainder of the afternoon.

I stomped through the garbage snow as fast as I could manage, attempting to catch up with my teammates. I tried to distract myself from my pain and exhaustion by designing the ultimate fantasy cheeseburger I would find once I reached Sonora. But my efforts to out-fantasize my reality weren't successful. With every trudging, slushy step, my frustrations rose. I just wanted to stop.

So why am I not stopping? I can do this alone. I was going to do this alone. It's nice being within the safety of a team, but what's that security worth? Being miserable for the next fifty miles?

I tried to shake it off. My irritation was just as much embarrassment from not being able to keep up as it was exhaustion and pain.

I can make it across Spiller Creek with these guys. That'll be three major crossings and over ten miles, more than enough for one day, damn near two days' worth of progress for my food supply. There's no way we'll keep pushing after Spiller. Maybe after a solid night of recovery, I'll feel up to another long day with them.

I was surprised to catch up to my teammates around a bend in the creek. Pete's pack was down on the snow, and Nick was watching him—*flip a large log end over end.*

"What's going on?" I asked Nick, whose face mirrored mine.

Pete heard me from the bank and called over with a zealous smile. "There's no good crossing; we'll make good crossing!"

He turned and flipped the log into the water, attempting to create his own logjam for us to presumably cross.

Pete was an interesting guy. My curiosity had been growing as I interacted more and more with the rugged teddybear. After all, what did I really know about Bulgaria? I assumed it was a country. Somewhere in Eastern Europe? Something about communism? With my American education where our teachers are paid in cafeteria lunch vouchers, what *didn't* I know about Bulgaria?

I was secretly grateful to watch Pete's logs float out of sight downstream. We continued trudging uphill past black-streaked granite canyons filled with cascading whitewater. The Spiller Creek drainage was gorgeous, and something I would've never seen in a lower snow year when the trail crossing was possible. I tried to keep that in mind through the nagging pain under my pack straps. Ninety-nine-point-nine percent of past and future PCT hikers would never see this mind-blowing sector of the Sierra—and there was something satisfying about that.

We passed many crossings, but all felt like a strong maybe, and none good enough for the three of us to clearly agree on, so we kept hiking. Every hundred trudging, uphill yards felt like a mile, but we stuck to our agreement: Either we all felt comfortable to cross, or we'd continue upstream. In theory, the further we hiked, the less water there was. The origin of ninety percent of these creeks was within five miles of the PCT. So in a worst-case scenario, we'd eventually reach the alpine lake feeding the beginning of Spiller Creek and simply walk around it.

The opposite seemed to be happening though. There might've *technically* been less water, but the terrain became increasingly aggressive, and the crossing options were shifting from "maybe" to "not-even-if-there-was-a-crateful-of-cheeseburgers-on-the-other-side"(-but-with-bacon-let's-talk).

Another large section of intimidating waterfalls ran through deep ravines, feeding our eyes, but further lowering our faith that continuing upstream was beneficial. Seconds away from turning around to go find out if Pete's logs ever stopped, the terrain finally flattened out. The creek went from ten feet wide to forty feet wide with many different islands and shallow spots. Pete continued pointing out logs he could throw into the creek and gaps he could jump across. If he were to spot a bear, he would've pointed out his intention to armbar it into submission.

I was no longer alone in my exhaustion, and our team struggled to agree on a crossing to attempt. Nothing gave us the warm fuzzy we were looking for, and this wasn't the place to risk it. Being swept off our feet would result in a quick deposit into the granite ravines downstream—a horrific prospect, at best.

One painfully slow mile from the trail crossing, a mile that had taken more effort than the nine before it, I was thoroughly wrecked. With every leaden step, my standards for safety slipped a little more. I stopped for a longing stare at a crossing clearly too deep and swift, but felt an absurd pull to just—go for it. I fantasized about what it would feel like to relieve the pressure on my shoulders, about the feeling of arriving at the end of the afternoon slush, and most of all—I fantasized about lying down. All I had to do was make it ten measly feet across an obstinate bit of whitewater.

Before I convinced myself to hop in and panic-dog-paddle my way into the ravines, I forced myself to hike onward.

Finally, a wide, thigh-deep section finally presented itself—finally. Thigh-deep wasn't perfect, but the current was a touch slower than anything we'd found so far.

There was no need for discussion. This was where we'd be crossing, what we'd been waiting for, an obvious yes. My two partners stripped down into their scandalous crossing outfits while I packed up my dry bags. With shaky, drained legs from the day's hiking, coupled with the adrenaline ups and downs, I was actually kind of worried about having the remaining strength to wade such deep water.

I sat down to rest for a minute, attempting to work up enough energy and psych to not be swept away by the tamest creek in North Yosemite. I took a few deep breaths, cycling as many positive, encouraging mantras through my mind as I could recall, as if there was a separate Danny sitting next to me who had a lot more faith in Danny than Danny did.

Crossing this creek exhausted was flirting with disaster. An involuntary noodlin' from my Jell-O legs and I'd be floating downstream. Crossing was a bad idea. Camping and then executing the crossing in the morning was a *better* idea. But Pete and Nick were already stepping off the bank. They seemed fine. I didn't want to be the weakling of the group, and I really wanted to stick with my team. I'd fought with everything I had, all day, to stick with them.

"Just one more today," I whispered. "You can do this. Just one more, then you can rest. You can do this."

Wielding extended trekking poles and equipped in his creek-battling attire of skivvies, bare feet, and a beanie, Pete lowered himself into the freezing water. The deepest, and thankfully slowest, section was right off the bank. Without pants on, it was extra uncomfortable to watch the snowmelt nip the bottom of his brief-wrapped bulge.

Not that I was looking.

The next step brought the water back down to his mid-thigh, and he sidestepped through the creek without issue. Nick went after Pete, also making the crossing look breezy.

With an elderly groan, I stood up and settled my pack carefully back on my shoulders. *Maybe this won't be so bad.* It was a rather optimistic perspective from a guy whose legs threatened to buckle in the alpine breeze.

I stepped my left foot down into the deep water and embraced the cold flooding my boots and rolling up my pant legs—a familiar feeling I was getting used to but wouldn't exactly miss once I departed the Sierra. I faced upstream, leaning slightly against the current and onto my trekking poles, allowing every step to settle before I took the next. Fighting the current was proving to be tough with the water above my knees. Every step took some serious effort to work against the strong pull of the crystal clear water. My planted legs rapidly lost feeling as the heat was sucked away, and sporadically wobbled against the strain. Glancing across the creek, I saw Pete and Nick were both facing away from me, focusing on redressing and recovering from their crossings, probably assuming the grown ass man behind them would be capable of wading through a long kiddie pool without dying.

In the middle of the creek, I planted a sloppy left foot, which skidded off the side of a smooth river rock before settling in the bed. Not a huge misstep—but enough to cause my left leg to tremor and come dangerously close to buckling. I wobbled and caught my balance with my trekking poles. My adrenaline exploded and I paused for a second to take a deep breath. My tired legs were both shaking uncontrollably, an odd sensation with most of the feeling numbed in my lower half.

You're going in, fluttered through my mind. *And nobody is going to see.*

In my frozen bubble in the middle of Spiller Creek, pure frustration and anger flooded through me. My teammates had so *easily* moved through this crossing. What the hell was wrong with me?

You're not going to be the guy taken out by the tiny creek, I commanded myself. *Now **move**.*

I took great care in settling and weighting each step. Without the strength to recover from a slip, a slip simply wasn't an option. After an embarrassingly intense internal battle, I stepped into the shallow water on the far side of the third major creek that day.

Pete looked back at me. "Not so bad, uh?"

I gave him a weak smile, then used all my remaining strength to squat my soggy butt up onto the bank. A beautiful, flat clearing of snow was just beyond, a perfect spot to setup camp for the night. I gladly sloughed my pack into the slush. It would be another twelve hours before I had to slide that torture device back on! I sat to empty the extra water out of my boots and wring out my socks, overjoyed and relieved I'd somehow stayed with my team the entire day.

But then Pete crapped all over my heart.

"We're three miles from Miller Lake. That would be a good camp."

Nick paused for a second but nodded and returned to strapping his water shoes to his pack, preparing for more miles.

Is he kidding? Is this some kind of sick, Bulgarian humor I don't understand?

There was a steep climb between Miller Lake and us. Without a literal gun to my head (and maybe a cheeseburger or two to sweeten the deal), I wouldn't be able to walk three more miles, much less *steep* miles through slush.

I sat silent, staring over the channel we'd just crossed. I couldn't believe the three gnarly creeks over almost eleven trudging miles wasn't good enough. I'd pushed as hard as I could, even pushing the bounds of my own safety—and these maniacs wanted *more*.

The solution wasn't ideal, but it was clear. We had to part ways. Pete and Nick were geared up for moving faster. I didn't want to hold them back, and I certainly didn't want to be death-marched forward. I'd had company for several dangerous creek crossings, and that was better than nothing. I could do the rest alone. That was the original plan anyway.

"Guys," I started, trying to find a hole big enough to cram my big, fat pride into, "I'm camping here. I'm exhausted. You two go ahead. I've got to stop for the night."

Pete glanced at Nick with obvious disappointment, but neither said anything. Nick threw his pack on, ready to keep going, but Pete hesitated. He seemed more conflicted than I was expecting.

"Seriously, no hard feelings. I don't mind being out here alone. That's what I'm geared up for. I'm way too heavy for fourteen-mile days and multiple creeks. What we hiked today was what I'd planned to hike over *two* full days. While I'd love to stick together, my pack is rubbing me raw, and I need a break from it."

"All right…" Pete seemed like he wanted to protest, but he didn't.

My short-lived teammates threw their gear on their backs, said a quick good-bye, and disappeared into the trees. With a heavy heart, I listened to the crunch of their boots slowly fade until the only sounds were Spiller

Creek and the mild wind rustling the pines. I stared into the pure water rolling through the bends in the snowbound creek, lost in thought.

What did I just do? I was lucky enough to find a team out here—and then I voluntarily quit on them? This could be a fatal error. Bolton Creek is still ahead.

My physical and mental states were on very opposite pages. I felt sick to my stomach, and it took some effort to swallow the hard lump in my throat. I was disappointed in myself. Disappointed I couldn't keep up, that I wasn't stronger. I couldn't quite tell if my insufficiency was more disappointing or embarrassing.

"Whatever," I sighed out loud. "It was the right choice."

I was unbelievably tired. I sent a satellite message to Mel to let her know Spiller was crossed safely and that I'd be solo again. That was a bit of news she wouldn't like. I gathered enough energy to stand, then grabbed my pack to drag it the short distance to the flattest part of the clearing. It was guaranteed I'd be sleeping on snow, but that was fine with me. At this point, sleeping on snow wasn't an uncomfortable thing. It had become just—a thing.

I turned to hike away from the creek and movement caught my eye. It was Nick. He was walking through the trees, back toward me. Pete wasn't far behind.

Confused, I walked toward them. "What's up? You guys all right?"

"We'll camp here. With you," Pete said.

I was reluctant to get too excited. I didn't want to be the designated team resentment sponge for the rest of Yosemite.

"Are you sure? I really don't want to hold you two back. It would honestly be better for me if I wasn't constantly feeling like the ball-and-chain of our team."

"No," Pete responded in his heavy accent, without the anger or frustration I expected. "We should stick together. We can stay here for the night. We're all tired."

Nick was already unpacking his bag and starting to set up his tent. He didn't say a word. He either was just as tired as I, or too pissed off to join the conversation. I hoped it was the former.

Pete went to work cutting a bunch of pine boughs to lie on the snow, then pitched his tent over them, a method used to provide a layer of insulation under his tent floor. It seemed an odd thing to devote such energy to.

Is that why Pete didn't want to stop here? Is sleeping on snow something he's trying to avoid? Is he not staying warm at night? Is he going to lose sleep sticking with me?

I tried to shake off the thoughts. I'd been as honest as possible with Pete and Nick, and if they were going to slow down to stick with me, that was their prerogative. I had to do what was best for me, and they were going to choose what was best for them.

Pete went to work gathering wood for a fire. I joined him in the hunt, snapping the lowest, dead branches off the pine trees surrounding camp. He started the fire right on top of the snow, and we both shed boots and hung our socks on axes, planting them right next to the steadily sinking fire pit.

Over steaming socks, Pete and I had another great conversation. I apologized up front for my American ignorance and asked him ridiculous questions like "Where is Bulgaria?" and "Bulgarian is a language, right?"

He answered all of my questions with good humor. I enjoyed the opportunity to talk with someone so different from me, to learn about his country and experience in the States. I was especially curious as to why he was so naturally set on connecting steps on the trail. His Bulgaria was a struggling country with little to no outdoor community, certainly no thru-hiking community. People weren't spending their time and money to venture halfway across the globe to go walk for six months; they were staying at home to feed their families. Since Pete was possibly the first Bulgarian to even attempt the PCT, I would've figured he'd adopt his ethics and hiking style from the long-distance hiking community in the USA, where the vast majority of hikers on the PCT didn't care to literally walk from Mexico to Canada.

I wasn't coming from a different country, but I *was* coming into thru-hiking from the climbing community, which was a fairly drastic culture change. Similar to Pete's experience, I knew almost nothing about thru-hiking when I started the trail, and quickly learned I was virtually alone in my quest to walk every mile.

And really, if hikers didn't want to hike 2,650 miles, that didn't bother me; 2,650 miles is *stupidly* far. That wasn't the problem. What rubbed me the wrong way was their inability to separate from their identity as a "thru-hiker." They wanted the accolade without the work—akin to someone starting their first marathon, hitching a ride past all the uphill sections, then arriving at the finish line with a victorious, "I did it. I'm a marathon runner!"

Pete and I fundamentally agreed the moment we skipped any open section of the trail, our attempt at a thru-hike would be over—*ergo* neither of us would be heading toward a successful thru-hike anymore. We'd be section hikers at that point, if the definition of a section hiker is someone with at least one section of a long trail they hadn't walked through yet. Skipping any part of the PCT instantly created a section to go back for later.

But oh brother, did being labeled a section hiker rub PCT egos the wrong way.

Section hiking held a negative connotation within the thru-hiking community, which I found rather irritating. Frankly, section hiking a long trail is *harder* than a straight thru-hike. It wasn't something to consider easy, or "less-than." A thru-hike is five committed months. In sections, completely hiking a trail as long as the PCT takes *years*, sometimes *decades* of dedication! Aspiring thru-hikers get into trail shape in Southern California and get to use that fitness through the remaining 2000 miles. On the other hand, section hikers have to stay in, or constantly rebuild, their "trail legs" season after season, often while balancing work, families, and other responsibilities.

For the most part, hikers who started in Campo had already awarded themselves the title of thru-hiker—and wanted nothing to do with being rebranded. Those weren't people I respected or admired. They weren't people who inspired me. They weren't people I wanted to hike with. They were people who represented the participation trophy world I was out there to separate myself from.

Pete was an amiable guy, but he also had an intensity to him that was refreshing. After eight years in the Navy, I knew I tended to be a relatively intense personality also. After leaving the military, I'd retained an instilled craving to be around people with ethics, impressive goals, and intense passion. Pete was one of those people.

After the fire pit had sunk several feet, and we officially had dry socks for the morning, we retired to our tents. I had no idea how much longer I'd have a team to move through North Yosemite with, but I was grateful to have Pete and Nick around while it lasted.

Alone in my tent, I had a blissful amount of food at my disposal. Really, there was way too much. The long day had put me far ahead of schedule with my rations, so like a child sitting cross-legged in a pile of Halloween candy, I ate. I ate and ate and ate. Every unwrapped ounce would be one less to carry, one less ounce digging into my sores, one tiny reduction in the energy required to mentally block out my life choices.

But again—the flavors were dampened.

"What is going on with my taste buds?" I asked, again studying the back of my Snickers Bar, as if I'd discover Mars had forgotten to add the sugar or something.

The action of eating was fun, and I loved the satisfaction of food stretching the walls of my stomach, but without being able to taste what I was eating, my hunger remained strong, as if my tongue was still waiting for the dinner that had already passed it by.

"Hang in there, body," I whispered. "This won't last forever."

I sat there silently for a while, my lower half warm in my sleeping bag, lost in thought, considering what the odds were I was causing permanent damage. I couldn't rationalize a connection between hard hiking and taste loss—but if there was, I really didn't want to spend the rest of my life gnawing on cardboard every meal. A surge of desperation to be done pulsed through me, in a place where an exit was still many days and many miles away.

I distracted myself reviewing my collection of pictures, maps, and notes about the upcoming crossings. The next day we'd have to cross Matterhorn Creek, Wilson Creek, and possibly Piute Creek. All were potentially dangerous.

"Tomorrow could suck."

I smiled. Something about that was exciting.

I found the energy to go brush the seven pounds of tasteless sugar out of my teeth, then fell asleep the minute my head hit my makeshift pillow. A final thought ran through my fading mind before I slipped into the black of a well-earned sleep.

I hope I wake ready to keep up.

32

BENSON

beep beep

beep beep

I pried one resistant eye open to find my phone and silence the alarm.

Before even trying to sit up, I could feel I was in for a hard day. Every muscle in my legs and hips was sore. My welts cracked and split sliding into my hiking clothes. I could've easily tucked back into my sleeping bag until the next three a.m. rolled around.

Excited for some breakfast, I fired off my Jetboil and opened up my favorite flavor Pop-Tart: a classic Brown Sugar. I broke off a big piece and threw it in my mouth, anticipating the wonderfully preserved, diabetes-encouraging flavor—but it never came. I was just moving a dehydrated flour-and-water pancake around in my mouth.

"Damn," I muttered through the unswallowable paste.

I gave the shiny pouch the stink eye, scanning for explanation. Maybe they'd accidentally put Pop-Tart-shaped carpet in the pouch? A kind of sick joke from some disgruntled employee's last day at the Pop-Tart factory?

The pastry looked fine though. It smelled fine, too. My loss of taste had gotten notably worse just overnight, and it was starting to freak me out. I finished that Pop-Tart, then forced down a second. I needed the calories.

Food was one of the bright points in my days, something I looked forward to. Having that taken away was upsetting.

Just a few more days, I thought, trying to talk myself down. *We'll figure this out once you get out of here.*

At this point, Sonora Pass was the goal. I wasn't thinking much beyond it. I wasn't on the PCT. I was in the Sierra, closing in on the finish line. There was still a tremendous amount of trail beyond Sonora, including a couple hundred more miles of snow—but Sonora Pass was all I cared about.

The consequences of my binging had arrived. Poops were usually reserved for the middle of the day, far off the trail, preferably perched over a majestic vista. But four daily pounds of backpacking food wasn't going to patiently wait until I found a five-star view. With urgency, I shuffled out into the cold, dark night to take the complete *opposite* of a boujee poop.

When I returned to camp, I took a minute to apply a few strips of duct tape over my welts. Between the scabs and the hair, I was in for a real treat when it came time to remove it, but I needed something more between my pack and my skin. Again, I shoved my foam sit pad into my pants for some makeshift padding.

Not long after we left camp, the dark blue tint along the horizon brightened into dawn. We huffed-and-puffed up the mountainside, aiming for a pass above the Spiller Creek drainage to reconnect with the PCT. The night had been a bit below freezing, so the slush was *almost* firmed—but Lord help us when the sun touched it.

We crested the top of the saddle as the rising sun ignited low-lying clouds wrapped around the surrounding peaks. The colorful display literally stopped us in our tracks. We took several reverent minutes to gaze over the incredible landscape together.

Dropping down from the saddle, I felt shockingly good—the byproduct of hard sleep and water-flavored Pop-tarts, no doubt. My sit pad was somehow staying in place (likely out of fear of slipping south again), and I easily held pace with Pete and Nick.

Navigation toughened in the hills heading to Miller Lake. Even after several intentional, anti-getting-lost team huddles around our phones, we still accidentally missed an important notch. It wasn't much of a detour, maybe an extra half-mile, but it brought up an exaggerated frustration inside me. Every extra-credit step expended a bit of my limited reservoir of daily energy, which I knew would inevitably run dry.

At Miller Lake, Pete wandered out onto the kind-of-frozen ice to give it a few hearty pokes, like any respectable Bulgarian would.

The snow started to lose its composition heading down toward Matterhorn Creek, and my snowshoes started unpredictably sliding. Not a huge deal, as I'd become fairly used to "snowshoe skiing" at times in the erratic conditions throughout the backcountry. Sure, the right answer was to stop and shift into crampons—but I've never been one to let right answers get in the way of progress. I finally felt good enough to keep up with the team, and really wanted to avoid making them wait on me before we'd even reached the first creek crossing for the day.

In soft slush, we arrived at a 70-degree chute where the last few hundred yards stretched down to the creek's drainage. Sitting to glissade was an option, but I'd all but stopped glissading. It always seemed like a fun idea, like a child flying down a giant slide, but refrozen slush is more abrasive than you'd think. The long butt glissades off Forester and Silver Pass had actually abraded holes in my pants and backpack.

I hesitated at the top of the steep chute. Nick and Pete's crampons were sticking well enough, so they kept kicking tight switchbacks down the snow. An adjacent grove of dense young pines looked like the better option for snowshoes.

"I'll meet you guys at the creek," I called down.

Pete turned his head with concern in his eyes.

"I'll be fine, this is just too slushy for my snowshoes."

A few yards into the pines, it became apparent that Pete's concern was justified. Losing elevation through the rolling snow mounds and tree wells was awkward, and kind of dangerous with so many obstacles to collide with.

Just put your damn crampons on! my subconscious commanded me.

My hiking shoulder-demon made an appearance. *Nah, you've got this. You stud.*

At one particular tree well, I lowered my right foot down to the edge of the well, and my left slid out of its slushy placement. I managed to securely plant my right foot, but the left kept sliding until I was facing uphill. In a reflexive move, I stabbed my left foot into the wet snow behind me, hoping for the points to penetrate deep enough to attach to solid ice.

They did not.

The momentum of my pack pulled my center of gravity backwards in slow motion. With the situation officially out of my control, my view went from my uphill skidmarks to the sky through the trees. I impacted hard, pack-first. My beanie vanished and my trekking poles ripped out of my hands. I slid headfirst downhill until my shoulder collided with a thin tree in the grove.

"Ughhh," I groaned, untwisting one of my arms and wiping the slush out of my eyes.

Upside-down and half buried, I watched big, white clouds effortlessly floating through the pine needles above. It took some effort to gather the motivation necessary to unbuckle my pack and somersault backward to set my world upright again. My snow-clad beanie sat ten feet up the slope, where the first impact had knocked it off my head. I felt liquid running along my skull, behind my ears, and dripping down my neck. I ran fingers through my hair and instinctually checked them for blood. Thankfully, it was just melting slush.

"Remember how bored you were of dry trail in Southern California?" I muttered, trying not to think about how far away dry trail still was.

With a few ambiguous vows of vengeance, I stood and trudged back uphill to wrap up my yard sale. I rushed to shoulder my pack and resume down through the trees, embarrassed knowing Pete and Nick were probably wondering what was taking their poky teammate so long. Not twenty feet later, I hit another loose patch, which *again* sent a foot sliding, depositing me into a small tree well.

For the second time in five minutes, I was half-buried in slush with my belongings sprinkled along the slope above me.

"Oh, right. Crampons."

The actual PCT made a brief appearance for just a few feet before Matterhorn Creek, right where it dropped down into the water. Nick was standing at the bank with his pack off.

"Crossing doesn't look good here," he said. "Pete's downstream looking for any options—but this might be another upstream slog."

The PCT crossed Matterhorn and took a sharp left, heading downstream and parallel with the creek. That meant every upstream step would be mileage and elevation we'd have to reverse to get back to the trail.

Pete returned without any good news, so we headed gently uphill through the Matterhorn Creek drainage. It took three-quarters of a mile hiking past many "maybe" spots before the creek finally widened. The beauty in the drainage was staggering. Waterfalls cascading down canyon walls and jagged mountain peaks surrounded us. We were three specs inching across an endless work of art. A forty-foot-wide section with one short, knee-deep crossing presented itself. It was further from the trail than we would've liked, but our effort was rewarded with a simple crossing all of us waded without issue.

Successfully on the far side of another notorious creek, Pete dropped his pack. "It's breakfast time, fellas."

The sun had risen above the high canyon walls, basking our bank in warm sunlight. I sat down, glad to take a sanctioned break. But no sooner than I'd sat, a familiar feeling returned.

It was a poop. I had to freaking poop again. It had only been a few hours since my anti-luxurious, icy, pre-dawn poop, and my system had already processed another load.

I let out an exasperated sigh. *I guess this is the time to do it.*

I groaned my way back onto my feet and shuffled into the woods for round two. It took quite a while to hike far enough to find somewhere dry to bury my goods. Proper Leave No Trace guidelines dictate digging a hole 200 yards from water, which wasn't looking likely as I waded through a never-ending string of shin-deep pools and marshes. Eventually, I gained enough elevation up a hillside to get onto some solid, dry ground.

This time, I got my majestic view.

I returned to my partners and shoved down another pound of cardboard-flavored food to keep the turd-factory operating at maximum capacity. When I lifted my pack, it was the first time since Mammoth where it actually felt lighter—*damn near* manageable. All the food I'd been eating was finally putting a noticeable dent in my load. My duct-taped shoulders, however, weren't celebrating quite yet.

Covering open sores on sweaty, dirty, unwashed skin with just duct tape wasn't exactly *ideal*. I was essentially draping an area rug over an overflowing toilet. But for now, the duct tape was helping me continue forward, and I was grateful to have the pain somewhat dulled. I could pull back that rug later.

Getting back to the PCT was uneventful hiking through pools of snowmelt and small, gushing tributaries feeding Matterhorn Creek. It took two hours and a mile and a half of effort to make it the fifteen feet from one bank of Matterhorn to the other. After reconnecting with the trail, the PCT remained visible for almost a whole mile, but most of it was unusable. If it wasn't multiple *feet* underwater, it was a small creek, running with water. We stayed on top of surrounding snow, using the submerged trail as a navigation guide.

The sun came out in full force for the day as we climbed toward our next major crossing at Wilson Creek. The snow returned with the gained elevation, and the sun's reflection went to work trying to burn our most sensitive places (I should clarify: our *exposed* most sensitive places—we were all wearing pants. This is a family-friendly story.). The pure white ground was almost as blinding as the sun itself.

Wilson Creek was wild, raging hard enough to run chills up and down my spine when it first came into view, but we were in for a happy surprise. The canyon walls lining the creek had been very active avalanche territory throughout the winter. Huge fields of bowed-over pine trees and pine tree debris covered the hillsides, residual evidence of a brutal season. Wilson Creek disappeared under massive snowbridges constructed by the avalanches, and our trio strolled over the intimidating creek with dry feet. That was cause for a brief smile.

All this snow really is worth it sometimes.

The trail gods had grown tired of all my smiling for the day. The roasting afternoon sun took its toll following Wilson Creek upstream, and I started struggling. Our pace slowed back into a familiar trudge through warm slush. Sweat stung my eyes and built under my duct-tape patches enough to wake the stinging pain.

A half-second before my motivation and morale took a major plunge, we stopped for lunch in a snowfield overlooking the buried creek. Too exhausted for conversation, I sat on a lone, dry boulder fixing myself a taco, trying my best to psych myself back up for more slogging. Getting through the rest of the afternoon was going to be a fight. Desperate for my food to taste like something, I dumped a small pile of salt on my cold tuna, along with horseradish, and then a packet of soy sauce to tie it all together.

I struggled against swirling negative thoughts that wouldn't stop reminding me we were willfully hiking through the awful afternoon conditions again, a lesson I just couldn't seem to stop learning—or at least stop subjecting myself to. It wasn't as if I didn't know better, but I also couldn't stop. I couldn't sort out whether I was being smart, simply doing whatever it took to stay safe within a team, or if this was cowardice to not be assertive and stop for the day, with or without my partners.

Had I *not* learned a valuable lesson on Pinchot? We were heading straight for Benson Pass during the *least* desirable time of day to attempt a steep, snowy climb.

And my tasteless monstrosity of a fish taco was pissing me off.

What am I doing? Am I out here to follow other hikers around or should I maybe hike the hike I'd planned? A snowy pass in the afternoon? Really, dumbass? I wouldn't voluntarily do this if I were on my own. So why am I allowing myself to be death-marched through North Yosemite?

"Freakin' Bolton," I muttered to my misbehaving taco.

There were many more creeks to cross, but Bolton was the big one. It'd been notoriously dangerous in past high-snow years, and this year it had already taken out one of the four hikers ahead—that we were aware of. There'd still been no news of the other three, which wasn't *necessarily* good news. Dead hikers can't report much.

Mel relayed that Roadrunner had left the backcountry after his accident in Bolton with a harrowing tale and zero encouragement for those behind him. Taking to the internet, his advice was clear: Get out of the backcountry with your lives while you still can. He'd sent a personal message to Pete and Nick stressing the same. No reassuring tips or lessons to pass along about Bolton, just a blunt message of impending doom. Whatever he'd encountered there must've been an absolute nightmare.

I'd seen a lot of big creeks, but I hadn't been forced to wade into anything deeper than my waist. I wasn't naïve enough to believe it would stay like that all the way to Sonora Pass. If there was one creek that would turn into a full-on swim across whitewater, based on past accounts and Roadrunner's warnings, it had to be Bolton. My confidence crossing creeks had grown, and I genuinely believed I'd be able to safely navigate and cross the rest before Sonora—with that *one* glaring exception. Problem was, Bolton was still a day's travel away. So I either stuck with my bullheaded teammates for the rest of the day, as well as most of the next, or I'd cross Bolton alone.

I tossed the other half of my taco toward a curious marmot and stood to put my pack back on, wincing as I weighted the inflamed, duct-tape bandages again. It felt like I'd taken a cheese grater to my shoulder, dumped sand on it, then tossed a fat child up there for a piggyback ride.

"Everyone ready?" Pete asked with a weak smile. Even his relentless enthusiasm was tempered.

I didn't say a word, just fell in line behind my partners to push back into the slush against every shred of my better judgment.

Just this one. You can do this one pass to stick with the team. It won't be that bad.

The terrain steepened, and I fell behind. I trudged uphill one miserable step at a time while my teammates pulled further and further ahead. My sit pad had helped so much through the morning, but refused to cooperate after lunch. The pad set off to explore down one of my pant legs, so I paused to again pull the sweaty foam out of my pants and strap it onto my pack for some air.

My mental state was buckling. I wanted to be alone so badly, to set my own pace, my own schedule—but there was just that one thing I wanted *slightly* more.

I wonder if I actually have the ability to hike beyond Sonora.

My teammates were turning into smaller and smaller silhouettes high on the pass. *If I can't even keep up with my fellow thru-hikers now, less than a thousand miles into this trail, how am I going to realistically get to Canada by October? And am I really going to go risk my life to cross Bolton Creek just to quit forty miles later?*

I didn't have to cross Bolton. There was an exit out to Highway 395 upstream from that Grim Reaper of a creek, the same exit Roadrunner had used after his accident. I could be sitting in our truck tomorrow. Sweet, sweet Mel could be driving me to sweet, sweet pizza—and I'd never have to walk another step along the PCT, never again have to submerge my body into snowmelt, never again have to trudge through slush.

My face flushed in shame behind my unkempt beard. Even the idea of sitting in the truck with Melanie after quitting was unbearable, pizza or no pizza.

"You're out here to be challenged. This is it. *This* is that challenge," I scolded myself.

My jumbled thoughts leveled off into one constant repetition:

This can't go on forever.

I numbed, losing all sense of time staring down at my cramponed boots taking endless steps. Each foot slid back downhill an inch or two before the points would find enough drag in the mush to stop. Every step was labored. Draining. Awful. But I kept moving forward. No matter what I wanted to complain about inside my head, I knew *damn* well and good that short of a broken leg—and maybe a frostbitten penis—I wouldn't be voluntarily quitting anything.

Okay, one *hundred* percent I'd be quitting at the first hints of penis frostbite. One chilly willy and I'd be sitting on my Jetboil like the world's tiniest heated bidet until the SAR team arrived.

And then I'd have to find a way to cremate Amped's Jetboil.

Or sell it on eBay.

The last open stretch of suncupped snow before the summit was the steepest. It felt interminable. An eternal hill of slush. A self-imposed version of hell I would never escape. The two dark silhouettes ahead disappeared over the horizon. Pete and Nick were clearly stronger hikers, but maybe that wasn't all bad. They were pulling me forward through terrain I'd be relieved to have behind me—at some point in the future. I pushed out the last section of the snowfield with everything I had to reach the mythical crest of Benson Pass. Pete and Nick appeared, packs off, taking a break in a small patch of snow-free ground.

I felt like I needed to apologize. I expected my partners to be pissed off or annoyed, but neither of them appeared even mildly irritated. I almost wished they *were* angry. It would've validated my whole self-assigned role as the team burden. But as usual, I was my worst critic. Pete and Nick didn't seem to care in the slightest.

"That was a bit tough, wasn't it?" Nick asked me with a calm smile.

I wanted to slap him, but in the state I was in, it would've been akin to a hot dog slapping a wolverine.

"I hate—everything," I responded, too exhausted for... words.

Nick laughed. "Well we've got a bunch of downhill ahead."

I was ready to drop my backpack right there and spend the night slumped over it like a fraternity pledge covered in Sharpie wieners tipped over a drained keg—but I knew my teammates were far from being on that same pathetic page. We'd hiked over twelve miles so far, beating the previous day, and four of those miles were through slush up a pass.

How much farther could these guys realistically want to hike today? A half-mile? Maybe a mile?

"I think we maybe hike four more miles today," Pete postulated to the group in his thick accent, crapping all over my damn heart again.

I laughed in delirious exhaustion. I couldn't even pretend four more miles was possible.

"There's no way. I've felt terrible for the last three hours. Four more miles isn't an option for me. I'll stop at the next access to flowing water. You guys are free to continue on, but man—I need to stop."

Pete nodded thoughtfully before a cheeky smile spread onto his face. "I think you can do four more."

I laughed again and stood. "You have too much faith in me."

Pete and Nick had stayed back with me the night before, but the odds of them holding back for another were pretty low. I'd be tackling Bolton alone, but I suddenly didn't care. After the effort it took to follow my team up Benson Pass, death only seemed mildly inconvenient. Endless sleep, no more physical effort, no more pain, and no more slush?

Sounds like a lifestyle I could get into.

I had to move slower. I wanted to hike passes in the nicest possible snow. I wanted to take more breaks, take more pictures. I wanted to scrape together some enjoyment through the North Yosemite section, obstacles be damned.

I shoved my sit-pad/diaper/ass-sweat-absorber/pink-eye-delivery-system back into my pants. Progress off the pass went quickly. The snow was in better condition, perfect for quick plunge stepping and boot-skiing. The sharp metal points on my feet combed through the mush like a fork through steaming mashed potatoes… with cheese, jalapenos—maybe a big dollop of sour cream.

I really need to find some non-dehydrated mashed potatoes in the next town.

I shook my head, trying to jar myself out of my food-obsessive daydreaming. It was a dangerous obsession to entertain still so far from civilization. The bear can on my back full of low-sodium, fat-free carpet wasn't going to be satisfying any cravings.

I kept my eyes peeled for the first chance to stop, ideally next to running water. Melting snow for cooking and drinking wasn't a chore I wanted to deal with, and not an ideal use of my limited fuel supply. But we cruised down hillside after hillside over solid snow, no liquid water in sight. Running water was actually audible at times but buried an unknown distance below the surface.

After two miles, we arrived at the beautiful, snowed-over Smedberg Lake. None of the shoreline had melted through yet, so I mentally braced for more hiking when a hole in the snow appeared above the inlet with easy access to water.

It was officially, irrefutably time to camp.

"All right, I'm going to stop here for the night," I announced firmly to my team, signaling it was time for us to part ways. "I'm beyond exhausted, but for Bolton tomorrow, maybe I'll just wake up an hour earlier so we could potentially meet up for that crossing still?"

Pete wasn't happy. "No, no Beta. Let's keep going, just two more miles!"

"Sorry, Pete. I'm too tired, my pack is killing me—and I'm sure I could find some other excuses. I've got to stop here for the night. There's water, flat snow to pitch my tent, and it's a gorgeous spot."

Both of my teammates stood silently, looking around—but not moving on.

"Look, just go ahead. Seriously, I don't want to be holding you guys back. I appreciate you sticking with me, but it's really not necessary. Both of you packed to move at a certain pace, and I packed to go at a different pace. No hard feelings, I swear. I would love to stick together all the way through Yosemite, but these days are turning into death-marches for me while you two are chomping at the bit for more. Splitting will work out best for everyone."

"I'm done for the day too," Nick dropped his pack with a rare show of assertion. "Let's camp here."

That caught me off guard. Pete stayed silent, hesitant. I sensed a bit of irritation, which I couldn't quite understand. What was two more miles going to do for him, or for us? We were next to running water in a beautiful camp—why was it so vital to continue?

Pete was clearly more motivated than Nick and I to get out of the Sierra, and with a pack astoundingly light for a full mountaineering setup, that made perfect sense to me. He *had* to be going without in one way or another.

"Are you worried about food, Pete? If you need more to stay out here a day or two longer, I know a guy," I said with a slight smile.

"Yeah… maybe."

Pete silently gave in. He dropped his pack and began wandering around, looking for a campsite. Nick and I set up our tents in the open snowfield overlooking the lake, which seemed like the obvious choice. Instead of joining us, Pete disappeared into a nearby gully. Over an hour passed while Nick and I rolled out our belongings and rehydrated meals, and our Bulgarian friend hadn't reappeared. Once I finished my dinner, I wandered over, curious what he was up to.

Before I saw Pete, I saw snow flying through the air. I peeked over the rim of the little gully with a raised eyebrow. Wielding what looked like the end of a broken snow shovel, he was digging a trench at the bottom of the gully.

"Uhh, Pete?"

He turned to me with a big smile. "I'm digging to dry ground! I'll sleep warm tonight!"

I chuckled and headed back toward my tent, but my smile lowered as a serious string of questions ran through my mind, *Is Pete struggling that much to stay warm at night? Digging down through feet of consolidated snow is certainly more work than I'd put into a campsite—unless it was absolutely necessary. Maybe I could've kept going if Pete really needed to find some dry ground to sleep on.*

Wait, I argued with myself, *No. You needed to stop and you made it clear they could've continued if they wanted or needed to.*

Conflicting feelings of compassionate guilt and stubborn self-preservation bickered inside me while I sat on my bear canister overlooking the lake. Fluffy, white clouds overhead darkened, and I emerged from an extended daydream to realize they'd been entirely replaced by a rolling overcast.

Precipitation had been nowhere in the forecast. Hoping the clouds were a random anomaly, I sent out a satellite weather request. After a few minutes of the signal struggling to transmit through the heavy clouds, a beep on the device delivered some startlingly bad news.

A seventy percent chance of snow.

A seventy percent chance—on *June 11th.*

It was also forecasted to get cold. *Really* cold. A low around ten degrees at our elevation. That would be the coldest temperature I'd experienced on the Pacific Crest Trail yet! In freaking *JUNE*!

In the late afternoon, I slipped off my sopping wet boots in the vestibule of my tent and slid into my sleeping bag. The sound of burning wood crackled from Pete's gully.

He must've built another campfire to dry his things.

I closed my eyes, feeling slightly overwhelmed. I was worried about keeping up with my team, worried about holding them back, about Pete staying warm, the impending storm, my stinging sores, Bolton Creek—but all that was no match for my exhaustion.

I should probably go dry my boots by the fire before…

33

BOLTON CREEK: PART I

JUNE 11, 2017
SMEDBERG LAKE

Bolton cycled through my dreams.

I hadn't seen it, but I sure was terrified of it.

The evening Pete and Nick had joined me, Nick showed me the ominous satellite message he'd received from Roadrunner, who'd recently emerged beaten and bruised from attempting Bolton solo. He had bee-lined back to Mammoth to find his friend Pete, to warn him not to go into North Yosemite. When it was clear Pete had gone against his wishes, he'd sent Nick (Pete didn't have an inReach) the message all but commanding them both to *immediately* exit the backcountry and quit their Sierra run. He was sure people were going to die.

I sat up in my tent and clicked on my headlamp. It took several minutes of yawns and headshakes to tear myself out of my comatose sleep.

It was cold. Really damn cold. A thick layer of frost clung to my tent. Every exhaling plume of breath drifted a couple feet from my mouth— and stayed there. A white haze of my suspended breath hung out with me while I lit my Jetboil and forced down another tasteless breakfast.

Recycling my ghosting morning breath was kind of gross—and I'd never been so terrified of my own flatulence.

Right on schedule, the first-in-line of my daily poops had arrived, impatiently tapping its little poop foot at the back door. When I could ignore it no more, I groaned and scooted over to the door of my tent and set my Jetboil cup out in the snow, and out of the way. I was permanently paranoid about knocking over food in the tent, so right after I finished my cowboy coffee each morning (as much as you can finish cowboy coffee. I couldn't quite man up enough to filter the grounds through my teeth yet), I would set the Jetboil outside. First order of business once I stood out of my tent was usually rinsing it out. Not today though.

"Uh oh," I whispered.

The wet boots I'd neglected to dry the night before were rocks. The low temps had frozen them incredibly solid—at a *really* bad time. I shoved a foot halfway into one and stomped my boot into the ice, pleading with my digestive system to wait for a little while longer, a tall order for a guy eating two guys' worth of dried, fibrous food each day. Hunched forward in my tent's vestibule, stomping away, I lost the battle to keep the toots back. I stomped and farted and stomped, then breathed the farts in and stomped, then exhaled the farts and stomped, then inhaled the exhaled farts and stomped.

Maybe Roadrunner was right. North Yosemite was indeed, horrific.

A reoccurring joke throughout the trail was every hiker had to shaterize themselves at least once during a thru-hike. That joke was no longer funny, and inching closer to full-blown, sobering reality. I fought valiantly to get my foot into the inflexible ice-brick that was once a boot. Only the sheer fear of the brutal, not to mention embarrassing, cleanup consequences of shitting myself at four a.m. in the fifteen-degree dark kept the poop factory on a teetering, slippery pause.

I couldn't get the boot on. Through unfortunately deep, meditative breaths, I retreated back into the tent to light my stove. Making careful passes over the strong flames, I cooked my boot with trembling hands until I could finally move the tongue and pry the upper section apart. I successfully wiggled a foot into the first boot, then continued on to the second.

"These are the times that try men's souls," floated out of my mouth.

It wasn't appropriate to compare my pinched colon to the patriots fighting in the American Revolution.

With one last courageous stomp-toot, the second foot slid into place. The untied laces remained frozen in gravity-rebelling poses, but that was good enough for a clenched sprint into the woods. Nick was sitting in his vestibule, also holding a boot over his stove.

"Man, it's crazy cold!" he called out to me with an amused chuckle.

I was grateful for the distraction, and knowing I wasn't the only one struggling.

When I returned from a strong contender for the Most Uncomfortable Dump Yet award, a smiling Pete emerged from his gully.

"That was great! I haven't slept that well in a long while."

"You haven't been sleeping well?" I asked.

"On snow. It's not *too* cold—but I don't sleep much," he replied with another cheeky smile.

I picked up my Jetboil and turned it upside down to dump out the remaining coffee and grounds—but nothing happened. With a hard shake, a solid black puck slid out onto the snow.

"Whoa," I muttered, "that's new."

Smedberg Lake was a sidewalk. Its raging outlet broke through the snowpack onto bare rock slabs. With more snow waiting below the slabs, we clacked and screeched our way down until our trio was stopped at the top of a short cliff. The deep snowpack had melted six feet away from the cliff, leaving behind a ten-foot-deep gap with no obvious way to get across.

Nick followed the cliffline until he reached a point where the snow was closest to the rock. The gap closed down to just a few feet, and—in honorary-Bulgarian fashion—he surged forward, hucking himself across onto the steep snowpack. With such a bulky load on his back, the force knocked his feet out from under him. It took a twenty-foot slide before he came to a rest.

He stood up and gave us the "I'm okay" signal—but failed to inspire those behind him. Pete disappeared around the corner, closer to the cascading waterfalls coming out of Smedberg Lake. Wherever Pete was headed, I figured it was safe to assume I wanted no part in it, and decided to tackle the cliff directly.

My climber brain saw an easy downclimb. A large crack in the granite cliff leading down into the gap seemed reasonable enough to jam my way down. I threw my trekking poles across the gap, took off my gloves, and carefully lowered a crampon over the lip.

The six-inch-wide crack had thick ice coating the inside, with a solid wall of ice inset about a foot, plenty of room for a clunky boot to jam into. I crimped down on a freezing rock hold at the cliff's lip and kicked the sharp front points of my crampons into the crack, then twisted my boot to lock it in place while I lowered the other foot. I repeated the familiar process to ladder down the crack, thoroughly enjoying the momentary escape back to my beloved world of climbing.

After descending a whopping ten feet, my hands were completely numbed. I lowered a crampon onto the bare rock floor of the gap and immediately put my gloves back on. With my axe, I climbed the snow wall up and out of the small crevasse, using the front points on my crampons to excavate steps.

I collected my scattered trekking poles and met up with Nick to traverse the snow slope toward the roaring outlet of the lake to locate Pete. I half-expected to spot him riding his pack down the whitewater like a rodeo cowboy wrangling an angry bull, but we found him strolling down the slabs after downclimbing a different small rock face.

A solid snowbridge took us across the outlet, but the snow disappeared as we lost elevation headed toward the next crossing at Piute Creek. Past journals I'd come across from the high snow years 2006 and 2011 told tales of a slow, extremely flooded Piute Creek, with crossings up to a *quarter-mile* of slow, waist-deep snowmelt! Not frightening in the life-threatening sense, but more frightening in the how-are-my-testicles-ever-going-to-trust-me-again sense.

And everyone knows how difficult testicle-trust is to regain.

BOLTON CREEK: PART I

We stuck to the north bank of the outlet, where the terrain shifted into a frustrating medley of snow, rocky outcroppings, and loose dirt packed with manzanita bushes. We stepped off one patch of snow onto a shale slab. Snow continued in the distance, so we clacked across the shale in our crampons, just like we always did. Why would we lose the time taking our crampons off, just to strap them back on minutes later? We were not *slaves* to pesky "good" ideas. We were masters of efficiency!

But this time, a light *clink* came from Nick's boot.

He lifted his right foot to reveal a crampon dangling in separate pieces. His well-traveled flex bar had snapped.

"You happen to pack any backup flex bars?" I hesitantly asked. The standard thru-hiker move was to leave the metal bars at home to save weight.

Nick sat down on a nearby rock to remove the shattered crampon. "Nope."

Crampons are designed with one spiked plate on the ball of the foot, and another plate on the heel. Connecting the two plates is a piece of springy metal—the flex bar. Its essential design allows the crampon to flex along with the natural flex of a boot, but it has limits. With every step, the bar flexes, and with enough cyclic stress, any metal will eventually break. Guaranteed. We were putting hundreds of miles on these crampons, amounting to *hundreds of thousands* of steps.

It wasn't great news. Snow traction wasn't going to be optional in the dozens of unknown miles ahead. Pete and I joined Nick in removing our crampons, collectively shocked and with a newfound sense of paranoia. It was quite the reality check to witness how quickly our precious snow gear could disappear. All of us were concerned about what that meant for the team, but nobody said a word.

I had the exact same pair of crampons as Nick. I hadn't dealt with breaking a flex bar yet, but I'd also spent most of the Sierra in my snowshoes, which didn't have flex bars or any sort of similar wear part. (But alpine snowshoes are stupid, I'd been so thoroughly assured.) I'd actually considered packing a backup flex bar but decided against it. Snowshoes were my primary mode of traction, with crampons as I backup. I'd rarely strapped on my crampons before Mammoth, so I figured bringing backup repair parts

357

for my *backup* mode of traction wasn't worth the weight. Nick's gear was certainly not my responsibility, but I would've loved to be able to reach into my bag to instantly fix the situation. As it stood, Nick had zero pairs of snow traction, while I had two.

Should I lend Nick my crampons? Is that something I'm obligated to do?

The crampons weighed several extra pounds, pounds I'd intentionally carried all the way through the Sierra, both for the ability to tackle terrain in the most optimal gear, but to *also* serve as a backup in case my snowshoes failed. Neither Pete nor Nick had any form of backup snow traction or even repair parts. They also had reaped the benefits of carrying lighter—but had just come face to face with the consequences.

Offering whatever I could to help was my gut reaction, but a big part of me resisted the idea. A cumulative irritation was building. I'd been wearing myself ragged trying to keep up with my heavier pack, but it was a load with everything necessary to stay safe, warm, and fed. The idea that I was not only death-marching behind my lighter-loaded, less-prepared teammates, but that my gear would serve as the whole team's backup gear was tough to swallow.

To be fair, nobody had asked anything from me yet. Pete hadn't asked for any extra food, even when I'd offered. Nick hadn't asked for my crampons. All of this was in my head, and if I didn't want to give away any of my food or gear, I didn't have to. *But*—there was a looming thought to contend with: The only thing worse than being the team's gear mule would be watching one of my partners suffer or die while the remedy sat unused in my backpack.

We were in a team, but I also had to prioritize self-preservation. After all, if I gave my crampons away, then broke my snowshoes and slipped and drowned in a river, I'd *probably* regret any altruistic decisions that got me there.

We made excruciating progress downhill through the dense thickets of manzanita. Any opportunity we had to get back on flat snow, we took. But the further we dropped into the Piute Creek drainage, the rarer snow became, leaving us to bushwhack along faint game trails. The loose dirt under the manzanita wasn't visible through the dense brush, and we took our turns launching into pokey slides. Untangling from the stiff, stubborn branches was testing everyone's patience. I was actually looking forward to Piute Creek. A quarter-mile of manzanita-free testicle-icing was starting to sound downright pleasant.

On the drainage floor, we entered a dark forest growing out of large, stagnant pools of water. Very briefly, we found the trail, right before it disappeared under a dirty marsh filled with brown ice, pine needles, and rotting logs. Heavy, gray clouds had massed overhead, masking most of the light, giving the forest a rather creepy vibe. I was relieved to have company.

Emerging successfully from the forest without being eaten by any candy-toting witches, we caught our first glimpse of the lazy, greenish-blue Piute Creek. Its typical banks were visible, only they were *five feet* under the surface. Adjacent to the PCT, a massive log spanned the first branch of the creek! It seemed our reproductive systems would remain un-iced for the time being, but other swollen branches of the creek were waiting through the trees ahead.

On an island separating the two largest branches of Piute Creek, we worked our way through a maze of fallen logs toward the second branch, praying for a reasonable crossing—and there was one. A gigantic log jam.

I didn't want to get my hopes up too soon—but in a shocking twist, it seemed the internet had gotten this one wrong too. After hopping across the log jam, we were technically on the far bank of Piute Creek, but the incredible swell of the waterway had overtaken the trail for hundreds of yards. We balanced our way atop more downed logs, doing our best to link a dry path through the mess. It took a moment of Bulgarian engineering to flip a log or two into place, but we stepped back onto the PCT with dry boots. So not only was a waist-deep, quarter-mile wade avoided, but our socks were still dry with *zero* steps hiking upstream.

Piute Creek was a confidence boost, and we needed it. Bolton was just a few miles away, on the other side of Seavey Pass. We would come face to face with the apex challenge on the PCT before the day was out. The only information we had on Bolton was from Roadrunner, if you could categorize a general proclamation of doom as "information." All three of us were doubtful we'd be able to actually cross it. Melanie was keeping an eye out for any news about Breeze, Monster, and Sneaky, but there still had been no updates. They were either getting very close to Sonora Pass—or they hadn't been as fortunate as Roadrunner. All three of us agreed we owed it to ourselves to at least go look the beast in the eyes before bailing. If we had to quit, we wanted to make that decision based on our own experience, not someone else's.

Just before the flat trail pitched upward toward Seavey Pass, Pete and Nick decided it was breakfast time. I welcomed the break—because any excuse to take my pack off was fully embraced. I took the opportunity to stroll into the woods for another disappointingly view-less poop, again not four hours after my last. Stepping through shallow patches of snow, I saw something I hadn't seen since Mammoth: bear prints.

Yosemite was typically a hotbed of bear activity during the summer months, but so far, I had only come across a couple tracks, total. It seemed most of the bears were still hibernating.

Not in Piute Canyon.

Track after track formed a crisscrossing mess through the mud and snow, no doubt from the big animals heading back and forth from Piute Creek. It was a bit rattling being alone under the dark forest canopy. I tried to tell myself they were all from the same animal, but there were many little prints alongside much bigger ones.

"Better make this quick," I said aloud, as if the bears needed reassurance that I'd soon be done defiling their forest.

I took a few extra steps away from Bear Highway before squatting down in the dark, damp woods. I couldn't stop looking over my shoulders, highly paranoid I was about to get mauled halfway through a doodie. Snowflakes started gently drifting down through the pines.

"Ohhh goody," I whispered.

I returned right as Pete and Nick were wrapping up their food, and the snow had picked up. We all threw on extra layers, but before we'd even hoisted our packs, the snow and wind had amplified.

Uh, buddy? It's snowing. Are you really about to go hike up and over a pass? It's windy and cold down here—what do you think it'll look like at a higher elevation? Sunshine and rainbows?

This time, I was easy to ignore. There was a dangerous creek only a few miles away, and the closer I got to Bolton, the more I wanted company. Normally, if I was alone and a storm started up, I'd setup camp and hunker down without a second thought, but with the plethora of bear tracks in Piute Canyon, camping was an easy no. Pitching a tent alone in Creep Forest and then spending the afternoon waiting to wrestle a black bear for my beef jerky sounded way less appealing than getting snowed on.

We climbed up and out of the canyon, snow thickening under our boots and over our heads. We stopped for Pete and me to don traction. Nick strapped his one good crampon to his left foot, ready to tackle the pass like a boxer entering the ring with one arm tied behind his back. My crampons sat on my back, unused.

"Nick, how about you take my right crampon so you have two to get up this pass?"

He looked surprised. "Uh, definitely. Are you sure?"

"Of course. It's not doing much good on my back."

I unstrapped my crampon and tossed it to him. From the angle of self-preservation, it wasn't smart. I'd equipped my pack for problems in the backcountry. I'd carried three pounds of crampons as a backup for hundreds of miles, which I wouldn't have any more. If I wanted or needed to use them instead of my snowshoes, was I going to demand them back from Nick? Actively endangering him at my whims?

Probably not.

But I couldn't push away the obligation to help a teammate in need. At the end of all my cold logic and reasoning, offering a crampon to Nick was barely a choice. He needed help, and I had help to offer. I couldn't be next to him struggling up steep, icy slopes with just one crampon while I harbored an unused pair.

Falling wet, heavy snow continued to thicken. Pack covers and rain jackets went on. Heads went down and we pushed higher into the storm. I trailed behind my teammates, once again chasing Skittles. Numerous gushing tributaries crossed our path, cascading down into Piute Canyon.

The snow improved as we gained elevation up steepening slopes. My snowshoes made catching up easy. While my partners switchbacked back-and-forth in their crampons, I flipped my heel lifters up and drew a straight line upwards. My shoulders had about had it for the day, and the pain was starting to push into the forefront of my focus. Whatever inflamed chaos was going on underneath the duct tape was getting louder.

You're going to have to deal with this before Sonora, I thought to myself. The thought of removing the makeshift bandages made my stomach turn.

Winds gusted with startling intensity closing in on the pass, swirling twisted flurries of fresh powder across the ice. Temps plummeted, but that was mostly a good thing. The snow was staying snow, and not melting into our clothes, and the low temperature was a perfect match for our exertion. Working hard uphill in both a fleece layer and rain jacket, I was warm but not sweaty. Unpleasant experience had taught me warm and dry was the goal—and crucial for staying safe in Sierra snowstorms.

Using the brim of my hat to block the weather, I lifted my head every so often to make sure there were still two Skittles ahead. I weirdly enjoyed the view and beloved **crunch** of my orange snowshoes biting into the powder-frosted ice. Hard ice was a rare treat these days.

We crested Seavey Pass in peaking winds. We didn't take too much time to celebrate before moving downhill toward the monster winding through the canyon below. Finding a safe path down proved to be slow, exhausting work. The terrain was surprisingly steep, and building snow was bad news for the guy with snowshoes. An inch of fresh powder had fallen, so the two-inch teeth under me were still able to reach through to grip solid ice, but another inch and my snowshoes would start floating dangerously on top. It was an ideal time to shift into crampons.

Oops.

Before it was within sight, Bolton Creek made its presence known. The concussive rumbling through the storm put us all on edge. It was a bout of thunder with no end. We dropped lower into the canyon with the solemn mood of three rookie knights headed into a dragon's den.

Flat snow was nonexistent, but a towering pine angling awkwardly out the side of the canyon wall allowed our team a place to drop our packs and get a bite to eat with the creek taunting just a hundred feet below. Four miles downstream, the buried PCT crossed Bolton, but we weren't going to head straight there. We hashed out an attack plan to first explore any upstream options. If there was a creek we'd be taking our time with, it was this one.

My appetite had again perished in a sea of nerves. I took out a Snickers, in hopes my day's dessert would be appealing enough to eat. But after a couple of bland nibbles, I folded the packaging back over the rest and returned it to my bear canister. Several built-up messages came in on my inReach as the GPS signal somehow broke through the bad weather and steep canyon walls.

One message was from Amped (or maybe he was going by "Miguel" these days), wishing me luck with crossing Bolton. The other three made my heart sink. Three short messages from Melanie obviously sent throughout the morning that hadn't been able to break through the storm.

Good morning! Are you going to make it to Bolton today?

The weather looks terrible. Will you guys be okay out there?

And the last, hardest message to read,

Please come back to me safe.

I read and reread the messages, staring at the inReach while Pete and Nick finished their lunch. What I was doing was incredibly selfish—I knew that. If something terrible happened to me, it wouldn't take much longer than a couple minutes before my pain and suffering would be over. But how long would Melanie suffer afterwards?

I mean sure, there'd be fewer socks left around the trailer. And the average smell in her life was bound to improve. But the thought of not having the rest of my life to adventure alongside my best friend was miserable.

I'll either find a knee-deep crossing, or I'll exit the Sierra—whether or not Pete and Nick are with me.

Bolton Creek flowed through Muir Canyon, and traversing the steep canyon above the torrent was clearly going to be an obstacle in and of itself. To afford us more mobility to scout our preferred crossing, we stashed our heavy packs in the tree well around our lunch pine and headed upstream unloaded.

The storm intensified, and fresh snow was accumulating quickly. Random snowshoe steps started floating on top of the powder and sliding a few inches before enough snow would plow aside for their points to bite. That loss of control was frightening. Crampons were the right tool for this job, and I officially needed *my* crampons on *my* feet.

Demand it back! My shoulder demon insisted.

*And what? Leave Nick to do this with one good crampon? Give him my snowshoes? The ones that are actively trying to send **me** for a slide into the creek?*

I continued along, taking extra time to kick my points through the deepening layer of powder. I made safe forward progress, but again lagged behind my partners. A mile upstream from our packs, the terrain eased and a glorious sight came into view.

Snowbridges. As in *multiple*—and they were all solid.

There was a safe way across Bolton Creek.

"Looks like we'll have our choice!" Pete shouted back to me with equal parts excitement and shock—but something wasn't right.

We glanced between each other with dwindling enthusiasm.

"Are we missing something?" Pete asked. "This feels too—*easy.*"

Snowbridges seemed like a godsend, but we were now *five miles* upstream from the summer crossing, and a lot of surprises could be hiding inside that much cross-country travel through a tight canyon.

"I don't want to rain on this parade, but if we cross here, it's *possible* Bolton Creek won't be traversable along the full length of its north bank." I opened the topographic map downloaded on my phone and scrolled along the bank on my snowflake-speckled screen. "The elevation lines along the other side of the creek accordion pretty close together at a point about three miles back toward the PCT. That could be a possible roadblock, maybe a spot where the bank turns into cliffs lining the creek."

Pete nodded. "And if we get stopped by cliffs, we'll have to reverse those miles to recross these snowbridges here, then traverse back along this bank to find another option."

"That could take a day by itself," Nick added.

"And if crossing Bolton were this simple, why is it so notorious?" I asked. "I'm not sure this is it."

Discouraged, we headed back toward our packs, unconvinced we'd found anything of substance. But we'd done our due diligence in scoping out upstream options, and now it was time to head downstream. Ideally, we'd find an option beyond those potential cliffs on the northern bank.

There was a sense of urgency retracing our fading tracks. The storm hadn't stopped building, and there was literally nowhere to pitch a tent along the slope—much less three. My pace slowed reversing the steeper sections. Kicking steps with my snowshoes was working well enough, but it was mentally taxing, slow work. I kept my fingers crossed that downstream from our packs, we'd find milder terrain.

The sky fully opened up just as we reached our packs. Thick snowflakes fell in a hauntingly beautiful display that would've been far more pleasant to be witnessing with our feet propped up in front of a ski resort fireplace. Pete threw his pack on with firm resolution, but Nick had doubt in his eyes.

"You think we're actually going to find anything better than those snowbridges?" he asked. "That creek doesn't sound very forgiving, and it's not going to get any smaller the further downstream we hike."

We stood silent for a few seconds, trying to sort our thoughts through the noise of the thundering creek. Snow was quickly accumulating around us.

"I don't know if we'll find anything better," I said. "The odds certainly aren't in our favor. Roadrunner must've seen the entire creek from this point downstream to the trail crossing. If there really was a safe way across, he would've crossed there. He must've been *forced* to try a sketchy crossing near the trail, simply because there were no other options—right?"

More silence.

"We need to see that steep section on the northern bank," Pete said. "We could keep our packs stashed here to quickly scout downstream until we can see it across the creek, then make a decision?"

Nick and I glanced at each other. "Sure, yeah," Nick replied, "let's do that."

Again, we hiked away from our snow-frosted packs into the storm. The canyon slopes led down to snow cliffs ten feet high lining the creek. We had two miles until the steepest section of the north bank was visible, but within the first hundred yards the slope steepened to forty-five degrees, slowing our pace to a crawl. The fresh layer of powder under my snowshoes made every step unpredictable. I was desperate to have my crampons under me but couldn't formulate a respectable way to get them back.

Pete and Nick again pulled ahead, fading into the storm. There was officially more snow on the ground than my snowshoe points could bite through. Even after multiple hard kicks, my steps slid an inch or two before compacting enough dry snow to take another. Instead of sinking metal points into ice, I was stepping along hastily compacted steps made of weightless powder.

My subconscious broke into the foreground for a scolding, *It was snowing back in Piute Canyon. That's where you should've stopped to camp, but you kept going. You were prepared with the proper snow gear, carried those extra pounds all the way here—and then you gave it away! How can you **still** be moving forward?*

I had no choice. Continuing on felt reckless, but so did moving back. Even if I stopped and returned to my pack, there wasn't a single spot along the canyon to pitch my tent well enough to ride out the storm.

Pete stopped before an even *steeper* stretch, patiently waiting for me to catch up.

"We've only made it a half-mile," Pete said. That was a generous overestimate. We might've still been able to see our packs if the storm hadn't been so dense. "These slopes aren't going to let us just wander up and downstream, not with any level of speed or safety, at least. I don't think this is smart. We should go back for our packs and fully commit to heading downstream."

"My snowshoes are trying to float on top of the snow, and it's starting to freak me out. Their teeth aren't biting anymore. I'm not sure where it would even be possible, but finding shelter is my biggest priority."

Both of them nodded.

"So if we return to our packs, and then hike back downstream," Nick took a frustrated breath, "what if we don't find anything better than the upstream snowbridges? Are we really going to risk hiking four or five miles through all of this—*fully loaded*—with the potential we'll have to *reverse* it?"

We froze again, silent in the driving wind and snow, trying to think, trying to stay calm and stick to reason. Maybe we should've just crossed the snowbridges. But maybe Roadrunner missed something. Maybe wherever he'd crossed wouldn't be so bad with teammates. Maybe it was going to take hiking twenty miles up and down along Bolton over the next two days to locate a safe crossing.

Maybe we needed to bail back over Seavey.

The options felt endless—not to mention terrible. The longer we waited, the more snow fell, and the more risky the south bank would become.

"Let's just go back to our packs and commit downstream," I said. "Everyone pray we'll find something Roadrunner missed. At the first flatish spot, we'll setup camp to ride out the storm."

It took twice as long to reverse what we'd just painstakingly crossed. In a complete whiteout, we dusted the inch of snow off our packs. The mass of large, heavy snowflakes dumping from the sky was erasing our tracks at an alarming rate. Without wasting any time, I led the way back across the fading depressions that were fresh footprints not two minutes ago. My teammates followed close behind to keep an eye on me. If a slip took me sliding toward the creek, there was little to nothing they'd be able to do, but their presence close by was still reassuring.

Every step was an ordeal. My team patiently waited for me to apprehensively weight each snowshoe, allowing it to slide until enough powder compacted under the platform to stop. Then, I'd stab my trekking poles into the snow as many times as it took to sink their carbide tips into ice, then hold a breath while I shifted my weight onto the impacted step to repeat the process on the other side. Inside, I begged every weighted shelf not to give out. It was sketchy, draining, frightening, slow work.

Thirty minutes in, Nick hesitantly asked, "Hey man, do you want your crampon back?"

I appreciated the gesture, but there was no point in even trying to switch out snow gear where we stood. The terrain was too steep, too unstable. It would be switching seats on a moving roller coaster. Besides, as it stood, one of us, whether it was Nick or me, had to traverse that slope without crampons—and it was me. That's just how the dice had landed.

"No, I'll be all right," I fibbed.

"Just take your time," Pete called out from behind Nick. "We're right behind you."

Only a few hundred yards in, I settled my right snowshoe, then planted my trekking poles as solidly as I could, like I'd done a thousand times before. I went to step my left foot forward—and it happened. The compacted snow under my right foot collapsed.

The unexpected slide lasted mere inches before enough additional snow compacted to stop it, but the unplanned, jarring movement sent me wobbling. I stabbed my left foot back into the snow, narrowly restoring my balance. Bits of my crumbled step tumbled down the slope, growing into snowballs that disappeared over the cliff lining the whitewater.

A hiker deposited into the creek would be in trouble. If they survived the trauma of the fall into the rocky rapids, there was no easy way to get back out. Even if that unfortunate, soggy soul gained their footing in a shallow section of the creek, the overhanging walls of snow guarding the banks would be almost impossible to reverse.

My heart jackhammered away, sure we were dead. My legs vibrated, desperate to sprint in the opposite direction from the danger. I paused for a few seconds, trying to calm my nerves enough to take the next step.

Nick broke the silence with a calm, "You've got this, bud."

"I need to find a place to stop sooner, rather than later."

Those words meant nothing. Stopping wasn't up to any of us. Steep hillside after steep hillside, one terrifying step at a time, we pushed downstream while our eyes scanned the creek in pleading search of a safe passage. Of course, it was highly unlikely we'd come across anything reasonable. Roadrunner hadn't.

The further downstream we hiked, the more snowmelt would be feeding the creek, and the more intense the whitewater would become. I'd promised to cross nothing deeper than my knees, but we were heading for something much deeper. Our sketchy progress downstream felt irreversible, a Chinese finger trap we were sliding deeper and deeper inside of. Reaching safety wouldn't be as simple as just turning around. A swim through rapids would *potentially* be safer than retracing our steps!

Roadrunner's dilemma was coming into focus.

But then, about a mile downstream from where we'd left our packs, and several miles shy of the PCT crossing—a snowbridge.

It wasn't the most robust bridge I'd ever seen. The middle was only a foot or two thick, not exactly ideal for a snowbridge spanning over 20 feet—but it *was* a bridge. Relief flooded through my whole nerve-wracked body, but it vaporized just as fast.

"There's got to be something wrong with it," I said. "There's nowhere else to hike through this canyon but within easy sight of this, so Roadrunner *definitely* saw it but couldn't use it. If he was forced further downstream to wade, that's a pretty solid sign he found out the north bank *isn't* traversable."

We stalled in silence, suddenly hesitant to use the heaven-sent bridge.

Pete had a wistful smirk on his face. "Wouldn't it be nice to be able to call Roadrunner right in this moment?"

"Well, at least it looks relatively flat over there," I said, pointing across the bridge. "I'm going to set up camp and wait out the storm. Again, you two are free to keep moving, but without crampons on my feet, I'm waiting until conditions improve."

"Might be good for all of us to camp here," Nick said. "I don't want to go on with your crampon, and I'm pretty sure I can fix mine if I have time to work on it."

Pete was hesitant—insane on the face of it—but not only was it well below freezing in the middle of the day, we'd also be camping on snow.

"Is that all right with you, Pete? You going to stay warm tonight?"

"Warm enough," he answered with a half-smile. "I'll stop here."

We all took turns walking over the bridge, just in case. In a surreal flash, we were all on the far side of Bolton Creek, safe and dry. No wading, no harrowing swims, no jumping—just a leisurely stroll over a perfectly situated skywalk spanning what we'd been fearing for weeks.

Not one of us believed we were done. Any celebratory thoughts were snuffed out by well-deserved skepticism. With steep canyon walls lining both sides of the creek, Roadrunner saw the bridge, almost guaranteed—but he hadn't been able to use it. I was positive we'd hit a roadblock along the north bank.

We settled in for a long, snowy afternoon after pitching our tents and diving inside, collectively relieved to get a break from the storm. Nick began his repair session, wrestling with duct tape, string, and whatever else he had to MacGyver his crampon back to health. The weather tapered off, but we stayed put.

I circled around camp, trying to find water. Although hundreds of thousands of gallons were flowing by in the creek thirty feet away, it was impossible to collect with the cliffs protecting it. Thankfully, I found a small stream trickling through a crack in a boulder, flowing just enough to fill our bottles.

I'd largely forgotten about the pain underneath my patches once we'd entered Muir Canyon, but safely in camp, it returned. In a below-freezing tent, I removed all my layers of shirts, dug a fingernail under one corner of my waist patch, and gave it a few hearty tugs to tear it off. That welt was looking surprisingly good. I scratched up the corner of my right shoulder patch, paused for a deep, bracing breath, and ripped through about half of the bandage before the dizzying pain stopped me. I took a few more quick breaths and tore off the rest, then repeated the same dizzying process on the left shoulder. I couldn't tell if ripping the scabs up, or the chest hair out, was causing the most pain. The combination of the two was just—lovely.

Covering the raw welts without anything between the tape and the oozing sores had been a terrible choice.

Surprising, I know.

The tissue was far from healed, and instead was red, bleeding, and inflamed; well on its way to being full-blown infected. On the bright side, there were awkwardly hot patches of baby-smooth skin on the upper corners of my chest, and as we all know—one cannot prepare too early for swimsuit season.

I needed a different solution. My waist would be fine with another duct tape patch, but I needed something more for my shoulders. I didn't have any large patches of gauze in my first-aid kit, but I *did* have a baffling number of small Band-Aids. So with my legs crossed, still shirtless, serenaded by the steady tap of snowflakes, I used the small scissors on my pocket knife to remove the sticky ends of a couple dozen of the small bandages, then arranged the gauze squares onto a piece of duct tape to create one big Band-Aid.

I stuck my janky masterpiece onto my right shoulder with a healthy bit of Neosporin, and sent a quick prayer out to the cosmos the infection would at least hold steady in the few days I had left before Sonora. I wasn't sure any wound could improve under the daily barrage of pack straps.

Through chattering teeth, I repeated the process to patch my left shoulder, then put all my layers back on. With a whole isolated afternoon ahead, I opened my bear canister to have some fun. None of it tasted like much, but now that we were safe, my appetite had returned with a vengeance. The death-marching had put me days ahead in my food schedule, so each meal was basically a free-for-all. It was almost impossible to eat enough to break into any future meals, so I spent a couple hours engaged in a heated eating contest with myself.

With a packed belly and a semi-subdued appetite, I tucked down into my sleeping bag.

What are we going to find ahead along this bank? If it turns out to be impassible, what do we do? Hike back to recross the snowbridge, then head downstream to wade? Upstream to bail? If a wade is going to risk the same accident Roadrunner went through, is it even worth going to look at?

CRUNCH

I hadn't even started to stress over the refreshed avalanche threat.

As soon as we'd crossed the snowbridge, I'd tried to send a message to Melanie on the inReach, but hours later, it still hadn't been able to break through the storm. My stomach was clenched into a knot. Our slow, sporadic GPS track stopping at a point along Bolton probably didn't look great. I would've given anything to assure Mel I was safe, but there was no way to update her. I also didn't know when I'd be out of Muir Canyon to have a clear-enough view of the sky to send a message out. It could be days.

It could be never.

I tucked down into my sleeping bag under the soft blue canopy of my buried tent and fell asleep to the sound of the storm.

34

BOLTON CREEK: PART II

JUNE 12, 2017
BOLTON CREEK

After twelve hours of sleep, it wasn't hard to wake up to the muffled alarm coming from whatever sleeping bag fold my phone was smothered in, but I hesitated to start packing. I'd set a standard three thirty a.m. alarm, but our team hadn't actually made a plan for the day. Once we'd disappeared into our tents to get out of the storm, the only communication we'd shared was Nick shouting he'd successfully mended his crampon.

It was dead silent, giving me a fleeting moment of hope the storm had passed, but then I noticed the walls of my tent were sagging. A couple of punches knocked the solid blanket off the walls, and the patter of snowflakes returned.

"It's still snowing?" I asked the dark walls of my tent.

I sank back down into my warm sleeping bag, running through my options for the forty-seventh time. The previous day had been bad. Really bad. I'd been playing with fire traversing steep powder in snowshoes. Now, I'd have my crampons back, but there was a new threat. It had never stopped snowing. Fresh powder over old ice was a perfect recipe for avalanches—and we were in the middle of a long, steep canyon. I'd seen plenty of examples of what happened in canyons when accumulated snow was sloughed. I don't know what kind of astronomical force it takes to fold a full-grown pine tree in half—but I *really* didn't want to be there while it was happening.

I wanted to move, to get out of Muir Canyon and out of North Yosemite as soon as humanly possible, but maybe the right move was to stay put. The terrain wasn't any safer than when we'd gone to bed. It was also cold. *Way* colder than we'd expected. We hadn't been able to start a fire because of the snowfall, so I'd removed my soggy footwear the previous night and set everything in the vestibule of my tent with a desperate prayer it would all somehow dry rather than freeze.

"Oh no," I muttered.

Smacking one of my rigid socks against the tent's center support sounded like I was wielding a monkey wrench, and not a hunk of sweaty wool. My backup pair of socks I'd pinned to the exterior of my pack never got a chance to dry in the storm, so I had two pairs of bullet-hard, unusable socks. My boots were in the same boat. I put two of my rock socks into a Ziploc bag, paused for a second to mourn the loss of comfort for the day, then threw the icy package of stink down into my sleeping bag for a miserable spooning sesh. I could use my body heat to soften the socks, but my boots were going to be another story. It was likely going to take another boot-roasting affair.

With my frozen plastic brick pushed against the warm skin on my stomach, I attempted another weather report request from my inReach. But after fifteen minutes of the device futilely trying to push a message out, I gave up and turned the inReach back off to save its battery. I pulled out a small mercury thermometer to check the temperature, but the thermometer only read down to twenty degrees—and it was pegged low.

With eyes wide open in the pitch black, all of the same unanswerable questions raced through my mind while I thawed my socks.

When is it going to stop snowing? I wonder how much accumulated on the slopes alongside the creek? What if Nick's mended crampon breaks? How long are these crazy low temps going to stick around? It is June, right? Should we be hunkering down through the storm? Take a rest day? What're the odds these guys would agree to that—especially Pete? Do they have enough food for an extra day?

I had plenty of food to go around, but I was starting to build a resistance to the idea of sharing. I'd offered to divvy up my rations many miles ago, and neither teammate had taken me up on it. If Pete and Nick remained hell-bent on staying with me all the way to Sonora, then splitting the weight of our combined provisions should've already happened. Trying to keep up with them under my load was literally wearing my skin away. Sure, a true man would probably be able to swallow the burden of carrying a few extra pounds of Pop-Tarts for his buddies, but all the cold, welts, and dehydrated food farts had left me rather—fussy.

By four thirty, I hadn't heard any noises coming from my partners. I peeked my head out into the biting cold, and there was a light on in Nick's tent. Pete's tent was the furthest away, but I didn't see any light or signs of life. It was safe to assume they were hunkering down until dawn. This wasn't a normal morning. We could all handle cold, we could handle snow, we could handle dark—but tackling all three at once seemed like the wrong move. I certainly didn't want to be the schmuck standing in the sub-twenty-degree dark with a dismantled tent, ready to go while my teammates were still snoozing.

At a quarter to five, I reached over for my Jetboil to get breakfast/boot-roasting started, and footsteps crunched outside my tent.

A croaking Bulgarian voice asked, "Beta, you almost ready?"

My heart jumped. *What the hell? Pete's up—and ready to go?! It's early even for our normal days!*

I instantly felt like a genuine, certified dick. "Damn, Pete. You really want to hike off into the dark in this storm? Why don't we wait until it's light at least, so we can see what we're up against? Is your tent already packed up?"

After a few seconds of tense silence, he replied, "Um... okay. My tent is still up. I'll go sit in there until you guys are ready."

I peeked outside again. Nick's headlamp was still moving around in his tent, which was reassuring, but guilt crept in with the knowledge Pete was up, ready, and—once again—waiting on me. I abandoned all my conflicting thoughts still entirely unsure whether leaving camp for the day was a smart decision, and launched into a packing frenzy. Breakfast was erased from my morning, and I hurriedly shuffled around in my tent, wrapping up my gear as quickly as I could.

The day hasn't even started, and you're already being pushed forward.

That was a souring thought.

Should I demand they leave without me? Would they do that? They certainly haven't been willing to leave me behind yet. Besides, is this a smart time to go solo? Do I really want to be alone to traverse this creek?

Unable to formulate any answers, the mechanical part of my mind took over and shoved it all aside. I pulled out my half-frozen socks from their Ziploc bag and forced my feet into the icy wool, then grabbed my left boot and started prying the inflexible leather and laces apart.

This is a bad idea. How can this not be a bad idea?

After several minutes funneling my anger and frustration into breaking into my boot, I'd only managed to open up the mouth of that frozen brick enough to hammer half of a foot inside.

My mind was desperate to sort out my situation and the best course of action, but nothing made sense. Again, I felt I was hiking out of obligation. I was being forced onto someone else's schedule out of my own fear of being alone. Partners were a mental boon to have around, but was I sacrificing the enjoyment of my hike because I was too scared to forcibly remove myself from the team?

Why do these guys want to stick with me? And why am I so scared to be alone? I know what I'm doing. I've read the past accounts. I have all the crossing information. I have enough common sense and risk management to make it through North Yosemite safely. So why am I so scared to just—try it?

With exaggerated force—which was one part necessity, two parts stress relief—I repeatedly hammered my boot into the ground. After enough stress relief to just about snap my own ankle, my numb, scrunched foot finally slid into place. With badly bunched socks and a half-assed attempt at tying the steely laces, I switched over to the right boot.

The repeated failed attempts to stay behind had made any further attempts increasingly awkward. Pete and Nick seemed determined to stick with their slower, heavier teammate, and the idea of confronting the issue even one more time was *possibly* more uncomfortable than hiking at five a.m. in a sub-twenty degree snowstorm. With one final, pissed-off kick, I winced as my right foot slid past the tightest constriction and into the bottom of its icy coffer.

I stood into the dark morning on a few inches of fresh powder. Any more than two fresh inches was when avalanche safety became a concern.

Perfect.

Snow continued falling while the three of us rolled up our tents and ground cloths. The extremely low temps left big, stubborn chunks of ice clinging to my tent. Whatever ice weight I packed up was likely to stay solid through the cold day ahead, so I tried to rip off as much as possible, but still ended up with a swollen tent roll that was *pounds* heavier.

Also perfect.

With my pack bulging at its absolute limit, I shoved my sit pad back inside my pants and cinched down my waist strap as tight as it would go. I strapped on my crampons, relieved to have them back. If snowshoes were all I had, the *only* option—no matter how awkward or uncomfortable—would've been for me to wait out the storm. I'd been taught a very clear lesson on where and when I could trust my snowshoes.

Nick bent down to strap his mended crampon onto his boot.

"How's your repair looking?" I asked.

"I guess we'll see, but I think I'll be good to go," he replied, standing and picking up his foot to show off the heavily taped flex bar.

Pete led the way out of our campsite and Nick followed close behind—but before we'd made it twenty steps, a soft snap was followed by a not-so-soft string of swears. Nick threw his pack down in frustration to remove his once-again broken crampon.

"Keep going guys, I'll be right behind you. I'm just going to go ahead with boots."

A familiar batch of conflicting thoughts rushed back into my mind. Nick was once again left without snow traction while I had two sets—but a permanent lesson had been seared into my mind: My gear was staying with me.

Aside from wanting to retain the ability to switch between ideal traction, my crampons were already strapped to my feet, and that wasn't going to change. The only gear I even had to offer Nick were my snowshoes.

I could've also handed him a revolver to play a bit of Russian roulette with.

Leaving a teammate behind was far from ideal, but the sub-freezing temps weren't conditions any of us had the luxury to stand still in. Pete and I took off together through the rolling snow along the north bank of the creek, doing our best to move fast enough to stay warm. Even with my thermal base layer, a second long-sleeve wool shirt, a fleece jacket, my puffy jacket, AND rain jacket—*while* hiking—I was just a half-notch up from shivering.

Pete and I managed to hike up a small reserve of body heat and stopped next to a trickling stream to give Nick a minute to catch up. The stream had been crippled by the low temps. A relatively large, cylindrical cavern of ice was hollowed out above it, evidence of the water flowing many times stronger during recent days.

The weather request I'd sent out on my inReach the night before finally broke through.

Eleven degrees for our location. The coldest on trail so far—in the middle of June.

Nick soon appeared, outwardly unfazed by the loss of his snow gear, but we were all worried. The terrain along the north bank was unknown, but likely either very difficult, or impassible. Since Roadrunner hadn't been able to use the snowbridge we'd crossed to avoid his horrific accident, bad news ahead was almost guaranteed, and would force us back onto the steep southern bank again with only two sets of crampons between the three of us. We were potentially wasting time and energy, but we had to see whatever roadblock awaited us with our own eyes.

Snow continued to fall in the dwindling storm, contributing to the several inches from the night before, but the air held almost completely still. Walking under lightly dusted pine trees and frosted cliffs was a visual feast. The metal points of our crampons made zero noise in the powder, a strange contrast to the hundreds of miles of scratched ice behind us.

It was quite the paradox to be on the far side of Bolton Creek, while still dreading crossing Bolton Creek. For almost a mile, we were in the trees several hundred yards from the water, but the canyon narrowed to where there wasn't much of a choice where we could walk. We caught a view of the creek for the first time that morning, where the full effect of the deep cold was revealed. The water was multiple *feet* lower than the previous afternoon. The overhanging snow roofs lining the banks, formed by the creek eating away at the snowpack, were now hanging *feet* above the water. The torrent had been choked into a tame, sluggish stream meandering through snowcapped river rocks. Unbelievably, Bolton Creek was now wadeable almost *anywhere*. Wading a creek in an eleven-degree snowstorm would obviously come with its own discomforts, and there was still the issue of getting up and down the snow cliffs to actually *access* the creek, but it was possible.

The fog of intimidation lifted off our team, and with my nerves calmed, my stomach was quick to remind me I'd skipped breakfast. To temporarily sate my hunger, I unclipped my water bottle from my chest to get a liter into my stomach—but the bottle was rock hard. What *had* been liquid water when we'd left camp was now frozen solid from riding on my shoulder strap.

I wasn't sure when, or even *if*, the temperature would rise above freezing throughout the rest of the day. I tucked the water bottle into my jacket to give it a chance to melt, and bent down to scoop up a handful of fresh powder to snack on.

With Pete far in the lead, the three of us hiked a bit apart, individually enjoying the peaceful morning. Nick and I lifted our heads to the faint sound of Pete shouting something back to us, but the sound-swallowing snow absorbed his words.

My heart sank.

CRUNCH

This is it. Pete found what's going to turn us around.

I couldn't have been more wrong.

As we neared our muffled Bulgarian, there was no clarification needed. Another snowbridge spanned Bolton Creek ahead. Not another kind-of sketchy one, but a *massive* bridge that from our vantage point, had no end. It didn't really even resemble a bridge, but more like a football field of snow the creek disappeared beneath.

Although we still hadn't reached the steepest terrain along the north bank, this giganti-bridge meant we'd be able to easily cross back over to the south bank, if necessary, without having to backtrack all the way to where we'd camped. Perhaps the *best* news was the terrain on the south side of Bolton had leveled out, which meant our crampon-deficient buddy wouldn't have to return to the steep, dangerous section of the south bank we'd been so relieved to escape the previous evening.

With 2.5 miles until the PCT crossing, we entered the topographical constriction along the north bank. The narrowing canyon forced us onto a single-track path of boulders and snowbridges sandwiched between the water on our left and a section of towering cliffs on our right. Our team was a bit on edge, expecting to find what would turn us around at every new vantage point. Certain parts along the steep cliffs took care, precision, and patience to navigate. Overhanging snow waves of questionable integrity hung over the creek, often times invisible to the hikers walking along their crests, but we took our time and focused on helping each other make it through each obstacle. We walked through tight hallways where the snow had melted away from the cliffs, and even had to do a couple easy climbing maneuvers up and over a collection of small boulders. But before long, the bank widened and we were strolling through easy, flat forest once again.

That was too easy. There's no way that was it.

An awkward sense of confusion hung in the air. I caught Nick's puzzled eyes and smiled, then Pete's, but we were hesitant to celebrate. We hadn't found anything *even close* to impassible yet, so it stood to reason we hadn't reached the hard part. Roadrunner had risked his life to wade this creek.

He'd willingly pushed into a section of whitewater that had almost killed him, and there had to be a *reason*.

But that reason—never came.

Muir Canyon remained flat, easy hiking along the north bank. Instead of finding an answer as to why Roadrunner had attempted a wade, we found more snowbridges. Several of them. *Massive* ones. Our spirits lifted with every new thick slab of snow spanning the creek. About 1.7 miles from the trail crossing, the creek *again* disappeared under snow for *hundreds* of yards. Bolton was more snowbridge than it was creek! The path of least resistance actually led us to cross *back* over to the south bank before zigzagging back over to the north! We soon reconnected with the Pacific Crest Trail alive and well—not to mention dry.

Pete turned around and shook my hand, followed by Nick's, a big smile behind his black beard.

"Congratulations, team. We've managed to survive crossing the most dangerous creek in the Sierra—with dry feet—three times."

We shared a relieved, baffled laugh.

That was it? The notorious Bolton Creek? That was the most dangerous crossing in the entire Sierra? The one that came with our choice of snowbridge??

I couldn't believe it. The stress lifting off our morning was a wonderful feeling. But the longer I pondered, the more my amusement slid into perplexion—and then irritation.

Roadrunner had gone out of his way to reach out to Nick and Pete, all but commanding them to exit North Yosemite in a seemingly altruistic effort to *save their lives*. Roadrunner, the person who'd seen the most of North Yosemite in 2017, who had almost been killed in this creek, told us we were walking into a death sentence—and I believed him. We all did. We had no reason not to. His words had been weighing heavily on all of our minds for the last week.

But now, we'd officially seen every inch of the terrain Roadrunner had, and his warning was—in the most apt of words—bullshit.

Leading up to Bolton, the creeks had been challenging to cross, but none of them unavoidably dangerous. Once Roadrunner reached Bolton, he had—for some baffling reason—attempted a wade, even *after* passing the six or seven gigantic snowbridges. He couldn't have missed every one of them. The narrow canyon didn't allow for hiking anywhere but right next to the creek. A blind man with a walking stick wouldn't have missed all of them.

So why didn't he use them? Or at least go back to cross the bridges once he'd laid eyes on the trail crossing? And the most haunting, disappointing question I struggled the most with: *Why didn't he tell us about the bridges?*

Conservatively, if Roadrunner had quite literally stared at his shoelaces for the four miles down Muir Canyon, he'd still seen *at least* half of the bridges before arriving at the point where the PCT crossed. The trail crossing must've been absolute chaos. I didn't have to be there to know how horrific this creek was in the early season, based on many past accounts and our own observations of the creek the day before. For Roadrunner, it was too deep and fast to attempt a wade, but despite knowledge of snowbridges upstream, he'd attempted it anyway.

He clearly made a mistake. It was a big one, one I couldn't find a reason behind, but we all make mistakes. Not a single shred of me thought less of him for making a decision—however catastrophic—or for the ensuing accident that decision caused. But the dawning realization of what he'd done with his experience was infuriating.

I didn't know many of the details, only that he'd narrowly escaped the creek with his life, then reversed back upstream along Bolton to bail out to the eastern side of the range. But now having laid eyes along the length of Muir Canyon, it was clear he'd unavoidably seen the snowbridges crossing "the most dangerous creek in the Sierra," not once, but *twice*.

Armed with that extremely valuable and promising information, he'd headed back to the PCT hikers in Mammoth preparing for their own run at North Yosemite. Rather than accepting his mistake and exiting the Sierra with a helpful message, such as, I don't know, "cross Bolton on the snowbridges," he'd arrived with only a message of doom awaiting anyone foolish enough to attempt what he had failed—conveniently omitting the part where his accident was 110% his own fault.

Now, if Roadrunner had chosen to stay completely silent about his traumatic accident, along with muffling the helpful information he had, that would've been understandable. I didn't know what level of embarrassment or humiliation he was dealing with—but he *hadn't* stayed silent. On the contrary, he'd gone out of his way to reach out to us, trying his hardest to scare everyone away from North Yosemite.

Why? Had he *wanted* to see us quit, to fail?

We'd spent *days* in mortal fear because of his words, *days* of marching toward the guillotine at Bolton Creek. It was hard to face the fact we'd crossed on the first downstream snowbridge we'd found, which had been solid *enough*—but certainly on the sketchier side compared to what was further downstream.

What if that bridge had collapsed under one of us? We wouldn't have touched it if we knew there were football fields of snowbridges within the next mile. Had he even considered that withholding the information he had could've resulted in a death? A death that might've included his friend Pete? What kind of person was this?

My entire outlook on the phrase "thru-hiking community" changed in that moment. There was a sense of betrayal from a collection of people I'd been largely convinced had each other's backs, in the same way I'd always felt the climbing community had mine.

I kind of felt like a dope. I'd spent so much effort providing the hikers behind me with extremely detailed Sierra information. Why was I so intent on helping the same bunch of people willing to hold back their own vital experience, potentially right up through my death announcement?

I also was struck with guilt. My time off in Mammoth had the potential to be the last days I'd have with Melanie and my pups, but that precious time wasn't spent relaxing with them—it was spent on my damn laptop, compiling and organizing all the information I could to help those behind me stay safe. It was an obligation I'd felt to my community, to do what I could to spread helpful creek crossing advice to my trail brothers and sisters, to keep them as safe as possible in the Sierra. None of the hikers ahead had made any kind of effort to help me or those behind me.

Once Roadrunner knew we weren't going to back down, he hadn't tried to help. He obviously knew how to send messages to Nick's inReach and just—hadn't. No one else had come out of North Yosemite. Roadrunner was the one person who had advice to offer. He could've spent all that fear-mongering thumb energy guiding us with information about McCabe, Horseshoe, and Spiller Creek. He could've assured us how safe crossing Bolton was going to be, maybe even given us a heads-up about the steep traverse through Muir Canyon, seeing as how that was *by far* the scariest part of Bolton Creek.

But he hadn't.

Even though he was just one hiker of thousands, realizing there was such a brutal hiker vs. hiker mindset out there—instead of the hikers vs. trail mindset I'd so romantically hitched my wagon to—was extremely discouraging. Even the attachment to the two great men I was hiking alongside changed, an involuntary shift that clearly wasn't fair.

The PCT made brief appearances from beneath the patchy snow and muddy marshes as we continued down through Muir Canyon. Pete led with a fury from snowpatch to snowpatch, marching with his head down. It might've been my already inflamed irritation, but the feverish pace Pete and Nick seemed insistent on maintaining wasn't helping. My partners were again slipping further and further away through the trees.

"*Why* are we moving so fast?" I growled.

It seemed like we were either nervously tiptoeing across dangerous terrain, or running toward the next obstacle. All of it was uncomfortable. I didn't want to sprint through the safe parts we could theoretically slow down and take in. I'd been looking forward to an intense but enjoyable trek through North Yosemite. That obviously hadn't happened. I'd spent almost the entire section either in a mess of nerves and adrenaline, or in a painful death-march to the next mess of nerves and adrenaline.

I was vaguely aware at some point, the PCT took an uphill turn to climb out of the canyon. The way Pete was confidently charging ahead, I figured he was aware. Rather than stopping to periodically check my GPS, I focused on pushing as hard as I could in a singular effort to keep up. Bear prints crisscrossed thinning patches of snow, and I was waiting to spot the PCT somewhere in the forest, but it wasn't showing. I lost more and more ground to my bullish partners, and soon was *sure* we'd missed something. Out of breath, I stopped next to a large pine tree, against which I rested my trekking poles, which wasted no time in tipping over onto the ground—like they'd done the previous 6,000 times I'd tried to rest them against a tree. My partners were too far ahead to notice, and kept on truckin'. By the time I took my phone out, turned on the GPS, and confirmed my suspicion, Pete and Nick had become dots on the forested horizon. We were almost a half-mile past where the trail had taken a steep right turn to start heading out of the canyon.

"PETE! NICK! STOP!" I shouted as loud as I could, but in competition with the rush of the creek, I might as well have been the chirp of a cricket. Not even like a *big* cricket, but a small, nerdy one. They continued Skittling along in their feverish pace—in the wrong direction. An exaggerated spike of anger flared up inside me.

"God *dammit*, guys."

I can't catch them. I can barely keep up with them! How far are they going to go before they figure it out?

Part of me was very tempted to head uphill to rejoin the trail without them. The idea of moving at my own pace for an hour or two felt wonderful—but I couldn't. I couldn't justify walking away from them. However, I *could* justify muttering impolite things under my breath.

I gathered my scattered trekking poles and started half-jogging through the forest. My pack bounced all over my bandages—exactly what my welts needed.

Fortunately, before too long, I spotted Pete standing still in the distance, looking down at his phone with Nick close behind. Pete's eyes rose to meet mine, and he pointed up the steep, rocky hillside.

"The trail. It's up there."

Reversing our steps to find the PCT might've been the easiest way to fix our mistake, but without a moment wasted on pesky deliberation, my teammates bulled straight into the vegetation on the melted-out, south-facing hillside, launching us into another session of steep bushwhacking. Trying to utilize faint game trails, we fought our way up and out of Muir Canyon, slipping and sliding in the loose scree and icy mud. The storm relented, and the snow finally stopped, but the cold remained. We climbed above a gorgeous blanket of clouds hung low over the canyon.

Eventually, we found the PCT, which ferried us uphill toward a small pass. The trail had clearly been melted out before the storm, so navigating along the lightly powdered path was thankfully simple, and quite beautiful.

Once again, I lost ground to my partners as we climbed snowy switchbacks, but the scenery served as a distraction to labored breathing and burning legs. As the trail gained more and more elevation over the cloud-choked canyon, the sun began peeking out through occasional breaks in the sky, bringing the fresh layer of sparkling snow to life, like a spotlight on a billion tiny disco balls.

At the summit of the pass, we found a perfect, bench-height rim of snow melted away from a large tree.

"Breakfast stop?" Pete asked with a smile.

In order to keep up, I still hadn't eaten, and my appetite was five minutes from collapsing me into a helpless sack of whimpering meat with only enough remaining energy to suckle on the nearest pinecone for sustenance. Not typically one for complicated midday meals, this time I broke out my Jetboil alongside Pete and Nick to make a huge pot of coffee combined with hot chocolate mix, a favorite comfort drink known as the Backcountry Mocha. But before I launched into Fattypalooza, I grabbed the inReach and used my vibrating fingers to let Mel know Bolton was safely in the rearview.

It took *three* packages of Pop-Tarts to start calming my hunger. I only stopped because logic and reason warned me I'd consumed an unreasonable hunk of preserved pastry—a claim my stomach found debatable. My taste buds were officially gone, a bizarre change I'd bizarrely accepted. There simply wasn't anything I could do about it. Not a single bite of food tasted like much, but the act of eating was enjoyable enough. Besides, every ounce I ate was one less ounce I had to carry—not a trivial benefit, by any means.

Heading downhill into Stubblefield Canyon, the angle of the snow was surprisingly steep. If we all had two intact crampons, it wouldn't have been much of a deal, but Nick had resigned to working through the terrain in only boots, his one good crampon enjoying the ride strapped to the top of his pack. We took our time to find the mildest path down the hillside to help keep our cramponless teammate from taking the least-desirable, highest-speed route to the canyon floor. The familiar rumble of a large creek reverberated through the trees.

The PCT crossed Stubblefield Creek after two large tributaries converged. Journals from heavy snow seasons had accounts of a full-on *swift water swim* across this one at the trail. At some naïve point in the past, sitting in front of my laptop, likely sipping a hot beverage in a warm coffee shop, I'd given my budding beard a stroke and had the rather manly thought.

Yeah, I could do that.

In the fifteen-degree morning, after a month in the snow, I had a less manly, more *over my dead body* kind of a thought.

Before reaching the PCT crossing, I called back over my shoulder, "Let's angle upstream to see if we can cross the two tributaries individually. If we stick to the PCT, we might be in for a swim."

Pete wasn't fazed. "If it looks slow enough, we'll swim."

I stopped and turned to see if he was joking, but that horrifying smile of his made it clear he'd swim across deep snowmelt without a second thought. If my teammates wanted to try even a deep wade in fifteen degrees, we'd be parting ways. Being beyond Bolton, my desire to be part of a team had evaporated. Our comically safe crossing over that "notorious" creek had erased the unease accompanying me since Mammoth. I'd seen enough of these creeks. I'd be able to handle the rest on my own.

A strong sense of disappointment had settled into the hollow left by my fear. While proud of my progress, I hated how much I'd let that fear dictate my decisions. I'd unconditionally stuck with Pete and Nick through recurring days of deathmarching, days far more tiring and painful than they were enjoyable. Most of that fear had revolved around Bolton. In cold reality, I'd ended up *less* safe with a team, for the only situation where I'd *truly* felt like

I'd toed the line was when I'd traversed Muir Canyon in failing snowshoes while my crampons were strapped to someone else's feet.

With only thirty miles until Sonora Pass, I was closing in on the end of the section I had looked forward to the most. By no one's fault but my own, I'd officially failed to balance the effort with the enjoyment. The uncomfortable truth was, this section hadn't been dangerous. Sure, there was plenty of danger to be *found*, and it was sure to teach the ill-prepared and egocentric a stiff lesson, but for those who had done their homework and were willing to stay humble and patient, there were many different safe lines through the snow and creeks in North Yosemite. It didn't deserve its reputation, and certainly didn't deserve to be labeled a death trap.

I led our team off the PCT, angling sharply upstream, trying to avoid a certain Bulgarian from even laying eyes on the trail crossing. Emerging at the bank of the first tributary of Stubblefield, there was a heaven-sent log spanning the wide creek. The low temps had also choked this creek's supply. It was evident that within the last twenty-four hours, the sunken middle of the snowcapped log had been underwater.

The crossing took nothing more than an easy balance capped off with a hop over a two-foot gap to the far bank. Just 50 yards later, we reached the smaller, second tributary, where we found an inarguably safe, knee-deep and slow section. After a failed search to find a dry crossing, we resigned to wade, much to the chagrin of our poor legs.

Pete and Nick stripped down into their underwear and bare feet, their red toes sinking into the powder along the bank. I stepped right into the creek, right into the arresting sensation of ice water flooding my boots. That feeling was a bittersweet acquaintance. Not exactly a *friend*, but there was something I mildly enjoyed about the familiarity—like seeing an overly political neighbor who's fun to greet, and maybe catch up with for a few minutes each month, but any more and you find yourself tossing dog poops over their fence.

The temperature of the sluggish water was at an impressive intensity I hadn't yet experienced. The brutal nighttime temps had transferred a new kind of cold into the creek, and I could actively feel the heat from my legs being sucked away from the skin in a bizarre, almost painful sensation. My legs wobbled a bit as I stepped onto the far bank, almost already devoid of feeling after a mere fifteen-foot wade.

I plopped down on the snow and removed my boots to wring out my socks, revealing beet-red, water-wrinkled toes. After so many months on the trail, I didn't recognize my own feet anymore. I'd put them through a special kind of foot-hell on this trek, and they were changing. Shape, size, appearance…

And smell. Mostly smell.

I dumped out the pool from my boots and wrung out my wool socks while my bare-thighed partners made their provocative way across the channel. We took a minute on the far shore to dry off and get back into our hiking gear. Pete wasn't as cheery as usual. He seemed a bit distracted, lost in thought.

"We should try to make more miles today than we've been making. I'm running a bit tight on food," he said. A fresh wave of irritation surged inside me.

That was me. *I* was the one restricting his miles.

"How many days of food do you have *exactly*, Pete?"

He shrugged. "Almost four days… probably."

"Four days of full meals, snacks—everything?" I asked, trying to paint a clear picture of what gritty Pete considered being "a bit tight."

"Oh no, light meals only. No snacks."

"That sounds like four days of *emergency* food rations."

"Ahh, it's not so bad. It's enough to make it to Sonora. It would just be nice to make more miles so I could eat more."

Good Lord, so he's not only having a hard time sleeping warm, but has also been operating hungry?

It further explained his pack weight, but it was still a shock. I actually respected that kind of mental toughness, to be in that elevated, elite mental stratum. It was impressive—but I wasn't going to push any harder. I couldn't.

The obvious fix was to divide our remaining food, and hike according to whatever pace that afforded us, but it had been *two days* since my offer to split my provisions had been ignored. Two long, heavy days of transporting that weight through difficult terrain on protesting sores, weight that could've been distributed amongst the team—weight that *should've* been distributed amongst whoever was going to consume it in the future. But instead, it had all remained on my back, like a subservient mule waiting for its prodders to get peckish. It took an internal fight to swallow my pride enough to offer once more.

"I still have way too much food on my back. If you both feel obligated to stick with me, we can divide it up, which would give you more days to hike while reducing my load. You don't have four days' worth of food, Pete. It sounds like closer to two or three. Once again, you two can push on ahead without me to get to Sonora faster, I **do not** mind at all—but those are our only two options. I'm already at my limit. I'm not going to death-march anymore. I'm certainly not going to even *entertain* the idea of death-marching *even further* each day."

Pete kept his eyes down as he cinched his boots laces tight, but didn't reply.

He'd been so resistant to the idea of parting ways in the backcountry but equally resistant to the idea of taking any of my food. Part of me understood. Most hikers—myself included—despise the idea of adding weight to their pack.

The conversation died there. An unspoken rift in our team had formed, but we all packed up like nothing had changed, and headed away from Stubblefield. Again, neither of them offered to take on any of my food. Something had to break, but I didn't know what—or when.

I led the way up and out of Stubblefield Canyon with a fresh set of frustrations circling through my mind. I was ready to be alone. I needed to move at my own pace to enjoy myself again. All of us were fed-up with the Sierra in our own ways. Nick was getting off the PCT for the season at Sonora Pass to return to work, and Pete was obviously ready for a break. That maniac had been gritting his way through the snow for almost 250 miles.

But how exactly were we going to split up? Pete seemed attached to an obligation to keep our team together. His intentions were undoubtedly good, but the harsh reality was the three of us had prepared *very* differently for this section.

With every step away from Stubblefield, I further regretted the words I'd chosen. I should've gone further—to clarify splitting up wasn't just acceptable, but would actually be *preferable*. Short of chasing them off with a trekking pole in the clubbing position, I couldn't think of a feasible way to split, much less an amicable way. I really liked these guys, and I didn't want to torch our friendship just so I could hike slower.

Luckily, the trail gods had it handled.

Over another small pass was Falls Creek, the last major crossing in North Yosemite. Past accounts told stories of a slow, waist-deep wade. I pushed with all I could to maintain an acceptable pace, and progress up and over the pass went well. We practically ran off the long decent, and stopped for lunch next to a creek that was more snowbridge than stream. My burning legs and stinging patches welcomed the break after a tough eight miles through boulders, dirt scrambling, two steep passes, and a couple creek crossings. Eight miles didn't sound like much, but I was on the verge of camping right then and there. And by "camping" I mean "slumping my pack onto my face and lying there until either death or morning arrived."

"We should shoot for a few miles up Falls Creek," Pete said, looking down at the GPS on his phone.

I'd never been so irritated. That would be six miles more for the day. Fourteen total, including three major creeks. There was no way in hell.

Nick gave his usual good-natured nod. I couldn't even bring myself to half-agree. I stayed quiet over my tasteless lunch, mourning another impending afternoon trudge.

It took some effort to stand and continue. Again, the team's Tiny Tim led the way with a racing mind, pushing legs, and panting breath. I hadn't done much of the leading in our team of three, mostly because I couldn't seem to keep up when keeping up was my sole responsibility. Being in front meant not only moving at a pace that wouldn't leave Pete and Nick nipping at my heels, but simultaneously navigating through the confusing hills and meadows.

We shot out of the forest onto a large, flat slab of white. Fresh snow masked the terrain, making it difficult to tell whether we were walking into a meadow or a lake. I tucked my trekking poles under an armpit and used the obstacle-free terrain to multitask, maintaining a quick stride while consulting my GPS. There were a handful of small lakes in the area, but we didn't seem to be on top of any of them. I steered our team toward the rim anyway, avoiding the middle of the large snowfield, just in case. I kept my eyes lifted toward the horizon, scanning the rock formations in the distance, searching out the optimal path to exit the field.

A crisp, sharp *crack* reverberated under my right boot, followed by a splintering cascade hidden under the innocent blanket of powder. Time slowed as the surface buckled under my weight.

My name was shouted in muffled panic. The sound seemed infinitely far away, far beyond the symphony of the cracks multiplying beneath me. There was no time to react. In numb acceptance, I watched my foot puncture the ice. The cold underworld swallowed my leg one bizarrely slow inch at a time, sinking deeper and deeper beneath the surface. I'd purposefully stuck close to the edge of the snowfield for just this scenario, figuring the depth of any water would be shallow enough to stay out of trouble—but my foot didn't find a lakebed.

My arms stretched forward, instinctually bracing to catch myself, but punctured straight through the thin ice with little to no resistance. I lazily turned my head to the side and closed my eyes while the insane cold of the subterranean water flowed up my sleeves. My torso slammed into the ice with a force that didn't match the speed of my world, violently expelling all the air in my chest. Everything fast-forwarded to align with reality in the millisecond it took for my right cheek to follow suit, also smashing through the ice and sending a pulse of blinding light through my vision that disintegrated into stars.

My leaden pack decided to become a buoyant flotation device, which fought to keep my body horizontal. I reached out to the rim of the unbroken ice, which immediately crumbled under the slightest bit of weight. I reached out with the other hand, and again, the lip snapped as if I were reaching out to a damn graham cracker. I paddled forward, fighting against the bullying flotation device enough to find the silty, soft bed of the lake with my crampons. In a surreal flash, I stood waist-deep in freezing, dirty water surrounded by bobbing chunks of brown ice.

Embarrassed, humiliated—and pissed.

Adrenaline sent my limbs trembling uncontrollably. I slogged through the mess of settling ice to reach the shore, which took a few high-steps to stomp a path through the rest of the ice. The side of my face stung like I'd given a six-foot-seven Amazonian a sneaky, unappreciated pinch to the behind.

I couldn't face my teammates. Their voices were buried in the background of my thoughts, cautiously asking if I was all right. I stayed silent, attempting to collect myself, to repress the vicious instinct to snap at them, to somehow offload my own humiliation on these two friends, guilty only of sticking by my side with remarkable patience.

"I'm all right, guys. Thanks," I forced over my shoulder.

I stepped over to a nearby rock and slumped my soggy pack onto the snow, then took a seat. I stared at the ground in front of me in a state of mild shock.

*What the hell was that? You wanted to enjoy this section. How's that working out? You wanted to stay safe at all costs. You promised **Mel** you'd stay safe at all costs—and you just fell into a frozen lake. If you were alone, you would've been moving slower. Hell, maybe even slow enough to look down periodically. You are the weak link in this chain. You are the problem, for both yourself, and your team.*

Pete and Nick stood next to their dripping teammate. Quiet, unsure what the next move was.

Pete eventually broke the silence. "Sorry, man. I saw the depression in the snow. I thought you'd see it too. I probably should've said something."

Great, they saw that coming from behind me.

"This isn't anyone else's fault." I struggled to keep my voice even. "You guys go ahead. I'm going to sit here and dump some of the lake out of my boots. I'll find you later."

But I wasn't going to.

It was time for Pete and Nick to move at the pace they needed to, so I could do the same. It was time for our team to split. There was again, concern in Pete's eyes.

"All right, Beta. We'll camp just a mile up from the Falls Creek crossing."

Doesn't matter.

"Sounds good," I replied.

With hesitation, both of them turned away and stepped up and over the small snow berm lining the edge of the lake. Just like that, I was alone.

I reached into my pocket where my phone had been, and it was wet. I still had my inReach and maps/compass to navigate with, but that soggy smartphone held all my photos and journal entries, which were as priceless as they were irreplaceable—and had no backups. I held the power button, then held my breath until it came to life.

The sun fully emerged for the first time in days, warming my freezing, drenched body, an olive branch being extended by the Sierra to a man at his limit. I slowly unstrapped my crampons from my squeaky, water-logged boots and tossed them in front of me. One at a time, I dumped an impressive percentage of the silty lake out of each boot, then wrung the reeking, lukewarm water out of my socks, creating a disgusting stain in the pure, white powder under me.

I closed my eyes and put my head down, desperately trying to get my bullying mind under control.

What a weakling.

This is pathetic.

How is just walking taking you for such a ride?

I sat in the warm sun with my head down for a long while, tearing myself apart. I had no outlet for the anger and frustration I felt. I only had my own ego as a punching bag. Negative thoughts circled around and around until they exhausted themselves. I remained slumped on top of my lakeside boulder in numb silence, waiting for any motivation to put my socks back on my stinging feet. An old Winston Churchill quote popped up in my head.

If you're going through hell, keep going.

I took a deep breath and shook my head. I felt like a failure, but I hadn't failed. Not yet, at least. Eventually, I calmed enough to accept my one option: keep going. After all, I was still alive. Falling into a frozen lake could've gone a lot worse. Being embarrassed is *technically* better than being dead—isn't it?

I put my boots and crampons back on, then my pack. I turned to face the jumbled hole I'd made—and forced a chuckle.

"Oh brother. What am I doing out here?"

I walked away under the gift of blue skies. Other than a soggy lower half, I actually felt really good. I was finally alone. I would be able to move at my pace, break when I wanted to break, camp when I wanted to camp, cross creeks where I wanted to cross—I was back on my own schedule. I hiked on with no one to worry about aside from myself, no one to keep up with, no one to impress, no one to disappoint.

It was just me.

I about broke into a skip along the shore of the beautiful Wilma Lake, but I suppressed the urge. I wasn't exactly sure what a steady diet of M&M's, Ibuprofen, and Pop-Tarts were doing to my bone health, but I had a sneaking suspicion it would take one attempted skip under my fat pack to discover my femur had taken on the texture of an expired churro.

I made it a point to stop as many times as I wanted. I took more pictures of Wilma Lake than I had the entirety of North Yosemite. I sat on every perfect stone overlooking the lake, not because I was particularly tired, but because I could. Taking my time was a priority. There was one thing that would spoil this newfound sense of freedom: catching up to Pete and Nick—and if I knew Pete, he wasn't feeling right about leaving me behind, no matter how much sense it made, so I took an extra long arc around the shore (of which I kept a rather paranoid side-eye on). After a cautious peek around each new turn, I paused to appreciate the view.

The outlet of Wilma Lake was impressively flooded. The snow gave way to a marsh, and I spotted a beautiful bit of PCT underwater, where polished river rocks had been mortared together. I resubmerged my freshly squeezed footgear to wade along the trail. The lowest point took me down to my upper thigh, but the flow was tame. I continued onto the snow, my boots squishing with every step, something I couldn't seem to get away from.

Just a few hundred yards later, I walked up on Falls Creek where the PCT crossed and took a hard right to follow its drainage upstream for nine miles. The current was slow, but I couldn't tell exactly how deep it was, somewhere around waist or upper thigh. Specifically, I couldn't tell if I'd be subjecting my shell-shocked genitalia to another ice bath, so I decided against it. I hadn't come across Pete and Nick yet, and that was how it needed to stay. If they were indeed camping somewhere along this creek, then it was time for me to stop for the night.

A flat patch of snow with some exposed granite slabs was nearby. I threw my pack down after a day *lightyears* from ideal, but I set up camp and rehydrated my dinner in peace.

Guilt and worry had been my nightly companion ever since I'd left Mammoth. I'd stressed about dragging Steve forward, about making it to Sonora without running out of food, about dying in creek crossings, about holding Pete and Nick back…

But I was alone again, and the simple love of backpacking was seeping back in. I enjoyed setting up my tent, accompanied only by the rush of the creek. I enjoyed laying out my solar panel in the fading afternoon light, collecting water to boil, pouring it into my dinner, and eating a warm meal along Falls Creek while watching the mesmerizing water roll through the canyon. I'd been so terrified of being alone, but it took a team to remind me—there were upsides.

"Tomorrow, my hike is back in my hands," I muttered, grinning as the sun slowly sank into the pines.

35
FALLS CREEK

Crunch

My eyes shot open at the sound of a heavy footprint compacting the snow close to my tent. Adrenaline ripped me from my deep sleep and sent my heart rate skyrocketing. I held perfectly still, trying to separate out threatening sounds against the background noise of the creek.

After a long, uneventful pause, I muttered, "Maybe it was just a dream."

Crunch

Another footprint. Closer.

"Shit," I whispered, tucking down into the false security of my sleeping bag.

My mind raced, trying to come up with a course of action better than hiding inside my delicate, nineteen-ounce down quilt. An unthrottled fart was about enough to turn that overpriced sack into a blown out mess of feathers.

Is it a bear? A mountain lion? Should I be making noise? Staying quiet? Should I turn on my headlamp? Keep everything dark?

CRUNCH

*The real-world odds of an animal trying to enter an occupied tent were almost zero, but if it **did** want to come in—there wasn't much resistance I had to offer.*

Crunch

Even closer. I could hear breathing. The massive, stuttering breaths of an animal much larger than myself.

It has to be a bear.

My entire body vibrated, ready to take action—action I hadn't quite figured out yet.

Crunch, Crunch

It was right outside of my tent, just feet away. Sniffing between labored breaths, it scanned back and forth across the front flap of my flimsy, opaque tent. I froze, not knowing what else to do, hoping the bear would lose interest. I desperately wanted to see what was going on, but had only the black canopy of my tent to stare into. The dim glow from the Sierra stars was just enough to illuminate plumes of white breath being cast from the bear's exhaling snorts as it hovered around the entrance of my tent, probably trying to figure out where that horrible smell was coming from.

You and me both, bear.

After what felt like an eternity, the giant animal wandered off into the woods beyond camp, its heavy steps slowly fading into the white noise of Falls Creek.

Relieved, I sat up and turned on my headlamp with a hand still trembling. In an attempt to take my mind off the close encounter, I pulled out my maps to plan out the next day, hoping the mental distraction would be sufficient to calm me down enough to get back to sleep.

A powerful, extended roar in the distance rose above the rush of the creek. The hair on the back of my neck stood on end, and I lifted my head from the maps to stare at the wall of my tent, adrenaline once again flooding my body.

The roar ended, but was followed by a far more terrifying noise: more footsteps. Fast footsteps. The earth-shaking steps of a heavy animal in a full run—headed straight toward me.

thud, thud, thud, thud, THUD THUD

There was no point in screaming. There was no one to yell out to. There was only me.

The barreling animal reached my camp at full speed. My world braked into slow motion as five sharp, massive claws penetrated the cuben fiber in front of my face. I turned my head and shut my eyes tightly, waiting for the impact. The incredible weight of the beast snapped my tent's center support like a twig.

I numbly braced for the mauling to start.

Will it kill me before eating me? Or start eating while I'm still alive to watch?

With an electric jolt, I shot up in my tent, firing plumes of panicked breath out over my sleeping bag. It took several confused seconds to understand what was going on, that I was safe, and not being eaten alive by a demon-bear.

"Ugh, *another* one?" I bitterly asked the darkness around me. I'd never experienced so many vivid nightmares so close together in my life.

I was drenched in sweat—not exactly ideal in a fifteen-degree night. I wiped the freezing beads off my forehead using the trembling back of my hand.

"I wonder if it's too late to catch up to Pete and Nick," I muttered, only half-sarcastically.

Having a bear attack nightmare was odd for me. I wasn't scared of black bears, and there were no grizzlies around. I hadn't been especially nervous about the increasing number of bear prints throughout North Yosemite, but apparently it was something my subconscious had been looking forward to torturing me with.

I picked up my phone to check the time.

"One thirty," I whispered into the dark tent. "Still got a couple more hours to sleep."

Ha.

I eggbeatered my way to three thirty a.m., then shut off my pointless alarm and sat up in the dark. I slumped my head into my hands, feeling completely exhausted, as if I'd spent the entire night running a marathon and not lying down in a warm sleeping bag.

While relieved to be hiking alone again, I'd always preferred camping with company. I wasn't naive enough to think having two tents for a bear to maul would be any safer than just one, but there was comfort with having others nearby that allowed me to mentally relax into a headspace where I just slept better.

It was far below freezing again, and I reached over to touch the socks I'd hung in the middle of the tent. They were rock hard.

"I can't believe it's still *this* cold."

I rapped the rigid wool against the tent's trekking pole support. The metallic clang gave me a millisecond of morbid amusement.

In spite of nightmares and ice socks, I was actually *looking forward* to hiking, which felt almost strange. I'd spent many weeks stressing over the passes and creeks through the Sierra, especially in North Yosemite, and the daily joy of waking up to an exciting new stretch of beautiful trail had been lost somewhere along the way. That stress was arguably a necessary evil to stay humble and safe, but now—with the most threatening obstacles behind me—the weight of the Sierra was beginning to lift off my shoulders. After all, if I had handled the *last* few hundred miles of snow, the next couple hundred couldn't put up much of a fight.

Could they?

My coffee grounds again froze solid in the time it took me to roll up my gear and cook some flex into my footwear. I stood up outside of my tent in a cloud of my lingering, white breath. I still couldn't get past the absurdity of it being the middle of June. With a smile on my Arizona-raised face, I slid the solid brown puck out of my Jetboil and into the snow.

Standing in the freezing temps in just a thermal top almost felt... *good*. I'd adapted to cold being the new normal. It signified positive things like hard snow and subdued creeks. It was familiar—oddly comfortable, even. My feet weren't on the same page. I was never going to get used to the sting of sliding frozen socks and boots on in the early morning. The boots had been heated over the Jetboil, but were still quite icy. I only used enough precious fuel to loosen the fabric. My skin would do the rest.

I collapsed my tent in the dark, involuntarily shooting glances into the spooky woods surrounding camp, scanning for gigantic, evil bears the logical sector of my brain absolutely *knew* weren't there—but this morning, the irrational sector was winning. I'd soon be battling a demon-bear with only my nail clippers and well-seasoned underwear to defend myself, I was sure of it.

I intentionally left camp just before five a.m., the same as Pete and Nick's preferred camp departure time each morning. They weren't going to spend any extra time in the cold waiting around for the chance I'd show up, so if we all started hiking around the same time, odds were good I wouldn't catch up, and we could avoid any awkward second break-ups. I didn't have another thin-ice-incident in me.

Wading Falls Creek in the below-freezing dark was an easy no, so I set off upstream. Since the PCT paralleled Falls Creek for many miles, whenever I found a spot to cross would be fine. I took my time through the woods on concrete snow. When it was time to remove a couple jackets, I just— stopped, no worries about holding anyone back, no stressing about sweating in my down jacket, and not a single guilty thought. It was wonderful.

The soft light of dawn illuminated the peaceful canyon. When I wanted a handful of trail mix, I stopped to enjoy it. When I wanted to take a picture, I took it.

I walked adjacent to Pete and Nick's deep footprint indentations they'd left in the afternoon snow. They led right to where they'd planned to camp, about a mile upstream of the PCT trail crossing. It was a nice, flat campsite with a couple large logs at perfect sitting height, covered in bright green lichen. Two freshly cut beds of pine boughs were still laid across the snow where they'd pitched their tents. A sunken pit of cold embers next to one of the sites was guaranteed where Pete had ignited his nightly fire to dry his gear.

A twinge of sadness ran through me. The campfire conversations, the camaraderie at the end of each hard day, the occasional idiot burning holes through his socks—they were fond memories. As much as I was going to enjoy hiking on my own, I wished I'd been strong enough to keep up.

A half-mile out of Pete and Nick's camp, I came across a large, obvious arrow made of tree branches laid out in the snow, pointing to the right. Two paths of their footprints were leaving from and returning to the arrow from the left, where they'd likely found a dead end of some sort. They'd taken time to make the marker, to save me from taking the same wrong turn.

I wasn't expecting any real obstacles before crossing Falls Creek, but two miles later I walked up to the bank of a large tributary with no easy way across in sight. My GPS told me it was the steep, cascading outlet of Tilden Lake. I followed Pete and Nick's crampon tracks uphill to find where they'd crossed, figuring I'd do the same—until I saw how Bulgarish it was. Their footprints disappeared where the creek narrowed to a four-foot wide gap of torrential whitewater, creating an ill-advised opportunity to jump across to a wet, angled slab on the other side—and if I knew Pete, he'd probably backflipped over it, possibly through a fire ring.

With my athletic skills, jumping there was only a fine choice for a suicide, so I continued on. Another rush of gratitude came over me knowing I hadn't had to look Pete in those sparkling, hopeful eyes to reject his jumping-across-whitewater proposition.

That said—I probably should've just jumped.

The angle progressively steepened along the outlet. My progress ground to a crawl fighting up patchy rock ledges and slabs, refusing to accept Pete and Nick's crossing could be the safest option—but every new bit of creek wasn't getting any safer. It took sweating my way up hundreds of feet of elevation above Falls Creek before I found a potential crossing where a section of the Tilden Lake outlet had split into two around a tall island of snow. From the shore, it appeared both branches of the creek had a stepping-stone path across. One line of idyllic stones led to the snow mound island, and another departed it.

A smug, self-assured smile spread across my face. "Looks like I'll be keeping my feet dry this morning—and *without* any leaps of death."

Back atop Dick Peak, the trail gods chuckled and kicked up their feet with a bucket of popcorn.

A stiff alpine breeze kicked up, highlighting the sweat soaked into my shirt. In a hurry, I tore open my snowshoe bindings and snatched them off the ground. Since I planned to strap them right back on once I'd skipped across the stepping stones, I settled on the brilliant idea to shave a heaping twenty seconds off of my day—and throw them across the creek instead of strapping them to my pack.

In a moment of pure complacency, I took one snowshoe off and helicoptered it across the first branch, aiming for the top of the snow mound island. As the orange and black, incredibly vital piece of gear flipped around in the air above the creek, a little angelic voice perched on my shoulder sing-songingly whispered, "This isn't smaaaaart."

But it landed spikes-down, *perfectly* on the apex of the mound, coming to a snappy rest *right* where I'd wanted it. My trail shoulder-devil showed up at my other ear.

"Not smart? Please. Like there's any way someone so strong and handsome could screw this up."

He had a point, so I grabbed my second snowshoe and confidently hucked it toward its other half. With a throw that left ten-year-old, little league Danny spinning in his grave (I'm not sure why he's dead), the snowshoe tumbled end over end, instead of helicoptering spikes-down. The flexible tail hit the top of the mound first, which sprung the snowshoe back toward me. I couldn't do anything but enjoy the flood of regret as half of my primary snow traction bounced down the slope, tumbled off the end of the mound, and disappeared into the creek.

I stood in confused shock, staring at the island with my widowed snowshoe perched on top, trying to recall the string of terrible decisions I'd somehow justified in order to throw away one of my beloved snowshoes.

"What did I just do?" I whispered to nobody.

In a slight panic, my mind ran in circles trying to calculate what losing a snowshoe meant. I still had my crampons, but they were crampons with well-traveled flex bars, likely ready to snap at any moment. I had zero replacement flex bars to repair them—and I'd just *voluntarily* thrown a snowshoe away?

I spent a minute expelling every swear I could recall from my thirty-one-year-strong collection, hoping I could generate enough self-denigration to get the point across.

I stepped up to the bank of the creek, eyeing the first stepping stone protruding from the whitewater. The large, smooth stone was a big target, but almost four feet off the bank, and had water continually lapping over the surface. It looked slippery—but the texture appeared rough enough to take a committing step out to. I extended my trekking poles and prodded the water around the stone, gauging the depth of the creek. To the right of the stone, it was a couple feet deep, but to the left, my four-foot pole couldn't find the bottom.

Well, whatever. How deep can it be? Besides, I'm not going to miss a stone that size.

I probably could've heard the overhead snickering through mouths jammed full of popcorn if the creek hadn't been so loud.

Another few neurons failed to fire (again, I blame dehydrated potatoes), and I forgot to consider how insanely cold it still was. The water lapping up and over the stepping stones was immediately freezing, forming an invisible layer of crystal-clear ice on everything protruding slightly above the surface. I planted my right trekking pole and took a committing step out to the first large stone—and my boot glanced right off of it.

In a record-setting attempt at a front split, my momentum from stepping forward carried me squealing beyond the stone and down into the black, rolling creek. I narrowly held on to my balance and caught myself upright in the rushing water, and while thankful I hadn't gone floating after my snowshoe, I was less than thrilled to be involuntarily standing in waist-deep ice water for the second day in a row. The swift current rolled the water up to my chest and I loudly cycled back through my well worn collection of swears. I retreated back toward the shore to try again. High-stepping out of the creek was met with an alarming amount of resistance, the feeling in my legs had faded in mere seconds.

Deja vu-style, I again stood staring across the first branch at my lone snowshoe stranded on the snow island, only this time, I was soaked up to my damn nips (which had assumed the fit and finish of two shards of glass), and cold. *Really* cold. The ambient was still at twenty degrees, the water I'd gone for a dip in wasn't much warmer, and the morning breeze was still flowing through the canyon.

I threw my pack down and after a moment of hesitation, took out my crampons. The only option to reach my lone snowshoe was to ignore the alarm bells going off and step across the stones with metal points to dig through the ice. It would acutely stress my aging flex bars—on the only form of traction I hadn't thrown into the creek. A better idea was to forget about it, to cut my losses and keep hiking upstream to find something safer and less stressful on my footgear—but I couldn't stomach the thought. Those snowshoes had been my lifeline for almost 300 miles. They'd kept me safe all the way up until the moment I'd voluntarily discarded them, a move I was feeling more guilty and stupid about by the minute. I felt an overwhelming obligation to retrieve the one surviving snowshoe.

I stood up and returned to the bank, irrepressibly shivering and ready to get moving again. I stepped back out across the initial gap to the first big stepping stone, grinning in satisfaction as the points on my right crampon easily pierced the thick, clear ice—shattering the slippery coating under my weight. Large plates of ice slid off the stone and into the whitewater. I stepped to the next stone, then the next, crushing through the flawless glass on each stone, every step spider-webbing the invisible surface into a thousand white veins.

After a shallow dunk at the end of the stones, I stepped up onto the mid-creek island with intact flex bars. Something orange caught my eye downstream.

CRUNCH

"My snowshoe!"

It had been sucked into an underwater thicket of reeds only a few yards downstream from where it had gone in!

I reunited with my beloved snowshoe atop the island snow mound, threw down my pack, grabbed my ice axe, and began kicking steps down toward the other snowshoe. A flurry of warnings fluttered through my mind, but I didn't know what was smart or efficient or safe anymore. I just wanted my snowshoe back.

I ran out of snow a couple feet above the water. Like most snowy banks, a sizable overhang had been worn into it by the creek. I sank my axe deeply into the mound to use as an anchoring handhold to lower back into the creek for a third time. I firmly kicked my left crampon into the snow, and then reached my right foot down into the water. My boot sank until it settled onto the thicket of submerged reeds my prodigal snowshoe was trapped beneath.

I stepped my trailing foot down and grimaced through the heat being sucked from my legs. It took another, deeper step off the reeds to pull my snowshoe out. I bent over and sent my left arm into the swirling water. The snowshoe was tangled deeper than it looked. I reached down into the creek until snowmelt was flowing around my left shoulder. The breath was sucked out of my chest in the seconds it took to wrap my fingers around the hard plastic. With a death-grip on the snowshoe, I pulled it up through the reeds with as much force as I could generate, snapping dozens of the thin, stubborn branches in the process.

I hurriedly reversed back out of the water, ripped the ice axe out of its placement, and rejoined my pack with two snowshoes and two crampons with intact flex bars. Successful—but dangerously cold, and more wet than I'd experienced in the Sierra yet. My entire left side was sopping from the shoulder down. My legs were completely numbed out below my thighs, and really, the only dry part of me was my head and right shoulder. The slight breeze rustling the pines sent my body into powerful tremors.

My fingers weren't working well enough to strap my snowshoes to my pack, so I grabbed them both in the semi-functioning palm of my right hand and headed off the island toward the smaller, second branch of Tilden Lake's outlet. The stepping stones looked nice, but I was already wet, so I opted to get the second branch over with as fast as possible.

And why not go for a fourth dip in a single creek in twenty-degree weather?

Without any further drama, I was on the other side of the outlet, strolling quickly through the pines with my snowshoes still gripped in my frozen hand.

I scoffed through trembling lips. "Well that went well."

I had no mobility or warmth left over to take my crampons off or to put my snowshoes back on. My only priority was to move with enough vigor to keep my blood flowing. With my head down, I half-walked, half-jogged down the shaded, windy canyon. Within a few minutes, my chattering teeth calmed and feeling began drifting back into my arms and legs. When I pulled back alongside Falls Creek, a beautiful sight opened up in front of me.

Sun. A whole, treeless snowfield of it.

The sky was open and blue. The powerful reflection off the pure, white snow all around me was like an oven. External warmth was a rare luxury these days, and chills ran up and down my body while the sun chased the rest of the cold out of my limbs. With no one but myself to convince, I embraced the opportunity to take a spontaneous break. Sitting on my pack, I drained the extra water from my boots, wrung out my socks, and shifted back into my workhorse snowshoes.

For almost twenty minutes, I enjoyed the chickadees chirping and the light babbling of the creek. When all feeling had returned to my fingers and toes, I tossed back a couple handfuls of trail mix for some energy, then shouldered my pack. I kept a bag of trail mix in my hand to continue snacking, but I soon tired of moving the cardboard-flavored, pasty mush around in my mouth.

My relationship with food had changed so much throughout the Sierra. It was sad, almost mournful, that I'd stopped looking forward to it. What had been the highlight of my days for *months* was now a bland chore. Without taste, I wasn't getting anywhere near the calories I needed, and my pack weight wasn't dropping much after each meal. Part of me wanted to ditch whatever I didn't want to eat—but abandoning perfectly good food wasn't an idea I was capable of entertaining.

The wide, snaking Falls Creek lowered as I made progress upstream. Eventually, I spotted a shin-deep opportunity to wade across, so I unstrapped my snowshoes and hopped in with them in my hands again.

I stepped up onto the far bank and threw my snowshoes into the softening snow for another break, enjoying the view back over the timid creek behind me. For the first time in the Sierra, I felt hopeful I'd reach Sonora Pass. There weren't any other obstacles ahead aside from snow, which felt as simple as hiking on dirt at that point.

Ahh, dirt. Just the thought of it brought up phantasmal daydreams of light packs, high miles, and comfortable sleeping—all the stuff I'd taken for granted in Southern California. Somehow, dirt was still hundreds of miles away, but I embraced the momentary mental escape.

I'd lost Pete and Nick's tracks, but they weren't too vital. Navigation was simple following Falls Creek, which would eventually lead to the creek's source at Dorothy Lake. The hard snow was softening but stayed in great shape for most of the morning. My morale was higher than it'd been in weeks. Moving across the pristine, white surface, listening to the beautiful sound of my crampon points dragging across the stiff snow, having no tracks to follow, no signs of any humans aside from the tracks behind me—it was all immensely satisfying.

I thought I'd found the perfect crossing for Falls Creek, but within a mile of my shin-deep wade, the creek narrowed and snowbridges began to appear. First just here and there, followed by the *entire creek* disappearing under the snow, still over a mile from Dorothy Lake.

Between the nightmare creeping me out, the super cold temps, and me fumbling my way across lake outlets like an honorary fourth stooge, my brain had miraculously suppressed my overloaded digestive system. But now, with just safe hiking ahead for the remainder of the day, my body turned to tasks it had put on the back burner.

Poop. I'm talking about poop.

Yes, again.

Trying to find a good, responsible place to poop in the snow is a tall order. A leave-no-trace hiker knows all turds need to find a home buried in the dirt for the bacteria in the soil to do their thing, to break down the waste into a less-offensive form. So standing on top of ten feet of snow without having an auger in your pack, finding access to dirt can be quite the challenge.

Luckily, tree wells exist. The steep cone of snow around most trees led straight down to mother earth, so I found a deep well, threw my pack down, and slid into it with my ice axe (i.e. the most incredible poop trowel ever). A quick second of manual labor and I'd dug down through the last bit of snow and into the dirt, creating a cantaloupe-sized grave for my, eh—*leavings*.

I scrambled back up to the lip of the tree well and went to work with the axe again, creating a sweet, ninety degree block in the snow to hang one cheek and a crack off of, which would theoretically allow my tree fertilizer to cruise down the steep side of the tree well and into (or at least within putting range of) its freshly manicured burial plot.

Of course, my manliness isn't anywhere *near* being able to bare-assed sit on ice, at least not while simultaneously being able to relax enough to relocate anything from the inside of me to the outside of me, so that's where my sit pad came in. Yes, that same, traumatized square of foam I'd been using to pad out my sunken waist, but that usually ended up straddling my unspeakables. Also the same foam I used under my head at night to keep my pillow from sliding around—but not before a leery eye each evening.

I loved that versatile chunk of foam. It'd always been one of my favorite pieces of gear. But as I positioned the faded, off-yellow square on the sharp edge, as a barrier between the white snow and my possibly whiter butt, I was greatly looking forward to throwing it in the trash. Mainly because emotional therapy for a sit-pad is a bit outside of a dirtbag's budget.

I settled onto my handcrafted perch, enjoying the view and my pro-level snow toilet. I glanced down at the alarming amount of ex-food snaking its way down toward, but not quite *inside* of, the hole I'd dug. Not a big deal. The only activity I was more proficient in than snow-toilet design was snow-golf-poop-putting.

The eye-watering mess scattered down the well stretched out for almost ten feet below me. I had just enough time to finish the thought, *should've gone watermelon size,* before North Yosemite finally unleashed a terrifying experience worthy of all the fear mongering.

The snow lip under my poor sit pad crumbled, sending my pants-around-the-ankles, bare-assed self on a squealing magic carpet ride of horror down into the tree well. Before I even fully understood what happened, I came to a rest at the bottom of the well, sitting directly over the hole I'd dug.

I was frozen in shock, holding perfectly still, staring straight ahead with wide eyes.

"Oh… **no**," I dazedly whispered.

I ran though the consequences of my afternoon poop going so horrifically south. I'd just slid down a slip-n-slide lined *with my own feces.* There was poop—*everywhere*? On my clothes? My sit pad? My skin? My—**gulp**—hair?!

Liquid water was super hard to get to, especially with the creek snowed over. How exactly was a clean up going to happen?! I didn't have any real soap even, just hand sanitizer, but certainly not enough to submerge my entire body in!

An involuntary "Nooooooo," crept out of my lips as I cautiously swiveled around to get my feet back under me, trying to limit any further spread of the disaster. I stood up, narrowly maintaining a hold on my balance with my ankles still in pant-cuffs. I started to assess the damage, examining my clothes, twisting around, searching for just how much biohazard I was going to have to slide into my $600 sleeping bag later. I carefully took my shirt off, prodded reluctant fingers into the hair on the back of my head, ran my hands along the middle of my back, cataloging the full extent of the bad news.

Standing in the bottom of a shit-filled, below-freezing tree well with my shirt off and pants around my ankles was certainly a new high point.

I turned my shirt over in my hands, in complete shock and disbelief.

There was nothing. Not even the slightest trace of doodie anywhere along my back, butt, shirt, hair, eyebrows—*nothing*! I dressed myself in complete suspicion, positive I'd soon come across the nightmare. There'd been a record-shattering, gorilla-esque pile below me, so I was mighty hesitant to accept there wasn't a stealthy streak hiding somewhere.

I bent down and peeled the shell-shocked sit pad off the compacted snow/shit mixture underneath, fully bracing to have to look my leave-no-trace ethics in the eyes and find the will to pack out a doo-drenched, bulky chunk of horrific trash all the way to Sonora Pass—*but there was nothing on the pad either*.

Somehow when the snow had given way, the sit pad had taken a good amount of loose snow with it and had miraculously smoothed a layer of snow over the awful contents below, like the stroke of an expert patissier floating a spatula of vanilla frosting over a—let's say—*chocolate* cake. I spun around over and over, checking every square centimeter of all gear involved—but there was still nothing.

Either I had gotten away with murder, or my eyes were lying to me. With no one else around to confirm or deny, part of me wondered if I'd slipped into some kind of shock-induced, alternate reality, whereas the *actual* me was one big shit streak with a thousand-yard stare and a strand of drool dangling from the corner of my poop-smattered lips—a brain-dead, toxic mess of sewage with four baby wipes and an ounce of hand sanitizer to his name.

I dressed the tree well the best I could before heading back to my pack, still stunned at the unbelievably fortunate outcome. I couldn't accept it. I just knew I'd eventually find a turd mushed into some unfortunate patch of hair I'd overlooked. With a suspicious eyebrow permanently jacked upwards, I checked my sit pad for the thirty-seventh time before tucking it back into the waist of my pants.

I spent the next mile hiking uphill through rolling fields of suncups, my mind repeatedly convincing itself it was catching whiffs of something poopy. At the top of the hill, I broke out of the trees into the huge, flat snowfield that was Dorothy Lake. A few patches of beautiful, light blue ice dotted the surface where the lake was close to melting through. Still shaky in my relationships with icy lakes, I opted to skirt around the shore, rather than attempting to walk across it, especially being alone.

Dorothy Lake was unbelievably gorgeous. I relished in the freedom to stroll slowly along the buried shoreline with my eyes up, to thoroughly appreciate my position as a tiny speck inside the grand arena of majestic peaks overlooking the lake. All the different shades of blue, against the pristine white, against strokes of black and grays along the cliffs—it was again, too much to actually be able to process with my human eyes.

I reached the western shore of the lake where Pete and Nick's semi-fresh footprints tracked along the buried Pacific Crest Trail. The snow had softened to where their steps had imprinted about six inches into the surface. I rejoined their path, stepping into the footprints to save me some frustration of forging a new line through the slush. But before I'd followed their steps even a hundred yards, I passed through an incredible campsite.

A small grove of trees lined the warm, sun-soaked shore of the lake. A precious patch of sweet, sweet exposed ground was lined by bench-height snow. There was plenty of dry, dead wood on the nearby trees for an easy fire, great water to filter right out of the lake, not to mention the stunning view.

I can't stop though, I've only hiked nine miles. It's only noon, so…

Wait, I came to an abrupt halt just past the campsite, *I sure-as-hell **can** stop. I've hiked far enough today. The snow is starting to turn into slush. I've got five days of food to make it through two days of hiking—and there's no one around to march me forward!*

My mind was instantly made up. I threw my pack down and set up camp with a smile on my face. It had been a while since I'd been on a schedule that allowed stopping before the afternoon suckfest, and I savored every second of it. I shook out my tent to remove the ice I'd been carrying all day, hung out my damp gear to dry, gathered water after a firm kick through the ice, and set out the solar panel.

I put together a modest fire and went to town drying my socks and boots for the first time in days. Another twinge of sadness joined me at the sight of my steaming socks hung over my axe. I hadn't been strong enough to keep up with the team, but I was comforted by the fact that alongside Pete, we surely wouldn't have stopped at noon.

I kicked back in the peaceful afternoon, taking in the still air and warm sun over a mug of backcountry mocha. I considered removing my shoulder duct tape patch, to have a look at what was happening underneath—but decided against it. The pain had leveled out, *maybe* even lowered, and I didn't want to push my luck. Whatever was going on under there, it could wait until I was out of the Sierra.

"Two more days," I muttered, looking out over the lake. "That's—nothing."

But Sonora still felt like an eternity away. I'd all but forgotten about the 1,700 miles beyond it. Exhausted from the last sleepless night, I ducked into my tent early, hoping for a long, deep sleep. A bit of fear lingered from the nightmare the evening before. I was less scared of an actual bear coming into camp, and more scared of closing my eyes to find whatever circus of horrors my subconscious had whipped up. Most fears in the backcountry were irrational, especially fears of animal attacks. One was more likely to walk away clean from a trip down a frozen slide of feces (or so the saying goes).

After one lingering, extended frown at my sit pad, I rested my head and blacked out into a heavy, thankfully dreamless night.

36

1000

Rising from my tent in the thick darkness was never going to stop being creepy.

I'd been waiting for a long time to get used to it, but here I was, about to step through the thousandth mile on the PCT, and I *still* fought to keep my thoughts rational while packing up camp in the dark. I shuffled around, tearing down my tent and organizing my pack by the small circle of light cast by my headlamp, allowing every twig snap or imaginary footstep to freeze me in place while I waited for more evidence of the creature coming for me.

Of course, it was inevitably just a squirrel, or a bird, or a—nothing. But one of these times, it was going to be the world's largest devil-squirrel, who had grown tired of its stash of nuts it had subsisted on through the long winter, and was coming for the rarest nuts in the Sierra, the last kind a lonely hiker wanted anything nibblin' on—my subconscious was sure of it.

The morning was markedly warmer, which was pleasant for morning chores, but never good news for the rest of the day. The snow wouldn't stay firm for long, so I hurried through my routine to get moving.

Not because of the nut-lusty, imaginary devil-squirrel—but because of the *conditions*, you see.

Unsure how much liquid water was in my future, I wandered back down to the lake to fill up my two bottles. The hole I'd kicked through the ice had refrozen, which was a strangely comforting sign. The temps felt warm through my warped perspective, but it must've still been below freezing, which meant the snow would be solid for at least a few early morning hours. After another hearty kick, I dipped my bottles beneath the calm surface of the lake, gritting my teeth against the shock of the water sucking the life out of my fingers.

After a few more imagined sounds and investigatory pauses later, I was out of camp, heading toward a small pass which also happened to be the northern boundary of Yosemite National Park. Alongside the shore of the lake, shallow pools of melted snow had refrozen into sheets of clear ice. The points on the underside of my snowshoes sent beautiful, white, spider-webbing fractures in all directions, a chorus of crisp cracking under the metal-on-ice crunch I'd grown to love.

I hiked alongside Pete and Nick's deep, refrozen steps, which told a familiar story of an unpleasant afternoon slog. Moving quickly across the sidewalk of bullet-hard, flat snow adjacent to my buddy's trudge-prints was quite gratifying.

THIS, right here. This is how you travel through snow.

It wasn't long until large dirt patches became more and more prevalent along the south-facing hillside, so I flipped my heel-lifters up and veered sharply west from Pete and Nick's steps. I wanted to maximize the utility of my snowshoes to gain elevation, which meant I needed to stay off dirt. I angled steeply uphill through a shaded, snowy forest lining the northern aspect of a mountain ridge, which formed the southern slope of Dorothy Pass.

The sun was close to cresting over the mountain peaks when I arrived at the broad saddle overlooking Dorothy Lake. Just enough light stretched over the terrain to give me my first glimpse to what awaited me beyond Yosemite.

This was it. North Yosemite was officially in the rearview. I'd connected my steps through the greatest obstacle along the Pacific Crest Trail in 2017, and I was alive to tell the tale.

The moment was oddly bittersweet. I took a minute to stare back over Dorothy Lake, reflecting on the many weeks I'd spent traversing through the mountains stretching out beyond the lake. I suppose I'd made good *enough* decisions. After all, I was exiting Yosemite in one piece, but my shortcomings were hard to ignore. Regardless, officially departing the infamous North Yosemite felt incredible.

To avoid a potentially dangerous crossing at Bonnie Lake's outlet, I broke away from the PCT and continued to contour around the north-facing mountainside into Bonnie Lake's basin. The lake was stunning. The surface was frozen solid with no signs of melting, and I walked confidently through the middle of it for what was likely the last time. I'd soon drop in elevation and hike deeper into summer, so walking across lakes probably wouldn't be in my future.

Well, at least without drowning, it wouldn't be.

Keeping to the west of Bonnie Lake worked like a charm. I reunited with the PCT almost directly above the buried 1,000-mile marker. It had been two hundred miles since I'd come across a visible marker, and this massive milestone wasn't going to be any different.

I took a break in the sunny, crisp cold of the morning to build myself a rough "1,000" out of my gear, snap some pictures with it, and force some calories past my uninterested taste buds. It was hard to process how far I'd walked. The furthest I'd ever backpacked before the PCT was 133 miles, and it hadn't happened without a healthy bit of whining. Truthfully, it didn't feel like I'd been walking for that long. Each day had just been some arbitrary chunk ranging between six and forty-one miles. It made sense after living on trail for several months, those numbers would inevitably add up to 1,000—but it was tough to fully appreciate.

Pete and Nick's melting, vague footprints crisscrossed back and forth across my path, along with the occasional set of bear tracks. None of the footprints looked very fresh. Even Pete and Nick's prints, which were no older than twelve hours, were faded into nondescript depressions by yesterday's sun.

A wide valley of rolling hills, huge snowdrifts, and snaking creeks gave me a frustrating maze to navigate. I kept finding myself on the wrong side of the creeks, forcing me to backtrack to try a different string of snowbridges. I picked up and followed Pete and Nick's tracks again, hoping they'd found a good path through the mess.

At least, I *assumed* it was their tracks.

The deep footprints were headed in the general right direction, but they soon began to climb steeply uphill away from the PCT—which would present itself as a red flag to most, but not to *this* dehydrated potato enthusiast. I figured they'd gotten tired of the same difficult navigation in the marshy valley and had possibly decided to skirt the hillside above. So I took a leap of faith, put my phone away, and committed to following the sunken dishes.

Melanie sent me several messages on the inReach, a rare treat in the middle of the day, but she didn't exactly have happy news for me. The messages were details about Longstride and Roadrunner's accidents—and their aftermath. Both hikers had apparently been doing interviews with national news agencies, megaphoning the same fear Roadrunner had sent directly to us. Roadrunner was calling for the coercion of government officials to *close the Sierra to everyone,* period, as if the Sierra were actively engulfed in flames or something. Melanie was seeing his interviews and words find traction online, and she felt like I needed to know. That was indeed bad news for a guy who was dedicated to connecting his steps, and still had hundreds of miles of Sierra left.

I angled out of the valley in a daydream. Sonora Pass was getting closer and closer, which was obviously exciting, but I was kind of dreading reconnecting with the PCT community. I wasn't quite sure what, if anything, my responsibility was. I wanted to share the information I had about the Sierra, to assist those who were fit and prepared to safely get through it, but didn't exactly want to go to war in defense of keeping the Sierra open. If I did, it would likely be interpreted as ipso facto encouragement for *all* hikers to head into the Sierra, no matter their skill level or preparation. In reality, all I wanted was for hikers to have information, to be equipped with creek crossing and mountain pass knowledge. It was information that could potentially save lives.

Of course, nagging in the back of my head was Roadrunner, and the complete lack of duty he'd felt to help me and everyone else behind him. Did I need to do—*anything* when I reached Sonora? Was everyone a self-absorbed Roadrunner? Or were there more people out there willing to pool information to keep everyone safe? It would certainly take a lot less effort on my end to just go home, drop my phone in the toilet, and kick my feet up for a week.

The more I thought about it, the more annoyed I became with the notion of the Sierra being painted as a murderous deathtrap. Maybe people *did* need someone encouraging them to try it. The backcountry had certainly been difficult, terrifying at times, but "impassible" (the word of the month in PCT Land) was ***not*** accurate. It was fair to say the vast majority of PCT hikers who had successfully hiked *700 freaking miles* to get to Kennedy Meadows were *physically* capable of traversing the Sierra. As for *mentally*—I couldn't know, but this wasn't a set of frail couch potatoes I'd be tossing an axe at and booting into the snow.

PCT hikers already had the legs, endurance, and commitment. If they wanted to tackle the Sierra, the odds were in their favor. If hikers were hearing discouragement from those who had messed it up, or from the underwear-clad, crumb-dusted Facebook enthusiasts spreading fear from their various basements, why couldn't I be the one encouraging voice? Hikers deserved to hear what the Sierra were like from someone who wasn't a career alpinist, who wasn't perfect, but who had still made it through in one piece.

Taking risk aside, skipping the Sierra was a shame. I'd never experienced a challenge like this before, but without a doubt—the rewards matched the effort.

I was pulled sharply from my daydream by a bear footprint. Not a melted-out, vague footprint crisscrossing my path like all the others, but a *fresh* bear footprint with perfectly clear imprints of large, circular pads and dotted claw points in the slush. I froze in place. The print was precisely inside of the tracks I'd been following. Something in the snow to my right caught my eye. It was another set of fresh bear tracks, but smaller. I looked to my left.

More tracks.

I lifted my head, following the deep depressions in the snow in front of me. Inside of every single one of Pete and Nick's tracks—there was a recent, clear imprint of a bear's paw.

"These aren't their footprints," I whispered.

A jumbled cluster of granite cliffs stood twenty feet from me, painted with black and orange streaks of lichen. The tracks disappeared into the rocks, along with dozens of others.

The hair on the back of my neck stood up. Pete and Nick's *actual* footprints were nowhere in sight. I might never have been following them. The converging highways of prints had tamped down the snow surrounding the rocks with tracks of all sizes, from the size of my head to some cute little prints only the size of my hand. Slowly, I backtracked away from the granite den, trying my best not to make too much noise. I was too close to Sonora Pass to get into a wrestling match with Mama Bear.

Once I'd tiptoed a few hundred yards back down into the marshy valley below, I started breathing again and picked up on Pete and Nick's *actual*, non-bear footprints—although I felt a fresh paranoia about trusting them.

The navigation eased and the familiar, adrenaline-spiking sound of a large creek reverberated through the trees ahead but this time, it was nothing to worry about. The raging Walker River appeared, followed shortly by a glorious bridge spanning it, the first bridge since the Tuolumne River.

The sight of a man-made structure brought up an exaggerated relief, as if I were a castaway seeing an approaching helicopter. I didn't have to devote a single iota of energy to cross the creek. I could just follow the PCT—no extra miles, no getting wet, no chasing after poorly thrown snowshoes… as Sonora was nearing, my patience for snow travel and creek crossings was definitely shortening.

Never mind the 200 more miles of snow *after* Sonora.

Eight miles into my day, my buddies' prints came to halt just before heading into Kennedy Canyon. Tamped down snow and a mess of bootprints meant I'd come across where they'd camped the previous night, totaling seventeen *miles* for them the previous day!

Another reassuring wave of relief hit me. I'd made the right choice. I couldn't believe their grit. I respected the hell out of it, but was happy to not be any part of seventeen miles of powder and slush. Eight miles of afternoon snow is a horrific endeavor. It couldn't have been easy—or fun.

Well, maybe for Pete.

I sat to eat some lunch and shift into snowshoes. Sonora Pass was only fifteen miles away, which meant Pete and Nick had likely made a push to reach the pass before dark. That provoked an undeniable, raw jealousy.

After lunch, I worked my way along steep ramps of softening snow in Kennedy Canyon. The dense pines occasionally opened up into avalanche zones, where more bowed-over trees remained pinned to their side. My snowshoes allowed me to move efficiently up wicked steep sections beyond the capability of my crampons, and I thanked my lucky stars I'd been able to rescue my snowshoe from my own stupidity at the Tilden Lake outlet.

With heel-lifters up, I made rapid progress, but was essentially walking up flight after flight of stairs in a reflective oven. Even with just my base layer on, I was sweating buckets and had to stop to chug water every few minutes. There was technically a creek flowing through Kennedy Canyon, but it was deeply buried, and I hadn't seen an accessible point yet. I'd actually skipped filling up at Walker River, because I'd assumed Kennedy Creek would be a safe bet.

Unfortunately for me, the further elevation I gained into the canyon, the less likely the creek was going to make an appearance. In the middle of an icy desert, I took the last sip of water from my water bottle. A massive, steep, sun-facing uphill would soon take me up to a high elevation ridge, where there was close to *zero* chance I'd come across any flowing streams. The effort of melting water with my stove seemed irrationally unbearable. Any additional effort to get to Sonora Pass felt like that. I pushed on, parched and continuing to soak through my wool shirt in the middle of an infinite sea of water in the wrong form.

Waves of dizziness eventually started overriding my stubborn resistance. I was seconds away from taking my Jetboil out when the glorious sound of rushing water appeared, bringing with it the elation of a Sahara wanderer stumbling across a Coke machine. A beautiful section of creek appeared for a mere twenty feet before ducking back under the thick snowpack. The water flowing over the grayish-blue, smooth cobbles was unbelievably clear, to the point where some shallow parts of the creek almost appeared dry. I set my pack down on the bank and chugged the pure water, liter after liter. All of the water in the Sierra had been about as perfect as drinking water could get, but this creek won me over as the best I'd ever consumed in my entire, thirty-one-year existence.

But what about my home municipal water supply in Phoenix, Arizona, you ask?

A close second.

Of course, being extremely parched from hiking thirsty for so long, a sticky puddle of bear urine—or say, my home municipal water supply in Phoenix, Arizona—might've been appealing.

I relaxed against my pack, thoroughly enjoying the rare luxury of a midday rest. Basking in the serene warmth of the sun, my eyes slid shut. Water babbled softly over the smooth cobbles and chirping chickadees sang me into an unscheduled snooze.

The sun slipped behind an overhead pine, casting a shadow over me and returning the reality of the low ambient temperature to the sweat-drenched hiker lying in the snow. I lazily opened my eyes and executed an elderly power-groan to sit back up, then did some more groaning in an attempt to shake the weight off of my eyelids. I slipped my fleece jacket on, trying to find the motivation to stand and keep walking. I was *exhausted*, which wasn't necessarily a surprise. I'd been running a recovery deficit for months.

I slumped forward, cradling my head in my hands. "I can't wait to get to Sonora. I'm going to sleep for a week straight."

I'd left Mammoth unsure of how many zeroes I'd need at Sonora Pass to recover, but whatever the number was, it was growing with every passing day. I'd originally figured maybe three or four days off the trail, but a week off was sounding more and more appealing.

*Could I afford two weeks? Could one take a full **month** off and still have time to finish the trail before eh, it started snowing in... in Canada?*

... ...

I jerked myself awake once again. "Ughh, I need to stand the hell up—or set up my tent for the day."

A curious eyebrow rose at the semi-sarcastic suggestion. It was barely noon; could I really make a solid case for stopping for the day?

You're damn right I could.

The huge, south-facing hillside above me climbed almost 1,500 feet up and out of Kennedy Canyon. The snow was already softening, and I wanted no part in trudging up a sea of slush in the heat of the afternoon. I was also sitting next to the last source of liquid water potentially until Sonora Pass—in short: I'd found the *perfect* place to camp.

CRUNCH

A flat patch of snow sat just above the white noise of the creek where I rolled out my tent and blew up my sleeping pad before preparing two lentil curry dinners from my bear canister. After I'd fully charged my electronics, dried my socks and boots, and completed every other possible camp chore I could think of, it was only two p.m., *definitely* too early to go to sleep—but after a heated staring contest with my tent filled with warm, fluffy, down things, I was tucked in and unconscious by 2:15 p.m.

37

SONORA

My eyes opened to my two a.m. alarm like a kid on Christmas, only I had much more to look forward to than a value-pack of Spiderman underwear.

Today's the day. I'll be at Sonora Pass by noon. I'll see Melanie by noon. I'll have a week of rest starting at noon. I'll attack untold pounds of food before the next time I go to sleep!

I turned over in my sleeping bag, puffing the standard witches brew of sweat-encrusted, sunburnt skin and dehydrated food farts into my face, melting my joyous exuberance into a watery-eyed frown. The fleeting thought of a shower brought one corner of my mouth up into a slight smile.

"I'll have more than just my own horrific stink to snuggle with tonight!" I croaked into the pitch-black tent, grateful Melanie wouldn't have to go through the ordeal of cuddling with me in my current state of sensory offense.

For *this*—was a marriage-ending stink.

Even after eleven solid hours of sleep, I still felt exhausted. Grimacing through the sore muscles and stink puffs, I sat up, excited to get the day started, but more excited to get the day finished.

I shoveled a couple Pop-Tarts into my mouth and washed the paste down with some hot coffee. My entire sense of taste had been relegated down to just hot and cold, but I still found some pleasure in that contrast. It had been chilly overnight, enough to firm the snow nicely, but hadn't been below freezing. Thankfully, my boots were still flexible, which drastically reduced the number of soul-damning words required to get dressed.

I stood up out of my tent in the eerie, still night, hurriedly shuffling around my humble home while mumbling incoherent thoughts to myself—not unlike a lunatic—as a distraction from all the forest monsters my mind wanted to introduce me to. I collapsed my tent, then pulled the titanium stakes from the ice one by one, then went down onto a knee to roll the cuben fiber back up for the day.

SNAP

My blood and I froze in place for several seconds. I didn't dare move. The sound was loud enough to echo twice across the canyon before fading into dead silence. After a very long minute, I slowly lifted my head to sweep the narrow spotlight of my headlamp through the pines. With darting eyes, I searched for any sign of movement—but of course, there was none.

With a jackhammering heart, I hesitantly resumed rolling up my tent while images of angry bears and hungry mountain lions danced through my head. I felt the full weight of just how alone I was. If something did attack me—how long would it take for another person to find my tattered thermals and perfectly intact, untouched underwear?

Days? Weeks?

My only partner was my own bullying mind, and no amount of slow hiking or falling into lakes was going to get rid of that guy. I quietly slid my pack on, doing my best to shake the fear. As much as I wanted to know exactly what had made the sound, wasting energy on it wasn't going to help anything. Regardless of what it was, only the one, tired option remained.

I missed having company for these morning hikes. I thought back to when Amped and I had executed our first two a.m. starts together. Even with him by my side, it had been creepy. Absurdly early wake-ups were still necessary to hike on the best possible snow, but I *could not* wait for the day I'd be hiking on dry trail again, where I'd be afforded the grand luxury of waking up and hiking with the sun.

I threaded my way through dense pines, trying my best to direct all my focus into efficiently navigating the snowdrifts. I emerged above the tree-line standing at the bottom of the massive, forty-degree snowfield stretching out of the canyon. My maps had the buried trail switchbacking up a lower-angled hillside further up-canyon, and then running back along the ridge a thousand feet directly above me. More than ready to leave Creepville Forest, I turned to my trusty snowshoes one last time and clicked my heel-lifters up.

Stair-stepping toward the stars, the snow hardened gaining hundreds of feet of elevation up a sweeping, treeless slab of ice. The metal points under me attached to the slope like tank tracks. I pushed my legs until I was out of breath and hunched over my trekking poles. I began counting my steps, breaking between every twenty. An imaginary, heartless Amped ordered me out of each rest.

The sky began brightening, and I gained the ridge with just enough light to take in the beauty of the icy moonscape surrounding me in all directions. Back above 10,000 feet, I was on top of the world. The last big climb before Sonora Pass was behind me. I was eight short miles from the pass, from safety—from Melanie. As a cherry on top of the ascent, in the most unlikely of places, the PCT appeared from under the solid sheet of white and stretched out along the southwest-facing mountainside as far as I could see. I excitedly unstrapped my snowshoes, attached them to my pack, and damn near skipped along the flat, high alpine trail at the breakneck speed of *over* one mile per hour.

The sun crested the horizon, sending beautiful, rainbow striations across the dark blue sky. The alpenglow arrived, and the snowy peaks all around me took turns igniting into ever-shifting purples, reds, oranges, and yellows. It was a grand finale, a final display from the trail gods, who I was glad had found something nice to do for a moment. They must've had some good coffee or something.

CRUNCH

The trail followed the spine of the ridge through massive cirques of rock and ice with incredible views at all times. Progress continued easily along dry trail and bullet snow. I'd sent Mel a message aiming to be at the pass by noon, but at eight a.m. I stood within five miles of Sonora.

Pretty much the only damper to my pace was selecting optimal traction. The trail continually shifted from the dry southern aspect of the ridge to the snowy northern side. My snowshoes were speed machines over snow, but patches of dirt wouldn't stop appearing. With a case of severe senioritis setting in, there was a lot of stubborn snowshoeing across not-snow to get to the next snow. I tried my best to not damage the aluminum crampon teeth, but not going as far as to *not* hike on rocks with my snowshoes— what some would call the "smart" thing to do.

Pff.

I crested a saddle between two peaks where I was treated to an expansive view to the northwest. Highway 108, the road that eventually would cut through Sonora Pass, was visible far down in the canyon below, which sent my heart aflutterin'—but the view wasn't all great news.

"God… *dammit*," I whispered northward.

There was still snow ahead—a *nightmarish* amount of snow, just as much as I'd been hiking through. I was even looking at the *southern* faces of all the peaks, where there was guaranteed to be the *least* amount of snow!

My reflexive first thought was, *It's time to quit.*

I found that wuss inside of me detestable. Why couldn't I think something cooler? Like, *Hell yeah! Let's roll, baby!* or maybe, *Snow? I eat snow for **breakfast.***

A vocalized, heated debate with myself ensued for the next half-mile. I presented my best argument to not quit the trail, and the weiner defense team presented their counter argument (in a rather weinery tone), which I had to admit was a strong one.

The idea of no more snow was *beyond* tempting.

Lost in the familiar rhythm of snow travel, I glanced up—and had to double-take to make sure my eyes weren't playing tricks on me.

428

People. There were *people*. Two of them. Not even people with backpacks—but two skiers, obviously out for just the day. So as not to alarm them, I stopped debating myself and suppressed my smile to a smooth, friendly level, a notch under the insane place it wanted to spread. I called out to the middle-aged couple with probably a bit too much exuberance.

"Hello!"

"Well hello there." The man eyed my pack with curiosity. "Where are your skis, bud?"

"I don't use—well, I mean—I don't *have* skis. Just my backpack!"

His curious look didn't go anywhere. I was overly excited to talk to someone who wasn't me, but I felt awkward and clumsy. I'd only been alone for a couple days, but having a normal conversation with strangers was more difficult than I remembered.

"Uh huh… Well I'm Oolie, and this is my wife Robin. We live in Mammoth."

My eyes lit up. "My wife and I spend our summers around Mammoth! Great spot… Uh, where are you going to ski today?"

"Not too much farther. But so—you're out here for an overnight?" Oolie asked. "Doesn't really seem like a nice time for a weekend of backpacking."

"No, I came from—Mexico. I'm hiking this way," I explained, raising a finger to point north.

The couple's curiosity was visibly shifting into concern. The lunatic wandering around the mountains was rambling about a country one *thousand* miles away.

"Sorry, it's been a minute since I've talked to people, except for Pete and Nick. But they're not here, eh—now." Oolie and Robin exchanged a worried glance. "Oh boy. I'm on the Pacific Crest Trail. I started in Mexico back in March."

Robin raised her eyebrows. "You've been out here for *months*? Oh my God. How long have you been in the snow?"

"Over 300 miles now."

An involuntary smile spread across my face. It was quite satisfying to hear that number out loud.

"Wow!" Oolie shook his head and looked at Robin. "I thought our ten miles to a drop was long."

They congratulated me and offered their extra snacks to fuel me for the last couple miles. As appealing as more tasteless bars were, I politely declined. I had a never-ending supply of greasy, salty, delicious food waiting for me in Mammoth. We talked for a few minutes until I felt like I'd convinced them I wasn't insane, then said goodbye. As much as I enjoyed conversing with people, a giddy energy inside was tugging me forward.

Steps later, I rounded a corner on the final downhill ridge and a beautiful sight opened up below me.

Sonora Pass.

It was real. There was a road lined with visiting cars. That was the road where Melanie would pick me up, the road I'd been chasing for what felt like forever, the impossibly distant objective that would never appear. It was sitting right there, within eyesight!

The remaining bit of the PCT wound down through very steep hillsides. I wasn't going to be able to track it through the snow. So my exhausted brain, capable of little to no critical thought, decided to beeline straight toward the road.

I suppose the trail gods were done with their coffee, and getting bored.

The terrain took a sharp dive, so I slowed my pace, but kept moving down the steepening hillside, hoping for good news the further I committed. That hope all but evaporated at the top of a seventy-degree snowfield. Hundreds of yards of steep snow was behind me, which wasn't *necessarily* irreversible—but sure to suck if I tried. Even the thought of hiking in the opposite direction of the asphalt winding through the white valley below turned my stomach. Summit-fever was in full swing, and I stared down the snowfield until I'd convinced myself I could make it down safely with sound, logical points like, "Don't be a coward" and "Man up, wusscake!"

From where I stood I couldn't know for sure, but the dizzying slope below *looked* like soft slush—easy enough terrain to commit to plunge-stepping down through. Hard ice at that angle would be quite dangerous, even in a seated glissade, but as long as the snow remained soft enough to sink my heels into, I'd be all right.

"Screw it," I muttered into my tunnel vision. "The pass is right there. You can do this, wusscake."

I launched into irreversible terrain. Plunge-stepping was second nature at this point, how I'd moved downhill through almost every steep, soft slope in the hundreds of miles behind me—and quite fun. I slid downhill with one heel pushed strongly underneath me, waiting for enough slush to compact under my crampon to decelerate to a safe speed. Then, I hopped off the planted heel, gained some free-fall momentum, and planted the opposite heel to repeat the process.

After dozens of steepening plunge-steps, right as I started to feel a *twinge* of confidence in my ability to make wise decisions, my eyes widened. The slush was thinning, and revealing a sheet of hard ice underneath.

"Oh crap," I muttered.

I ground both of my heels into the dwindling slush and reached behind me to dig the handles of my trekking poles into the snow in a desperate move to stop my momentum. My four points digging into the slope sent up a spray of ice all around me. I gritted my teeth and closed my eyes against the barrage of flying slush, and thankfully came to halt. I opened one cautious eye, then shook my head to clear the slush away from the other. I was perched at the top of a fifty-foot section of near-vertical ice. My four heel spikes were my only attachment to the slope. It took just a slight extension of my elbows to stand essentially straight up. I scanned the ice around me, wobbling slightly, searching for an escape.

There was none.

My adrenaline started pumping. The windswept, glimmering ice under me was *clearly* too dangerous to slide down, but reversing my path wasn't any less risky. The plunge-stepping had left my compacted footprints almost ten feet apart, eliminating the option of climbing back up through them. The steep ice and thin slush between my footprints was beyond the capability of my crampons.

I turned to face squarely downhill, wobbling through strong vertigo. Making a decision felt impossible, even with just the one option. I needed to slide out of the hole I'd dug myself into—but my inner weiner was being mighty assertive.

I took a breath, sat back, and grabbed my trekking poles by the base, close to the carbide-tipped points. I clearly hadn't chosen the optimal path down to the pass, but I was committed now, and down was the only reasonable way out. I wanted my axe in my hands, but it sat useless, strapped to the side of my pack, and I had no safe way to get to it.

"*Please* don't let me break my leg within eyesight of the pass," I begged the universe.

I swear, if a SAR team has to helivac me to the hospital only a mile from the road…

I yanked my heel spikes out of the ice, which instantly sent me accelerating onto the vertical pane of cold glass. The situation was out of my control in a millisecond. I dug in the spikes of my trekking poles, leaving an arcing tail of ice shards behind me. I wasn't going to be able to stop, or even slow down. All I could do was provide as much drag as I could, while hopefully keeping my careening body on my butt, and not tumbling end over end.

My crampons went from helpful to a liability in a hurry. They were all-or-nothing; either disengaged, or fully engaged. With all of my focus, I kept the spikes floating above the ice flying underneath me. If even one point caught, it would send my entire crampon into the ice, bringing that boot to an instant halt while my momentum would keep the rest of my body moving, tearing apart every ligament in that leg before sending me rag-dolling down the slope.

As fast as the half-terrifying, half-exhilarating slide had flown out of control, it was over. The angle softened to where I was able to safely arrest my momentum and come to a stop. The unruly world I'd launched into evaporated, and I sat on the snow under blue skies and chirping chicka-dees with a jackhammering heart, wide eyes, and rapid breaths.

SONORA

I slumped my pack off and took a quick inventory. Although my shirt and waistband had been packed with ice, there were no tears in my pants, which I was grateful for. My romanticized arrival at Sonora Pass hadn't involved homemade assless chaps. My backpack wasn't so lucky. The bottom had taken the brunt of the slide, and almost *half* of the bottom of my bear canister was visible through the fabric. After countless glissades eating away at it, I was surprised the pack had enough material left to keep the canister from sliding right out.

"Only one more mile, pack," I soothingly consoled my inanimate, shell-shocked Gregory. "It's about time to take you to that farm upstate."

Ridiculous as it sounds, the thought of throwing that pack in the trash was heart-wrenching, like throwing one's child in the trash—only worse. I don't know a single child that would carry a 50 pound load of M&M's hundreds of miles through the Sierra.

I was now pretty much at the same elevation as the pass, which sent a huge surge of energy flooding through my body. This was real—I was *minutes* from **the** Sonora Pass. Wonderful thoughts of touching the asphalt, taking pictures of the signs, and seeing Melanie fueled a near-run shuffle across the remaining snow between me and civilization.

My senses were assaulted nearing the road. The sound of revving engines and giddy people piling out of cars was a bit overwhelming. I placed a glorious, unforgettable step onto the asphalt, wincing at the shouts of tourists taking pictures next to the fifteen-foot-tall walls of snow still lining the highway. Converging genres of music blared from multiple cars as groups of shirtless dude-bros geared up for a bluebird day of backcountry skiing. Parents shouted loudly at gaggles of mildly obedient children playing in the snow and chasing each other back and forth across the winding highway.

The over-stimulation was weirdly difficult to process. The smells of suntan lotion, deodorant, and laundry detergent were almost nauseating—coming from the guy who literally hadn't touched soap in two weeks. I removed my crampons and bent over to grab them.

HONNNK

I shot up at the deafening blast of a car horn right behind me. The bald, dickhead owner of the vehicle waved frantically from behind the wheel of his immaculately shiny SUV, shooing me out of his parking spot. The animal in me wanted to use the crampon in my hand to carve ten simultaneous dicks in his hood, like one of those fancy, detention-hacking chalk holders from grade school. I thought better of it, and instead shot a death-glare to the driver, who could care less as he crept his polished car into the small pull-off, his bumper inches behind me until I'd fully vacated.

My return to civilization wasn't going *quite* as planned. I set off east along the shoulderless, two lane highway, unsure where I was headed, but I needed to *not* be in the middle of the noise. Across the road from the barely uncovered Sonora Pass sign, I set my pack down, pulled out my foam pad and set it on a perfect sitting-height bank of snow. Although worn and excessively compacted—and *barely* able to hold back the cold from seeping through—I slid the loyal foam under my butt anyway, for old times' sake. Frankly, a sheet of newspaper would've been more insulating. I stared at the green highway sign, fixated on the white lettering.

"I made it."

An unexpected flood of emotions emerged from wherever I'd been suppressing them. Without really knowing why, my eyes welled up.

I was alive—grateful, and beyond proud. I was sitting at Sonora Pass. The High Sierra were behind me. I'd successfully traversed the 300-mile monster that had haunted my thoughts for *so long*. I honestly had never attached to the idea I'd see that sign. I'd pitted myself against forces much, much bigger than me. I hadn't *wanted* to die, but a deep, dark part of me had accepted that as a possibility—even craved the opportunity to step into the arena with that ultimate fate.

I missed Melanie to an incredible degree. A haunting thought I hadn't allowed to surface in the backcountry appeared.

You risked never looking into Mel's eyes again—never hearing her voice, never touching her, never holding her…

434

It was unbearable. If absence does indeed make the heart grow fonder, risking a forever absence had taught me just how lucky I was to have her in my life. My impromptu breakdown was embarrassing, and I was glad to be alone while my subconscious finally was allowed to claw its way to the surface. With my head down, tear after tear left my blurred vision, leaving spots on the asphalt between my tattered boots. It wasn't sadness, exactly—it was guilt.

I'd made a promise to Melanie I hadn't kept. Risking our life together for a selfish, arbitrary trek wasn't fair to her. I reached back into the past, over-analyzing the worst of the obstacles I'd stumbled my way through. I certainly hadn't been the heroic badass I'd planned on being. So many moments hadn't been fully within my control. The more I thought back, the more flashes my imagination created of tumbling into creeks, snow-bridges collapsing, logs buckling, and my feet being swept from under me.

What exactly is the worth of what I just accomplished? Anything?

And did I actively keep myself safe? Or did I simply get lucky?

The "what-ifs" came in an unstoppable wave. I let my emotions collide and work themselves out while car after car of staring occupants crept by, no doubt curious as to where the hell a lone backpacker had come from—or was going to. Luckily, Mel was a couple hours behind my early arrival at the pass. I had no idea simply sitting at Sonora would be such an emotional trainwreck for me, and I was thankful she wasn't going to drive up before I'd had the chance to get a grip on myself.

My subconscious eventually ran out of grievances and settled into the background. I processed my thoughts and tried to forgive myself. Maybe I hadn't held up my end of the bargain to a degree I found acceptable, but I was still in one piece. That had to be good enough.

My stomach turned over on itself again and again in impatient anticipation of the pizza and cheeseburgers in my immediate future. Sure, maybe I was forgetting about my checked-out taste buds, but I couldn't wait to be in the mere presence of warm food that hadn't come from a Ziploc bag that'd spent thirty minutes tucked into my crotch.

CRUNCH

A smile crept onto my face at the thought of what was ahead: Melanie, food, the pups, food, resting, food, and gearing up for a MUCH lighter pack for the miles ahead.

Did I mention I couldn't wait for food?

My fingers shook in giddy excitement as noon approached, knowing I'd soon be wrapping my wife up in the stinkiest damn hug she'd ever experienced.

That lucky girl.

With walls of snow lining the road on both sides, the only place she would have to pull over would be in the one parking lot. With a bracing breath, I walked back into the chaotic collection of loud music, cars, people shouting, and children screaming. I kept my head down, trying to appear normal in the overly stimulating environment, but my eyes involuntarily darted toward every noise. It was a scene likely to be described as "average" or even "peaceful" by a city dweller, but I felt like an introverted mental patient strolling through Burning Man.

One SUV had every door wide open, surrounded by several beer-bellied, hairy-chested guys lathering themselves up with sunscreen, bobbing their heads in unison to music blaring from the vehicle's speakers. Skis and snow gear were scattered around the vehicle.

One of the guys with a second-trimesterish beer bump looked up from his lathering boogie as I approached and froze, staring at me through his reflective, red sunglasses.

"Bro," he started, his jaw hanging slightly open, "where are you going? You know there's like, not any *dirt* to hike on, right? It's not time to go backpacking yet. There was like, a *really* big snow year this last winter."

… … …

He wasn't wrong.

I fought every urge to laugh out loud. "I'm actually *exiting* from the backcountry. Looking forward to *not* being on snow for a bit."

All four of the skiers froze, staring at me through variously colored sunglasses long enough to make it awkward.

"Um—where are you guys headed today?" I asked.

Ignoring my question, the red-sunglassed guy blurted out, "No, you don't mean you came *out* here. There's only snow, bro! You didn't hike through the snow, right?"

One corner of my mouth again crept up into an amused smile. "I did. I'm on the Pacific Crest Trail. It comes right through here, somewhere under all this snow."

From the other side of the SUV, a green-sunglassed bro shouted over in a heavy beach-bum accent. "Brahh, you're tellin' us you hiked through the backcountry like this?! Where'd you come from?"

This question was getting more and more awkward to answer. Where *had* I come from? Mexico? Kennedy Meadows? Mammoth? Yosemite?

"Well, the trail runs through Southern California to Kennedy Meadows—and then through the Sierra. It runs right by Mammoth and through Tuolumne…"

I hoped they were familiar with at least one of those places. Four simultaneous jaw drops told me they understood perfectly.

Red-sunglassed dude-bro softly asked, "From—*Mammoth*? Through the snow? How far is that?"

"About a hundred miles, but I've been in snow for over 300."

"WHOAAA!!"

In a coordinated shout of shock, psych, and disbelief, the skiers erupted into stoked praise, high-fives, and congratulations. Two of them reached into nearby coolers and demanded I take as many beers as I could possibly handle. I thankfully accepted a couple cold Coors Lights and answered question after question from the deeply intrigued group, who'd seemingly lost all interest in their backcountry ski prep.

I did my best to quickly sum up such a massive experience, fielding their curious questions, which ranged from the typical to the ludicrous:

"Were there any creeks?"

"Did you ever have to drink your own pee?"

"How many bears did you see?"

"What kind of gun did you bring?"

"What kind of food did you eat?"

"What's that smell?"

Before too long, the purr of a familiar diesel engine rose above the questions, and our silver truck appeared around a bend in the highway. Mel and I locked eyes and my heart skipped a beat—and this time, it wasn't the Pop-Tarts' fault. Both of our faces lit up, and she gestured toward the parking lot just down the road.

I thanked my new friends profusely for their generosity, then spent at least ten no-thank-yous refusing the truckload of beers they wanted to send me off with. In a half jog on my suddenly painful feet, I chased after our truck. Mel got out of the driver's seat with a big smile and her long, blonde hair floating in the breeze.

I'll never forget that hug. I wanted to hold her beyond forever. I wasn't tired, wasn't hungry, wasn't in pain—nothing else mattered. We hadn't specifically talked about it, but it was a hug neither of us were sure would ever happen. I fought to keep the returning flood of emotions at bay.

A familiar Australian voice came from the other side of the truck. "Ey, Beta. Congratulations, mate."

"Thor!" I released my tight hold on Melanie and limped over for a big hug from my gentle giant buddy. "You're still alive!"

I was overwhelmed with love and gratitude, and narrowly maintained a grip on myself. We rapidly shot updates back and forth through big laughs and bigger smiles. Thor had been resting for the twelve days since we'd last seen each other in Mammoth. The creeks in North Yosemite weren't worth the risk to him, and he took the offer from Melanie to hitch a ride to resume his hike at Sonora. Part of me was disappointed I wasn't leaving with my Aussie friend. Looking back on how tough my partnership with Pete and Nick had been, I'd grown a renewed appreciation for just how well Thor, Amped, and I had clicked.

As good as it was to talk with two people I loved so much, my obnoxious stomach was in a mood. I said good luck to Thor, gave him one last hug, and hopped into the truck. Minutes into the ride to Mammoth, my mind finally began allowing me to feel what I'd done to my body. My eyes refused to stay open, and I struggled to hold a conversation in my beaten-down state.

Mel smiled and turned up the radio. "Close your eyes for a bit."

I only mustered half a thank-you before I was out cold, but the exhaustion was no match for my stomach. Before long, I was dragged out of my nap by a vicious hunger still an hour from Mammoth. We pulled over in the tiny town of Lee Vining for an emergency sandwich.

At a heavenly little eatery tucked into a garden (the rather appropriately titled Epic Café), the assault of freshly squeezed lemonade and a strongly seasoned panini managed to break slightly through the barrier of my dulled senses, and I tasted my food for the first time in a week. I was struggling through a primal concoction of overjoyed emotion, exhaustion, excitement, and ravenous hunger. I wanted to forever sit in that cafe with Melanie, to look at the beautiful girl in front of me—to hear her voice, to have her hear mine, to eat amazing food, to take in every possible second I could, all while fighting the most forcible drowsiness I'd ever experienced. I was on the high of a lifetime.

Back in the truck, I watched the jagged, snowbound peaks flow by in a daze. I couldn't believe it was over. From here on out, my pack would be lighter, I wouldn't have to stress about creek crossings or food rationing or bail points.

Everything would be easy.

What I *didn't* know, was that the 2,000 remaining miles along the Pacific Crest Trail would cause me to reflect wistfully back on the days where I was falling into frozen lakes, sledding over my own fecal matter, and cooking my boots over a Jetboil.

Pooling hoards at Kennedy Meadows had continued to escalate the sense of fear and hopelessness at the southern gates of the Sierra range. Social media had an amplifying effect with the near-miss accidents in the snow. Success stories were easily lost behind hysteria surrounding the failures. Resolves were shaken, and many heart-wrenching decisions were made. Capable hikers gave in to the fear and bitterly abandoned goals of a border-to-border thru-hike. My fellow hikers were shotgunned all across the trail in desperate attempts to avoid snow, in a year where snow travel wasn't optional.

Longstride and Roadrunner's stories had dealt a heavy blow to the psyche and camaraderie along the trail. Roadrunner had continued to be especially vocal, both online and in the news. A massive percentage of hikers readily sided with the attractive notion that the Sierra were essentially not part of the trail in 2017. The range was too dangerous for anyone. Impossible. Those 460 miles were an optional (and maybe even a bit *idiotic*) stretch of the PCT. Hikers could hitch around that trivial twenty percent of trail and still claim a successful thru-hike, technically making 2017 the *easiest* year yet to complete a PCT hike!

I—was *not* on the same page.

I saw no harm or issue with skipping the Sierra, if that's what hikers wanted to do, but claiming a thru-hike anyway? My opinion was 2017 would simply be a near-impossible year for a successful PCT hike, one demanding a monumental effort by a dedicated few. The notion of changing the definition of a successful thru-hike to suit the majority was obvious nonsense.

If ninety percent of a group of marathon runners decided five of the 26.2 miles are unfairly steep, should that matter? Should that change the definition of a marathon? Or should those ninety percent either suck it up and push through those five miles, or simply be okay with not completing that particular marathon?

I'd be called a moron—*to my face*—for my success in the snow, a self-absorbed lunatic with too little brainpower to have understood the peril I'd put myself in. And on a gross flip-side, I would catch hikers in bold-faced lies, taking advantage of the fact most hadn't seen the Sierra backcountry, and professing to have traversed the snow when they clearly hadn't. I would experience swollen egos from track-shorted trail heroes, brave enough to loudly boast about hiking forty-five miles every day—between their hitch-hikes to skip the hard stuff.

Quite contrary to my experience in Southern California, my fellow *hikers* would prove to be the most formidable obstacle I'd find along the Pacific Crest Trail in 2017.

Of course riding along the beautiful Eastern Sierra with a full belly and a dazed smile stuck on my face, I had no idea. My eyes again grew unbearably heavy, and my conversation skills took another sad dive. Mel insisted once more I take a nap, and I would've thanked her—but I was already asleep.

EPILOGUE

On September 16, 2017, I made it to Canada.

If you're looking for a happy ending—there it is. I successfully stuck to my goal of connecting steps from border to border, which ended up taking 2,808 miles and 144 days. Over 150 miles of my trek was spent walking on highways around wildfires and getting in and out of the Sierra in Lone Pine and Mammoth. The summer in the Pacific Northwest saw one of the worst fire seasons in history, and my feet were plagued by relentless plantar fasciitis. But my stubborn nature won the fight, and I arrived in Manning Park, Canada having laid eyes on every open, legal mile of the Pacific Crest Trail.

I was, and will forever remain, proud of my PCT hike. It was far from easy, *massively* rewarding, but four years after stepping onto Canadian soil, I remain uninspired to hop on another long trail.

It wasn't the terrain. The PCT runs an absolutely *incredible* path along the western crest of the United States. That trail is nothing short of a miracle. I will never forget the wonderful views, the wildlife, the alpine lakes, and drinking the best water on the damn planet for five-and-a-half months. If there weren't any people involved in thru-hiking, my life would likely revolve around it.

That's not to say every single human out there rubbed me the wrong way. Far from it, the majority of people along the PCT were wonderful. Many have become lifelong friends.

But imagine being at your favorite fast-casual Italian eatery, and the waiter drops in to deliver a steaming basket stuffed with dozens of golden brown, butter-brushed breadsticks. But for some perplexing reason sure to affect the waiter's tip, tucked in between all those beautiful breadsticks is a fresh terd.

Now, that one terd may be in the minority, but it makes it *powerfully* hard to enjoy nibblin' on the rest of those breadsticks.

That minority of obnoxious hikers put such a bad taste in my mouth (not the best phrase to use there), it was genuinely difficult to enjoy the culture of the trail. By the end I found myself hiking and camping away from *all* my fellow PCT hikers, just to avoid the worst of them. Almost six months of digging into that basket of hikers and occasionally taking a bite of butter-brushed terd, my apprehension of those around me grew—understandably, by my estimation.

For whatever reason, poor ethics and self-absorbed egotism is endemic in those who choose to go hike 3,000 miles in this modern age, and I'm not alone in that observation. It was brought up in lowered voices around dozens of campfires throughout Northern California, Oregon, and Washington. Popular books and movies, like *Wild* and *A Walk in the Woods*, were often the scapegoats. Many hikers believed those two pieces of media in particular had brought in a flood of hikers looking for a New York Times bestseller to write about "finding themselves" or whatever, but I don't think that's correct. From my vantage point, social media was—and remains—the problem. Its attracted a sea of hikers who seem to care much less about *hiking* the PCT, and much more about *people seeing* them hike the PCT—which invites a particularly terdish kind of person out onto that trail.

It might sound odd, but my accomplishment in the Sierra was something I ended up hiding from fellow thru-hikers. Although internally, I was immensely proud of what I'd done, externally, it was an invitation for insults. Being labeled a "purist," a term I'd initially accepted as part-and-parcel of attempting to connect my steps, became a derogatory term for those who had pushed through the snow, for those unreasonable chaps who had the audacity to hike *all* the miles, instead of *most* of them.

I compiled all of my mountain pass and creek crossing information on a website I shared as far as I could, and many hikers expressed gratitude for helping them stay safe through the snow. But that information also invited a lot of hate from those who didn't want to hear the Sierra weren't a guaranteed death sentence, or accept they'd skipped a possible, open section of trail. The collective agreement was the snow miles weren't needed to claim a successful thru-hike. Hundreds of hikers used that convenient loophole to justify skipping around the Sierra, and as long as everyone was on the same page, everyone would arrive in Canada as a bona fide "PCT Hiker." That participation-trophy groupthink left a guy like me on the outskirts.

The Pacific Crest Trail Association maintains the sole, rather unofficial record of those who have ever completed the trail. The list is on the honor system, and as of this writing, 537 people self-reported a successful, complete thru-hike in 2017 (defined as 2,600+ miles by the PCTA). By my estimations, and others who also put in the hard work to hike an honest, border-to-border hike, the actual number is well below one hundred. I personally met *three*—out of the hundreds of people I met on that trail—so a hundred is a generous estimate. It took me several months (and maybe a prod or two from Melanie) to swallow my pride and insert my name into a list of people I recognized as those whose hard work ended at typing their name and hitting "enter." Several were hikers who had trimmed off over *a thousand miles* between avoiding the snow and wildfire smoke, and still shamelessly claimed a full thru-hike.

I didn't need or want every hiker to hike every mile. But if you, dear reader, are considering or maybe even actively preparing for a thru-hike: take credit for what you earned. If you want credit for doing a hard thing, then do the hard thing. If you don't care to do the hard things, then don't take credit for doing the hard things.

Hard stuff to follow, I know.

The self-evident nature of the above feels painfully obvious, but maybe it's not. I personally watched hikers skip hundreds of miles (miles that were invariably through snow, smoke, or aggressive terrain—a.k.a. the hard parts) then unabashedly claim a full thru-hike right alongside those of us who had actually put in the work—risked our lives even—to traverse the entire trail.

But a runner isn't a marathon runner for merely standing on a track wearing running shoes—and a hiker isn't a PCT hiker for merely standing on the PCT with dirty legs and a tiny backpack.

If the accolade is attractive, put in the work. If it's not, then don't.

But don't put in the work because you read a book by some random 34-year-old with a developmentally delayed sense of humor—do it for that beautiful creature staring back at you in the mirror. That guy/gal is the only person you need to stay true to. No matter what you convince your friends, family, or social media followers of, that face staring back at you while you brush your teeth at night knows the *exact* truth. You'll have to trust me that it feels a hell of a lot better to be able to smile and say, "We did it," rather than, "We convinced everyone we did it."

To give some closure on my taste bud erasure—just in case Melanie would prefer I be a present father for the next four years instead of writing another book—it ended up being from a powdered toothpaste product I was using. On the Fourth of July, I was off the trail at a buddy's cabin near Truckee, California for a barbecue. One of the guests was a nurse who narrowed it down. I'd considered the toothpowder as the problem but had dismissed it. It seemed too inane a culprit. I'd figured the exertion was to blame, that I was doing so much damage to my body that certain "luxury" parts, like taste and the will to live, were being shut down.

Malnutrition was another theory. I'd done my best to add in nutritious food to my pack, but the reality was for every fleck of dehydrated mushroom in my bear canister, there was a pound of chocolate, peanut butter—or sometimes chocolate-covered peanut butter.

EPILOGUE

Turns out, instead of grabbing the plain ol' toothpowder I was looking for, I'd grabbed the *whitening* version—and on the side of the bottle (which I didn't have with me, since I'd repackaged it into a tiny Ziploc) in microscopic words, it read: Do not use for more than two weeks.

I'd been using it for fourteen.

And with that, I vowed to never brush my teeth again.

The End.

ABOUT THE AUTHOR

Daniel Winsor hasn't won any literary awards, but he *did* manage a B- on his high school senior essay—and with minimal tearful begging.

A nuclear Navy veteran, Daniel decided to utilize his highly sought-after skillset to leave the military and move into a trailer in the Eastern Sierra desert, where he spent six years growing beards and becoming intimately familiar with the beautiful Sierra range. After hundreds of miles exploring mountain peaks and backcountry rock climbs, Daniel wouldn't stop complaining about the hiking, so he decided to tackle the 2,650-mile Pacific Crest Trail.

All good things must come to an end, and Daniel has left the rewarding world of risking his life between uncomfortable poops to settle in rural Alabama with his wife, Melanie, and brand new daughter, Zoey. He spends his time writing, climbing, woodworking, and dadding. Hearing his daughter laugh for the first time was the most exhilarating moment of his life.

More of his writing and general maturity can be found at:

www.hikerbeta.com

CONSIDER REVIEWING THIS BOOK ON

If you enjoyed reading Crunch, please take a few minutes and give it a review on Amazon.com.

The almighty Amazon algorithm (hallowed be thy name. Amen.) is the gate-keeper to whether or not my book gets suggested to other people online. And to please it, Crunch needs as much attention on the Amazon site as possible.

You see, when Timmy throws a few too many back, then types into Google "how to hike the Pacific Crest Trail if you hate yourself," my book only appears if the algorithm has seen that a lot of other people have interacted with Crunch—and reviews are a *huge* part of that.

Now, I would obviously prefer all five-star reviews, and if you're feeling lazy after all this reading about me walking with wet feet, I've prepared a review for you to give a quick copy and paste:

"Wow! I've never read such an exciting and handsome piece of literature!"

If it's not five-stars, I'd still appreciate the review... but did you miss the part where I talked about my bowel movements sixty-three times?

The algorithm rewards eyeballs, so every review—no matter the stars—every click, every share, every time you say Crunch by yourself while your phone listens to you—it's all gold.

Thank you in advance. I really can't wait to hear what you thought about Crunch. Even if by page three you'd decided it was a one-star book, I hope I at least made you smile once or twice.

ACKNOWLEDGMENTS

This book wouldn't have been possible without the support from:

Doranne Tay and Donovan Wood—I'll never forget your overwhelming kindness and generosity.

Brian and Micki Winsor—thank you for your love and encouragement through this project, as well as raising a boy who values hard work and dedication. I can only hope I can pass those values on to Zoey (and any other littles who may arrive).

Other fine souls who provided generous support along the path to publishing this book:

Leon Grams	Kevin Carroll
Michael O'Brien	Laura Olmstead
Rebecca Gau	Kels Roberts
Jennifer Walt	Jake Chaney
Molly Donnellan	David Xiao.

But to anyone who offered even a single encouraging word along the way, thank you. It meant more than you know.

-Daniel

Made in the USA
Monee, IL
03 March 2022

92195347R00267